D1335669

Royal
Horticultural
Society

E S S E N T I A L
GARDEN PLANNING
& CONSTRUCTION

Royal
Horticultural
Society

ESSENTIAL
GARDEN PLANNING
& CONSTRUCTION

Edited by Deborah Parker

Editor-in-Chief
Christopher Brickell

MITCHELL BEAZLEY

**RHS Essential Gardening Planning
& Construction**

First published in 2006 by Mitchell Beazley,
an imprint of Octopus Publishing Group Ltd,
2–4 Heron Quays, London E14 4JP

Copyright © Octopus Publishing Group Ltd 2006

All rights reserved. No part of this work may
be reproduced or utilized in any form or by any
means, electronic or mechanical, including
photocopying, recording or by any information
storage or retrieval system, without the prior
written permission of the publishers.

ISBN-13: 978 1 845330 59 0
ISBN-10: 1 845330 59 5

A CIP catalogue copy of this book is available from
the British Library

Executive Art Editor **Sarah Rock**
Commissioning Editor **Michèle Byam**
Designer **Terry Hirst**
Editor **Deborah Parker**
Production Controller **Jane Rogers**
Picture Researcher **Nick Wheldon**
Indexer **Sue Farr**

Set in Meta.

Printed and bound in China by
Toppan Printing Company Limited

Contents

Introduction   6

Planning   **8**

Information gathering and the plot   10

The function of a garden   18

Design principles   22

Structure, space, and movement   32

Garden style and tailored plans   42

Construction   **78**

Choosing materials   80

Drainage   86

Types of foundations   88

Building a patio   94

Surfaces   98

Steps   116

Walls, fences, and gates   128

Changing levels   162

Pergolas and arches   168

Water features   178

Family areas   192

Other garden features   198

Lighting the garden   210

Furniture   220

Glossary   224

Index   226

Acknowledgements   230

Introduction

The elements of *RHS Essential Garden Planning and Construction* have been drawn from the popular series that comprise the *RHS Encyclopedia of Practical Gardening*, and have been revised and updated in this practical guide. It brings together the principles vital to successful garden planning, with an explanation of how to put these into practice in constructing elements and structures in the garden. In this book, techniques are explained to give a basic but thoroughly comprehensive guide to this subject. As it takes a "hands-on" approach, the techniques shown in this book are copiously illustrated – often with step-by-step diagrams – and fully explained.

ABOUT THE BOOK

The book is divided into two sections: Planning and Construction.

It begins by looking at the starting points for creating a new garden: conducting a full assessment and surveying of the plot, combined with the planning that needs to be undertaken at this stage. However big or small a garden project you are embarking on, the basic principles apply – whether you are starting with an absolutely blank canvas, reworking a small part of a garden, or revitalizing a front garden. Thorough planning is essential, particularly when considering the functions the garden must fulfil, and it provides a firm basis on which to begin the project.

As well as looking at the principles underlying good garden design and the concepts of scale and proportion, it explains in practical terms how to draw up your plan. Various examples of good garden plans are given throughout this first section, from functional designs for a small town front garden with a parking area to a large informal garden that meets the needs of a family.

In addition, differing locations, needs, and their appropriate design solutions are discussed, ranging from cold exposed sites to hot dry gardens and low maintenance plots. The problems created by dealing with a sloping garden are also answered.

Planting is such a wide ranging and detailed subject that it could not possibly be covered by the scope of this book: there are many other titles devoted to the cultivation and placing of plants.

Your own tastes will influence your plan, but ideas for your approach can be garnered from many places. Magazines, books on significant gardens, television programmes, and garden centres are good sources of inspiration, but perhaps the most valuable way of assessing how gardens work is by visiting other gardens. The internet is a particularly good source of information when assessing the materials available for use in the garden.

Fashion has always played a part in garden design. The positive side of this is that it encourages suppliers to promote an ever increasing range of materials and objects to tempt gardeners to update their garden. Manufacturers create lower cost alternatives to more expensive traditional materials, making these available to gardeners working to a tighter budget. On the other hand, fashion can colour your views as you plan your garden. Crazy paving, for instance, may seem a little outdated if you are creating a path or a patio. Yet if crazy paving is an appropriate style for the garden design and you like it, then there is no reason not to have it. It is pointless having the very latest in garden design if you don't like it or it does not function for you. And remember, what looks of the moment now could appear very dated in five or ten years' time.

Whatever materials are selected for construction, every good garden owner should be mindful of environmental issues. Incorporate wildlife-friendly features into your garden plan. If clearing a site, consider where you can reuse those materials you no longer need. Recycled alternatives are available to replace quarried stone and gravel, whether used in the garden for construction or for decorative effect.

CONSTRUCTION

The second part of this book deals with hard-landscape elements and other garden structures. Guides to selecting appropriate materials and designs, such surfacing for use in paving and paths, are supplemented with instructions on how to lay a path, build foundations or a brick wall, and create a deck, pool, or pergola.

Practical information on selecting and building steps, walls, fences and gates is given, together with a section dealing with the siting of water features in the garden and the creation of pools. Other garden structures, such as pergolas, play apparatus, and garden furniture, are explained, as is the use of lighting and electricity in the garden.

Although many gardeners prefer to bring in professional help for construction jobs, the basic skill required to erect a fence, lay a path, or create a timber deck can be learned by almost anyone. This "do-it-yourself" approach is invariably less expensive than employing someone else, and there is a great deal of satisfaction to be gained from making something yourself.

SAFETY IN THE GARDEN

Regulatory changes now limit the use of certain chemicals within the garden, so ensure you treat timber with a non-toxic preservative, following the manufacturers instructions carefully. And don't forget that some constructions require permission from the local authority, and that certain electrical work must be notified. It is up to the garden owner to ensure that these rules are adhered to.

Accidents are mostly due to carelessness – tools and cables can be tripped over – so get into the habit of putting away all equipment after use. Although there is no need to be wary of using power tools provided you take sensible precautions, take special care when using electrical equipment near water. Installing electricity in the garden should always be done by a qualified electrician. Wear sensible clothing, in particular stout footwear as you undertake any construction work in the garden.

PLANNING

Creating a garden is an exciting prospect; you may be full of ideas and keen to see them take shape. Yet, as with many enterprises, the planning stage is the most important. It is not a process that cannot be rushed. Undertaken thoroughly and carefully, it will allow you to make changes and adjustments as your plan comes into being. Rush it, and you could find you make mistakes that prove costly in both money and effort. The following section outlines, in appropriate order, the steps you need to work through to fully assess the site, the principles underlying good garden design, and how to choose and develop an appropriate design for the size, shape, function, and location of your garden.

Function

Governing the design of any garden is the question what is the garden to be used for? It might be a garden for a family, a cottage garden for a plant-lover, or a front garden that has to include a parking area. Within the garden itself will be a number of functional areas – for example, for relaxation, access, recreation, or for growing vegetables. If the garden is not functional, it will not be used and therefore will be neglected.

To develop the function plan of the garden into a an aesthetically pleasing space, the basic principles of design should be adhered to, enabling you to create harmony and continuity, and balance proportion, scale, and perspective in your garden. There are practical solutions to problems such as a sloping garden or screening unattractive features.

Style and location

The function of the garden will have an effect on its style, but other factors will influence this: its shape, proportions, the architecture that will associate with it, the amount of maintenance required, and its geographical location. Examples of garden designs of differing styles and functions in various locations are illustrated, from suburban plots to wildlife or hot, dry gardens.

Conservation

When selecting materials to be used in the creation of your design, ensure that these come from sustainable sources. Where possible, re-use materials from gardens that are being renovated. An added benefit is that recycled stone and wood will already have weathered and immediately soften the appearance of any new construction. Quarrying has an impact on the environment and, with a little research, recycled alternatives can be found for gravel and stones. Timber products should be certified as originating from sustainable sources.

Where to begin

Think about your perfect garden in terms of an analogous design triangle. To begin with, the garden must be functional and fulfil all the needs of the owners. This suggests that it must also be feasible. Think also about the style of garden you prefer, not only in terms of your own expectations, but in terms of how it will harmonize with the site and associated architecture. Finally, consider how the functionality and style of the garden might be affected by the constraints set by the site – its shape, size, aspect, climate, and so on. Bringing these three design factors together harmoniously should result in your perfect formula for success.

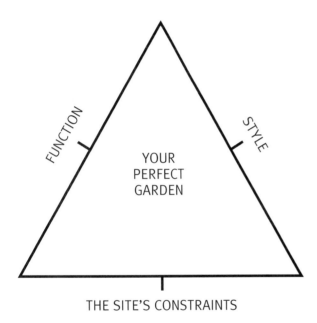

Some designers, both professional and amateur, design "on the ground" – that is to say, without actually recording their design or thoughts on paper. This approach can work, but it calls for a great deal of skill and a good memory. Mistakes are much more expensive and difficult to rectify on the ground than on paper and, more to the point, to a budding designer even a modest plot can be intimidating.

The importance of a drawn plan cannot, therefore, be emphasized too strongly.

Making a photographic record
When starting to assess your garden, it is helpful to make a full photographic record of the plot in all directions. The prints or digital print-outs can then be pinned to a large board,

preferably as a panoramic view. This can be especially helpful if the move to a new house and garden has not yet taken place and you are trying to prepare the garden plan in advance. Later on in the design process photographs can allow you to test the visual effects of your ideas. By overlaying them with tracing paper you can sketch in various options such as different tree shapes, path routes or an arch or pergola, and decide which look best. Take photographs from a normal standing or sitting position, since this is the height from which you will most frequently view and appreciate the garden. Photographs provide the most accurate evidence of the garden features' relative positions, and "before" and "after" photographs create a useful and interesting record of the progress and development of the garden over time.

The importance of a survey
It is vital to have an accurate record of the size and shape of the plot and of the features in it. Always start by taking measurements of the plot. This will ensure that every nook and cranny is recorded and, in the process, every view seen and remembered, for it is important to get to know the garden intimately.

Always check first to see if a measurement or survey plan exists before compiling your own. If the site is fairly new or extensive alterations have been made recently, there may well be a survey of the house and its plot held by the architect or developer involved. If this is the case, and if the survey is sufficiently detailed, you can use this plan instead of making your own. Check the scale and at least a few of the measurements before using an existing plan, for it may have been enlarged or reduced, making the stated scale false. If this is the case, use a photocopier to reduce or enlarge the copy of the survey until it is to the correct scale.

Calling in a professional
If your garden is particularly large, or if the plot is very steep or complex in shape, it may be too difficult to measure by yourself. Calling in a professional surveyor will probably be more cost-effective and accurate in gardens of over about 2½ hectares (1 acre). Laser instruments and computerized plotters can make light work of problems that would be almost insurmountable to the amateur surveyor.

It is best to find a surveyor through recommendation, or you could contact a relevant professional association as they will hold details of qualified and accredited members.

On sites of several acres or more, an aerial survey undertaken by a professional is an option, although a costly one. This will give you a detailed analysis of your site and will even show, if requested, changes of level.

The measurement plan

Starting to take measurements

The information to be collected forms the basis of the measurement plan and of the final design, so it is essential to work methodically and carefully. Start by pacing out the plot with approximately 1m (3ft) strides, roughly measuring the longest distances lengthways and across the garden. This will help you to decide on an appropriate scale. The larger the scale the better, and remember that 1:50 is a larger scale than 1:100. Once you have decided on the scale, record it.

A garden of half an acre or less can be measured by one person, but enlisting help should speed up the process.

Plotting the house

Again by pacing, determine the approximate size of the house and fix its position on the site, then pencil it in on the graph paper. Start measuring the house using the tape measure and, using the scale rule, draw it in on the graph paper.

Many of your subsequent measurements will be taken from the house, using the walls as "base lines", so be as accurate as you can. Include items such as drainpipes, windows and doors (noting whether they open inward or outward). If there are deep eaves, indicate with a dotted line how far they project beyond the house wall as they will create "rain shadows" that result in dry areas underneath.

Triangulation

After measuring the house and plotting it, give each house corner a code letter, as shown opposite, and write the letters clearly on the plan. Next, establish and plot the corner points of the garden, then join them with lines to represent the garden boundary. The most convenient way of measuring the corners is to use a method called triangulation. This involves drawing a series of triangles on the plan using a scale rule and a pair of compasses, or a beam compass. It is based on measurements taken on the ground using a 30m (100ft) tape and a 3m (10ft) steel retractable tape.

In the example shown opposite, a physical measurement is taken from house corner A to the boundary corner, in this case corner 1. The measurement from the tape is converted at the chosen scale using the scale rule, then plotted on the graph paper plan using the compasses, opened so that the radius (the distance between the compass point and the point of the pencil) accords with the scaled-down measurement. The compass point is placed on the plan on house corner A and a generous arc is drawn in the general location of the boundary corner 1 using the pencil in the compasses. Following the same process a second measurement is taken, this time from house corner B to boundary point 1 again. The true measurement is scaled down to give a radius for the

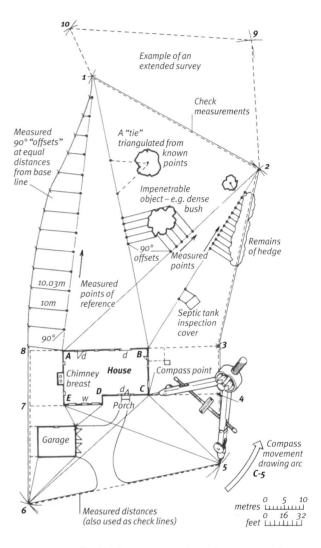

Example of an extended survey

Check measurements

Measured 90° "offsets" at equal distances from base line

A "tie" triangulated from known points

Impenetrable object – e.g. dense bush

90° offsets

Measured points

Remains of hedge

10.03m

10m

90°

Measured points of reference

Septic tank inspection cover

Compass point

House

Chimney breast

Porch

Garage

Compass movement drawing arc C-5

Measured distances (also used as check lines)

metres 0 5 10
feet 0 16 32

compasses and, with the compass point at house corner B, a second arc is drawn, bisecting the first. The point at which the two arcs cross gives the precise position of boundary corner 1.

On your plan, establish and record each boundary corner in this way. As each boundary corner is fixed, draw lines to join them. Check the accuracy by taking a measurement between the points of the boundary corners, scaling it down and comparing it with the distance you have plotted on the plan.

Occasionally a corner or object may be out of sight of the house, as is the case with corner 6 in the diagram. To establish its position, the position of the garage must be fixed, then the garage corners used as the reference points.

The measurement plan

In a very large garden with distances well beyond the scope of a 30m (100ft) or even 50m (150ft) tape measure, or where areas are partly or wholly hidden from view, triangulation can still be achieved using a "leap frog" method. In the example shown on page 11, an established distant line 1–2 is used as a base line for the next section of the measurement plan. In the extended survey, further triangles have been constructed to fix the hypothetical corners 9 and 10.

Offsets

To plot curved boundaries or features, "offsets" are taken. Offsets are measured lines running at 90 degrees to the base line, usually at regularly spaced intervals, say 1m (3ft 3in), 2m (6ft 6in) or 3m (10ft). The more complicated the curve, the closer the offsets need to be.

In the measurement plan on page 11, the boundary line 1–8 is plotted by taking offsets from A–1, the nearest base line, but if there is no convenient line on which to base the offsets, you may have to establish one for the purpose.

A dot or cross is drawn on the graph paper to represent the end of each offset line drawn away from the base line. These dots or crosses are then joined with a pencil line to represent the curved boundary. It is important to ensure that the tape for measuring the offsets is at 90 degrees to the base line: this can be done by laying a second tape along the base line

on the ground, making sure it is flat and taut. Then use a large set square or a builder's square to check that the offsets are perpendicular to it. An alternative method is to lay the offset tape over the base line tape with its edge along the printed calibrations on the base line tape. If the offset tape is not at 90 degrees the tape and calibration lines will not align.

Offsets can be used in conjunction with triangulation to establish the precise positions on the measurement plan of, in the example on page 11, a tree.

Sighting off

If the plot is square or rectangular with the house sited squarely on it, and the boundaries are close to the house, you may not need to use triangulation to establish their positions. A method known as "sighting off" is adequate, but two people are needed. One person looks along the appropriate house wall until it appears as a single vertical line while the second person, under instruction from the first, places a range pole or cane against the object or boundary to be plotted. The second person pushes the pole or cane into the ground at a point where it and the line of the house wall appear to align, then measurements can be taken between the two.

Range poles

Range poles or canes can be used as mobile points of reference and are especially useful if there are no other physical reference points in the plot being measured.

When using range poles for triangulation, however, remember to position the poles or canes forming the triangle so that they are clearly visible and the space between them is clear. Remember also to stretch the tape measure straight between the points being measured since the results will be inaccurate if the tape is curved or bent.

Adding detail

The "flat" measurement plan, giving a bird's-eye view of the plot and the features in it, is important, but there are other pieces of information that have a bearing on your design. This extra data can be recorded either on the measurement plan, or separately. One of the most important details you need to measure and record is any rise and fall in ground levels.

Positioning tapes for offset measurements

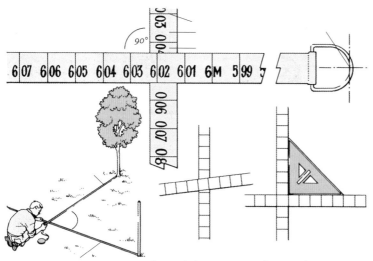

Establish the precise position of the tree using offset measurements.

Incorrect: these tapes are not at 90° so will give incorrect readings.

Correct: using a set square to check the tapes are at right angles.

The measurement plan

Changes of level

Whatever the style of garden you intend to design, you must take account of any changes of level in the plot.

If you are designing a sloping garden along formal lines, perhaps with terraces, walls and steps, for example, then you need precise information on the degree of slope. If you propose to build steps up the slope, you will have to calculate the number needed, their dimensions and the angle of ascent and descent. Without accurate measurements it would be easy to make some serious and expensive mistakes.

Establishing changes in level

Changes in level can be measured using simple equipment. This is especially so if only "spot" level measurements are required, indicating the relative levels of specific points in the garden: for example, the patio door relative to an inspection cover or to the base of a tree, or the four corners of a garden relative to each other.

Professionals use the "grid system", which calls for a comprehensive set of readings taken and recorded at the points of intersection of a series of equally spaced, notional parallel lines running at right angles to form squares over the site (the grid). A measurement plan like this would probably have to be carried out professionally, whereas a spot measurement plan is much easier to achieve.

Implementing the plan

On completion of the design, work out a strategy for its implementation. You will need to draw up a timetable of tasks, some to be carried out by yourself, others by contractors. This will probably show a series of overlapping phases.

Choose nurseries, suppliers or contractors who are known or recommended to you. Obtain references for contractors and follow them up. Check whether your contractor is a member of a recognized professional trade body: such organizations supply lists of their members.

Estimates and contracts

Estimates should always be sought before orders are placed or instructions given. Obtain several estimates and, in the case of a professional contractor, a quotation if possible.

A quotation sets out a mutually agreed fixed price, whereas an estimate can change and is more likely to rise than to fall. Contractors' estimates can vary according to instructions to include labour only, or labour and materials. Ensure that everyone asked to quote or estimate is given the same information. At the same time agree the payment terms and the timing of payments. Alterations made to the plan during the contract period will have cost implications. These should be agreed before the event and not afterwards, since misunderstandings of this nature can easily lead to dispute.

SEQUENCE OF ACTION

A logical sequence of events for the realization of a garden would be as follows:

1 **Complete garden plan** to detail.

2 **Prepare a work schedule** taking into account normal seasonal variations. Build in time for delays

3 **Order construction materials** and plants requesting delivery dates appropriate to the timetable and season. Some may have to be ordered months ahead – for more unusual plants this can take up to a year.

4 **Clear the garden** of unwanted materials, weeds and plants.

5 **Carry out major ground contouring,** taking care not to mix subsoil and topsoil together.

6 **Install underground service lines,** pipes and drains, removing excess materials from the garden to use for infilling elsewhere. Excavate for ponds. Lay foundations and bases, erect fences and so on. Line out, finish and fill ponds.

7 **Construct all vertical elements,** such as steps, walls, and pergolas, followed by the hard horizontal elements, such as patios and paths.

8 **Finalize soil contouring** and bring to adjacent path and patio levels. Cultivate areas to be planted, importing additional or exporting surplus topsoil as required. Incorporate organic materials and fertilizers if and when appropriate.

9 **Implement the planting plan** and mulch on completion. Plant the trees in the proposed grassed areas. Finish planting around pools.

10 **Finely cultivate the areas to be grassed,** incorporating organic matter, fertilizer and surface drainage material appropriate to soil type and intended use, for example ornamental sward or hard-wearing grass for a games area.

11 **Turf or seed** the areas to be grassed. Reuse turfs that have been removed during contouring or construction work.

12 **Make final checks** and any final adjustment.

14 **Work out** a maintenance schedule.

15 **Enjoy the garden** and watch it develop. Keep a photographic record of it as it changes during seasons and evolves over time.

Site assessment

Using a wall or buildings to establish ground levels

In order to be appropriate for this technique, a wall must be constructed with its courses and mortar joints level and clearly visible. Where the ground is at its highest relative to the wall, make a note of the brick or stone horizontal mortar joint it reaches. Run your finger along this horizontal joint to the end of the wall and mark it. Measure vertically down to the soil at this point (H in the diagram, below). The reading indicates by how much the ground has sloped relative to the starting point. The distance over which the slope has occurred is equal to the length of the wall.

Using panel fencing

The tops of any ready-made fencing panels used in the garden should be level. This means that the rise or fall in the ground level of the garden can be calculated by adding together the measured steps $h_1 + h_2 + h_3$ and so on (see diagram, below).

Base the measurements on relative tops of panels rather than on the vertical posts since they often project unevenly and may have caps or finials attached.

Using a spirit level and straightedge

Choose a timber or metal straightedge about 2m (6ft 6in) long. Check that it is straight by looking along its length with one eye; any bows will be apparent immediately. Lay the spirit level on top of the straightedge, then, resting one end of the straightedge on the ground at the highest level, lift the other until the bubble in the spirit level shows that it is horizontal.

Drive a stake into the ground just under the lifted or raised end of the straightedge. When you can place the raised end on top of the stake and the spirit level shows the straightedge to be horizontal, measure from the top of the stake to the ground. This indicates the fall over the entire length of the straightedge. Repeat the process to measure the entire slope.

Using a garden hosepipe and two funnels

The hosepipe used must be at least as long as the distance over which the fall is to be measured. Drive a stake vertically into the ground and attach one end of the hose with the funnel attached to it. Ask someone to hold the other end of the hosepipe with its funnel or, if the slope is particularly steep, it is better to attach the funnel to a hand-held pole (see diagram on page 15).

Using a watering can or a second hose, slowly pour water into the fixed upper funnel A until the lower funnel B overflows. Move the lower funnel B up and down, carefully, and slowly add more water until it is brimming, but not overflowing, in both funnels. At this stage the funnels are at the same level. Now ask a third person to measure from the top lip of the "lower" funnel B to the ground using a steel tape. Subtract the height of funnel A from the height of funnel B to establish the groundfall between the two. One advantage

Using structures to establish ground levels

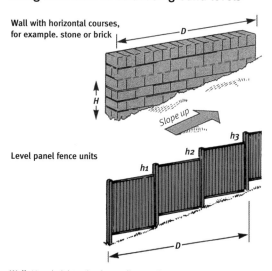

Wall: H_1 = height gained over distance D
Fence: $h_1 + h_2 + h_3$ height gained over distance D

Using a spirit level and straightedge to determine groundfall

The length of the straightedge multiplied by the number of measurements taken indicates the length of the garden, provided that the straightedges do not overlap.

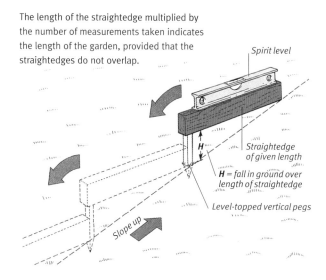

H = fall in ground over length of straightedge

Site assessment

EQUATION 1

Length of garden: 78m (256ft)
Length of wall: 16m (52ft)

x

groundfall
wall length: 0.45m (18ins)

= fall over entire garden: 2.19m (7ft 2ins)

78 (256) ÷ 16 (52) = 4.87 (4.92)

4.87 (4.92) x 450mm (18ins) = 2.19m (7ft 2ins)

EQUATION 2

Calculate as follows:
Total length of the garden divided by the multiple of the length of the straightedge, multiplied by the sum of the heights, straightedge measured to ground.

Example:
The garden's length is 72m (234ft) approximately. The length of the straightedge is 2m (6ft 6in). Therefore, the length of the garden requires 36 separate straightedge readings.

The total fall measured from beneath the straightedge to the ground adds up to 4.15m (13ft 6in approximately). The groundfall may vary a little down the slope so the 4.15m (13ft 6in), when divided by 36 straightedge lengths, shows an average fall of 12.5cm (5in) every 2m (6ft 6in) equivalent to 6.25cm (2½in) every metre (3ft 3in).

A typical hand-held level

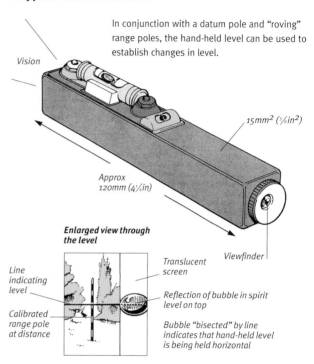

In conjunction with a datum pole and "roving" range poles, the hand-held level can be used to establish changes in level.

Vision

$15mm^2$ (⅝in^2)

Approx 120mm (4¼in)

Viewfinder

Enlarged view through the level

Line indicating level

Translucent screen

Calibrated range pole at distance

Reflection of bubble in spirit level on top

Bubble "bisected" by line indicates that hand-held level is being held horizontal

Using a hosepipe and two funnels to establish ground levels

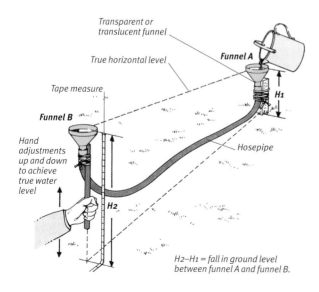

Transparent or translucent funnel

True horizontal level

Funnel A

Tape measure

H1

Funnel B

Hand adjustments up and down to achieve true water level

Hosepipe

H2

H2–H1 = fall in ground level between funnel A and funnel B.

Using a hand-held level and range poles

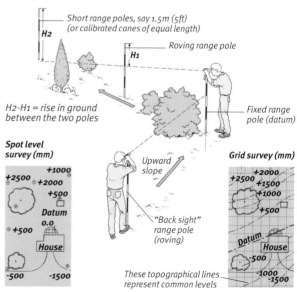

Short range poles, say 1.5m (5ft) (or calibrated canes of equal length)

H2

Roving range pole

H1

H2-H1 = rise in ground between the two poles

Fixed range pole (datum)

Upward slope

Spot level survey (mm)

+1000
+2500 ⊕+2000
+500

Datum
0.0

⊕+500

House

-500   -1500

"Back sight" range pole (roving)

Grid survey (mm)

+2000
+2500 +1500
+1000

+500

Datum

House

-500

-1000
-1500

These topographical lines represent common levels

Site assessment

of this method is that the hosepipe need not be straight and this makes it possible to measure around corners. The method will not work properly, however, if there is a kink in the hosepipe or if any section of the hose is higher than the funnels, since either situation would affect the flow of water.

Using a hand-held level
The hand-held level (illustrated on page 15) is an inexpensive optical instrument. By gently tilting the hand-held level up and down, the black line indicating level will eventually coincide with the bubble of the reflected spirit level. This shows that the instrument is level and can he used in conjunction with a couple of range poles to detect changes in level.

The range poles must be the same height, preferably about 1.5m (5ft) and calibrated identically. One is pushed into the ground at the lowest point to represent datum and remains there while all measurements are taken.

Note by how much the datum pole is driven into the ground. Then drive the other pole, known as the "rover", into the ground by the same amount at the point where the increase in ground height is to be measured. Rest the handheld level on top of the datum pole and look into the viewfinder. Move the level gently up and down until the horizontal line within the instrument bisects the bubble. Now look beyond the line and bubble to see where the horizontal line appears to coincide with the calibrations of the rover pole. You can estimate the change in level by noting how many calibrations appear above the horizontal line of the hand-held level and record this on the measurement plan as a plus quantity, such as +450mm (18in) or +750mm (2ft 6in).

Reposition the rover in any part of the garden to establish spot levels, but make sure it is clearly visible from the datum pole. You may occasionally need to measure levels that are lower than the datum. Under these circumstances, position the rover in the lower spot and take the reading from there back to the datum pole, but record these measurements on the plan as minus quantities, such as -300mm (1ft) or -900mm (3ft), since they are lower than the datum.

Assessing a mature garden
If you inherit a mature garden and intend to make changes to meet your own requirements, do not make any immediate decisions because at any time of year there are bound to be plants that are dormant and features and effects that are not immediately apparent. If you assess a garden in winter, there may be no evidence of bulbs or herbaceous plants. Similarly, in summer, paths, paving and ornaments may be lost under luxuriant plant growth or grass. It is wise simply to observe the garden for a year.

Soil testing with pH meter or "test tube" kit

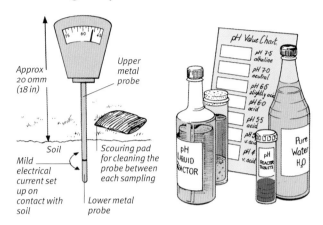

Testing soil type
The best garden design is useless if no attention is paid to the soil, as the soil must be in good condition if the plants specified in the design are to thrive. In general, plants should be chosen to suit the local soil type, but it is not unknown within new housing developments for the native soil to have been removed and replaced with a token layer of soil from elsewhere, or soil of poor quality.

In any new garden make a proper check of the soil rather than relying on superficial observations. First check the soil structure (see also page 89). The scope of this book does not cover in-depth details of the methods of identifying the clay, sand, silt and organic material content of soil. However, other books will cover this, and give advice on correcting any deficiencies. Then assess its texture and, if necessary, take steps to bring it closer to the ideal open crumb structure that allows optimal movement of water, air and roots.

Testing soil pH
The pH is a measurement of soil acidity or alkalinity and it will dictate the types of plants that are likely to thrive in it. A pH of 7.5 or higher is alkaline, 7 is neutral, while figures lower than 7 are acid, with 4.5 representing a very acid soil. You can establish the pH of your garden soil using a pH meter or using a simple "test tube" type kit available at garden centres.

Take several samples, as soil conditions can vary across the plot. Take the samples from approximately 150mm (6in) down, then carry out the test as soon as possible, as leaving the soil may alter its condition. Avoid taking samples from areas where fertilizers or herbicides have been applied as these chemicals may result in an unrepresentative reading.

Tools for garden construction

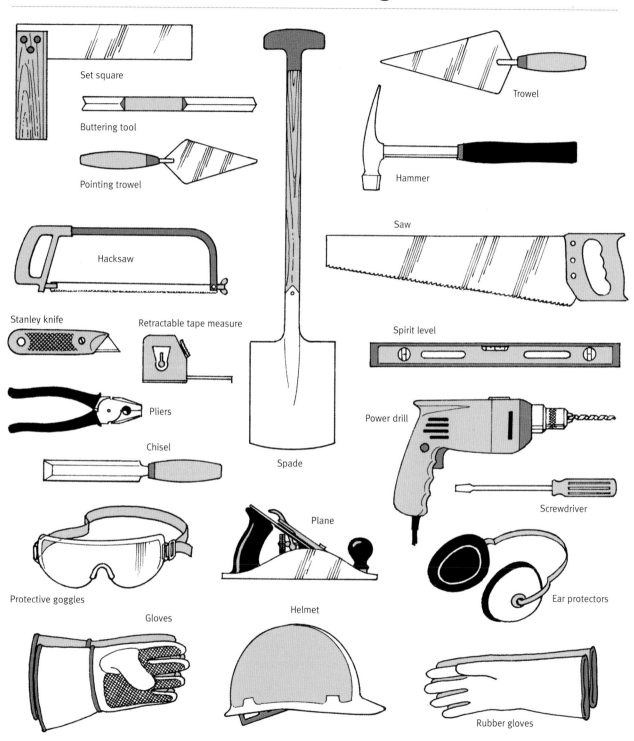

Set square

Buttering tool

Pointing trowel

Trowel

Hammer

Hacksaw

Saw

Stanley knife

Retractable tape measure

Spirit level

Pliers

Chisel

Spade

Power drill

Screwdriver

Protective goggles

Plane

Ear protectors

Gloves

Helmet

Rubber gloves

The function of a garden

Estimating costs

When designing a garden, you must consider the costs involved. Try to form an idea of the costs of plants, materials and services by visiting builders' merchants, garden centres and nurseries. You must decide how much of the work you are prepared or able to do yourself or you may decide to consult a professional garden contractor for some of the work. The contractor must be fully briefed in order to estimate accurately, so provide as much information as possible.

Try to set a realistic overall budget at the outset; then, as the design develops, research the cost of implementing each area. Certain details of the design may have to be trimmed or adjusted to ensure that the work stays within budget.

Needs and requirements

Start by making a list of everything that is required from the garden. Such a list can become complicated: it must include but distinguish between what is needed, what is desired and what is expected. What is truly needed must take top priority: for example, a vegetable garden may be a necessity. What is desired might include a rose garden, a pool, or a velvety lawn and this is where style and aesthetics come into the equation.

A garden for everyone

Bringing the needs, desires and expectations of all the family members together into an harmonious whole is one of the most difficult parts of garden design. To begin with, the drawing up of a family requirement list should be a "free for all" session. This list may not be entirely feasible or affordable, but without it there is little chance of satisfying even one individual, let alone the whole family. Spend plenty of time studying the requirements list with the function plan (shown on page 21) – then take a sheet of tracing paper, lay it over the site assessment plan and mark the areas that would best suit the proposed facilities. Do move things around on paper. Take as much time as you need to get them exactly in their right place as you have one opportunity to get it right – it might be too late after installation.

Always ensure that each "functional" area is of an appropriate size, proportion or shape. As with the proportions of vertical elements, certain functions cannot be performed without a reasonable amount of space. At this stage we are not concerned with form (this is the next stage in design), simply where and how things are going to happen.

The logic of garden function

When designing rear and side gardens, many professional designers commence drawing their function plan from the house, perhaps starting at the main point of access. The most important view of a rear garden will probably be from the house doors, windows or terrace, so this is the logical place to begin. Starting here and moving outwards introduces a degree of logic to the process. The same principle can be applied to the front garden, but here it is a good idea to start at the entrance to the drive and work towards the house.

This, then, is the value of the function plan: it allows ideas to be explored and areas or features to be moved around on paper until they are allotted their most appropriate place.

Example of a function plan

The example of a function plan (on page 21) was produced by overlaying the assessment plan with tracing paper and drawing over it. This is where garden designing really begins.
Front garden Starting at the front of the house, the drive needs upgrading to accommodate extra car parking or a turning area. The garage should be visually softened from the direction of the road. The opposite side of the drive could be planted simply or given a more formal treatment.
Access Good access is called for at each side of the house, as is a screen between front and rear areas. The shady side of the house provides an opportunity to grow ferns and other shade-loving plants, while the sunny side of the house is the best place for growing vegetables and herbs, especially as it is close to the kitchen door.
Placing the terrace The area immediately to the rear of the house, being in full sun until well into the afternoon, is designated for activities including dining and sunbathing. The area needs to be large to accommodate this. Even a simple item such as a table 900mm (3ft) in diameter with four chairs, requires a surprisingly large space: you should set aside an area of up to 4m (12ft) in diameter.
Away from the house Beyond the terrace is an open area of lawn with the other features arranged at its periphery. The left side of the grassed area is reserved for children's play. Trees and shrubs have been planted in the far corner to link with those in the neighbouring plot. The idea is to create the effect of light woodland while concealing the boundary fence. Functionally, this planting will also create an effective barrier to the cold winter winds. On the far right more trees will be needed to screen the neighbour's house from view. This same general area will accommodate a second sitting area.
Problem features Unsightly but necessary features such as septic tank covers frequently have to be incorporated into gardens; the skill of the designer involves including them but making them as unobtrusive as possible.

In addition, access routes around the garden must be planned with care as these form the "skeleton" of a garden design. And at the next stage routes will need to be precise.

Above: Professional designers
usually draw a function plan for
a rear garden from the house
looking outwards. This design
moves seamlesslessly from a
patio area up steps into an
open area meant for relaxation.

Far left: This small town garden has a straightforward if unadventurous design; a redesign might well provide a larger terrace for sitting, as well as curvy paths and borders to provide visual contrast.

Left: When adding constructed elements such as a pool or decking it is essential to work out the correct proportions.

Below: In any style of garden it is vital that key structures such as glasshouses are easily accessible and thoughtfully sited.

The function of a garden

The basic garden's function plan (on tracing paper)

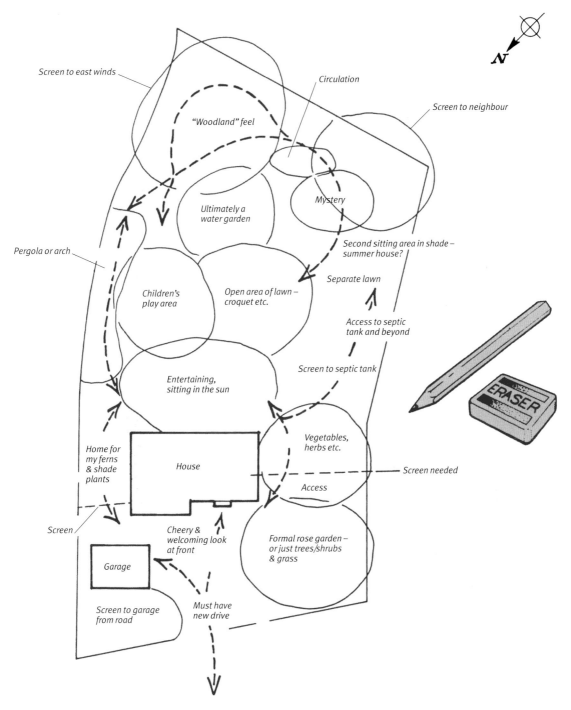

Screen to east winds

Circulation

Screen to neighbour

"Woodland" feel

Mystery

Ultimately a water garden

Second sitting area in shade – summer house?

Pergola or arch

Separate lawn

Children's play area

Open area of lawn – croquet etc.

Access to septic tank and beyond

Screen to septic tank

Entertaining, sitting in the sun

Vegetables, herbs etc.

Home for my ferns & shade plants

House

Screen needed

Access

Screen

Cheery & welcoming look at front

Formal rose garden – or just trees/shrubs & grass

Garage

Screen to garage from road

Must have new drive

ERASER

Theory and technique

To develop the function plan into a successful and pleasing outline or schematic plan you need to appreciate the basic principles of garden design.

Continuity

Individual garden spaces or rooms should never be designed to be totally independent of each other. Continuity is essential within the garden, even when one space may be hidden from another. It helps to form a pleasing structure, and the more informal the garden, the greater the need for this kind of coherence as, without it, a garden will lack harmony.

Harmony

Perhaps the most important and intangible of garden design principles is harmony. Harmony is a just and balanced adaptation of all parts one to another, forming an agreeable whole. The creation of harmony in a garden, particularly a new one, can be slow. Paved surfaces and constructed vertical elements produce more or less instant effects but trees and plants generally take years to mature and gain their full stature and mass. Though harmony may take a long time to achieve, the designer must have it in mind from the outset.

Different types of harmony

Colour and texture For many gardeners, harmony of colour is paramount, but there are many other types: harmony should exist not only between one plant and another, but also between the plants and the constructed elements and between the constructed elements themselves. The concept of harmonious design also extends to textures and forms. This does not mean that these need to be safe or uneventful. Quite the opposite can be true: schemes using exciting colours, textures or forms can be brought together harmoniously. Remember, harmony is not synonymous with conventionality.

Unity A facet of harmony, unity can be thought of as a thread or theme running through a garden, drawing its disparate parts into a whole, where architecture, hard and soft landscaping, planting and features come together to form a single coherent entity.

Balance

Balance must be present in all aspects of a garden design. It often goes unrecognized when it does exist, but when it doesn't, it is all too obvious. A simple example of balance would be a matching pair of conifers marking the entrance to a pathway, or two identical flights of steps at each end of a formal retaining wall.

Balance is virtually intrinsic to symmetrical designs, but it can be harder to see how to achieve it in asymmetrical or informal design. This is where the hidden laws of balance come into play. For example, large masses can be balanced against smaller but "weightier" elements; in a garden context this may mean planting some large "frothy" trees at one side to strike an aesthetic balance with a "heavier" building at the other, the trees in this instance being the "mass" and the building the "weight".

A garden with a slope across the main view can be disconcerting, as the garden seems about to slide into the next property. This type of imbalance can be rectified by placing a much greater mass on the lower side than on the higher.

Planning for balance

Where plants and trees are concerned, a rough sketch of the proposed arrangement in vertical form indicating ultimate height, form and, if possible, texture will give an idea of how a balance will eventually be achieved. As with harmony, balance is often lacking in the formative years of a garden, but it is important to plan ahead for it.

There is an unwritten law stating that groups of trees planted in odd numbers achieve balance. This does generally work, but rules of this type need not be followed

Creating harmony in garden design using different shapes

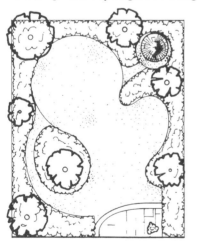

Harmony using curvilinear shapes in a large garden.

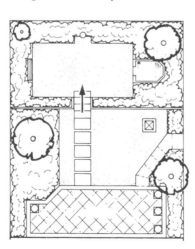

Harmony using rectangular and polygonal shapes in a small garden.

Theory and technique

slavishly. Always follow your own design instincts rather than those of others — it is your garden after all.

Balance in planting design
Before embarking on your own design make a point of visiting as many gardens as possible. Study those which, in your opinion, are well balanced and try to analyse why you feel that they are, so you can apply the same techniques.

Colour balance is not easy to achieve and it certainly cannot be sustained unless a proper planting plan has been prepared. Drawing up a detailed planting plan allows you to consider each subject individually and in the context of the whole planting. Make notes of foliage and flower colours, including shades and tones, stature, form, habit, cultural requirements and flowering season. This last characteristic is especially important since a scheme based on flower colour alone will lack harmony if the plants selected to complement each other bloom at different times of the year.

Since flowering periods can be relatively short it is also important to take into account other characteristics of a plant or tree. Make sure that the plants still combine well together when flowering is over.

Before re-design

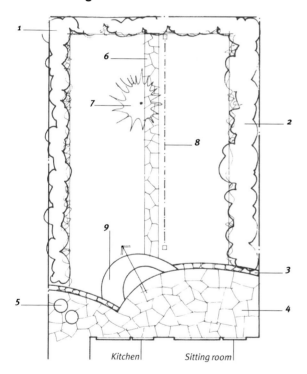

Several features spoil the garden and the whole layout adds up to a poor use of the site. The badly laid crazy paving terrace (4) clashes with the shape of the house. Retaining walls made from broken concrete (3) are unsafe, as are the steps (9). The central path (6) divides the rectangular garden into unrelated sections, as do the shrub beds (1, 2) around the lawn and the washing line (8). Other existing features are a sumach tree (7), and an open corner for dustbins (5). The aim of the designer is to provide a family garden, with safe, attractive steps and paving. The design should distract from the straight boundaries.

After re-design

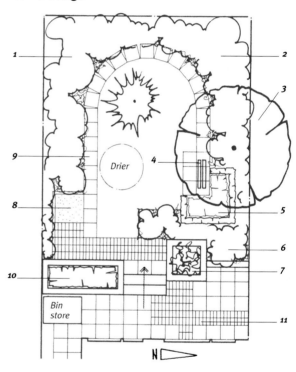

The terrace has been reshaped to provide room for sitting and eating. It has been resurfaced with neat precast slabs and bricks to provide contrast. The path (9, 11) now sweeps round the garden, ending at a seat (4) under a *Robina pseudoacacia* 'Frisia' tree (3) which provides a focal point. The shape of the lawns and the borders now give strong, flowing curves rather than straight lines. Raised beds are provided for annuals (7) and shrubs and trailers (10). There is a bed for salad or herbs (5), one for roses (6), and a mixed shrub and herbaceous border (1, 2). A play area with sandpit is provided for the children (8).

Scale and proportion

Good scale and proportion within a garden is dependent on several factors, including the size of the plot relative to the house and surroundings, and the proportional relationship between the garden and the elements within it.

Constructed elements

At a practical level too, constructed elements can suffer from being wrongly proportioned. For example, a summer house must be large enough to accommodate the number of people likely to use it and the supports and beams of a pergola must be in proportion to its overall size. Such features would not function below a certain size, so they might have to be excluded from a very small plot.

Take plenty of time to make sure that everything fits well into the plan. Rough sketches of the features on tracing paper can be laid over photographs of the area or areas concerned and give an indication of how they will look.

Vertical proportions

Any single oversized element will make part of or even the entire garden appear smaller. For instance, a large tree growing in a relatively small plot diminishes the area. Oversized hedges, fences and walls can also adversely affect the sense of space and movement within a garden.

Horizontal proportions

Horizontal surfaces should also be designed in proportion, not only to the area but to their function. Wherever possible a path should be a comfortable width with an allowance made for any adjacent plant overgrowth. The main pathways of a garden should be wide enough to accommodate the passage of garden equipment and to allow two people to walk side by side. The dimensions of a patio or terrace should be as generous as possible not only for practical purposes but to provide a satisfying visual foundation to the house. Any paved area must be constructed using units of a size proportional to its overall dimensions. Paving units which are too small make a large area appear fussy, while units which are too large make a limited area appear smaller (see page 35).

Proportion in a small garden

In pursuit of good proportion, certain compromises may have to be made in a small garden between the size of the paved areas, lawn and borders relative to plot size.

A horizontal surface which is too large relative to the overall size of the site will draw attention to the lack of space. Lawn and paving areas made deliberately large to increase the sense of space will often have the reverse effect, leaving little or no opportunity to screen or camouflage the boundary with planting. Where boundaries are obvious the sense of enclosure is increased.

Undersized elements are as unwelcome as those which are oversized. For example, a small flower bed in a large expanse of lawn will look incongruous and a small piece of sculpture at the end of a long vista will fail as a focal point because it looks insignificant.

Simplicity

A common fault with gardens is that they are too fussy or complicated. It may be that no proper plan was made in the first place, resulting in a collection of disjointed ideas, often following impulse-buying at the garden centre. Or the garden

A round pool which is too small for its surroundings.

A round pool sized so that is in proportion to its surroundings.

This pool is too large, both practically and visually, for the space in which it sits.

Scale and proportion

may have been over-designed, with too many features each competing for attention. Indecision or a lack of direction could be the cause, as there is often a compulsion to fill every available space. Try to resist this, as simplicity is an essential part of good garden design.

Restraint in planning
When aiming for simplicity, be decisive and design your plan along simple lines, resisting the temptation to cram in too many different plants and materials. Simplicity should be applied at all levels of design from the basic layout to the final choice of building materials and plants. All gardens benefit from simplicity, but small gardens particularly so.

Interest
What is interesting to one individual may not be so to another, but this is one of the joys of designing your own garden. The purpose of your design is to create an environment in which specialized interests can be integrated with the overall scheme while satisfying aesthetic and practical needs. This can stretch the imagination but is attainable only if the specialists and enthusiasts, as well as other family members, are involved at the initial planning stage.

Creating suspense
Every garden should be interesting in its own right. Gardens which can be seen in their entirety and at one glance will inevitably become boring. Of course you will know what lies behind the screen or at the end of a curving path – but the sense of intrigue will remain. Try to create certain areas which are not so readily seen or places which have to be visited – making sure that they are worth visiting. In the smallest of gardens, low walls, disappearing paths or planting can suggest hidden spaces even though they may be non-existent.

Focal points
Focal points play an important role in providing garden interest. An attractive focal point, glimpsed at a distance, will have the effect of drawing the visitor from one area to another.

If the garden is large and contains several focal points, arrange them in such a way that, having arrived at one, another can be glimpsed further on. It is unacceptable in terms of good design for more than one focal point to be plainly visible at the same time as this will cause confusion, leading to a lack of balance and harmony.

A focal point need not necessarily be an artifact. A distinctive tree, an area of water or a composition of natural or naturalistic elements can be equally entrancing. A beautiful or dramatic view lying outside the garden will almost

inevitably become the principal focal point, reducing any others in the same field of vision to mere interruptions.

Functionality and feasibility
A garden may look attractive and exciting in plan form but if it is not feasible or does not function properly then it cannot be deemed to have been well designed. Keep in mind the old adage "form follows function". Research every element of the plan thoroughly, including the cost of creating the garden and also of maintaining it.

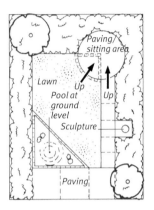

An asymmetrical formal design based upon geometric shapes. Many permutations are possible.

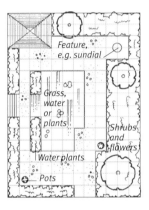

A garden based on the "grid" system. A useful early route to harmonious and unified design.

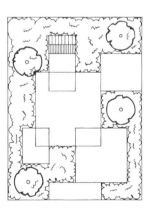

Using overlapping squares and rectangles. The example does not designate the areas for specific purposes, but your own ideas can.

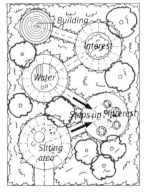

Circles are popular, although, if touching, they can create awkward shapes between them. Here each circular area has its own function.

Drawing up the plan

The outline plan represents the penultimate stage in the planning process. It must take into account the information derived from the site measurement and assessment, the requirements list and the function plan and be based on the principles of functional and aesthetically pleasing design.

How to set up for plan drawing

From now on, all versions of the plan need to be drawn with a greater degree of precision. Remember that the plan is not only a means of recording your thoughts but will be useful for calculations and for the quantification of plants and materials. It is important to draw the plan so that it can be photocopied or duplicated in some way: on tracing paper, for example. The original is unlikely to last the entire period of the garden's construction, particularly if it is regularly used outdoors.

The preparation of a garden plan is time-consuming, but to what degree depends on its complexity, size and the amount of detail involved. Because of this a centre of operations is needed. This could be based around a professional drawing board or simply a rectangle of smooth hardboard.

Drawing symbols

A garden plan is obviously more meaningful if the various elements have their own distinct symbols. You will probably develop your own graphic style but the symbol examples shown right may help at first. If the drawing is intended also as a visual realization, then make the graphics more realistic, perhaps introducing colour.

Adding detail

To make the plan even clearer, give existing shrubs or trees a different symbol from proposed additions. Draw the symbols for proposed trees to scale, with outlines representing their estimated spread at a reasonable stage of maturity, say in five to ten years. Draw existing mature trees to scale so that their true spread is represented – this is especially important if plants are to be placed under the canopy.

Shrubs and herbaceous plants can also be represented. At the earlier stages, use a general symbol simply to indicate how a bed or border will appear. Later, when deciding precisely what plants are needed, their exact location, their estimated size on maturity and consequently their spacing and numbers, draw in labelled symbols indicating each plant group or tree.

Do the same for other structural details: show the vertical features and surface materials drawn to scale to give an accurate idea of intended sizes.

When inventing symbols of your own, begin by imagining the bird's-eye view of the particular object or element and keep the symbols as simple as possible.

Standard tree symbols

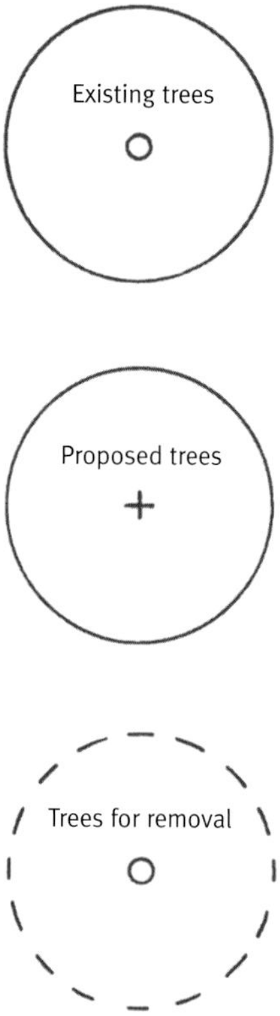

Existing trees

Proposed trees

Trees for removal

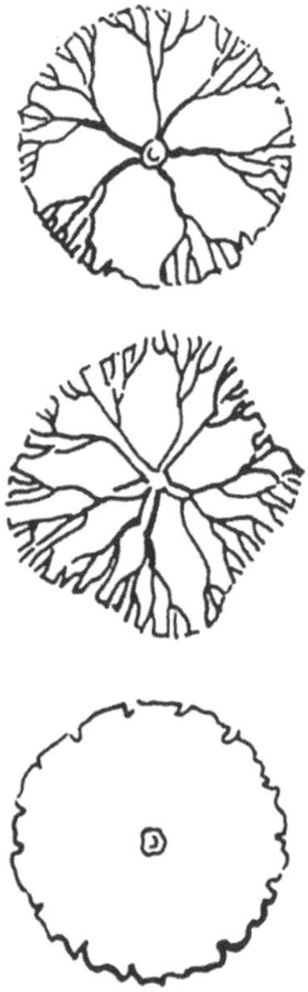

Coniferous types

More realistic tree symbols

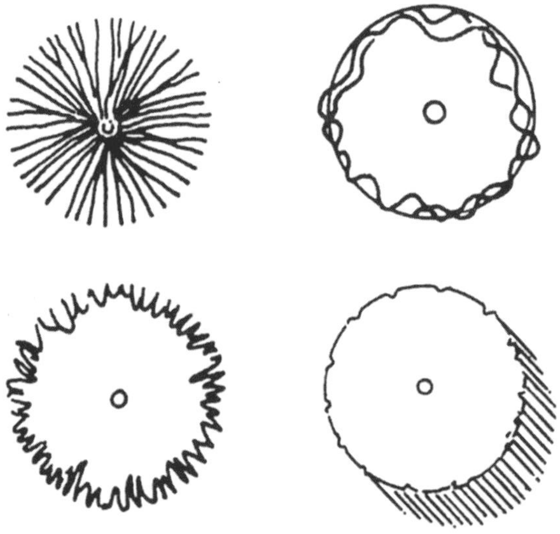

Drawing up the plan

Ground cover symbols (in plan)

Mown grass

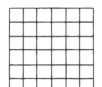

Square or rectangular paving

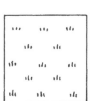

Rough grass

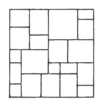

Random rectangular paving

Gravel

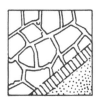

Random natural (crazy) paving, brick edging

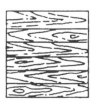

Timber decking

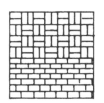

Brick paving, various patterns

Plants and bare soil

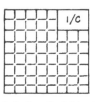

Setts (granite, brick, etc., with inspection cover)

Plan symbol examples

Boulders

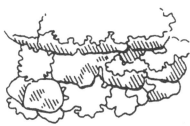

Stratified rockery (plan)

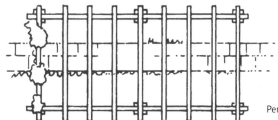

Pergola (plan)

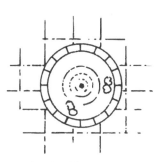

Formal pool and fountain

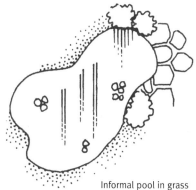

Informal pool in grass

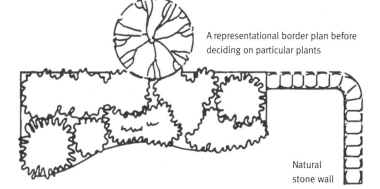

A representational border plan before deciding on particular plants

Natural stone wall

Drawing up the plan

The example opposite of an outline plan shows how a harmonious composition might be achieved by following the design planning processes we have already outlined.

Front garden

The existing driveway needed to be enlarged and resurfaced, preferably with material linking it visually with the house. On its left (seen from the road), an informally shaped lawn has been positioned in front of the garage from which access is gained to the area at its rear, at the same time leaving room for shrubs and a tree to distract the eye from the unattractive garage wall. To the right there is a formal rose garden and a weeping tree to attractively frame the house.

Paths and services

A path to the right of the house serves both the kitchen door and the vegetable garden, with a surrounding hedge acting as a screen (but not so high as to exclude too much light).

Space has been found on the shady side for a glasshouse. It is usually better for a glasshouse not to be in full sun-on the south side of a wall, for example, nor positioned in permanent shade either. The glasshouse and small toolshed next to it are reached via a path and rose arch. Beyond this the path veers to the left, passing the shrub- and tree-screened septic tank cover. Reasonable access is always needed to the tank from the front drive. A minor cranked or angled path leads to it and this, in conjunction with planting, obscures a direct view of the unsightly septic tank cover.

Recreational areas

Eventually the main path links with the shaded, secondary sitting area, which incorporates a small summer house backed by trees. These trees screen the house next door, but also ensure that the summer house sits well in the design, making it a subtle focal point. Close by, the grassy "glade" is completely hidden from view, forming a secret garden. This has a simple bench within it.

Beyond the glade the path divides. The main path continues and eventually reaches a bench seat, positioned as another focal point and for rest and contemplation. The narrower path, meanwhile, veers to the right, passing through the "woodland" planting. Here a variety of plants and shrubs, all appropriate to and thriving in the same moist, shady conditions, may be enjoyed at close quarters.

Taking care of wildlife

The proposed informally shaped wildlife pond echoes the general theme of the garden. Because there is a natural mound on the far side of the area earmarked for the pool, some means of retention was thought necessary to allow a flat walking surface to be cut into it so that the path can circle the pool. To achieve this a dry-stone or rock retaining wall is constructed and planted with ferns and other shade-loving plants. A false spring creates movement and sound.

House and garden

The left side of the garden seems to be the ideal place for the gently curving pergola, which harmonizes perfectly as it is made of rustic poles. After emerging from the pergola, the path leads back to the front door via a gravelled area designated for shade-loving plants such as ferns, hellebores and hostas.

The terrace is formal in shape, but even though the rest of the garden is informal a degree of formality is acceptable this close to a house. Even so, sharp angular shapes have been avoided and planting visually softens the terrace outline.

Trees occupy the open areas but they have not been randomly planted. Viewed from different places, in particular the house windows, they have been positioned to frame various garden "pictures".

USING A DRAWING BOARD

Pulleys to facilitate movement of rule

Parallel-motion transparent rule

Drawing boards are usually tilted when in use as this makes drawing easier. The degree of tilt is a matter of individual preference. Some boards are designed for use on flat tables, while others have special stands with height-adjustable supports beneath. When using a flat, table-top drawing board or one made from a piece of hardboard, place a length of square or rectangular timber beneath the farthest side to tilt it. "Professional" drawing boards incorporate adjustable parallel rules, but with table-top models, a T-square will do just as well. For the smallest plans, using the printed squares on graph paper will make even a T-square unnecessary.

Drawing up the plan

The outline plan

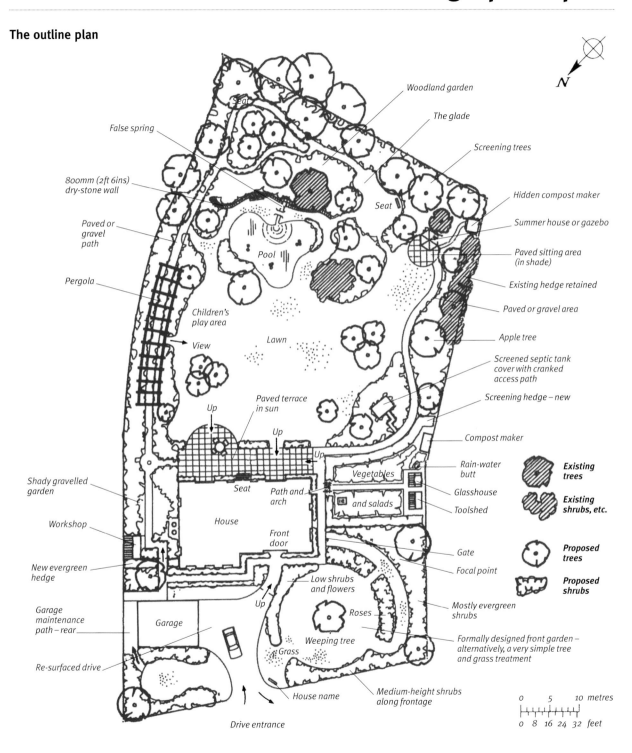

Woodland garden

The glade

Screening trees

Seat

False spring

Hidden compost maker

800mm (2ft 6ins) dry-stone wall

Summer house or gazebo

Paved sitting area (in shade)

Paved or gravel path

Seat

Pool

Existing hedge retained

Pergola

Paved or gravel area

Children's play area

Apple tree

View

Lawn

Screened septic tank cover with cranked access path

Screening hedge – new

Paved terrace in sun

Up

Compost maker

Up

Rain-water butt

Up

Vegetables

Glasshouse

Shady gravelled garden

Seat

and salads

Toolshed

Path and arch

Workshop

House

New evergreen hedge

Front door

Gate

Focal point

Garage maintenance path – rear

Up

Low shrubs and flowers

Mostly evergreen shrubs

Roses

Garage

Re-surfaced drive

Weeping tree

Grass

Formally designed front garden – alternatively, a very simple tree and grass treatment

House name

Medium-height shrubs along frontage

Drive entrance

Existing trees

Existing shrubs, etc.

Proposed trees

Proposed shrubs

0   5   10 metres

0   8 16 24 32 feet

N

Cross-sections

Some gardens are on fundamentally awkward sites, and for these the designs have as much to do with overcoming environmental problems as with satisfying aesthetic or practical needs. This is certainly the case with sloping gardens. Slopes tend to foreshorten the view of the garden and this foreshortening effect can be worsened if the site is terraced in an inappropriate way. It can be difficult to visualize changes in level. This is where cross-sectional drawings become an invaluable aid to the designer.

Measuring up for a cross-section

Cross-sections are based upon axes drawn through and across the garden plan at right angles to each other. If the garden slopes evenly or its design is simple then possibly only two cross-sections will be required, one drawn latitudinally and the other longitudinally. If, on the other hand, the slopes are uneven or the plan is complicated, then a series of cross-sections will be necessary. To ensure success in a sloping garden, full information on the extent of the problem is needed, so, before drawing a cross-section, establish precisely what the fall or rise in the ground is and over what distance it occurs. Always use the same scale, such as 1:100, for the cross-section as for the horizontal plan.

Using the cross-sectional drawings

First draw a cross-section to show the way the garden slopes naturally, then another to show what is proposed. The proposed cross-section can be done in two ways – either in the form of an overlay or as a separate drawing. The overlay, especially if drawn on tracing paper, allows immediate comparison and is therefore more useful.

Cross-sections showing proposals cannot usually be devised independently of the flat plan at the design stage. The two must be worked on together, testing ideas on the flat plan by observing their effects on the slopes, at the same time ensuring that the ideas are feasible.

Designing for slopes

The diagram right, top shows a plan with the various axes of the cross-sections drawn in. The axes are positioned where information is needed about the existing ground falls. Circled dots indicate points at which the original level measurements were taken. Datum has been fixed immediately outside the patio door and is expressed as 0.0.

Since the garden slopes downward relative to the house, the measurements are mainly expressed as minus quantities, for example -2.5m (7ft). When a garden slopes up from the house level it is usual to express levels in plus quantities, for example +1.48m (4ft 6in). Occasionally elements or objects not

The existing garden before development

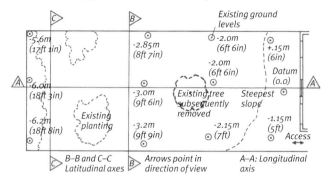

Existing garden contours (before development)

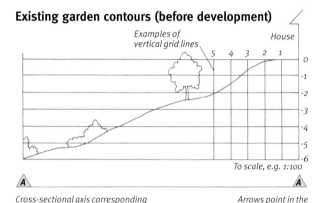

Examples of vertical grid lines

House

To scale, e.g. 1:100

Cross-sectional axis corresponding with that on plan (above)

Arrows point in the direction of view

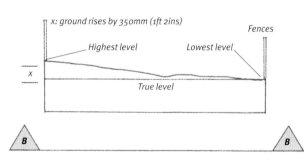

x: ground rises by 350mm (1ft 2ins)

Highest level   Lowest level

True level

Fences

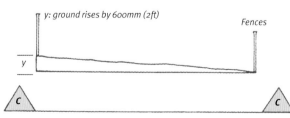

y: ground rises by 600mm (2ft)

Fences

Cross-sections

strictly on the cross-sectional axis are added in the form of an elevation to help with the comparison between the "before" and "after" plans, or to act as landmarks.

The diagrams left show cross-sections of the garden in its original state. In the first, longitudinal cross-section (A–A), the terrace (next to the house) has been chosen as the level for datum and is at almost the highest point. The far end of the garden is the lowest point. The distance over which the ground falls is known because it was measured and recorded during the original surveying process (see page 14).

Cross-sections, especially of very steep slopes, are best drawn in conjunction with a horizontal grid, evenly calibrated at appropriate spacings, for example 300mm (1ft), 450mm (18in) or 1m (3ft 3in). The steepness of the slope and exactly where it occurs is then quite clear from the plan, but whether or not a grid is drawn a "true level" line is always necessary: without it, it is mentally difficult to compare the slope with a level. To make the cross-section even clearer, vertical grid lines can also be introduced at the same spacing as the horizontals. These help to indicate comparative distances.

Cross-sections of the planned design

The plan of the proposed design for this garden (right) has three cross-sectional axes corresponding with those drawn on the plan of the existing garden (see page 30). A–A is drawn longitudinally, running the length of the garden, while B–B and C–C run latitudinally. Their precise routes are chosen at locations where it is necessary to know the effects the plan might have on the slope.

The cross-sectional diagrams on the right show the effects of the planned proposals on the slope and vice versa. The dotted lines indicate the original ground contours, and the parts of the original slopes that will need to be reduced or built up are clearly visible. Wall heights, numbers and proportions of steps and the size of the flat areas can now be accurately calculated or assessed. The effects of making flat areas, such as the patio, on slopes can also be better appreciated on the cross-section.

To help visualize the practical and aesthetic aspects of the plan and the height of the various features, add "stick people" to cross-section drawings. Make sure they are drawn to the same scale as the cross-section and arrange them sitting and standing. An adult seated, stick person's eye-level will lie approximately 1m (3ft 3in) above the ground, and standing approximately 1.5m (5ft). These approximations are enormously helpful in calculating what is likely to be seen from different places within the sloping garden. A ruled pencil line drawn from eye-level to tops of walls, or slopes will indicate sight lines reasonably accurately.

Examples of sections with directional arrows

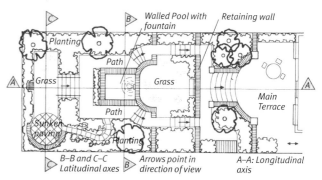

The effects of planned proposals on the slope in cross-section, A–A, B–B and C–C

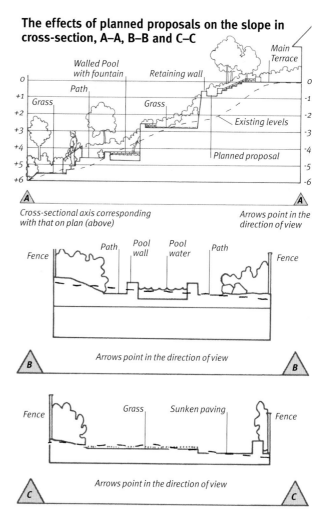

Designing the vertical

By this stage of the design process, the importance of composition and harmony can be more fully appreciated. But so far we have dealt only with the flat plan, in other words, designing on the horizontal plane. From this point onward, you need to start thinking about the garden's vertical planes.

Vertical elements

The juxtaposition of vertical elements creates structure in a garden by interrupting the sight lines and by enclosing or compartmentalizing the garden. Vertical elements create spaces, interest and movement. During the early planning stages all vertical elements must be imagined, yet they are as important as those on the horizontal plane and in some cases more so.

Selecting verticals

Some vertical elements, sheds for example, may be required for practical purposes only; others, like pergolas or gazebos, have practical and aesthetic roles to play, while others are simply decorative. Take care, as with ground shapes, that compositions of vertical elements are pleasing and harmonious as differing styles might easily conflict or compete for attention. Too many structures and features will confuse and make a garden look overpopulated (see illustration below): this risk is greater in a small garden. Individual vertical elements need space if they are to succeed on both practical and aesthetic levels and overcrowding will interfere with this.

Style and positioning

Continuity between existing architecture and proposed garden elements is essential in terms of style, materials, textures and colours. This is important for vertical features sited close to the house, which must be styled appropriately for the architecture of the building and not look out of place.

When positioning any vertical structures, including trees, take account of the views from all directions. To form an idea of how their relative positions appear to change when seen from different viewpoints, move the plan around frequently during the design process and look at it from all angles. This also helps to prevent the plan from becoming one-directional.

As far as possible, arrange vertical elements as pleasing compositions or, where appropriate, as a series of goals to tempt the visitor through the garden: pergolas or planted tunnels are excellent for this.

Identical paths, one (left) with an open, airy feel, the other (right) enclosed, more mysterious and atmospheric.

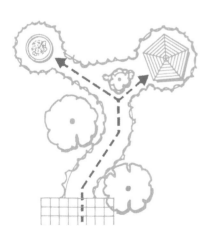

A zig-zag arrangement of vertical elements within the garden leads the eye (and feet) from one point to the next to provide interest and movement.

An example of an "overpopulated" garden with too many vertical features, each with its own unrelated style and form, and each demanding individual attention.

A simplified version. The arch now forms a "gateway" and the summer house is glimpsed invitingly. The seat is partially hidden so as not to conflict visually with the arch.

Designing the vertical

Constructed and natural features

Of the vertical elements, those that have been constructed usually have the greater impact, since they tend to be more definite in shape and form than trees and shrubs. Trees and shrubs are, however, more versatile and especially useful for informal boundaries and partitions. Some plants are trimmed formally, topiary for example, and so become architectural features, while some constructions such as rustic dry-stone walls appear almost as though they grew out of the ground.

Creating spaces

The open horizontal spaces of a garden are defined by the vertical elements and features which surround them. Without this definition, an area will lack identity and possibly even a sense of movement. However, spaces can be inadvertently "lost" as well as created. For example, conical or pyramidal trees, such as conifers, numerously planted make a small garden look even smaller, as the conical shapes act as distance gauges. Set against a formal boundary this visual phenomenon is exaggerated. The use of more rounded-shaped trees and shrubs has the opposite effect.

Using verticals for definition

The vertical elements creating garden spaces need to be chosen or designed at such a height that the area they surround functions as an independent space. Some areas can be planned to work as entities in their own right, but without obscuring nearby features which also contribute to the same design. Alternatively, the garden can be compartmentalized by creating a series of enclosed, individual outdoor rooms.

Compartmentalized gardens can be exciting places with each "room" having its own function and proportion. Add character by choosing appropriate surrounds: a leafy unclipped hedge will suggest informality; a clipped hedge, gentle formality; while walls or fences are far more formal.

Height and scale

On a practical level, in compartmentalized gardens, vertical elements need to be tall enough to define the space properly. Too low and the area within can be overlooked, losing its individuality relative to the rest of the garden. The divisions must reach at least eye level to ensure that the spaces within are not overlooked (see diagram, below far left).

Sloping sites

On sloping sites it is often necessary to create flat areas but always avoid over-terracing. When any flat area is created upon a slope, there is an inherent risk that the rest of the garden may be partially lost from view. If distant areas of garden are removed from view in this way, they frequently remain unvisited.

For structural and aesthetic reasons, it is usually better to have a stepped retaining system rather than a single vertical system such as a blank wall. The single system, usually taller, will appear closer and more uncompromising, while a stepped system will appear less so.

In a small patio garden, the use of offset screens makes more of the available space and extends the depth of the plot.

Space is easy to lose when terracing ground that slopes downward. Terracing can remove almost an entire garden from view.

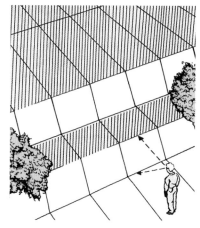

Terracing on a steeply sloping site must be planned with care if most of the garden is not to be lost from sight.

Movement

The way that spaces are shaped in a garden can suggest movement, but to what degree depends upon their proportions and perspective. The height of the surround relative to the size of the area within is critically important. The higher the surround, the smaller the area within it appears. A high

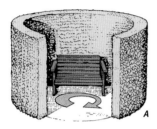

An equally proportioned area such as a square or circle (above) appears static. The height of the surround changes the quality of the space within. Both the horizontal spaces above are the same size and proportion, but A appears enclosed while B is open and airy.

surround will cast more shade within, to the extent that very small areas with high surrounds could be in permanent shade and feel claustrophobic.

Spaces can be used to determine the route or speed of progress through a garden. Try to encourage a sense of speed and movement appropriate to an area's function, whether it is a linking corridor or a place to meander. Long, narrow areas evoke the greatest sense of movement and are often used to link "calmer" areas, although they can also be used to help to create atmosphere and structure.

Since vertical elements surrounding a space affect its sense of movement and the atmosphere within, height is the most influential factor – but form, texture, and colour all play their part.

Choosing ground coverings

Grass or gravel are neutral in texture and leave an area's inherent sense of movement (or lack of it) intact. Some paving materials or units are laid in patterns and the direction of the joint lines are significant in suggesting movement.

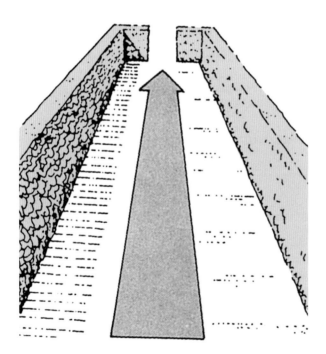

A broad rectangular area viewed "end on" encourages a slow, measured pace along this part of the garden: the same shape entered or viewed from the side gives an impression of greater breadth but less depth and encourages movement around it.

The sense of movement is very strong indeed here because of the height of the surround. Even though the space is exactly the same proportion as that of the diagram on the left, the feeling of enclosure means this situation is almost oppressive.

Proportion and perspective

When choosing paving material, you must decide whether the space needs to be static or should have a dynamic effect. Parts of the garden such as sitting areas, for example, need to be static in feel: here a sense of movement could be unsettling. The choice of the ground surface and its associated patterning in these areas, has an important role to play, in addition to the height of the surround.

Consider the proportions of the paving in relation to the area to be covered: it can radically affect the area's apparent size. Drawing paving units to scale on the plan can help to indicate the most appropriate size.

Proportions of covering material

The principles of suggested movement and of the relationship between the proportions of constructed elements and their overall shapes apply as much to the vertical as they do to the horizontal plane.

The examples shown right illustrate the importance of the relative proportion of the covering material and the area being covered.

The illustrations below show similar principles at work on a vertical plane: shadow lines introduced on the wall primarily by the joint lines, but also by associated planting, affect the perceived

proportions. Achieving perfect relative proportions is more difficult when using manufactured products. These will probably conform to multiples of 100mm (4in) or 75mm (3in) – for example, a flat brick is approximately 225 x 100mm (9 x 4in).

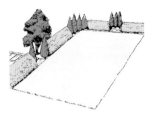

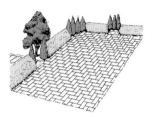

Gravel (or grass) is neutral and keeps the area's proportions intact, subject to perspective.

Small units relative to the overall size can seem fussy and the plot therefore appears smaller.

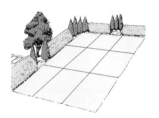

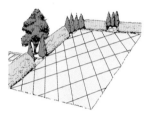

While the area still appears spacious, the units here are, perhaps, too large.

A satisfactory relationship between the size of the units and the host area.

Diagonally laid paving of this relative proportion sits well and appears comfortable in the area.

This wall appears longer than the same sized wall illustrated right because the mortar joints or predominant shadow lines are horizontal. The introduction of plants which have columnar or upright forms exaggerates this effect and is helpful in smaller gardens.

This wall is the same length and height as the illustration left, but it appears higher and not as long due to the verticality of the shadow lines. This effect is exaggerated by the associated rounded and horizontal plant forms.

Proportion and perspective

When designing your garden, bear in mind that although the plan is drawn from a bird's-eye viewpoint, the realized garden will rarely be seen from directly overhead. A plan drawn to scale indicates the garden's size and proportion but suggests much more space than will actually be seen. This is due to the effects of perspective, which can make a garden appear anything between two thirds and half its actual size.

Designing with perspective in mind
To appreciate the foreshortening effects of perspective on your design, lay the plan flat on a table and look across it with your eyes 15mm (⅝in) above the surface. This represents, at a scale of 1:100 (⅛in:1ft), an eye-level view from about 1.5m (5ft) in a standing position. Positioning your eyes 10mm (⅜in) above the paper represents an eye-level view from about 1m (3ft 3in) in a sitting position and further exaggerates the foreshortening effect.

False perspective
When the amount of available space is limited, introducing false perspective effects can increase the sense of distance.

When a garden is viewed from one place, such as a window or patio, the eye tends to follow a specific axis. The view terminates at the "vanishing point", where all uninterrupted visual lines appear to converge. It is rare for a perspective vanishing point to be visible, as in most cases boundary walls or other features intercept well beforehand.

Objects in the line of vision appear smaller the further away they are and this phenomenon can be used to create false perspective. Actively decreasing the size of features as they are seen from a chosen viewpoint makes them appear to be more distant, making the garden appear larger. An arch, seat or other focal point at the end of the path could be made smaller than usual to add to the impression of distance.

Planning for perspective
Sketching perspective diagrams allows you to test the effects of the planned vertical elements. Several different views are usually needed as it is difficult to draw an entire garden in perspective from one viewpoint. Start sketching at the front of the picture to avoid drawing over things which occur further back and are obscured by planting or by nearer objects.

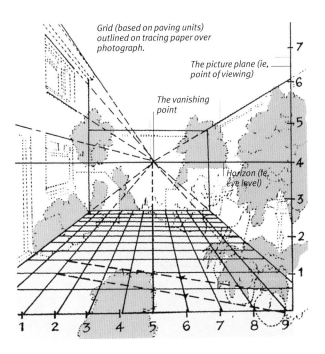

Grid (based on paving units) outlined on tracing paper over photograph.

The picture plane (ie, point of viewing)

The vanishing point

Horizon (ie, eye level)

A perspective sketch gives an impression of the way a garden might look from a particular place. In this instance, the view (from a standing position) at a patio window is taken as the picture plane (or frame).

The lines leading from the picture plane toward the vanishing point cannot be drawn to scale beyond the picture plane. Scale calibrations can also be drawn along the vertical axis to achieve good proportion.

Proportion and perspective

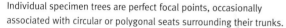
Individual specimen trees are perfect focal points, occasionally associated with circular or polygonal seats surrounding their trunks.

Borrowed focal points, such as these distant hills, have been used for centuries to extend boundaries.

Alternatively, photographs of the garden can be used. Enlargements are best at, say, 150 x 100mm (6 x 4in) or larger. Clip tracing paper of the same size over the enlarged photograph, then, taking the relevant information from the plan, sketch your ideas in pencil over the tracing paper. Start by sketching in ideas at the front of the picture. Sketch your proposals accurately but not in minute detail: an impression is all that is required.

Within the garden, structure can be created with a number of features, but partitions, focal points and more diffuse compositions create the sense of interest and excitement that makes even the smallest plot worth visiting.

Partitioning

Surprisingly, introducing partitions into a garden can make it appear larger rather than smaller. Imaginative partitioning can make a tremendous difference to small and medium-sized gardens and can be used to create spaces. Garden compartments should be linked in a way that allows them to retain their individuality and sense of enclosure. Entrances and exits should be arranged adjacent to seats rather than opposite them, where they are in full view of the sitter.

Compartment size relative to the height of the surround profoundly affects the sense of enclosure. A large space with a relatively low enclosure feels far more open than a small space with higher partitions, which may also create more shade (see Movement, page 34).

Focal points

Focal points are objects or plants lying inside or outside a garden that demand special attention. More often associated with formal than with informal gardens, they are best sited individually as, when two or more focal points are seen together, a visual conflict is inevitable. Focal points are used in large gardens as goals forming part of a planned route and arranged as a progressive series.

Practically any individual object or tree will serve as a focal point provided that it is significantly different from its background or immediate surroundings. Therefore this should be carefully considered. Normally, a background of neutral colour and relatively uniform texture will ensure that the chosen focal point is displayed to the best effect.

Borrowed focal points

Focal points are useful for terminating a view within a garden in a satisfactory way, rather than it appearing as a dead end. But views lying outside a garden can also be incorporated into the design. These "borrowed" focal points can be as varied as a church spire or a coastline, but may be so dominant that the importance of other elements or lesser focal points within the garden is diminished.

Before designing a garden around a borrowed focal point, check what the implications might be. If there is a possibility of development in the surrounding area, the plan may have to be changed to conceal the view rather than to incorporate it.

Compositions

In informal gardens, individual focal points may be out of place and their role taken over by more diffuse compositions, for example, a grouping of several plants. These plant compositions are often subtle in effect but they must still be distinctive and distinguishable from the general planting. Some compositions can comprise trees and shrubs in combination with seats, garden buildings or other structures. Compositions can be made with works of art or structures, provided that they are carefully presented as such and have an affinity with one another. The rule regarding two visible, individual focal points also applies to compositions: it is best to site different compositions individually, so that the one does not detract from the other and to avoid visual conflict.

Most buildings, however large or small, can be improved by good foils and framing. Focal points need not be single objects; compositions are often more effective. Focal points and compositions can be used to draw attention away from unsightly features which could become focal points themselves.

It may be tempting to hide large, unattractive features with a "wall" of fast-growing evergreens, but this usually only draws attention to the fact that something is being screened.

A better solution would be to use densely planted informal tree and shrub forms in combination with a small alternative focal point, such as a seat, which would tend to draw the eye downward. Informal tree forms break up unsightly architectural shapes. In winter, the bare branches of most deciduous trees can still soften hard outlines. Evergreens could also be used but most take many years to become sufficiently mature to be effective. In temperate climates, indigenous trees would blend in better since, as part of a screening arrangement, a degree of visual anonymity is an advantage.

Instead of being screened, this shed has become the centre of a composition. Its most visible side now has a light pergola attached. Bold planting and a seat now make this an attractive focal point.

A pavilion reflected in a still pool, with trees and shrubs acting as foils. Their forms are indispensable, both individually and as components of the unified composition.

A single bench seat is at the heart of this composition, yet it would not work so well as a focal point without the contrasting shrubs and trees that surround it.

Screening

Sometimes it takes more than a focal point to counteract an unsightly feature. In many cases, screening can remove the offending object from view.

Curving paths can be used to screen unsightly objects provided they are densely planted, or can be combined with a decorative fence or wall to become an eye-catching feature.

Tall unsightly objects or unattractive views just outside the garden can be concealed by screens placed near the main viewing position rather than closer to the offending object itself. The height of a screen close to the viewing position can be lower than one positioned further away. In principle, the further away the object relative to the screen and the closer the screen to the observer, the easier it is to disguise the object. But in many cases, even a relatively low screen maybe inconvenient near the house. An alternative might be a constructed screen above a certain height.

Planning for screening

Deciding on the form and position of screens early in the design process ensures that the main part of the garden does not become obscured from view as planted elements mature. Sketches and annotated photographs should help the process.

In the example below, there is a commercial unit just beyond the garden boundary and the aim is to screen it from the house. The lines drawn from eye height to the chimney stack represent the angle of view and indicate the minimum height the screen needs to be. This changes as the viewer moves further into the garden, but not too dramatically. A planted bund (soil mound) or raised bed positioned at a distance can speed up the screening process by immediately giving plants extra height.

Overhead screening

In the smallest gardens screening may have to be achieved using tall planted trellis or with pergolas and arches. Vertical screening over 1.8m (6ft) or so may need planning permission.

The problem of being overlooked can be eased by using overhead screening: horizontal beams set on uprights to support planting. The direction in which the beams run and their spacing is determined by the position of the overlooking building. For example, where, say, a patio is overlooked on at least two sides, cross-beams should run at right angles to each other to form a grid pattern. When viewed obliquely from above, these beams obscure any view of the area beneath, but anyone underneath can look up and see the sky – if the planting is not too dense.

Screening for mystery and concealment

Gardens benefit from the addition of a little mystery: gardeners who can see their entire plot at one glance run the risk of becoming bored with it. The smaller the space, the greater the need for some hidden corner. Where all space is at a premium, a separate hidden area may not be feasible but it can still be suggested. Screening thus makes a positive contribution to the design, whereas screening unwanted or distracting objects from sight is more a means of returning emphasis to the garden.

Unattractive features may lie inside as well as outside the garden, such as compost and dustbins and garden sheds. Whatever the unwelcome object, take care not to draw attention to it inadvertently by using the wrong type of screening. The screen should visually break up the lines or form of the offending object, making one wonder what lies behind rather than being a feature in its own right.

Screening unsightly objects

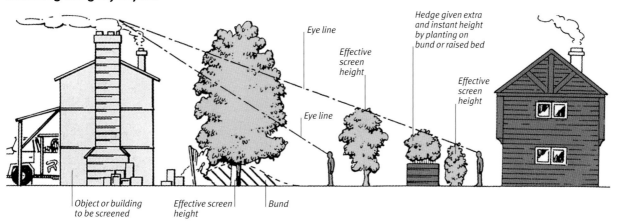

Eye line

Effective screen height

Eye line

Hedge given extra and instant height by planting on bund or raised bed

Effective screen height

Object or building to be screened

Effective screen height

Bund

Coping with sloping gardens

Sloping gardens, usually more difficult to design and maintain than flat ones, have the advantage of being potentially more interesting. The design solutions for a garden which slopes upward from the front of a house, however, are quite different from those for a front garden sloping downward.

Slopes and visibility

Gentle upward slopes bring more of the garden into view than an equivalent flat area, but if a garden slopes so steeply that it has to be terraced, it effectively disappears from view once the slope reaches eye-level. The idea is to bring as much of the garden as possible into view.

Access and safety

Access is one potential problem, especially for machinery. Maintenance at the higher level may only be possible if a set of tools and equipment is permanently stored there. If access is poor and the upper reaches of the garden are uninteresting, the chances are that no one will go there.

Steps (see pages 116–127) and ramps must be as safe and convenient to use as possible. Ramps should preferably be no steeper than 1:20. Straight flights of steps and ramps are not always feasible in extremely steep gardens, in which case choose sideways, zig-zag or curving steps or ramps, as they allow a more gradual ascent or descent.

Focal points

Close retaining walls can look uncompromising, but there are various ways of softening their appearance by the introduction of planting or other focal points. Wall fountains are fascinating, especially when associated with bold plants such as bamboos, fatsias, grasses and irises, most of which could be evergreen to ensure year-round interest. Enliven the wall with hanging baskets, pots and containers. If it is feasible, design the wall to be stepped with a series of flat planting areas in its face; this will both soften its appearance and provide planting opportunities. Night-time lighting, too, can create dramatic shadows to emphasize the wall's architecture.

Planting for slopes

Planted or grassed embankments are softer in appearance than walls and may be more appropriate in informal gardens. Choose grass mixes and plant varieties that thrive in a well drained situation, allowing for whether the embankment is in sun or shade. Grass is never easy to cut on a slope, so is usually a second choice to ground-cover plants.

Planting plans should allow for closer planting than would be usual in horizontal sites. The closer the plants are, the more rapidly they will spread and merge to inhibit weed growth. In drier conditions growth rates tend to be slower, so close planting also speeds up the ground-covering process.

Reducing the negative effects of close retaining walls

Planting of alpine and rock garden plants among the crevices of a wall can enliven a retaining wall in a less formal setting

A sitting wall, with tiered planting spaces to soften its appearance, adds interest by affording different planting spaces at different levels

Coping with sloping gardens

Downward slopes

Where a house is at a higher level than the garden, the means of retention will be seen with the house as part of a composition. Ensure that materials used for steps, walls and paths are in harmony with the architecture of the house and bear in mind the colour of the hard landscaping when choosing the colour of flowers.

Gardens which slope down from the house appear more spacious than upward-sloping sites. The physical problems connected with steeply downward-sloping gardens are similar to those sloping upward, but the design solutions are different. On looking back towards the house, embankments, walls, and lawns are seen as a composition.

Upward slopes

Gardens which slope upward close to the front or rear walls of the house present only a restricted view. If retaining walls must be positioned close to the house, make them attractive enough to be a feature of the design (see pages 128–9).

Drainage is an important aspect of design. If the house is at the bottom of a slope, an efficient drainage system is essential if flooding is to be avoided at times of high rainfall.

Always slope the paving down from the house to ensure that water does not collect close to its walls. The retaining wall should have drainage holes (weepholes) at its base which discharge into a rainwater channel at its foot. From here the rainwater can be conducted to a ditch or drainage system.

If the slope is really steep, a series of intercepting lateral drains may be required. Under these circumstances, you should seek expert advice.

Creating flat surfaces in sloping gardens

Think very carefully before creating a flat area on a sloping site. A cross-sectional sketch (see pages 30–1) will be of great help in illustrating exactly where the flat area might best be placed – minimizing unnecessary and expensive earthworks. Access, too, will have a bearing on the costs and feasibility of major earth moving.

The creation of the flat area can be done either by removing soil, building it up or "cutting and filling" – where soil is dug out on the high side, then heaped up and consolidated on the low side. New slopes created by the levelling operation intended for growing or planting should not exceed 40 degrees, to ensure stability. The question whether to grass, plant or pave the newly created level is up to you. Even if you choose paving, the area should not be truly flat to aid surface water drainage. You are also likely to need an intercepting drainage channel on the high side, beneath the wall or embankment.

Sloping garden with an asymmetrical theme

In the illustration below, the garden slopes downward from the front to the rear, and all the shapes (except the terrace and paths) are derived from polygons. Main steps are shaped to make an easy transition from the rectangular to the polygonal and are attractive features in their own right. Two levels of flat lawn are separated by the necessary retaining wall. At the bottom left is a secondary sitting area complete with a small summer house. A small, screened garden shed occupies the opposite corner.

When a sloping garden is large, then different styled sub-gardens can exist together, providing that they are are not in visual conflict. There might be a unifying factor – perhaps a paving material common to each. The idea of a varying style, sloping garden works well on steeper sloping sites when steps or paths lead from one area to another. As always, it is better to have the more formal areas near to the house.

Sloping garden with an asymmetrical theme

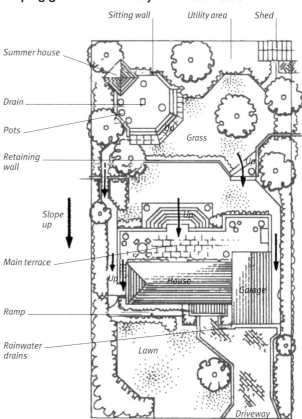

Style in the garden

The dictionary defines style as the "manner or expression of ideas". Most gardens conform to one style or another if they have been consciously designed. In some, the design follows the function, as is the case with most family or domestic gardens, while in others, such as ornamental gardens or bedding schemes, the design is intended purely for visual appeal. Some gardens are totally functional and are essentially without style, for instance a basic vegetable garden.

The style of a garden is often influenced by factors such as function, the environment, geographic location, shape, proportion, levels, associated architecture, the amount of maintenance required or the cost of realisation. But there can be other influences – themes such as water features, roses, rocks or herbs.

If particular needs are to be fulfiled, this will also affect style. Gardens for the elderly will be different in style from a garden for a family. The style will be further influenced by the number of people for whom the garden is intended, whether an individual, a family or a community.

Formal gardens

1 A symmetrically formal garden with a single line of symmetry is illustrated below. One side appears as a mirror reflection of the other. The line of symmetry in this example passes through the centre of the garden lengthways, although alternatively it could pass centrally from side to side.
2 There are two central lines of symmetry in the second example, that quarter the garden. To be truly symmetrical, each of the four quarters must be an exact image of the others.

To achieve an area of true formality in an informal plot, a separate sub-boundary or boundaries must be created inside it and structured symmetrically within.

Informal gardens

3 Asymmetrical formality is a popular style in modern gardens. The formally or geometrically shaped planes do not conform to any lines of symmetry but are juxtaposed or overlapped to create interesting sub-shapes. Asymmetrical formality is the ideal style if a sense of order is preferred but without being too strict. To achieve this, try experimenting with different geometrical ground shapes.
4 Informal gardens can be very appealing, with natural forms and curving lines creating the vertical and horizontal planes. A degree of underlying order can be achieved, however, by linking curves based on part or whole circles and ellipses and allowing them to develop as flowing lines and free forms.

Achieving style in the garden

Having decided upon the style you wish to achieve, the next problem is how to interpret it.

In some cases, the particular style may not result from free personal choice but may depend on what is appropriate to the situation. A formal "wild" garden, for example, would seem as incongruous as a "natural" rock garden in the corner of a town garden surrounded by high brick walls. Style must work on a practical and an aesthetic level. This is another aspect of garden "style" not based on the form or function, but rather on the garden as a setting.

1 A symmetrically formal garden

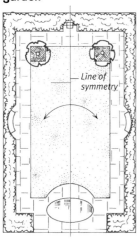

Line of symmetry

2 Two central lines of symmetry

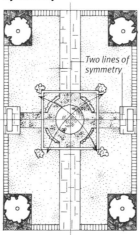

Two lines of symmetry

3 An asymmetrically formal garden

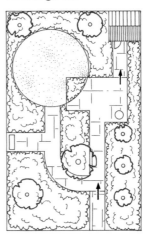

4 An informal plan

Style in the garden

A garden combining symmetrically formal, asymmetrically formal, and informal areas

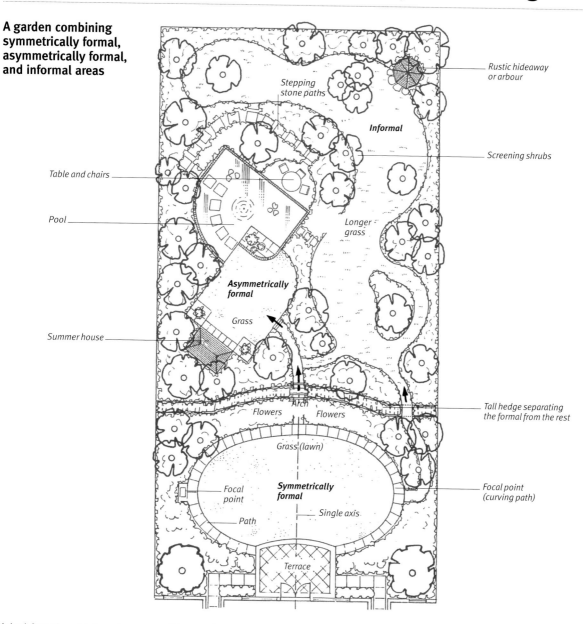

Rustic hideaway or arbour

Stepping stone paths

Informal

Screening shrubs

Table and chairs

Longer grass

Pool

Asymmetrically formal

Grass

Summer house

Arch

Flowers   Flowers

Tall hedge separating the formal from the rest

Grass (lawn)

Focal point

Symmetrically formal

Focal point (curving path)

Path

Single axis

Terrace

Linked formal and informal areas, as illustrated in the example above, create gardens of contrasting moods.

Traditionally, the area closest to the house is treated formally. A single line of axis terminates at an arch, from which point a path curves invitingly to the left, its destination tantalizingly invisible from the house. The path leads, via the arch, to the next section, which is designed along asymmetrical lines.

Ground shapes are geometric and are based on straight lines and true arcs. To the right is an informal garden where hidden areas create a sense of mystery and where wildlife is encouraged. Although each section of this garden is different in character, style and shape, there is no visual or intellectual conflict. They are complete entities occupying their own spaces yet contributing to the garden as a whole.

Small town/patio gardens

When a garden is small or enclosed, there are strategies that can be used to increase the sense of space.

When the boundary opposite the house in a wide, shallow garden is a wall or fence, this increases the sense of enclosure. In the illustration below, this rather high wall is integrated in the design by fixing a mirror to it to create a *trompe l'oeil* effect or illusion. The mirror appears to be an opening to another part of the garden, an illusion enhanced by subtle adjacent planting and by the positioning of a sculpture in front of it. To reinforce the illusion, the octagonal area in which the terracotta figure stands is paved with flint and pebbles and set at a lower level than the rest of the garden.

Grass or paving covers the more open area. On the right lies a secret sitting area, reached by an arch lightly clad with plants. On the ground flint and pebbles are used for continuity.

A town garden

In the garden illustrated (page 45, left) the main view from the patio doors is of the table and chairs which form the focal point. The paving has been laid diagonally to increase the sense of space and is pale in colour to reflect the available light. Part of the paved area is screened from view so a sense of mystery is created. Only when visiting this area do the raised pool and wall fountain come into view. The side of the

A wide, shallow patio garden

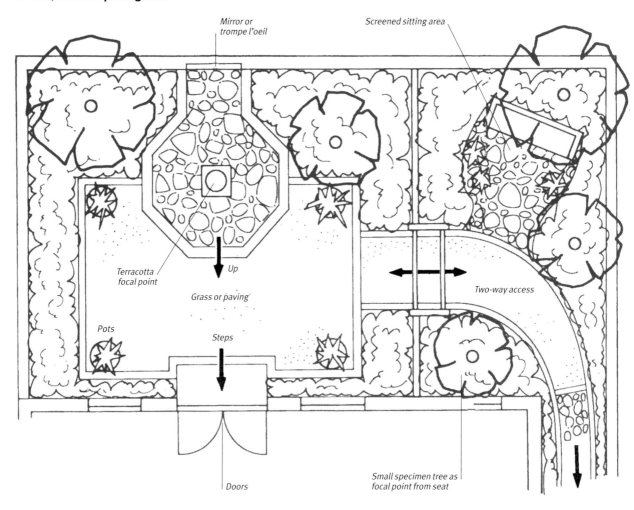

Mirror or trompe l'oeil

Screened sitting area

Terracotta focal point

Up

Grass or paving

Two-way access

Pots

Steps

Doors

Small specimen tree as focal point from seat

Small town/patio gardens

screen facing the house has a sculpture or plaque attached to it, a focal point seen only from the kitchen window. This area between the screen and the kitchen window is a little lower than the rest of the garden and the paving is laid with uninterrupted joint lines leading away from the window to create an illusion of greater distance and to direct the eye toward the screen with its sculpture or plaque. Potted plants placed in groups or individually offset any sense of formality.

A small, informal town garden
Provided that the formal boundary lines are concealed from view, this "jungle" garden (below, right) is the perfect solution for even a very small plot. Despite its lack of size, a sense of mystery is created, with the farthest area concealed by the winding path and bold planting, which includes a high proportion of evergreens. Their year-round foliage screens the garden from neighbouring plots. An arbour positioned in the top left corner is the perfect place for solitude, while the decked area is ideal for summer relaxation.

All paving is of roundish natural stone, which echoes in shape the many curves in the garden and acts as host to low carpeting plants in the less frequently used parts. If the garden is overlooked from above, the decking could have a pergola over it to provide privacy.

A town garden

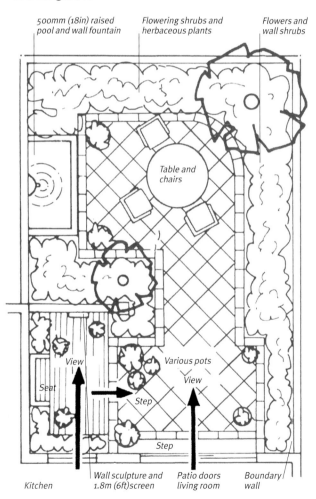

500mm (18in) raised pool and wall fountain

Flowering shrubs and herbaceous plants

Flowers and wall shrubs

Table and chairs

View

Various pots

View

Seat

Step

Kitchen

Wall sculpture and 1.8m (6ft) screen

Patio doors living room

Boundary wall

Step

A small, informal town garden

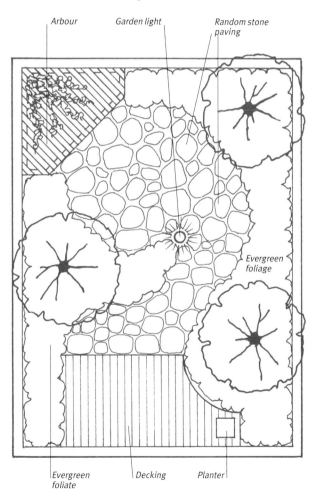

Arbour

Garden light

Random stone paving

Evergreen foliage

Evergreen foliate

Decking

Planter

Front gardens

Regrettably, front gardens are often the poor relations in terms of garden design, yet their function is equally important. Front gardens should bid visitors welcome and frame the house, complementing its architecture and acting as a setting for it. Another function of a front garden is to give importance and direction to the front door. On entering from the road or foot-path, the front door should be the main focus of attention and never be hidden or its position obscured. When there is little or no side or rear garden, the front garden may have to take on a recreational role as well and this must be combined with the more functional requirements so that, as far as possible, these apparently conflicting uses are integrated in a coherent whole.

A small terraced-house garden

Boundary wall

Setts or brick edge

Porch

Access for window cleaning

Evergreen sphere or favourite shrub rose

Flowers

Close evergreen ground cover, grass or gravel

Pot, sundial, bird-table or other focal point

Gate

Path surfaces with textured concrete, tiles, brick, stone or gravel

A small terraced-house garden

In the tiny garden shown below, there is no room for parking. the garden has been designed to be compatible in style with an older house. The formal appearance of the surrounding walls sets the tone and their lines have been reflected within the garden. A path leads from the gate straight to the front door and could be surfaced with various materials. In this instance, exposed aggregate concrete is used, edged with granite setts. On either side of the path, within the scalloped rectangle, low ground cover is used. Small-leaved ivy (*Hedera*), *Arenaria*, *Sedum* or *Vinca*, would all be suitable. Alternatively, grass or gravel could be used.

Because of the strength of the design, mixed herbaceous or annual, colourful planting is both appropriate and cheerful for the borders which flank the walls, in conjunction with the contrasting box tree spheres. Halfway along the path is a paved circle and terracotta pot. This is large enough to be a focal point, but not so large as to impede visitors.

Parking and driveways

Many front gardens have to function partly as a parking area, increasingly so in towns and cities as on-road parking space is at a premium. This calls for imaginative design solutions to avoid creating a harsh, totally utilitarian look. There is a wide choice of material that can be used for driveways, with brick or block paving becoming a popular choice. Dry-laid brick surfacing on a drive must have the joints running diagonally to the traffic flow (see Paving, pages 84–85). Whatever the medium chosen, it has to be capable of supporting the weight of the car without suffering damage, and sloping drives, particularly those sloping downward to the house, need an extra-efficient drainage system to avoid the risk of flooding.

For safety there should always be an uninterrupted view of the road when driving out and, conversely, a good view from the road of cars emerging from the garden or driveway, although this often depends on the shape of the road.

A front garden with a parking area

The double gate of this uncomplicated suburban front garden includes a pedestrian hand gate for convenience. Where driveways slope upward, check that the gates will not snag the rising surface before they are fully open. To help avoid this a pair of gates (rather than a single gate) is better since the gate length is effectively halved.

There are two reversing bays, positioned at either end of the drive, each illuminated with a lamp. The drive could be brick paved in a diagonal pattern that is suitable for its strong and graceful curving shape. In keeping with the simple design of the garden, a pergola is used here as a car port, planted

Front gardens

with climbers to soften its outline and make it an attractive yet functional feature in its own right.

The shape of the grass areas in the borders also balances the shape of the driveway. The parking area is approached directly, yet there is sufficient space in front of the porch for unloading or for quick access to the house in bad weather. Trees screen the front door from the road and provide vertical balance to the pergola, whereas low-growing plants and shrubs and a grass verge are positioned nearest the gate for clear visibility when approaching the drive from the house or the road.

A front garden with parking area

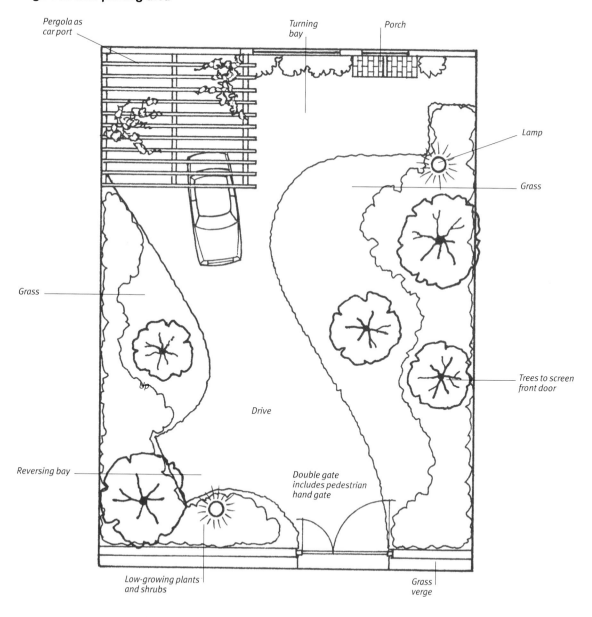

Pergola as car port

Turning bay

Porch

Lamp

Grass

Grass

Trees to screen front door

Drive

Reversing bay

Double gate includes pedestrian hand gate

Low-growing plants and shrubs

Grass verge

Cottage gardens

Cottage gardens are popular, particularly as their style associates well with most types of informal architecture, yet the style originated as a matter of economic necessity. Their original function was to supplement the diet of their owners with fruit and vegetables, while herbs were grown, too. Flowers tended to be planted only in odd corners to bring cheer to the otherwise strictly utilitarian productive areas. Victorian watercolourists produced a romanticized image from which the popular concept of the cottage garden was born.

Structure in the cottage garden

They can be very beautiful, but the notion that a successful cottage garden can be created simply by gathering together a random selection of flowers and plants is a false one.

The anarchic appearance of some cottage gardens belies the usually strong underlying structure, which must be able to cope with the seasonal nature of most flowering plants in terms of their colour, shapes and proportion relative to their neighbours' and the structure of the garden itself. The routes of paths and the positions of boundaries are important factors in this structure, which is usually formal but with any unwanted appearance of functionality being offset by carefully selected plants.

Framework and features

Always start by working out the horizontal framework of the garden, deciding the routes of paths according to their function. Then decide on the positions of seats, ornaments, sundials, bird baths and so on. Finally, think about the plants.

Plant the taller subjects at the back and the smaller at the front, but leave room to experiment; the cottage garden is not the place for too much conformity. Check flowering seasons or, if grown for foliage effect, when a plant looks its best. A balanced mixture of flowering and foliage plants will extend the garden's annual period of interest considerably.

Colour is a matter of personal taste; some prefer controlled themes, others a riot. There will be a time when the cottage garden is at its best, probably during early to midsummer in temperate climates, because of the prevalence of biennials in the typical planting scheme.

Use traditional materials such as gravel, clay, brick, natural stone, terracotta and rustic timber for paths and edgings as these are in keeping with the cottage garden style.

A small cottage garden

Many cottage gardens are very tiny. In the example illustrated below left, the gateway is not opposite the front door; a problem which is resolved satisfactorily by the construction of a graceful curving path. As the path is of uniform width, brick "running bond" is not only achievable but wholly appropriate, since it is strongly directional and has the effect of drawing the visitor towards the house.

To the left, waiting to be discovered among tall plants, is a hexagonal gravelled space edged with blue-grey (or red) Victorian "rope" edge tiles, as are all the paths. At the centre of the hexagon is a strawberry or herb pot, which fits in perfectly with the theme. Alternatives would be a small terracotta figure or sundial, depending on the aspect of the plot. A fruit tree screens the view of the less attractive side path and, in conjunction with the smaller ornamental tree situated nearer the front boundary, frames the cottage (or house). No soil is visible in the borders, since these are completely planted up with typical cottage garden favourites, including climbing roses.

A small cottage garden

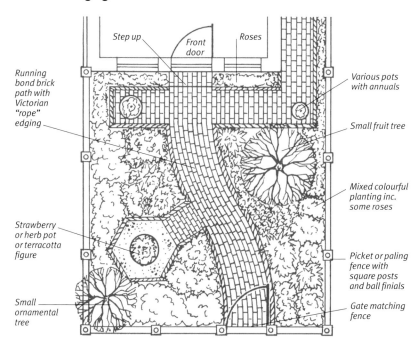

Step up

Front door

Roses

Running bond brick path with Victorian "rope" edging

Various pots with annuals

Small fruit tree

Mixed colourful planting inc. some roses

Strawberry or herb pot or terracotta figure

Picket or paling fence with square posts and ball finials

Gate matching fence

Small ornamental tree

Informal gardens

Informal gardens are difficult to design because they lack the order inherent in the geometric shapes and straight lines of formal designs. The results, however, are by definition much closer to nature. Creating an informal garden within formal boundaries is difficult unless the boundaries can be effectively and permanently screened or camouflaged.

A large informal garden

This large, informal garden could be adapted to most tastes or interests. For example, a variety of plant species could be housed for the collector or, alternatively, species planted and features included to attract wildlife for the conservationist. The drive and front garden are the only truly formal elements while the terrace, retaining a modicum of formality, is shaped to integrate with the general theme.

One feature, intended as a surprise, is the small cave or grotto at the bottom of the two flights of steps facing each other, set some 1.8m (6ft) down. The dry stone retaining walls at each side have shade-loving ferns and mosses growing in the cracks, further softening the outlines of the walls.

In the corner of the garden another surprise is provided by a sunken dell, which is home to shade-loving woodland plants, and this, too, is approached by winding paths and steps. The use of materials such as stone for the steps and walls is appropriate to the informal style of this garden, as is the use of gravel for the paths, as this lends itself to their meandering forms.

A fairly large, reflective pool is set within lushly planted borders and areas of less frequently mown grass. From the secluded shelter or gazebo (bottom right), there is a view back across the pool and grass. A mixed hedge surrounds the property, trees and tall shrubs forming the vertical structures. They could be indigenous shrubs, ornamental or fruiting trees, or a mixture of different types.

A large informal garden

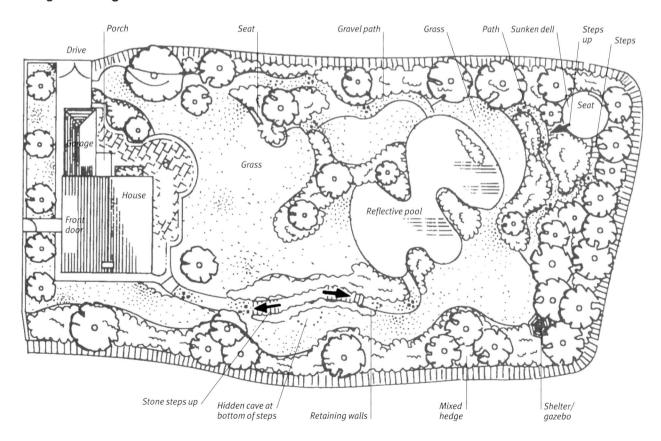

Drive · Porch · Seat · Gravel path · Grass · Path · Sunken dell · Steps up · Steps · Seat · Garage · House · Front door · Grass · Reflective pool · Stone steps up · Hidden cave at bottom of steps · Retaining walls · Mixed hedge · Shelter/gazebo

Family gardens

One of the most common types of garden is for a family with children of different ages and with different needs and expectations. Family gardens always make interesting projects. Following the guidelines set out in this book will not only make the process easier but more enjoyable too.

When designing a garden for a family, think ahead and consider how the garden's elements could be updated as the children grow older and, ultimately, the garden could be modified to fit solely with the parents' needs.

Gardens for different age groups

A garden designed entirely for children needs to account for various age groups. Where children with a wide range of ages are expected to use the garden, it is advisable to separate one age group's activities from another. Very young children will generally not be able to join in with, or make use of,

older children's games or play equipment because of their smaller size and restricted ability, and older children may scorn to take part in what they perceive to be "childish" adventures.

Underlying any design for a children's garden is the unavoidable and obvious fact that children grow older and what they enjoy one year they may well have grown out of by the next. In a communal garden, successive generations of children will pass through and a wide range of equipment will be used to the full. This is not usually the situation in a private garden (unless an owner is willing to await the arrival of grandchildren) and by definition all children's gardens are transient constructions. Bear this in mind when designing, as toys and play equipment will be used for a relatively short time and can never compare with games and activities born of the imagination.

A garden for older children

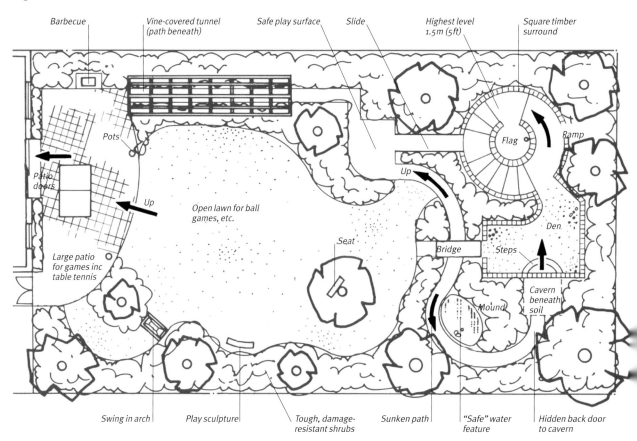

Barbecue   Vine-covered tunnel (path beneath)   Safe play surface   Slide   Highest level 1.5m (5ft)   Square timber surround

Pots   Patio doors   Up   Open lawn for ball games, etc.   Large patio for games inc table tennis   Seat   Up   Flag   Ramp   Den   Bridge   Steps   Mound   Cavern beneath soil

Swing in arch   Play sculpture   Tough, damage-resistant shrubs   Sunken path   "Safe" water feature   Hidden back door to cavern

Children's gardens

Above all, children's gardens should be challenging, intellectually stimulating and exciting places and, it goes without saying, they should also be safe places. Parents will not be able to relax and enjoy their garden if they worry about potential dangers. For older children safety features should be in place but not be made too obvious, since a sense of adventure and imagined danger can be an enjoyable part of growing up.

Designing "secret" and concealed areas within the garden will appeal to children in this way – they are still within the boundaries of the garden yet away from the parental gaze. Densely shrubbed and wooded areas let them escape into a forest or jungle in their imaginations. Children enjoy games that involve hiding, and as well as secret garden areas, trees and hedges can provide places to hide, and individual plants can also become favourite spots. For example, a weeping tree, such as *Prunus pendula* 'Pendula Rosea', positively invites young children to hide from view beneath its umbrella of dense trailing branches.

Pathways, as well as leading the visitor around the garden, have their part to play in a children's garden. Changes in level add to their "play" potential, and the more circuitous the better. Partially or fully covered, they become tunnels. The material used in and the construction of paths – suitable for small bicycles or tricycles as children learn to cycle in the safety of their garden – must be considered.

Planting for children

When designing the planting with children in mind, choose robust, child-resistant shrubs and trees – ones that can sustain some damage and will not die off if they get hit by footballs or are brushed against during play. Select plants without spikes or barbs, or place these in areas which are away from places the children will play, and choose only those that are non-toxic. Remember that any plant that forms fruit or bears berries will attract the attention of small children who may want to "taste" them. But whatever flowering plants and shrubs you choose, they still need to be attractive to the adults who will also enjoy the garden.

Wildlife in the garden excites any child, so trees should be included in your design, and a nest box can be fitted to the largest trunk. The habitats described on page 55 (Natural and wildlife gardens) will interest children, especially once the creatures have made their homes in them.

Thought should also be given to encouraging children to garden, perhaps by providing an area to be cultivated purely by them. A raised planting box might be incorporated into the plan for your budding horticulturists. Inspire them by letting them cultivate plants that grow quickly, such as sunflowers, pansies and primulas, or crops that they can eat – including wild strawberry, dwarf beans and salad crops such as lettuce and radishes.

Structures for play

A play house in any garden will always be well used by children. These can be either permanent or temporary features, but either way, place these as far away from the house as possible to provide the children with a degree of privacy. Smaller structures, such as a robust, rounded "play" sculpture – perhaps a climb-on animal or fantasy figure – can add to the overall design of the garden: it not only brings pleasure to the children but can also act as a focal point.

A number of easy to construct play structures, such as a climbing frame, detailed in this book (pages 192–197), can become part of your garden design. Siting them and their environment needs consideration, for example, immediately beneath the equipment grass could be replaced with one of the many "play safe" impact-absorbing paviours.

A garden for older children

Older children will appreciate the garden illustrated here because its design emphasizes adventure and exploration. The patio is generously proportioned for general use and for games like table tennis, chess, and hoopla. The barbecue is a permanent feature and the focus of summer parties.

A large open lawn can be used for more boisterous ball games and makes an aesthetic contribution to the entire scheme. In this area, the main focal point is a tree with a seat in its shade. A concealed path leading from the left of the patio immediately enters a vine-covered tunnel, providing dappled shade and occasional glimpses of the garden. On emerging from the tunnel, the path curves sharply past the end of the slide then dips beneath a timber bridge, continuing past a "safe" water feature to arrive at the rear entrance of a cavern constructed beneath an earth mound.

The alternative route across the lawn and over the bridge leads to a den enclosed by square section timbers set vertically into the ground to an approximate height of 1.5m (5ft). From here, the entrance to the safe, properly constructed subterranean cavern is reached by descending semi-circular steps. Opposite the cavern is the entrance to the sunken path, to the right via a ramp and to the left by steps. These also provide access to the top of the slide.

The entire garden is surrounded by hardy, child-resistant shrubs and trees. These unify the otherwise disparate elements and also provide year-round colour and interest for the adult members of the family.

Natural and wildlife gardens

Wildlife conservation as a theme for a private garden is an exciting concept. All conscientious gardeners recognize the serious effects of the continuing loss of wildlife habitats. and know that gardens can provide opportunities to create alternative habitats for some species.

Surprisingly, wildlife gardens need to be as well managed as any other type of garden. A well-planned wildlife garden accommodates a wide variety of animals and native plants, plus a few trusted strangers. In a tiny plot, planting a single shrub chosen to attract insects and birds can help, while at the other end of the scale some owners of large gardens are developing them as miniature eco-systems.

Wildlife ponds

A wildlife pond will inevitably become the focus of a garden, and can be created with a flexible liner sandwiched between protective geotextile layers resting on the native soil. The lining should be well concealed all around. The sides of the pond must be sloped very gently (at a maximum of 20°), to provide easy access for animals and amphibians.

Having gently sloping sides means that the pond will have to be quite large to achieve the minimum ice-free water depth of 600–750mm (2–2ft 6in) at the centre. An allowance also has to be made for a 150mm (6in) soil layer at the sides and bottom for growing plants. The soil layer should be of low-nutrient clay or sub-soil and free of stones which might penetrate the lining.

Wildflower meadows

Wildflower meadows are not simple to achieve. Herbicides or fertilizers must not have been used in the immediate area for at least 18 months, and existing lawn grasses are unlikely to be a good basis for the meadow, so will need to be removed. Turf can be lifted for use elsewhere or composting and, before sowing, the ground must be thoroughly cleared of weeds.

The wild flower seed mix to be sown should be tailored precisely to the garden soil type, pH, and aspect. Consult a specialist in advance for advice about this and about sowing rates and times, which are also critical. Never expect the meadow to become established quickly – it can take two years before it begins to match expectations. Even then some flowers will need to be resown annually such as the field poppy (*Papaver rhoeas*), which self-sows only on newly-disturbed soil.

Cutting the wildflower meadow is also important and the appropriate frequency and season will vary according to the kinds of plants grown. Make sure the clippings are always removed to prevent too much plant food returning to the soil and to inhibit fungal growth.

Where suitable indigenous grasses are already growing and herbicides or fertilizers have not been used, wildflower "plugs" (of small plants) available from some nurseries, can be used. These succeed in established grass sward when seed may not, but if seeding is preferred, the existing grass must be thoroughly and deeply scarified beforehand and all debris removed before sowing takes place.

PROVIDING HABITATS

Rotting logs can attract invertebrates and fungi.

A flowerpot, angled so that rainwater cannot get in, is an ideal home for bees.

Nest boxes should be located beyond the reach of any predators.

Left: Even the smallest water feature can provide focus in a garden. Here, a waterfall over grey slate that ends as a shallow pool brings movement and excitement to an area of this garden.

Below: Despite its relatively small size, this garden with its curvy lawn, mixed borders, pond, and paved area shows successfully the basic garden principles of balance, unity, form, and colour.

Above: Paving fulfils many functions. For easy access to different parts of the garden concrete paving is versatile, available in a wide range of colours, shapes, and styles and can be laid in a wide range of patterns and bond.

Left: Gravel is the simplest form of flexible paving. However, a good way to prevent it spilling onto borders is to combine it with edging material that harmonizes, such as bricks.

Natural and wildlife gardens

Providing habitats

Trees and plants for a wildlife garden should be selected not only to attract birds, insects and animals as visitors but as permanent residents. This is probably the most important function of a wildlife garden.

There are many ways in which a garden can be made attractive to wildlife.

Bird tables These range from the basic DIY types to the sophisticated. What is important is that the table is accessible to birds yet safe from predators.

Decomposing logs attract various forms of wildlife including insects, small rodents, and fungi. Small ferns and various algae can also take hold, adding further interest.

Bumble bees are usually welcome in a garden. Create a home for them by fixing a flower pot into an embankment, angled so as not to collect rainwater. A layer of fine wood shavings at the bottom will be appreciated by the bees.

Various nest boxes encourage bird species whose precise nesting requirements may not be met by the trees. The RSPB provides information on the dimensions of the boxes, hole sizes and perches to suit particular species. Boxes, like bird tables, should be positioned well beyond the reach of any predators. Pergolas, arches and redundant swings all qualify as supports from which to hang bird-seed containers. A thorny climbing rose might be used to discourage cats.

Some wildlife pond owners may have mixed feelings when they receive a visit from a heron. To minimize fish losses, provide a refuge for the fish by placing a number of pitch fibre pipes (pipes used in road drainage works) open at both ends and 100mm (4in) or more in diameter, at the bottom of the pond. As they are black they soon merge into the soil at the bottom. Alternatively, make the pond extra deep, remembering that a heron is a wader, not a diver.

To encourage moths and other insects to come to feed, paint a slurry patch onto the side of a tree or two. The slurry is made from a mixture of treacle and ripe bananas with a dash of beer or stout to give added incentive. To attract nocturnal moths and insects, hang a translucent light in a tree or on a pergola. A clear outer cover is essential to prevent injury to insects and moths through direct contact with the hot bulb.

Dried moss, hay, and short pieces of string are good nesting materials for birds. Loosely bundle a mixture in some wide mesh sacking, then tie it to a tree branch from late winter onward.

An informal, natural garden design

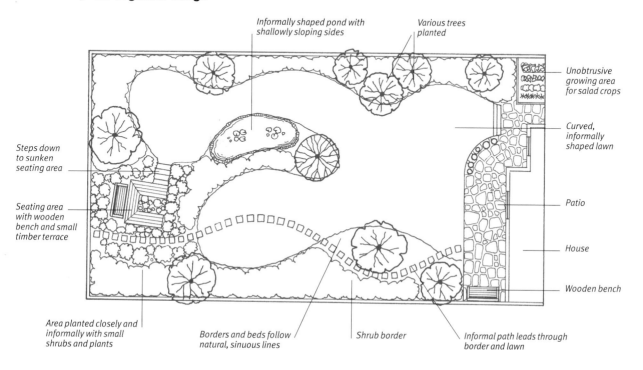

Informally shaped pond with shallowly sloping sides

Various trees planted

Unobtrusive growing area for salad crops

Curved, informally shaped lawn

Steps down to sunken seating area

Seating area with wooden bench and small timber terrace

Patio

House

Wooden bench

Area planted closely and informally with small shrubs and plants

Borders and beds follow natural, sinuous lines

Shrub border

Informal path leads through border and lawn

Water gardens

There is little doubt that, whatever form it takes, water becomes the main focus when it is included in a garden. Because of this, its form and placement must be chosen with the utmost care. Water has such an irresistible appeal that where other eye-catching features exist its introduction will be a potential distraction. To prevent this, think about how the existing features might be brought together in a mutually complementary way, perhaps using the water's reflective properties or water plants as the catalyst.

Where a design does not have other features to consider, or is starting from new, this almost magical element can be exploited imaginatively to the full.

Water in perspective

The principles of space and movement in the open areas and horizontal surfaces in the garden are equally important when expanses of water are being designed. When horizontal land forms are viewed in perspective they appear to close up and look smaller than when seen on plan (see page 54). The phenomenon tends to be exaggerated where bodies of water are concerned. This is because the surface of the water is often below that of its immediate surround, so from a distance less water is seen. This is true also when water is raised closer to eye level, as in a raised pool.

Try to take this effect into account during the design stage by laying the plan on a flat surface close to eye level, then viewing it end on (see diagram opposite). Another technique is to mark out the pool on the ground, go back to the house or patio, then sit down and look at the proposed pool shape from this level. This gives a realistic impression of the finished shape as it will appear from a frequently used vantage point.

The diagram (right, top) shows an informal pool in plan form with surrounding planting and an island. Also illustrated

is how the same pool will appear from a standing, then a sitting, position. Plants at the front of the pool conceal much of the water surface, as does the island. For this reason avoid creating islands in small ponds. The fact that the water surface is lower than the ground exacerbates the problem. Achieving the planned effect would involve making the pond larger from front to back by as much as two or three times.

Viewed from further back even less of the water surface would be seen. Even a short grass surround, combined with the lower level of water, can greatly reduce the view of the pool. Water plants in the foreground could conceal it completely.

The effects of perspective on ponds

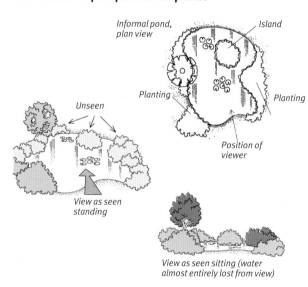

Informal pond, plan view

Island

Unseen

Planting

Planting

Position of viewer

View as seen standing

View as seen sitting (water almost entirely lost from view)

Viewing the water surface

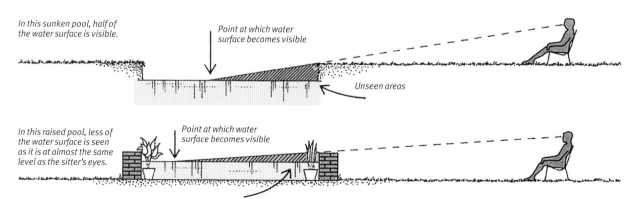

In this sunken pool, half of the water surface is visible.

Point at which water surface becomes visible

Unseen areas

In this raised pool, less of the water surface is seen as it is at almost the same level as the sitter's eyes.

Point at which water surface becomes visible

Water gardens

SAFETY FIRST WITH WATER GARDENING

Safety factors

Because water is so attractive, especially to children, safety must take priority over appearance in water features. It is well known that even the shallowest water can prove fatal to the very young. Rather than take any risks, a pool or pond should be omitted from your garden plan altogether, or its inclusion postponed until a more appropriate time when the children have grown.

If a water feature is already present in a garden that is to be used by children, then it should be securely fenced off with lockable gates at the access points. Alternatively, cleanly puncture the bottom in one or two places to ensure adequate drainage (these punctures can be repaired later) and fill the pool with soil. It can then serve as a moist shrub or flower bed until the children have reached an age where the pond can be reinstated.

Raised shallow pools with walls 600mm (2ft) or so high are not quite as dangerous but, even so, these are not suitable in an area where young children will be playing unless constant supervision can be guaranteed.

If children will use the garden, then consider using a mesh or grille.

This is a strong, rigid structure that should sit above the surface of the water. This mesh needs to be strong enough to support the weight of a child, so materials such as chicken wire or plastic mesh are not suitable. In addition, the mesh needs to be lockable and fixed into place, so that it cannot be removed by a curious child.

Designing water features for safety

Conventional sunken pools or ponds should not have plain sloping sides, especially if they are constructed using smooth liners. These can be very slippery and once a child or even an adult has fallen in, it is not easy to climb out. The deeper the pool, the more difficult this is. Instead, arrange the sides as a series of inward-sloping steps, which will make it much safer.

Where concrete is used to line the pool, texture the steps by very rough brushing or tamping before the concrete dries, to make it even easier to climb out.

If a pond is too deep for an adult to wade into, then suitable rescue equipment such as a throw line or a pole of at least sufficient length to reach the centre of the pond should be provided.

Design for a water garden

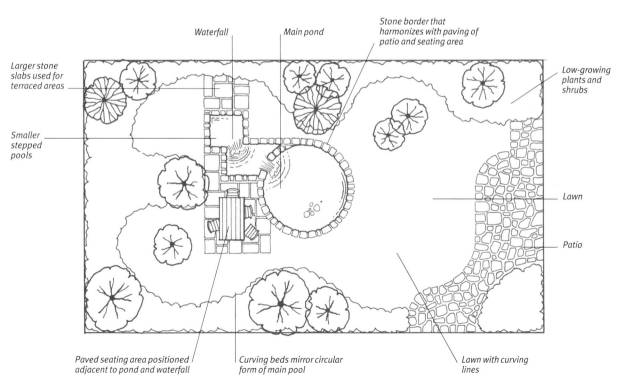

Waterfall

Main pond

Stone border that harmonizes with paving of patio and seating area

Larger stone slabs used for terraced areas

Low-growing plants and shrubs

Smaller stepped pools

Lawn

Patio

Paved seating area positioned adjacent to pond and waterfall

Curving beds mirror circular form of main pool

Lawn with curving lines

Holiday or seaside gardens

Seaside gardens must be designed within quite specific parameters. The plants have to cope with strong, salt-laden winds and, where holiday homes are concerned, periods of time out of season without regular maintenance.

In season, when there may be other more interesting things to do, seaside gardens can still suffer from neglect. This should be borne in mind at the design stage if relaxation is the main purpose of the garden.

Coastal conditions

In temperate zones, proximity to the sea usually means moderated temperatures, enabling more tender plants to be grown, but the effects of strong, salt-laden winds may offset this advantage. In selecting plants for a maritime garden, observe which plants thrive in other local gardens and also consider those that grow wild nearby if considering a more naturalistic design. If the garden will not be regularly maintained all year round, and will not be watered out of the holiday season, research plants that will grow in dry areas.

It is common practice to include windbreaks in the designs for maritime gardens – indeed it is sometimes not possible to

create a seaside garden without them. Plants and trees usually perform this function better than solid objects such as fences or walls. The former can, by filtering the wind, reduce its force while the latter creates turbulence in the garden, sometimes resulting in more damage than if there were no screen at all. Any screens, whether planted or constructed, should make a positive contribution to the design of a garden as well as being functional. In addition, a colourful, striped canvas awning would be an attractive summertime alternative to a pergola.

If it is planned to leave, say, a table and chairs in the garden on a permanent basis, ensure that the furniture is manufactured from sunlight-resistant plastic or aluminium. Alternatively, timber furniture will survive being outdoors all year round and should weather in the salt-laden winds if it is properly treated with preservatives and is regularly maintained.

A low-maintenance seaside or holiday home garden

In the garden illustrated below, the main paved area around the house is reached via a raised, paved rectangle with a low planted bowl at its centre. In the corners are short stone

Low maintenance seaside garden

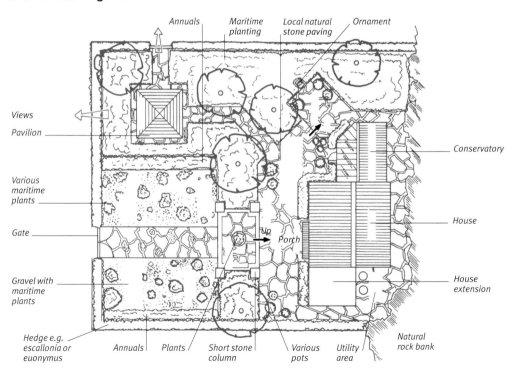

Annuals · Maritime planting · Local natural stone paving · Ornament

Views

Pavilion

Various maritime plants

Gate

Gravel with maritime plants

Conservatory

House

House extension

Natural rock bank

Hedge e.g. escallonia or euonymus · Annuals · Plants · Short stone column · Various pots · Utility area

Up · Porch

Holiday or seaside gardens

columns. The caps form the plinths supporting matched plants or pots. To one side of the house is a conservatory, glazed only at the front to prevent overheating in summer. One angled side looks toward an ornament or sculpture at the far end of a paved rectangle with planted pots.

The area at the rear of the house, being close to an embankment, is utilitarian but, although it is not seen as much as other parts of the garden, indigenous plants growing in rock crevices provide interest, as do sea birds nesting higher up. The planting has been chosen to cope with strong, salt-laden winds.

The best view of the sea is afforded from the pavilion which, set with in trees and shrubs, is a feature in its own right. Every care has been taken to link its style architecturally with the house. Trees and shrubs will inevitably be sculpted by the prevailing winds to become an integral part of a seaside garden's character.

A small, decked seaside garden

The seaside garden of modest proportions illustrated below is completely decked on three levels. The surround is formed on one side by the house or apartment walls, two side walls 1.5m (5ft) high, one longer than the other, and tinted, ultraviolet-resistant glass panels supported by coated aluminium or timber frames. This is a garden for recreation and the major feature, second only to the sea views, is a raised circular plunge pool or jacuzzi. This is viewed not only from the windows but also from the seat set against the wall beneath the canvas awning, with a light to extend the use of this space into the evening. Between the decked surfaces and the surround grow a variety of colourful maritime plants, seasonally supplemented with others growing in pots.

Although the timber decking is afforded some protection from salt-laden winds by its being enclosed by the walls and panels, it will still need to be treated regularly with a timber preservative or wood stain to help it withstand the bleaching effects of both the salt and the sunlight.

An efficient irrigation system would be an advantage in a garden of this style, particularly if the property is not inhabited all year round, and raised decking can be designed in sections so that it can be lifted to allow irrigation lines to pots and planters to be introduced underneath.

A decked seaside garden

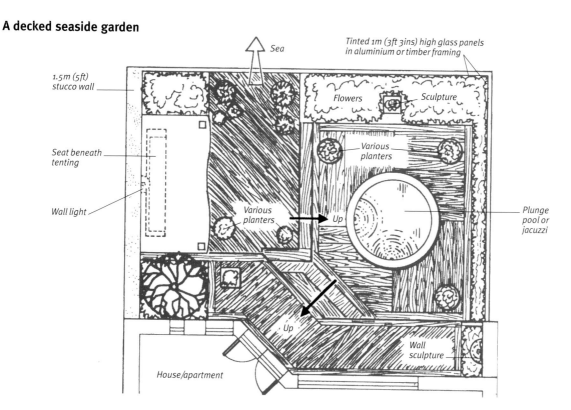

1.5m (5ft) stucco wall

Seat beneath tenting

Wall light

Sea

Tinted 1m (3ft 3ins) high glass panels in aluminium or timber framing

Flowers

Sculpture

Various planters

Various planters

Up

Plunge pool or jacuzzi

Up

Wall sculpture

House/apartment

Cold, exposed sites

Apart from the personal discomfort involved, strong winds can cause structural and plant damage in a garden. When associated with high or low temperatures, dehydration becomes a possibility. Low temperatures introduce a wind-chill factor, which lowers the temperature even more. If the soil at ground level or in pots is wet, the problem is exacerbated further. For this reason, only the hardiest of plants should be used in cold, exposed gardens. Take your lead from what is growing naturally or successfully in the area. Native plants and trees, having evolved under such conditions, are an obvious choice but may lack the variety preferred by many gardeners.

Creating shelter

A shelter belt can improve the situation but lack of space may leave room only for a constructed screen. There is often a dilemma when screening exposed gardens as many have dramatic views which are lost in the process. Under these circumstances, it would probably be better to decide which are the best views, then plant the shelter belts or erect the screens to leave a series of "windows". This not only enhances the views by framing them, but also creates sheltered areas.

Where a garden is cold because of its orientation (on the shaded side of a hill, for example, or because of local climatic conditions), the best solution may be to set about creating a series of microclimate-creating hedges, shelters or buildings. The garden can then be enjoyed with a degree of comfort.

Choosing plants for exposed sites

The more exposed, cold and wet a garden is, the more limited the choice of plants and trees that can be grown successfully there. Under extreme conditions, indigenous species alone may have to be relied upon. This presents a challenge, but can still result in a garden that is interesting, attractive and functional. In such adverse conditions, a fundamental change of gardening philosophy may be necessary. For example, there is no reason whatsoever why a shelter belt should not be thought of as a contribution to the garden's visual appeal as well as acting as a foil to any formal elements within.

A small patio garden for an exposed site

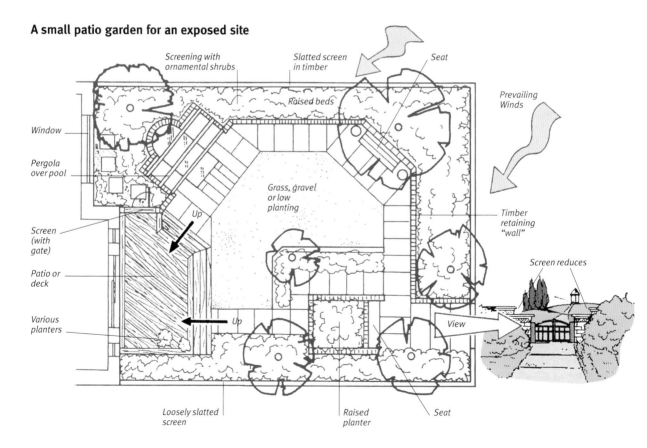

Screening with ornamental shrubs

Slatted screen in timber

Seat

Raised beds

Prevailing Winds

Window

Pergola over pool

Grass, gravel or low planting

Up

Screen (with gate)

Timber retaining "wall"

Patio or deck

Screen reduces

Various planters

Up

View

Loosely slatted screen

Raised planter

Seat

Cold, exposed sites

A small patio garden for an exposed site

An architectural solution makes the best of the garden illustrated on the oppposite page. Immediately outside the patio doors is the timber deck, furnished with various planters and with a broad step leading down to the main garden. This area has been lowered to provide greater protection from the prevailing winds. The excavated soil has been re-used to fill the raised beds which are supported by vertically positioned square-section timbers.

In the raised borders, screening trees and plants give instant height. These trees and plants supplement the small-aperture trellis which screens and surrounds the entire garden. To the left of the deck is a small formal pool, backed with a continuation of the timber "wall", and over the pool is a vine-clad pergola. A path on the left leads to an inward-looking seat (a focal point viewed from the house), and to the right there is a raised planter for flowers and herbs. Unseen behind the planter, a seat looks out over the open land or townscape.

Protecting cold, exposed sites

On the windward side, an arrangement of dense, hardy shrubs rising to a planting of trees makes the best shelter belt. Any shelter belt will be further improved if some permeable screen is added at its centre. To be effective, however, there must be a dense mass of planting and this is simply not possible in small gardens. Under these circumstances, a slatted screen or "pierced" wall probably provides the best solution, especially if hardy plants are established on one or both sides

A permeable barrier (illustrated below, right) such as a hedge, slatted fence or row of trees allows the wind to filter through, dissipating its force.

A solid barrier (shown below, left) is inappropriate in exposed situations. On impact, the wind increases in speed as it travels up and over the solid barrier; then, as it plunges down, it can cause extreme turbulence on the supposedly protected side, reducing air and ground temperatures there as well as battering any planting. Few plants can withstand strong winds from above.

POTENTIAL TYPES OF BARRIER FOR AN EXPOSED SITE

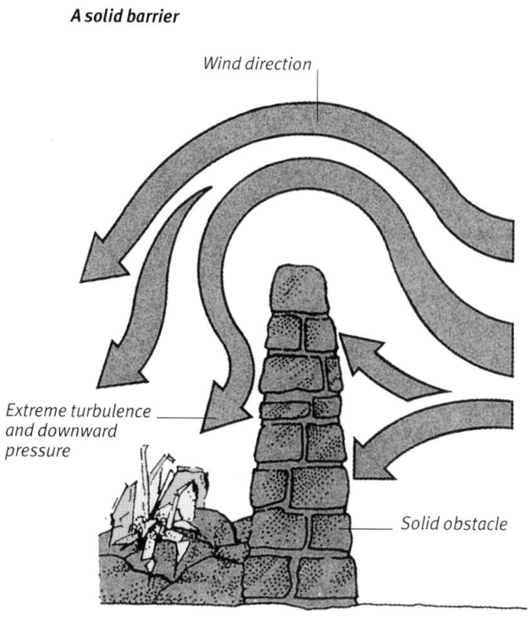

A solid barrier

Wind direction

Extreme turbulence and downward pressure

Solid obstacle

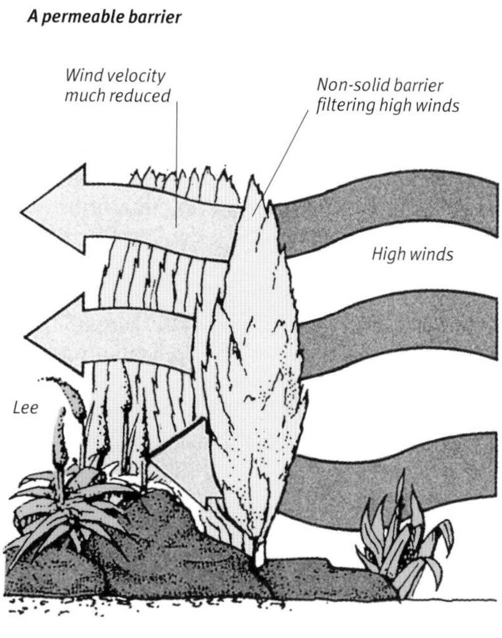

A permeable barrier

Wind velocity much reduced

Non-solid barrier filtering high winds

High winds

Lee

Hot dry gardens

Shortage of water is always a problem in gardens in hot, dry climates and for those which have to be left unattended for considerable periods. Climate change is increasingly affecting gardeners who may find that the amount of rainfall their gardens receive during summer is lessening, combined with higher average temperatures and extended growing seasons. To combat this, gardens (or areas within your garden) can be specifically designed with drought-resistant plants.

This is known as xeroscaping, a modern word created from the Greek *xero*, meaning dry. Tough plants which are xerophytic, or naturally tolerant of dry conditions, are used in preference to delicate ornamental subjects from more temperate climates. These xero-phytes, some of which have hitherto been considered weeds, include grasses, succulents and cacti and many narrow-leaved plants from dry, hot places. These are generally more efficient at conserving water than those with shiny or waxy leaves. Grey or silver-leaved plants are also a common sight in hot, dry places, having adapted to their environment by developing light-reflective leaves. Colour in this type of garden is provided through the variety of foliage as much as through flowering plants.

Hot, dry conditions are not confined to gardens close to the equator: temperate zones can be dry and hot in summer but damp and cold in winter. This poses problems for the designer, since there are comparatively few subjects that will tolerate such extreme weather conditions.

Creating shade

Shade must be created in a hot, dry garden if it is to be enjoyed in comfort. Parasols, pergolas, arbours, and shade trees can all make a valuable contribution, but the selection of horizontal and vertical surfaces is also important. White house walls reflect sunlight, making the interior of a house cooler, but they can be dazzling to those sitting outside.

Similarly, paving that is too light in colour can be so reflective that people in the garden are uncomfortable without sunglasses. Conversely, dark or non-reflective paving absorbs heat from the sun and may be too hot to walk on, especially with bare feet. Pale "earth-coloured" pavings, including grey, are probably the best choices for surfaces in hot sunny situations, or gravel or chippings in a neutral colour.

Areas of shade can also be created through planting: including high-growing plants and shrubs in the design will provide shady spots for both visitors to the garden and for other plants. Although it may seem contradictory, the arid atmosphere that may exist within a hot, dry garden can be counteracted by the inclusion of a water feature within the design. The sound of water bubbling over stones or the cascade of a wall fountain promotes a feeling of coolness.

Position any fountain or pool in a shady position to ensure that evaporation is kept to a minimum, and water should be recycled by a pump.

Establishing a xeroscaped garden

An irrigation system might seem an obvious solution for the hot, dry garden but this would oppose the concept and function of xeroscaping, and conservation of water. The idea is to work with the dry conditions rather than to try to change them, but there are steps that can be taken to help the xerophytic plants to thrive. A layer of gravel used as a mulch over soil has the advantage of storing any available water, which is then released as a vapour that will rise up through the plants. It also reduces evaporation from the soil beneath. Polymer granules can be incorporated into the soil, where they store water to be used by the plants with minimal loss through evaporation. As there is a risk that birds may eat polymer granules left on the surface, make sure they are well dug in or covered by a mulch.

Creating the traditional "lawn and beds" design in some locations will become increasingly difficult because of climate change, therefore xeroscaping is an attractive alternative to be considered.

Informal hot, dry rock and decking garden

Although the diagonal timber deck and associated exposed aggregate concrete paths are angular, the general feel of the garden is informal. Shade is provided by a large parasol and a shade tree growing through the deck, with its roots in the cool soil beneath.

The main area is gravelled and surrounded by large boulders and xerophytic, ornamental and indigenous trees, and plants. The textured concrete zig-zag path at the left, hidden for most of its length, passes beneath a pergola constructed of sun-bleached driftwood. This supports climbing plants and vines, creating dappled shade beneath, while the choice of sun-bleached material adds to the dry atmosphere of the garden. Other timber used in the construction of the garden, such as the decking, could be stained or treated with a coloured preservative to tone in with the colour scheme of the garden and the texture of the concrete and gravel.

Boulders and rocks are appropriate to the ambience of the dry garden and where possible these should be recycled or even created from simulated stone.

In the far left corner is a concealed gazebo with open-slatted roof and sides to ensure that it remains comfortably cool within. Steps from the gravelled area disappear in a short tunnel below a large rock garden which is home to dwarf or prostrate sun-loving plants.

Hot dry gardens

Informal hot, dry, and decking garden

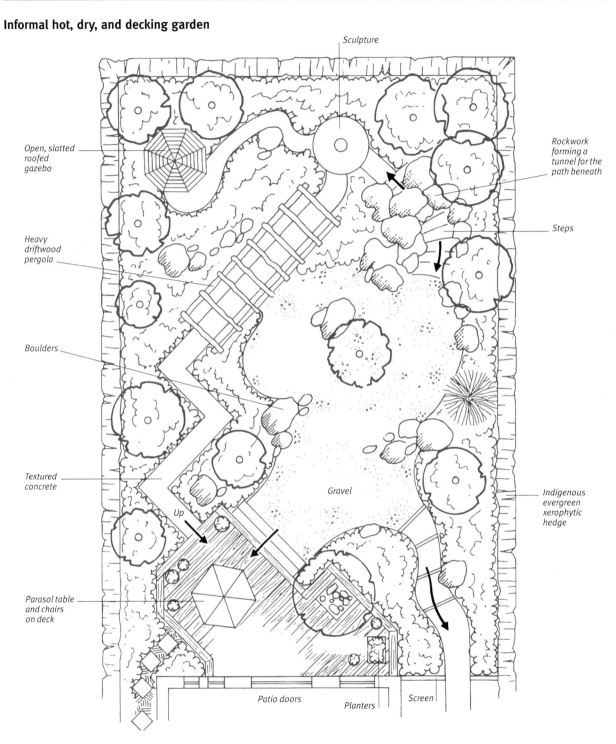

Sculpture

Open, slatted roofed gazebo

Heavy driftwood pergola

Boulders

Textured concrete

Parasol table and chairs on deck

Rockwork forming a tunnel for the path beneath

Steps

Indigenous evergreen xerophytic hedge

Gravel

Up

Patio doors

Planters

Screen

Informal alpine and rock gardens

An informal alpine and rock garden

Some alpines and dwarf conifers are so individualistic in form and cultural requirement that it can be difficult to incorporate them into a small, formal garden where well defined or straight boundaries are clear. Nevertheless, alpines, dwarf conifers and rock gardens are popular as garden themes.

The small garden illustrated below has been designed with walls and rock garden forming the structure; the alpine plants and conifers simply furnish it. As the garden is small, the plants can be placed individually. A paved path runs along the house wall, both for access and to limit the amount of gravel which might otherwise inadvertently be carried indoors. In the rest of the garden, gravel or crushed stone is the main horizontal surfacing because of its natural association with alpine plants.

The spiralling beds rise to approximately 750mm (2ft 6in), supported by dry-stone walls which are similar in type and colour to the boundary walls. The spirals create vertical areas of light and shade, thus increasing the range of planting

conditions in the soil joints. The areas at the top of the walls are suitable for growing a variety of subjects where well-drained conditions and soil types can be finely tuned to meet individual plant needs.

Dry-stone raised beds at the sides of the garden contain more robust alpines and conifers, while the surrounding walls host climbing plants which may be too invasive when grown horizontally. A small pavement rock garden in the corner near to the house can be enjoyed from the nearby windows. Diagonally opposite, angled steps lead to the rock garden. Alongside the conifer bed, a circular window has been constructed in an extension of the boundary wall, providing a view of an interesting tree or shrub beyond.

The rock garden itself is constructed in a naturalistic, stratified way using stones similar to those used in the boundary wall but much larger. This makes for visual harmony and helps to integrate both the formal and informal aspects of the garden. The rock garden could be planted with undemanding alpine favourites or rare and more difficult

An informal alpine and rock garden

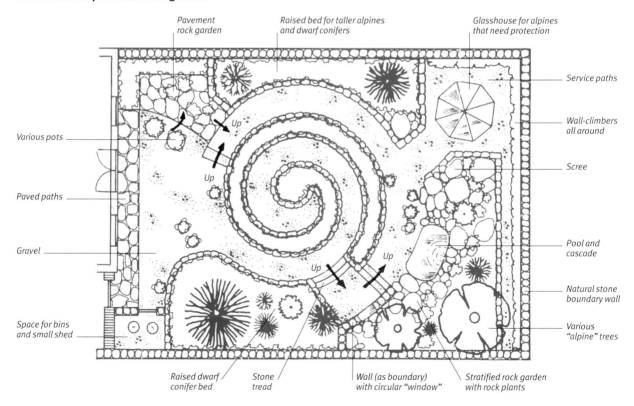

Pavement rock garden

Raised bed for taller alpines and dwarf conifers

Glasshouse for alpines that need protection

Various pots

Paved paths

Gravel

Space for bins and small shed

Service paths

Wall-climbers all around

Scree

Pool and cascade

Natural stone boundary wall

Various "alpine" trees

Raised dwarf conifer bed

Stone tread

Wall (as boundary) with circular "window"

Stratified rock garden with rock plants

Informal alpine and rock gardens

species, according to the owner's personal enthusiasm. A small rock pool invites the visitor to pause and enjoy the sound of water gently cascading from the false spring above. A well-ventilated glasshouse provides winter protection for plants that are moisture- or climate-sensitive.

Blending a rock garden into the garden
Rock gardens made up of equal-sized stones heaped up in the corner of a brick wall never look convincing. Even in the smallest garden a rock garden should be designed to have the most natural appearance possible, using recycled stone if possible or local stone where available. A couple of rocks can be introduced nearby but independent of the main rock garden to help blend the feature into the garden as a whole. There are various forms a rock garden can take:

Stratified rock garden This type is designed to resemble eroded bed-rock with the strata of the rock clearly visible, or an escarpment with soil pockets or plateaux which are ideal for planting up. Use the largest rocks that can feasibly be imported, ensuring that they are well founded and laid so that they slope inward toward the centre of the rock garden. This makes the structure more stable and safer to maintain and encourages rainwater to run back into the soil pockets where it is needed, rather than draining off. By adding different compost mixes and grits, plants with different cultural requirements can be grown.

Boulder rock garden Boulder stones, shaped by glacial activity or water erosion, are not generally found naturally in a stratified state. Because of this they lookout of place in a conventional stratified rock garden, but they can be arranged in a way that allows their sculptural qualities to be enjoyed. The tone of a boulder rock garden is determined by the surrounding and associated planting. For example, the same group of boulders planted with different grasses, yuccas, and succulents in a gravelled setting creates the impression of an arid zone, while a planting of hostas, ferns, and rodgersias in a mossy, shaded setting will suggest moist conditions.

Pavement rock garden This is an excellent way of growing favourite alpines, especially when a conventional rock garden cannot be accommodated. Large flattish stones are the most suitable (but not of protected limestone) and must be of sufficient size to step on safely and to allow for the sideways spread of the plants. The joints between the stones should be approximately 25–50mm (1–2in) wide and a lime mortar (one part cement to two parts lime and ten parts sand or stone dust) can make them stable.

Boulder stone arrangement

Boulder rock garden (cross section)

Gravel, moss or close ground cover as preferred

Pavement rock garden

Pavement garden (cross section)

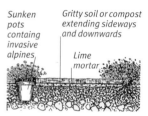

Sunken pots containg invasive alpines

Gritty soil or compost extending sideways and downwards

Lime mortar

Compost pockets can be created, wider than the finished joints if necessary, before the stones are laid, then planted up once the pavement is in place. Given adequate drainage, individual cultural conditions can be created between the pavement stone joints in the same way as the soil pockets of a stratified rock garden. Invasive alpines should be confined by clay pots sunk into the soil, again before the stone is laid. Pavement rock gardens can also be established at the periphery of a patio: a useful device when space is limited.

Scree A natural scree is a mixture of soil and eroded stone debris which has fallen from rock outcrops above. These conditions can be recreated in a garden either as an independent feature or in association with a stratified rock garden, providing the perfect opportunity for growing a range of xerophytic and other plants (see page 62) that have adapted to suit these gritty, dry, free-draining conditions. Most types of crushed stone can be used, but do consider using recycled aggregates.

Dwarf conifer gardens Dwarf conifers vary so considerably in shape, habit, and colour that it can be difficult to make them part of the structure of a garden. This is why they are more appropriate as an individual collection or as features in an alpine garden since there is a natural affinity between them. Always check the ultimate height and spread of conifers sold as "dwarf" varieties: some can still reach 2m (6ft 6in) in height.

Low maintenance garden

An important part of good garden design is a fair calculation of the time required for maintenance. No garden, however delightful initially, will continue to be so if it is not properly maintained. The amount of maintenance a garden will require can be reduced in two ways: firstly by incorporating labour-saving devices into the fabric of the garden construction (and conversely not including in that design high-maintenance planting, structures, or areas); secondly, by using efficient techniques during day-to-day maintenance procedures

"Designed-in" maintenance devices

Paving surfaces These should be designed to be easily cleaned by brushing or washing off. If the surface is too rough, detritus will become trapped in the surface holes and hollows; too smooth and the paving will become slippery in wet or icy conditions.

Mowing edges Where grass grows directly against a wall or steps, cutting it is difficult and both hands and equipment can suffer knocks and abrasions when doing so. Electric string trimmers can cut lawn edges, but the most low maintenance method is using the mower while the lawn is cut. A good mowing edge has its upper surface set just below that of the adjacent grass turf, so that no contact damage is inflicted on or by mower blades. The mowing edge itself can be of practically any flat material, such as brick, stone or concrete.

Laying the mowing edge on a bed of mortar ensures that it is stable and remains level or at least even if on a slope. For low walls up to 900mm (3ft) high, a 100–150mm (4–6in) wide mowing edge is appropriate. Above this height, a 225mm (9in) wide edge is more accommodating to mowers.

Lawn edging Some lawns need to be physically contained to preserve their shape. This is particularly important in a formal layout. If you do not want a mowing edge, use a timber or steel edge set just below the level of the turf. Where paths cross lawns, lay them so that the upper surface is at or just below that of adjacent turf levels. Where a bed or border abuts a path, ensure that the soil level is below that of the path. This will discourage soil migration onto the path itself by acting as a mini retaining wall.

Mulching

This helps to suppress weed growth and reduces the need for watering. Mulches are useful for most plant situations and can be applied around shrubs, borders, vegetables and fruit. Where trees are planted in areas of long grass a proprietary flexible mulch – such as bitumen felts and natural fibre that will break down eventually – is effective.

Organic or gravel mulches conserve moisture and inhibit weed growth. Most plants benefit from mulching, although bulbs or rhizomes do not like mulches immediately around them. Mulches should be applied at a minimum depth of 75mm (3in) and just left on the soil surface, not dug in. In open areas where the mulch becomes a ground cover in its own right, gravel, pebbles or stones can be used.

Weed growth can be inhibited by placing polythene sheets, or a geotextile membrane (which is self draining), beneath the mulch. Save time on planting and maintenance by choosing permanent plants such as shrubs, trees and perennials rather than more time-consuming annuals or bedding plants. Where slopes in the garden are steep or inaccessible to mowing equipment, use a vigorous groundcover plant and plant closer together so that the establish quickly and spread.

Irrigation systems

Watering is the necessary but potentially most labour-intensive maintenance operation. In summer pots and containers need to be watered at least once a day. Mulching and incorporating organic material into the soil helps to retain moisture. However, in areas of low rainfall or where summers are hot and dry, it is worth investigating the possibillity of installing an irrigation system. The larger the garden, the more labour-saving and worthwhile this is. There is a choice of types ranging from simple tap-operated DIY kits to sophisticated timed multi-systems that must be designed and installed by professionals. The "leaking pipe" system, where holes are made along the length of the hosepipe from which the water will seep out is basic, but it can be less wasteful of water than using a garden sprinkler. What ever type you use, remember that water is a resource that should not be wasted. Irrigation systems operate most efficiently and cost-effectively at night, when watering is achieved with least water loss through evaporation.

Sloping areas

When a grass embankment slopes downward to finish at a fence or wall, conventional mowing can be impossible. Creating a level area at the bottom of the slope wide enough to accommodate a mower is better, especially if a mowing edge is placed against the fence or wall.

String trimmers are easy to use to cut grass in awkward places, but both the operator and any young trees and shrubs in the lawn need to be protected. Goggles should be worn to protect the operator from flying stems, gravel or soil, and the trunks of trees should be protected from lacerations by plastic guards at their bases.

Structures

Structures of stone, concrete and brick will call for the least attention, apart from cleaning. Timber structures, decking and

Low maintenance garden

fences need to be checked regularly for signs of rot and deterioration and dealt with appropriately. Soft woods can be pre-treated with preservatives, but these are only guaranteed for a limited period of time, perhaps up to 15 years. Therefore many garden structures will need a "follow up" treatment with preservative. Hardwoods are a more expensive alternative, but ensure they come from renewable sources. Stained wood preservatives are quicker and cheaper than applying paint, which must be applied on a more regular basis. Treating any existing structure necessitates the removal of any climbing plants from it, which can be awkward.

A low maintenance garden

A garden requiring little maintenance to keep it in good order does not have to be dull. The differing textures and use of space in the garden illustrated below create an interesting yet simple design. Curves and circles dominate the centre, with a circular gravelled section, which soften the formality of the rectangular garden.

The area nearest the house is paved with square slabs, in the centre of which is a slightly raised bed. As with other beds and borders in the garden, these are edged to keep the soil in place. Bricks provide a change of texture, leading to the gravelled area (an alternative to a lawn). This contains a brick-bordered circular pool, softened with planting around its edges. A simple seating area of timber and gravel forms part of a circle and provides an ideal place to enjoy the pool and the bed beyond it – also shaped to mirror the circular gravel section.

All beds in the garden are closely planted with low-maintenance shrubs and perennials. The lack of gaps between plants prevents the growth of weeds, and the borders at both edges of the garden are filled with slow-growing, evergreen shrubs that will need minimal pruning. A number of smaller trees have been selected to add height.

In the hidden seating area at the farthest point of the garden, the use of bricks to border the gravelled seating area adds to the unity of the garden design, reflecting their use elsewhere in the garden.

A low maintenance garden

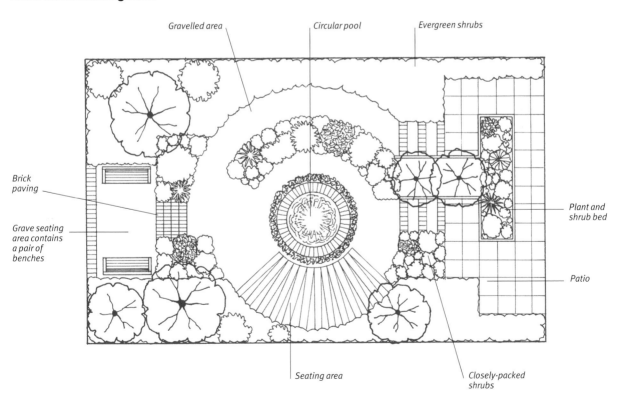

Gravelled area

Circular pool

Evergreen shrubs

Brick paving

Grave seating area contains a pair of benches

Plant and shrub bed

Patio

Seating area

Closely-packed shrubs

Productive gardens

The tendency with productive gardens is to hide them away. Neglected or out-of-season vegetable plots contribute little to the visual attractions of a garden, especially if all other areas are well planned and maintained. This is a pity, since well grown, healthy crops can, given the right conditions, be as appealing as the other plants, with the added attraction of their being edible. Few will argue that fresh produce, taken from the garden and eaten straight away, can be bettered.

It is the tradition in some countries to ensure that productive areas make a positive contribution to the appearance of the garden as a whole, and they are given pride of place alongside the strictly ornamental areas. With a resurgence of interest in growing vegetables, these plants are even being used in ornamental planting schemes, and the sight of vegetables such as brassicas growing in ornamental beds increasingly common.

To ensure that productive gardens are both aesthetically pleasing and horticulturally successful they will need to be given the same consideration at the planning stage as all other parts. Detailed information regarding the siting, size, orientation, soils, and climate of productive gardens is not within the range of this book. There are, however, a number of gardening titles available which provide a thorough explanation of the best ways of establishing and maintaining productive gardens.

Designing productive gardens

From the point of view of their design, it is usual for productive gardens to follow formal lines, as this makes planning, crop rotation, cultivation, and maintenance far easier than it would be in a plot laid out in an informal style. But there is no reason why a degree of informality should not be introduced.

Herb plots are extremely popular in modern gardens. Although grown mainly for culinary purposes, some herbs have great visual and aromatic appeal, and an increasing range of herbs from all over the world is now available. Even though this may mean growing the more tender types in protected pots, from seed, or as annuals in a border, the wider choice adds an extra dimension to herb garden design.

Formal productive garden

In a symmetrical, formal garden vegetables could be grown in geometrically shaped areas arranged around an axis running longitudinally down the garden. In keeping with the formal symmetry, productive plants such as dwarf fruit trees can be grown in large terracotta pots, and be pruned either to form a pyramid or a spherical shape. These trees, of matching shapes, should then be placed so that they mirror each other across the garden. A circular herb bed will also suit the style of this garden and perhaps provide a place for smaller or miniature vegetables.

As part of the formal design, yet reflecting the productive nature of the garden, pathways can be edged with lavender, cat mint, parsley, or other herbs. In addition, any trellis or archway can be used to support various plants, some ornamental, others fruiting. The view of structures such as cold-frames, sheds or soft fruit cages can be concealed by the use of trellis screens, but in a productive formal garden an ornamental glasshouse can provide the perfect focal point.

Informal productive gardens

While formal areas are probably best suited for vegetable-growing, informality is the preferred style for most gardens. The design should encourage a visit to all parts of the garden on the basis of visual appeal quite apart from the need for maintenance. All trees will be selected to produce fruit or nuts, but these are often as beautiful in flower as their strictly ornamental counterparts. To screen, say, a utilitarian glasshouse or cold-frames, place fruit trees to obscure them from view. If constructing a large fruit cage to protect soft fruit, build it from black steel framing and netting. Black is the least obtrusive colour under these circumstances and by growing screening plants in front of it, runner beans perhaps, render the fruit cage almost invisible.

Small herb gardens

A garden, devoted entirely to herbs, could exist in its own right, or as part of a larger garden. Herbs are excellent container plants and these can be incorporated into the garden plan. Most herb gardens are informal simply because it can be difficult to assess the height and spread of different herbs and more difficult still to keep them within their limitations. However, you can give your herb garden a formal structure by hedging it all around with rosemary, or another woody-stemmed herb such as lavender or hyssop. Keep the hedge neatly trimmed and it will serve as an excellent barrier to cold winter winds. Indicate the entrance to the herb garden with an ornamental feature such as an archway supporting a climbing, perfumed rose.

Access is very important when planning your herb garden. You do not want to tread across wet grass or rummage among other plants to get to the herbs, although some herbs release a wonderful scent when brushed against or trodden upon. A gravel path dividing the garden into quadrants provides access as well as form. It could lead to a seat, or highlight a central focal point such as a sundial. In a simple, balanced arrangement such as this, different herbs can be grown in each quadrant without the risk of disharmony.

Productive gardens

Small garden 2cm=1m ($\frac{3}{4}$in=3$\frac{1}{4}$ft)

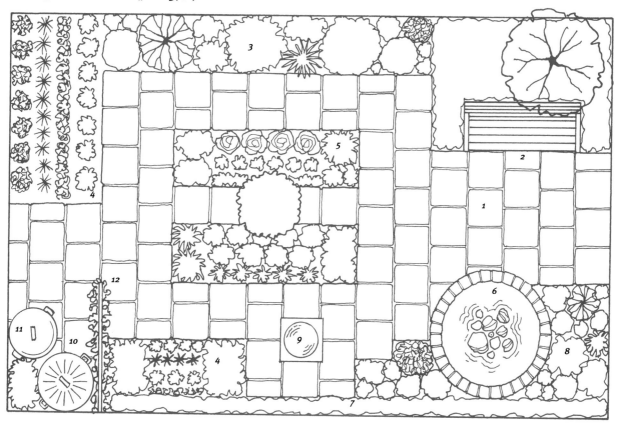

This is a small, semi-formal organic town garden approximately 7 x 5m (23 x 16$\frac{1}{2}$ft). Despite its size, it is possible to grow salads, herbs, a few vegetables, and fruit as well as ornamentals in the space available. It is also a place to relax in, as well as being a wildlife refuge.

The central bed is given to fresh salads and culinary herbs, and other plants in the border are chosen to attract bees and other beneficial insects. Paving takes the place of a lawn, with space betwen slabs for creeping herbs in the crevices. A low fountain bubbles over stones; as well as being a pleasant garden feature it attracts birds and insects. Damp vegetation around the water will also harbour frogs and the fences are covered with climbing plants, giving leafy height and nesting sites for birds.

Although space is at a premium, there is a worm bin for recycling kitchen waste and a small compost bin. These are screened off at the wider end of the garden. The compost bin takes the garden debris and any bags of brought-in manure.

Key

1 Paving with space for crevice planting
2 Garden seat
3 Small tree/large shrub and ground cover
4 Vegetable beds
5 Annual herbs/salad beds
6 Bubbler fountain over stones
7 Cordon fruit trees/climbing plants/nesting hedges
8 Ornamental/attractant plants
9 Bird table
10 Compost bin
11 Worm bin
12 Trellis with climber

Roof gardens

For a variety of reasons, roof gardens need a different design approach and a different set of construction techniques from those used in ground-level gardens. Not least of these is the weight of the garden, which clearly has to be supported by the roof.

Even if there is a suitably sited flat roof available, it may not necessarily be constructed with enough strength to support anything more than the waterproofing system and the occasional visitor to carry out maintenance. Even then special timber walkways (known as duckboards) are normally required to spread the weight of anyone walking on the roof, and any further loading could invite serious structural damage to the building, even collapse. Never embark upon a roof-garden project without consulting a structural engineer. He or she should be qualified to decide whether or not the roof is suitably supportive, or what measures might need to be taken to make it so.

Placing roof garden features

Generally speaking, if a roof structure is not already strong enough, the necessary modifications are costly and disruptive. Where new houses are concerned, facilities for a roof garden can be part of the architect's brief at the outset, so avoiding extra expense later.

The strongest, most supportive areas of a flat roof are those close to the supporting walls. Usually these are at the periphery but, depending upon the size of the roof, supporting walls may cross under the roof as well. All the weighty elements of a roof garden should be designed to be as close as possible to the supporting walls with only the very lightest items at the centre. Unfortunately, there is always a risk of objects placed near the edge falling off the roof, so ensure that nothing top-heavy is included in the design and that anything that could be displaced by strong winds is secured to the decking. Do not secure heavy items to the structure of the building as this could cause structural damage in high winds or interfere with damp-proof courses (DPC).

Drainage

Never interfere with rooftop waterproofing, drainage systems, or the DPC, including those in adjacent walls, either at roof level or beneath copings. To do so may result in the main house structure being penetrated by water. Unfortunately, this can happen when trellis, safety rails or deckwork are fixed.

A roof garden must be designed to ensure that rainwater is quickly discharged from all horizontal surfaces, as damage may be caused not only by water penetration but by its weight. Even a shallow depth of standing water can amount to an immense weight on larger roofs, especially if you bear in mind that just 1 litre of water weighs 1 kilo (1 gallon weighs 10 lbs, or 8 lbs for a US gallon).

Exposed situations

Wind funnelling and the wind-chill factor can present far worse problems at roof level than they do on the ground, damaging plants and causing discomfort to visitors.

In summer, a lack of shade combined with normal dark roof surfaces that absorb rather than reflect heat, can result in swiftly rising temperatures that will cause the compost in plant containers to dry out very quickly and also make the roof garden an uncomfortable place to sit. An irrigation system can help solve the former problem, while pergolas, awnings, and planted trellis provide welcome shade and shelter for visitors.

Planting

Permanent plants for roof gardens must be tolerant of the cold stormy winds of winter. In very low temperatures the plants' roots and the compost in which they grow can be frozen. In summer when the compost heats up it can dry out completely. Either situation is detrimental to normal plant growth.

Since compost-filled pots and containers lack the mass of the soil at ground level, they are subject to greater temperature fluctuations. Only the toughest plants such as berberis, buddlejas, and cotoneasters should be used on a roof unless year-round shelter, seasonally appropriate watering, and a high level of maintenance can be provided. Annuals are popular choices for summer to supplement the

A decked roof garden

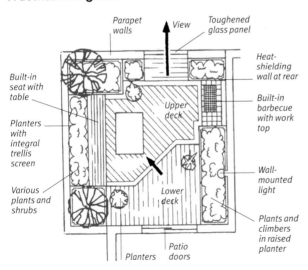

Parapet walls
View
Toughened glass panel
Heat-shielding wall at rear
Built-in seat with table
Upper deck
Built-in barbecue with work top
Planters with integral trellis screen
Various plants and shrubs
Lower deck
Wall-mounted light
Plants and climbers in raised planter
Planters
Patio doors

Left: One of the most decorative kinds of paving, herringbone paths usually need some kind of edging to ensure that the bricks do not fall away with use; here, the path is edged with gravel.

Below: Even tbe most attractive informal garden benefits from a path taking the visitor from one area to another. However attractive a surface a lawn is in dry weather walking on it after heavy rain, frost, or snow can soon turn it into a muddy quagmire .

Below: Informal paths help create a relaxed and restful atmosphere. Irregular or crazy paving is especially appropriate for informal or cottage gardens.

Left: Timber decking is the perfect surface for sitting, dining, or sunbathing. Planks do not have to be laid out in parallel lines as there are numerous, often complex, patterns to choose from.

Below: The combination of rounded pebbles and flat stone slabs, of different shapes can create a striking path of different shapes, especially in a more formal setting.

Roof gardens

tough structural plants that form the permanent roof-garden landscape, since they do not have to suffer the rigours of winter. However, winter need not be cheerless as winter-flowering pansies, bulbs, and evergreens can all be used to great decorative effect.

When a roof garden is used only in summer and for the rest of the year is unvisited, then year-round plant displays are less important.

Automatic irrigation can be a boon on a hot roof garden where regular watering is essential. At ground level hand watering is problematic enough but on a roof, especially if water is not readily accessible at that level, it becomes even more of an onerous and time-consuming task.

A decked roof garden

In the roof garden illustrated (left), timber decking has been placed over the roof but it is made in sections so that it can be lifted should the need arise. Gravel makes a good alternative surfacing, ensuring good drainage, reasonable reflection of heat and an even weight-loading.

A built-in seat is positioned between freestanding planters which have trellis panels built in as part of their structure, thus overcoming the problem of instability and fixing. Ideally, trellis or similar structures should not be bolted to parapet walls as this increases the risk of structural damage to the wall in high winds.

The planters have gaps underneath to allow water drainage and are raised on feet. The more points of support there are, the more evenly their loads are spread over the surface of the roof. The permanent barbecue is a focus in summer but is screened from immediate view from the patio doors as it may appear less attractive in winter. A toughened glass screen allows an uninterrupted view beyond the garden and lighting extends the use of and the view of the garden at night.

Freestanding planter for a roof garden

Integral trellis

Parapet wall

DPC

Roof surface

Gardens for people with disabilities

The aspirations, needs, and pleasures of gardeners with disabilities are no different from those of anyone else. Gardens can be enjoyed both passively and actively, to varying degrees, by everyone, but what is different for the disabled person is the degree of access possible, and this depends upon the form of disability. As they grow older, many gardeners may find that they are less mobile and less able to tackle heavier tasks in the garden, yet still wish to enjoy their interest, so much of the advice in these pages applies to any gardener who finds themselves less able than they once were.

The design of the garden must, as always, be tailored to meet an individual's preferences and needs but, unfortunately, communal gardens for the disabled can only ever be geared to the most common forms of disability.

Most people associate gardens for those with disabilites with raised flowerbeds or work benches. While these may be suitable for certain gardening activities, for older gardeners who find it difficult to bend down, and for particular forms of disability, they are by no means the universal solution. For example, where wheelchair users are concerned, a raised bed containing even low-growing plants blocks out the view of the rest of the garden which is visible to those who can stand.

Design criteria

Maintenance of raised beds can also be more difficult for wheelchair users, as tools have to be lifted and used at waist level. Even specially adapted tools can seem cumbersome and heavy under these circumstances. Downward movements, in which the ground supports the weight of the tools, are usually the easiest for everyone to handle.

Work benches, on the other hand, are generally more convenient raised to waist level, whether for disabled or able-bodied gardeners. For the partially sighted or blind, different design criteria are applied but, again, the provision of easy, safe access to plants and other elements in the garden is most important, especially when the garden has been designed to have plenty of interest in terms of touch, smell, and sound.

The cost of implementing a garden needs careful thought: the construction of a raised bed, for example, costs far more than the creation of a bed at ground level.

When constructing such a garden, safety is an even more important part of the design equation than is generally the case. Paths need to be wide and easy to negotiate, areas to sit and rest – and enjoy the garden – should be provided. Access to all parts of the garden should be straightforward and low-maintenace techniques (see page 66) should be employed where possible.

Information and help for gardeners with disabilities is readily available from specialized organizations and relevant charities.

Elements within the garden

Paving in the garden for the less able must have a non-slip surface, yet be as even as possible. A flat natural stone is a good selection, first for its pleasing and warm appearance and secondly to allow the curvilinear paths to be formed easily. A reconstituted stone would be an equally valid and lower-cost choice. Not all borders within the garden need to be raised since this would be both costly and unnecessary, but those that are should be broad and built to wheelchair height. The top of the wall can also be used as a seat, which is useful for maintenance and allows closer contact with the plants. There should be no sharp corners in paths and any curves must be gentle enough to be easily negotiated.

Any garden shed in the garden designed for those with disabilities needs waist-high benches, and choose a glasshouse with a sliding door for easy access. Any sitting areas should be designed to have room for wheelchairs and conventional seats.

Any ramps in the garden should, ideally, not be constructed with a gradient steeper than 1:20 for reasons of safety and comfort. Depending upon the time available or the ability of the owner to maintain the garden, open areas can be gravelled for very low maintenance, turfed, or planted with some kind of ground cover such as camomile. Areas of border out of immediate reach should be planted with more robust shrubs which have trouble-free characteristics.

A garden for people with disabilities

Such a garden need not be bland or uninteresting. It is not necessary to sacrifice stimulation and interest in the pursuit of absolute safety. A well-designed garden will incorporate these characteristics. In the example shown on the right, the main terrace is laid with a non-slip surface, making it suitable and safe for sitting, entertaining, alfresco meals and sunbathing.

Where the main terrace ends, there is a change in the texture of the paving intended to signal the change of direction or circumstance. This safety technique, important to the visually impaired, is repeated throughout the garden. In this instance, timber decking signifies a change of area from the patio, with gently sloping ramps (that have handrails attached) to assist with the change in level.

The raised beds near the terrace make the plants more accessible to touch and smell. Taller plants do not, of course, need to be raised in this way. Places to relax have been provided on the decked part of the garden with a tree seat placed around each of a pair of trees. The trees themselves shelter and shade the seats. Among the sitting areas in this garden is a seat opposite a raised pool; further across the garden the view terminates with an appropriate focal point. A

Gardens for people with disabilities

sculpture could be selected if this garden was created for blind or partially sighted visitors, chosen for its tactile appeal. A semi-circle of lawn at the far end of the garden is surrounded by a gravel path to signify another change of area.

The beds in the garden contain plants and shrubs chosen for their textural qualities and aromas. Trees have been selected to attract birds, bees, and insects, the sounds of which will be particularly attractive in summer.

A garden for people with disabilities

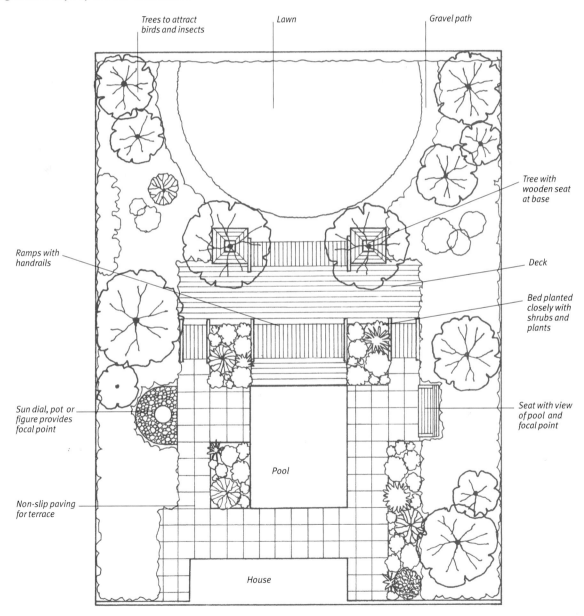

Trees to attract birds and insects

Lawn

Gravel path

Tree with wooden seat at base

Ramps with handrails

Deck

Bed planted closely with shrubs and plants

Sun dial, pot or figure provides focal point

Seat with view of pool and focal point

Non-slip paving for terrace

Pool

House

Placing plants

Having decided on the layout of the garden, it is time to consider exactly which plants will be grown where. Take time to research the habits of the plants you plan to grow: their appearance through the year; the growing conditions they need; the height and spread they will attain, and the maintenance they require. Consider also how they will work in combination, throughout the year, with other plants in your design.

Trees

Site trees where their form can be appreciated and avoid specimens that will outgrown their space. Plant trees away from buildings. Consider the habit of the tree (see below), as well as flower, foliage and berry colour. Evergreen trees provide form and interest year round, though deciduous trees can be attractive when bare.

Shrubs

Shrubs can be useful to build up the framework of the planting scheme. When designing shrub and mixed borders, plot plants on a plan and number them from one to twelve according to which month they are at their best. This shows what will be of interest at any time of year and which gaps will need to be filled.

PLANNING

Plan a border by numbering plants on a plan according to the month they will be at their best.

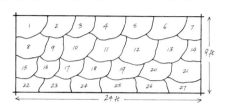

(1) 3 Aster 'Fellowship'. Soft pink, September. 4 ft.
(2) 5 Helenium 'Moerheim Beauty'. Rich crimson, July-Aug. 3 ft.
(3) 3 Echinops 'Taplow Blue'. Metallic blue. July-Aug. 5 ft.
(4) 5 Heliopsis 'Incomparabilis'. Golden orange, July-Aug. 4 ft.
(5) 4 Delphinium 'Blue Jay'. Mid-blue. June-July. 5 ft.
(6) 3 Aster 'Crimson Brocade'. Deep red, September. 3 ft.
(7) 5 Polygonum amplexicaule 'Astrosanguin...

Tree forms

It is important to know the habit of a tree before planting it. Trees can be spreading (a), weeping (b), fastigiate (c) or conical (d). Check the eventual height and spread of the tree and allow it adequate space when planning the garden.

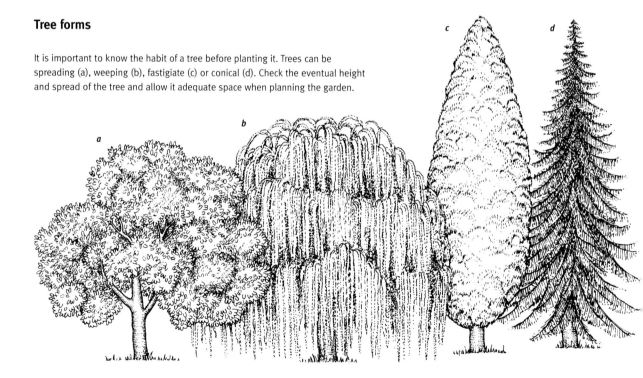

Low planting

The shape of a horizontal surface creates its own sense of movement, which is influenced further by the chosen covering: grass, plants, water, or paving.

As far as plants are concerned, once they have grown to a height that obscures other parts of the planted horizontal surface from view – the far side of a flower bed, for example – you must start to consider them vertical rather than horizontal elements. Under this circumstance, even the most carefully shaped bed or border on plan will not appear as such in reality. This point is also worth bearing in mind when shaping truly horizontal areas which are formed by surrounding plantings, or any other vertical elements, for that matter. Harmony should always exist between horizontal and vertical elements.

Horizontal plantings

Planted horizontal surfaces take on functional roles too; grass is the most common ground cover because of its attractiveness and its usefulness as a foil to other garden features and plants. Choice of grasses depends on many things: use, appearance, climate, siting, soil type, and the maintenance it is likely to receive. Some grass mixes are chosen for their appearance alone, others for their wearing qualities – where ball games are to take place, for example. In damp shade or on hot dry banks, different mixtures will be required.

Where grass is unsuitable, other low-growing plants can be used. As with any plant, its ability to grow well under given conditions will prevail over its appearance, and compromises have to be made according to circumstance. Plants having the appearance of grass can be selected but many will not have its semi-evergreen properties. However, it is worth considering subjects such as the low-growing thymes, sand-worts (*Minuartia verna*), *Arenaria balearica*, mossy saxifrages and camomile (flowerless cultivars are best). Moss is used extensively in Japan as a close semi-evergreen cover but it enjoys being constantly shaded and moist. In warmer or more sheltered places, taller subjects with more distinctive textures or colourful flowers can be used. These include poached egg plant (*Limnanthes douglasii*) and, for frost-free climates, succulents such as hottentot fig (*Carpobrotus edulis*) or Livingstone daisies (*Mesembryanthemum*) grown in well-drained soils are colourful. The more permanent subjects include the prostrate cotoneasters and low-growing hybrid roses such as *Rosa* 'Nozomi'.

Taller ground-covering plants include heathers, geraniums, cytisus, genistas, vincas (usefully evergreen), a multitude of low conifers and ivies, ajugas and so on.

There are books devoted to the subject of groundcover plants but, whatever is chosen, it should make both a useful and an attractive contribution to the garden. Subjects are often chosen simply for their ability to facilitate garden maintenance or to fill awkward corners, but consider how they might make a good foil for other plants or trees growing nearby.

Consider first the visual effect you are seeking to achieve from ground-cover plants, their function, the soil conditions and aspect, and then make the choice. Willing a particular favourite plant to perform the task to which it is unsuited is not the answer.

Dry shade

Plants such as *Lamium maculatum* 'Beacon Silver' can thrive in dry permanent shade: some other varieties of lamium do equally well.

Hot dry areas

Low plants for areas which are hot and dry often have bright flowers and silver leaves. Many of the heathers and heaths thrive here.

Underplanting

Low growing plants as foils or for underplanting include lesser periwinkle (*Vinca minor*) and ivies. Bulbs such as crocuses are also useful in this context.

Decorative effect

Useful plants for low planting for permanent decorative effect include ivies, evergreen euonymus (which can be pruned into shapes) and low hebes.

CONSTRUCTION

When you are satisfied with your garden design, having created a functional and stylish plan, then the hard work of constructing it begins. Planting up your garden might be your idea of relaxation rather than a chore, and you may intend to leave the fencing, paving, walling, or creation of a pool to contractors. However, by tackling some of the building work yourself, following the guidance given in this section, you may gain new skills together with a sense of satisfaction at having created something yourself.

BEFORE YOU START

Most gardeners, except those with rural plots, find themselves in close proximity to their neighbours. If you are about to undertake any large projects (which can create noise during construction) it is worth outlining your plans to your neighbours. At worst you may find yourself being able to avoid potential disputes, and at best you may find you have gained willing helpers. In fact, large building projects such as the creation of a substantial timber deck may even require planning permission from the local authority before you go ahead.

TOOLS

Your own toolkit may well already comprise a number of items – spirit level, hammer, trowel, saw – that will be utilized in the construction of your garden, or you may be able to borrow additional items. It may be worth considering purchasing some new tools if they are likely to be well used in the future. Hire shops offer equipment such as concrete mixers, block cutters, and motorized compactors. These can save a lot of time and effort – using a compactor will give a better finish with far less effort than using a mallet and batten.

SAFETY

Whichever tools you use, always use them safely. Ensure that your eyes, hands, and ears are well protected. Wear suitable protective clothing and shoes, regardless of the weather conditions – on warm days it may be tempting not to keep yourself fully covered. Take your time on your construction tasks, tidying as you go along to reduce possible hazards. If you are having large amounts of materials delivered, have them deposited as close to the working area as possible. Be careful when lifting, bending at the knees and be aware of what you can manage with reasonable ease. When moving large blocks and slabs, "walk" them on their corners to the place they will be laid. And don't be tempted to always fill that wheelbarrow to the brim – just make more journeys instead.

Choosing materials

Making a garden usually involves a great deal more than organizing the planting and laying the lawn. All gardens must have basic structural elements – walls, fences, paths and so on – in order to link, separate, or screen various areas of the plot. When choosing materials for these, bear in mind that they vary enormously in cost, durability, maintenance requirements, and aesthetic appeal.

Buying timber

Timber is one of the most popular materials used in gardens, and is suitable for numerous kinds of structure. It is cut from many varieties of trees, but for practical purposes can be divided into two main groups: hardwoods and softwoods. These terms can be misleading, as they are not necessarily an

Stone, brick blocks and concrete

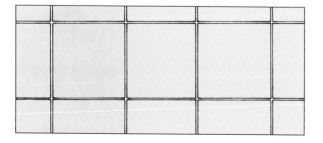

accurate guide to actual hardness of the wood, but in general terms softwoods are usually softer than hardwoods.

Softwoods are derived from coniferous, or cone-bearing, trees, which include pine, fir, and larch. Hardwoods come from broad-leaved trees such as beech, mahogany, teak and oak.

Softwood Economical to buy and easy to saw, plane and sand, softwoods will also hold screws well. Nails, however, can cause the wood to split along the grain. Sold in a vast range of lengths and sections softwoods are available in two forms: "sawn" or "planed" ("prepared"). The sawn type is less expensive than the planed type and is generally used where a smooth, fine appearance is unnecessary. Sawn wood is suitable for most of the timber construction work mentioned in this book.

Timber is usually obtainable in metric lengths, although some suppliers confusingly offer it in units of 300mm, which is often referred to as a "metric foot". This, however, actually measures 11¾in. So beware when ordering: 6 metric feet of timber might measure only 5ft 10½in.

Hardwood Less common and usually much more costly than softwoods, hardwoods are not normally used for general garden construction. They are used for garden furniture, where their natural beauty enhances the appearance of a table or seat. All hardwood and hardwood products should be certified as having been obtained from sustainable sources.

Preserving timber

Most timber will eventually succumb to rot or insect attack unless properly treated with a suitable preservative. When ordering softwood for outdoor use, it is best to ask for 'pressure-treated' timber which has been injected with a preservative fluid against fungal decay and insect attack. However, pre-treated timber is more costly than untreated timber, and you may prefer to buy the latter and treat it yourself. Preservative can be brushed on, sprayed on or – the most effective method – you can soak the timber in a makeshift bath of preservative. Where possible use water-based preservatives as these are kinder to the environment.

Avoiding timber defects

All timber should have been "seasoned" in order to reduce its sap and moisture content. This makes it easier to work with and gives it greater resistance to rot, but it also often introduces certain defects which could mar your work. Select your timber carefully to avoid the following common faults.

Knots Knots can present real problems when you are working with wood: if the knots ooze resin you will not only find the timber difficult to saw but also the sticky resin is likely to bleed through any subsequent paint finish you apply. Applying a shellac knotting compound will seal "live" knots against oozing. Dry knots often fall out, leaving a hole in the timber.

Warps Hold one end of a piece of timber and peer down its length to look for bad warping across or along the grain, and reject any badly misaligned timber.

Shakes Look out for splits along the grain, or between the annular rings of the timber, which could become worse and even cause the timber to fall apart.

Surface checking A covering of fine cracks need not be a serious fault; very fine ones can be planed away or filled before painting – but reject timber with wider cracks.

Bricks and blocks

For walls, barbecues, planters, flights of steps, and other solid structures in the garden, bricks and blocks are widely used. Durable in damp conditions, masonry structures also have strength and stability, enabling them to support loadings from other constructions – the timber roof of a pergola, for example. Strength is not only inherent in the density of the brick or block: the bonding arrangement in which the individual units are laid provides rigidity as well as a decorative face for the structure.

Bricks Made in standard metric sizes, bricks measure 225 x 112.5 x 75mm (8^{7}/$_{8}$ x 4^{3}/$_{8}$in). The measurements are nominal and allow for the mortar joints: the actual size of a brick is 10mm (³/₈in) less all round. This makes calculation of the height of a wall or structure much easier: if the mortar joint allowance were not part of the brick's nominal dimension you would have to allow for each mortar joint independently.

Bricks are commonly made of clay. Clay bricks are produced in two main qualities: "ordinary" for general use and "special" for exposed sites. Calcium silicate bricks are graded from Class Two (weakest) to Class Seven (strongest). Dense, hard engineering bricks are essential for use in damp conditions, or below ground level. Impervious to water, they are produced in Classes A or B, which refer to strength and water resistance. Class A are stronger, and class B more water-resistant.

If possible, choose bricks of a colouring that matches, complements or blends with local brick types. Choose "facing" bricks, which have attractive face textures, where appearance is important.

Blocks Some walling blocks resemble natural stone and offer a softer, more natural appearance than bricks. They are moulded from concrete and may have natural stone aggregate added for a more authentic appearance and texture. Various colours are available usually mimicking local stone colours: buff tones, greens, yellows, reds and greys are popular. Only one long face and one end face are usually textured, by being either "split" (having the appearance of split stone) or "pitched" (artificially chipped to give rougher appearance). These faces are used on the visible side of the structure.

Most blocks conform roughly to brick sizes for ease of laying and matching to areas of brickwork.

Breezeblocks Where the building requirements are purely structural and the appearance of the blockwork itself is immaterial, large, grey breezeblocks may be needed instead of bricks. Moulded from concrete in various densities, breezeblocks measure 150 to 225mm high x 450, 600 or 620mm long x 60mm thick (6 to 9in high x 18, 24 or 24¹/₂in long x 2¹/₂in) thick.

Natural stone

Bought from a quarry or large garden centre, natural stone can be used to construct features such as a traditional dry-stone wall (see page 134) or a rock garden (see page 64).

Used for building walls, natural stone is both heavy and expensive – and it requires some skill to use it successfully. It is usually laid without mortar, relying on the weight of the stones and the way they are laid to create a rigid, long-lasting structure. A manufactured type of "dry-stone walling block" is available from some suppliers. This offers an easier way to create a country-style wall: The blocks are lighter and fairly regular in form, but are still laid without mortar.

More irregularly-shaped stones and boulders should be used to construct a rock garden or to create natural-looking rocky outcrops.

Concrete

Cast concrete is versatile and economical. It can be used as a means of forming a base for a garden structure, or as a surface in its own right. It consists of a mixture of Portland cement, the aggregates sharp sand and stones (known as "ballast" when combined), and water.

For small jobs, simply buy pre-bagged dry mixes, which contain all the ingredients, properly proportioned and ready for mixing with water. You can buy pre-mixed bags containing between 2.5kg (5¹/₂lb) and 50kg (1cwt) of concrete.

For large jobs, it is more economical to buy the ingredients separately in bulk and mix them yourself. You can mix by hand, or use a hired motorized mixing machine. However, for a job such as casting a driveway or large patio slab, which will require over 3 cubic metres (4 cubic yards) of concrete, it is best to buy ready-mixed concrete. Ready-mix is delivered to your house by mixer lorry and – given suitable access – it is possible to have the load dumped directly onto the prepared foundations. With such a large amount of wet concrete, speed in spreading and compacting the mix is essential before hardening (curing) commences, so assistance will be needed.

Choosing materials

Paving is laid to fulfil many functions as paths, drives and as patios. There are many forms to choose from. Inorganic paving materials include gravel, natural stone, pebbles, setts, bricks, concrete, tarmac or asphalt and resin. Organic pavings include grass, sawn timber, bark, ground or chipped coconut shell and rubber compounds.

When choosing paving material, decide whether the space needs to be static (such as sitting areas) or have a dynamic effect. Some paving materials are laid in patterns and the direction of the joint lines suggest movement, whereas gravel is neutral in texture.

Flexible paving

Flexible paving systems, such as shingle, are usually made up of loose stone aggregates and not bound within a rigid matrix, such as cement. To prevent them from spreading outward, flexible pavings normally require restraining edges.

Gravel

Gravel is the simplest form of flexible paving. There are three basic types:

Shingle Rounded stone pieces worn smooth by natural causes are available in sizes ranging from 5mm ($\frac{1}{4}$in) to 20mm ($\frac{3}{4}$in). Pea shingle is the best known type, similar in shape and size to a garden pea, hence its name. Besides being a good path or drive surfacing, shingle makes an excellent foil for plants or pots. It is not so suitable for sloping paths or drives as it tends to migrate downward. Shingle paths need a firm base with the surfacing itself approximately 50–75mm (2–3in) deep.

Crushed stone Crushed stone is derived from crushing larger rocks into flakes or shards. It is multi-faceted and does not have the same tendency as pea shingle to migrate on a slope. Pieces vary in size but tend to range from 25mm (1in) to 50mm (2in). Its colour depends upon the rock source.

Path gravel (self-binding) This consists of pebbles, shingle or stones held in a matrix of soil having a high clay content. It is best raked and rolled to produce a cambered surface, again over a stone base. Path gravel material is laid as a wearing surface to a depth of up to 75mm (3in), depending on the volume of traffic. Path gravel needs to be re-raked and re-rolled following heavy rain or frost. The camber allows rainwater to drain harmlessly away.

Tarmac

The main ingredient of tarmac is shingle or crushed stone held in a matrix of tar. The numbers and depths of the courses or layers in a path or drive depend upon the expected traffic. Each course is made up of different sized stones and thicknesses: the largest at the bottom.

Tarmac surfaces can be 'dressed' with rolled-in gravel or marble chippings. Coloured tarmacs can be vulnerable to damage from vehicle tyres so consult an expert first.

Asphalt Asphalt is closely associated with tarmac. Usually black or grey, asphalt paths are more closely textured than tarmac, but less resistant to damage from oil and petrol spillage. "Bull-nosed" units are an attractive and appropriate choice of edging, but as they are relatively thin they need to be backed up (haunched) with concrete.

Natural stone

Any stone used for paving should be frost-resistant and durable, so you should check both these properties with the supplier before ordering. The shapes of paving stones will depend upon the source and how the rock was created. Some paving stone is naturally flat and occurs in suitably thin strata; other types have to be sawn from larger blocks, and are more expensive. There are hundreds of stone types, among the more common of which are Portland, a limestone, York, a sandstone type, and granite, an igneous rock.

Natural stone paving patterns

Random rectangular This pattern uses slabs (or flags) that are basically rectangular in shape but of different sizes. The skill comes in laying the slabs so that uninterrupted joint lines do not extend too far in either direction, detracting from a random appearance. As a pattern, this tends to be static.

Regular sawn one size This regular pattern uses square or rectangular slabs of one size. The pattern can have either a widening or lengthening effect depending on the direction from which the paved area is seen.

Regular coursed rectangular stone Blocks of stone set on edge form this positive and interesting pattern. It is made up of stones of differing lengths but similar widths in each row. Edging stones of the same type provide a stabilizing and attractive finish.

Random (crazy) paving This pattern comprises random-shaped pieces of stone set onto mortar, and is useful in informal schemes and where a path or terrace curves or is irregular in shape. For terraces, it is essential to choose stone with a flat, even surface. Where random stones are flaky, as some are, and therefore liable to be damaged by frost, fill the mortar joints right to the top of the stone surface.

Setts Setts are cubes or rectangular blocks cut from very hard stone, usually granite, varying in size from a cube of approximately 75 mm (3in) to a rectangle of 150 x 150 x 250mm (6 x 6 x 10in). They can be laid in a wide variety of patterns. "Regularly coursed", using small units, creates a rather static appearance.

Choosing materials

Pebbles Pebbles are smooth, water-worn stones. When imaginatively used and laid in mortar they can make beautiful and sometimes intricate patterns, especially when pebbles of different sizes and colours are used. Small pebbles need to be edged for stability, perhaps with brick, stone, setts, or timber. In some circumstances, pebbles are simply placed loose upon the ground for textural appeal.

Reconstituted stone

Reconstituted stone paving is a mixture of natural stone aggregates and cement. Most units are moulded to resemble natural stone, and the range of shapes and sizes available is very wide. There are also countless different textures to choose from: for example, smooth, brushed, stippled, and exposed-surface aggregates. Brightly coloured reconstituted slabs should be used with discretion as they may clash with the colours of adjacent architecture or plants.

Irregular rectangular paving The units shown below have been laid in a linear pattern which is made up of parallel rows of different widths, resulting in a strong directional feeling. The units themselves have a "rubbed" texture leading in the same direction as the uninterrupted joints.

Octagonal paving Octagons are a traditional paving shape for use in the garden. Octagonal pavers must be combined with small square units between them to be laid in a continuous pattern.

Hexagonal paving A wide variety of colours and textures are available; the example illustrated on page 84 has a stippled finish.

Diagonalized square paving Diagonal patterns are used to minimize the sense of movement of paved areas. In the example on page 85 square units resembling terracotta tiles have been used. A stabilizing edge of brick or tiles prevents the triangular pieces at the sides from being dislodged.

Mixed sizes Two sizes of paving are used in the example shown on page 84 to achieve a Flemish pattern. Brushing the surface of the paving units during the manufacturing process results in an attractive "non-slip" texture. This pattern tends to lack a sense of movement.

Equal-sized paving These can be square or rectangular, and laid with uninterrupted joints in either direction. If the slabs have the surface cement washed away during the manufacturing process to expose the aggregates within, the result is an attractive finish and a safe walking surface. The pattern is strongly directional.

Shingle

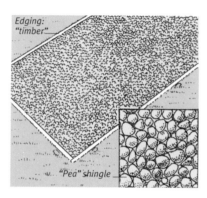

Edging: "timber"

"Pea" shingle

Crushed stone

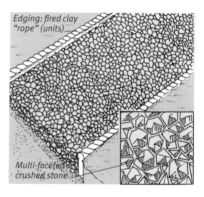

Edging: fired clay "rope" (units)

Multi-faceted crushed stone

Timber decking

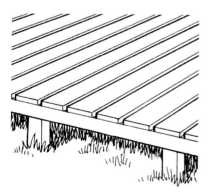

Path gravel (self binding)

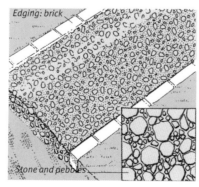

Edging: brick

Stone and pebbles

Tarmac

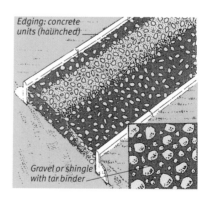

Edging: concrete units (haunched)

Gravel or shingle with tar binder

Paving

Concrete laid *in situ*

In the right context, well designed areas of concrete can enhance a garden's appearance. Being a "rigid" material, concrete must be properly supported with a solid stone base. Continuous concrete paths and paving must incorporate any thermal movement joints at intervals of not more than 5m (16ft). Without these it may crack. Thermal movement joints are made during the casting process by placing a timber strip horizontally between the shuttering to leave narrow open joints between sections. A 10mm (⅜in) width is adequate.

Texturing, marking or colouring concrete will determine its final appearance, but expect colours to fade gradually.

Brushed and trowelled Texturing concrete before it sets will provide a non-slip surface. Path edges can be smoothed and rounded using a special trowel. This gives a neat finish and emphasizes the brush marks, the depth of which vary with the stiffness of the brush and the pressure exerted.

Brush texturing Soon after laying the concrete, effects ranging from swirling patterns to fan shapes can be produced by using a soft brush on the trowelled surface.

Marked out By marking out unset, textured concrete with a rounded-end metal rod or pebble the effect of pre-cast paving slabs, random paving or even an abstract-patterned path can be achieved. Concrete brick laid diagonally at the sides in a traditional way suggests authentic stone paving.

Exposed aggregate concrete A basic or specially formulated concrete mixture can, prior to setting, have its surface washed and brushed to remove some of the cement, so exposing the gravel and other stone particles that make up the aggregate.

Mechanically impressed concrete Coloured concrete is impressed using a mobile hydraulic press. Most paving types can be imitated using this type of finish, ranging from natural stone to brick paving patterns.

Brick paving

Choose bricks and patterns to match or harmonize with the colour and textural qualities of nearby architectural features.

Running or stretcher bond Depending upon the direction of the path relative to the direction of the uninterrupted joint lines in the paving pattern, this bond is described either as "stretcher bond", which makes the paved area appear wider, or "running bond", which has a lengthening effect and creates

Irregular rectangular

Octagonal

Hexagonal
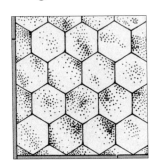

Continuous/stack bond

Diagonalized square
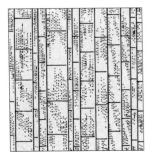

Mixed sizes
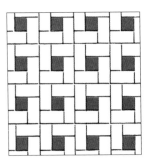

Equal sized

Running/stretcher bond

a strong sense of movement. Running bond is particularly suitable for paths with gentle curves.

Straight herringbone This usually needs some kind of edging to ensure that the half-bricks used do not fall away with use.

Diagonal herringbone This is the same as straight herringbone except that it is set at an angle, usually of 45 degrees to the main view or to the direction of the path. It needs an edging to secure the small triangular bricks at the sides. The pattern is useful for patios and for curving paths.

Continuous or stack bond This has a modern appearance, and the brick direction can be varied to suggest widening, with the bricks laid with the long edges horizontally, or lengthening, with the long edges leading away from the viewpoint. Alternating panels of this pattern with bricks laid at 90 degrees to each other result in a chequered effect.

Basketweave This is probably the most "static" paving bonds. The bricks can be laid flat when each unit is made of two bricks or laid on edge where each unit made up of three.

Stable paviours Not a laying pattern, this is rather a description of a particular shape of hard, impervious brick which was originally used in stables. Stable paviours are

available either as "doubles", with chamfered edges and a centre valley, or "singles". They are butt-jointed (touching) rather than having mortar-filled joints. The chamfers (angled corners) give the appearance of conventional joints.

Diamond paviours This type of brick is normally manufactured in blue, red or yellow fired clay. These bricks are usually butt-jointed, and can be laid in practically any pattern. The name "diamond" refers to the pattern on the upper face which provides a non-slip surface.

Timber paving

Known as decking, it should be treated with preservative, or a naturally weather-proof wood, such as oak or cedar should be selected. The longevity of decking is increased by raising it off the ground or laying it on a free-draining gravel base.

Board decking Decking is usually left in a natural state when constructed of hardwood, but other types of timber can be stained and treated. Textured boards, such as those with a sawn finish, are safer to walk on than those planed smooth.

Timber setts Hardwood cubes or setts can be used in the same way as conventional stone setts. To add to their attraction, cubes can be laid with the end grain uppermost, preferably in a gritty sand bed. Sand should also be brushed in to any small surface gaps on completion. Setts laid in a diagonal pattern require a stabilizing edge.

Log rounds When sawn to 75mm (3in) or thicker, log rounds make excellent stepping "stones" in an informal situation. If softwoods are used, they will require regular treatment with preservative, but laying them over a free-draining layer of sharp sand will give them a longer life. Fill the gaps between with carpeting plants, granulated bark or gravel.

Coconut shell chips or granulated bark These are both good path materials for an informal situation, but must be laid on a proper base of stone or gravel if they are to last. The edging could be constructed from logs, laid longitudinally and fixed with pointed stakes driven in at their sides. This arrangement defines the path well and prevents the overspill of pedestrians or plants in either direction.

Other more unusual paving types include:

Clear resin-bonded aggregates Aggregates selected according to shape, colour and size are mixed with a clear, inorganic resin, then smoothly spread over a prepared base. The resulting appearance is of wet gravel, but the surface is fixed. It is a popular finish for swimming pool surrounds.

"Safe play" composite material paving This impact-absorbing paving system is invaluable around play equipment of all types. It is based on recycled rubber products and available in a range of styles, sizes, and dark colours.

Basketweave – flat

Basketweave – on edge

Straight herringbone

Diagonal herringbone

Drainage

For plants to survive, soil must contain both air and water. In poorly drained soil, plant roots are restricted to the top few centimetres/inches so they cannot anchor properly or search far for nutrients. The causes of bad drainage may be due to a heavy clay soil, a hard pan in the subsoil, through which water cannot percolate or a high water table. The water table is the level in the soil below which the ground is saturated. The water table is higher in winter than in summer; normally it is about 2m (6½ft) below the surface. Where the water table is high, artificial drainage will help move water to a lower level.

Installing a land-drain system

> **CAUTION**
>
> Do not be tempted to fill the trenches merely by returning the excavated earth. otherwise soil will enter the pipes and slowly block them with sediment.

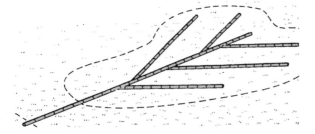

1 First mark out the drainage pattern in a herringbone pattern, using sand or spray paint. The number of side branches is mainly determined by the size of the site.

2 Dig out the trenches and clear off loose debris. Check the fall using a 2m (6½ft) plank and spirit level. Where trenches meet their bases must be at the same level.

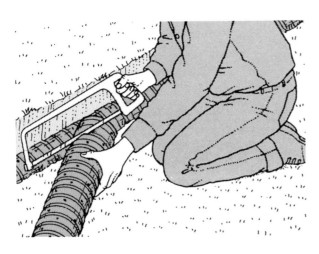

3 First lay the central pipe, which must lead to the soakaway. Then cut the plastic branch pipes at an angle so they fit roughly against the main pipe.

4 Cover the pipes with gravel and a layer of fine plastic mesh to prevent the land-drain system silting up. Finally, fill in the trenches with topsoil and replace the turf.

Cultivation

To improve the drainage of clay soils (see page 89) dig them deeply and incorporate plenty of grit and organic matter. Hard pans, a hard layer of soil which can occur naturally, may not be far below the soil surface and can also be broken up by deep cultivation. If they are too hard for piercing with a fork they can be penetrated with a steel bar, which should be hammered through the impermeable layer at intervals to aid drainage. Where these measures do not work or the water table is high, artificial drainage should be considered.

Artificial drainage

Ditches are the cheapest way of draining land. They should be dug 1–1.2m (3–4ft) deep on sloping land, so water is carried to a receiving ditch at the bottom of the slope linked in turn to a soakaway or stream. Ditches can be left open as long as they are cleaned out annually or used to accommodate a covered, land-drain system, as shown on page 86.

In small gardens or for small-scale drainage problems a rubble-filled pit or "French drain" should help. Lining drainage pits with a geotextile membrane allows water to seep in but prevents them from silting up with particles of soil.

Land drains

Originally land-drain systems were built of lengths of clay pipe, called tiles. Now it is more usual to use perforated corrugated plastic piping. This material is easily cut to length and can be bent round slight curves. The pipes are laid in trenches excavated in herringbone fashion across sloping land, with the main pipe leading to a soakaway situated at the lowest level. The trenches should be dug 60–90cm (2–3ft) deep and about 30cm (12in) wide. The distance between side branches depends on the soil type: on clay soil space them about 4.5m (15ft) apart; on loam space them 7.5m (25ft) apart; and about 12m (40ft) apart on light sandy soil.

Retaining walls

Waterlogging may also occur behind retaining walls. These may also retain a reservoir of water behind them if no provision is made for drainage. To provide weep holes leave one vertical joint unmortared every 1.5m (5ft) along the wall in every second or third course of bricks or stones. Backfill the base of the wall with rubble and install a drainage gully in front if the wall abuts a path or patio, to carry off the water that seeps through to a drain or soakaway.

Ditch

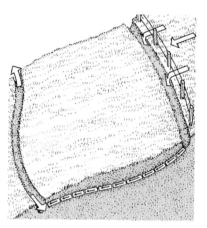

If the land slopes, dig a ditch across the top of the plot to intercept water from higher ground. Connect it, via other ditches or land drains, to another ditch that has been dug at the bottom of the slope.

Rubble

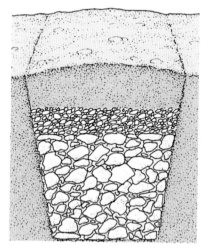

Line a 60–90cm (2–3ft) deep trench with a geotextile membrane and half fill with broken bricks or rubble. Cap with a layer of gravel and the excess geotextile. Replace the topsoil.

Soakaway

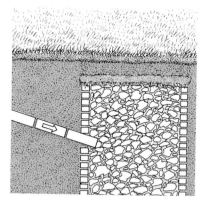

A soakaway must be constructed if there is no suitable watercourse for a drainage system to run to. Dig a hole up to 1.8m (6ft) deep and across. Lead the pipe into it. Line the hole with a geotextile membrane or unmortared bricks and fill it with rubble. Top with a geotextile membrane or upturned turves and cover with topsoil.

Types of foundation

Foundations are necessary for any structure that you build in the garden, in order to support and spread its load on firm ground. Whether you are constructing a solid footing for a boundary wall, or laying the base for a garden building, the basic principles are similar.

Strip foundations

Small structures such as brick planters and masonry garden walls must be built on strip foundations. These consist of a trench filled with a layer of compacted hardcore (which comprises broken stones or bricks) topped with fresh concrete.

The foundation is built wider than the wall, so that the weight of the wall is spread out at an angle of 45 degrees ("the angle of dispersion") from its base. To gauge the correct width of foundation for a given wall width you should, as a rule of thumb, allow two times the width of the masonry. The depth of the concrete foundation depends on the height and thickness of the wall and on the condition of the soil, but in general it should be half as deep as it is wide, and project beyond the ends of the wall by half the width of the masonry. For example, a wall over six courses of bricks high would require a trench about 400mm (16in) deep.

Brick foundations

There may be no need to build concrete foundations if your wall or other structure is less than about six courses of bricks high and less than about 6m (20ft) long. A foundation strip consisting of bricks laid crosswise on a well-compacted subsoil base topped with a thin layer of sand will probably be sufficient. The bricks are grouted with a "slurry" comprising a creamy mixture of cement and water.

Foundations for steps

Garden steps built into a bank (see page 122) will require a cast concrete footing at the base of the flight, beneath the first riser (the vertical part of the step), to prevent the structure from slipping downwards. The treads (the part on which you walk) should be laid on well-compacted hardcore, while the intermediate risers can be built either directly on the back of the tread below, or else on a base of compacted hardcore behind each tread.

For freestanding garden steps (see page 116), which lead, say, up to a raised area of lawn from a lower level, it is acceptable to put down concrete strip foundations to support the outer walls of the structure, with the inner area filled with compacted hardcore.

Paving foundations

Paving slabs, block pavers and other paving materials must be laid on a surface that is firm, flat, and stable. In many cases a

Slab foundations

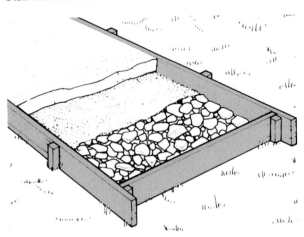

Slab foundations comprise a layer of hardcore to firm up the soil base, a blinding layer of sand to fill voids in the hardcore, and fresh concrete moulded and levelled in timber formwork fixed to stakes at the perimeter of the slab.

Strip foundations

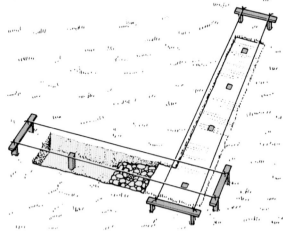

Strip foundations, used as a base for small structures and garden walls, comprise a trench containing well-rammed hardcore topped with a blinding layer of sand and fresh concrete levelled to guide depth pegs in the base.

SOIL CONDITIONS

For the foundation to provide adequate support for the structure, the concrete must be laid on firm subsoil. This lies beneath the softer topsoil, the depth of which varies from area to area, but which could be anything between 100 and 300mm (4 and 12in). What this means is that you have to dig down to the subsoil before you start to dig out enough for the depth of the concrete itself, which is another 75 to 150mm (3 to 6in).

Types of subsoil also vary in their load-bearing capacities: for example, chalky soils can support more weight than clay soils, but sandy soils support less weight. Basically, the weaker the subsoil the wider you must make the foundation slab.

If you are unsure about the prevailing soil conditions in your area, consult your local authority's Building Control Department for advice.

Climate plays an important part in determining how deep to place your foundation. Shrinkage and swelling of the earth due to prolonged dry spells or periods of rain can cause sufficient ground movement to crack the foundation concrete. For this reason you have to lay the foundation below the point at which it can be affected by these conditions.

Once you have dug the trench you can either lay the minimum thickness of concrete required for the size of structure you are building, and be prepared to lay extra courses of bricks to reach ground level, or else fill the trench to ground level and save on the number of bricks that you will use.

base of well-compacted subsoil is sufficient for laying paving, but where the soil is soft it will be necessary to add a layer of compacted hardcore to prevent the paving from sinking.

Hardcore contains many hollows, even after consolidation by garden roller, which are filled by spreading a blinding layer of sand or a lean concrete mix (i.e. 1 part cement : 3 parts sand) over the surface and levelling it with the back of a garden rake. (Always remember to clean tools thoroughly after dealing with wet concrete. It is very difficult to remove traces once the concrete has had a chance to dry.)

Paving slabs or other small-scale pavers can be laid directly on the blinding layer using mortar, although it is possible to lay some block pavers loose on a prepared sand bed without mortar.

Cast slab (raft) foundations

Whereas a small, lightweight garden shed or solid fuel bunker can be erected on a foundation of paving slabs on a hardcore base, larger structures such as a garage or a summerhouse must be built on a firmer base. A slab (or raft) foundation consists of a cast concrete surface laid over the prepared base.

Slab foundations are also used in drive- or path-laying, where no above-ground structure is involved but the top of the cast concrete forms the top surface of the drive or path, or creates a suitable base for another surfacing material.

The slab is formed by erecting a timber framework or formwork at the perimeter of the site, fixed to stakes driven into the ground (see page 92). The wet concrete is poured onto the prepared base, compacted and levelled to the top of the formwork, which is removed after the mix has hardened or cured.

Correct compaction and curing of the concrete slab are essential if the slab is to be strong enough for its intended purpose (if it is a driveway it might have to support the weight of a car or a caravan) and to withstand the extremes of weather to which it will be exposed.

SOIL TYPES

There are three basic soil types, classified according to the amount of sand or clay particles they contain.

Clay

This soil type usually contains a rich supply of plant foods because clay particles have the ability to retain nutrient elements until they are released to plant roots.

Clay soils are sticky when wet and hard when dry – lack of moisture can lead to cracking – so they can prove difficult and heavy to cultivate. Slow to drain, clay soils are prone to waterlogging and are slow to warm up in spring.

Silt

Typically alluvial in origin, silty soil is deep, fertile, and has a good water-holding capacity.

Silt soil packs down easily, so it becomes airless. The amount of moisture it receives affects silt soils, as it is sticky and cold when wet and dusty when dry.

Sand

Easy to work, sandy soil is free draining. It is relatively quick to warm up in spring.

This soil type does not retain moisture, and it can be naturally deficient in nutrients as many are easily washed out.

Concrete

Choosing a concrete mix

It is vital that you mix the concrete ingredients – sand, cement and aggregates – in the correct proportion to give the most suitable strength of mix for the job. There are three mixes:

A: *general purpose* for surface slabs and bases where you need a minimum thickness of 75–100mm (3–4in).

B: *light duty* for garden paths and bases less than (75mm) 3in thick.

C: *bedding* a weaker mix used for garden wall foundations and bedding in slabs.

What to order

When ordering the ingredients to make up 1 cubic metre (35 cubic feet) of the three different concrete mixes described above, consult the chart below which shows the composition of the three mixes:

DIFFERENT CONCRETE MIXES AND THEIR COMPOSITION

Mix	Cement: number of 50kg (110lb) bags	Sharp sand plus aggregate	OR	All-in aggregate
A	x 6	0.5cu m (17⅔cu ft) + 0.75cu m (26¼cu ft)		1cu m (35½cu ft)
B	x 8	0.5cu m (17⅔cu ft) + 0.75cu m (26¼cu ft)		1cu m (35½cu ft)
C	x 4	0.5cu m (17⅔cu ft) + 0.75cu m (26¼cu ft)		1.25cu m (45cu ft)

What to mix	Mix A	Mix B	Mix C
Concrete mixes are made up by volume, and it is convenient to use a bucket as your measure. For the concrete mixes previously listed, mix the following, remembering that each mix requires about half a bucket of water (although this does depend on how damp the sand is).	1 bucket cement 2½ buckets sharp sand 4 buckets washed aggregate OR 1 bucket cement 5 buckets all-in aggregate	1 bucket cement 2 buckets sharp sand 3 buckets washed aggregate OR 1 bucket cement 3¼ buckets all-in aggregate	1 bucket cement 3 buckets sharp sand 6 buckets washed aggregate OR 1 bucket cement 8 buckets all-in aggregate

Making a strip foundation

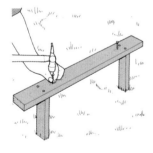

1 Fix profile boards at each end of the proposed trench, with nails attached to mark the trench width.

2 Attach stringlines to the width markers, linking both sets of profile boards at each end of the proposed trench.

3 Sprinkle sand along the strings to mark width on the ground. Remove strings but leave profile boards in place.

4 Dig out the trench to the required depth, making sure that you keep the base flat and the sides upright.

Strip foundations set in a trench are used as footings for garden walls and small structures. First mark out the position of the trench on the ground.

Setting up "profile" boards

Profile boards are used to set out the position of the trench on the ground. Hammer pairs of 24in (600mm) long pegs of 2 x 1in (50 x 25mm) rough-sawn softwood into the ground at each end of the proposed foundation and nail cross-pieces on top. Hammer nails partially into each cross-piece to correspond with the width of the trench and link with string. Transfer the positions of the strings to the ground by by sprinkling sand along the lines. Remove the strings but leave the profile boards in place as a guide to bricklaying later.

Digging the trench

First remove the topsoil and set aside for possible re-use elsewhere in the garden. Dig the trench to the correct depth. Lever out any large stones carefully, possibly retaining them for use elsewhere in the garden.

Keep the base of the trench consistently deep and the walls vertical. If the soil is very friable you might have to shore it up with plywood shuttering and until the concrete is added.

Hammer 25mm (1in) sq wooden pegs into the base of the trench so that they protrude by the depth of the concrete (plus the depth of any hardcore) needed for the foundations.

Tipping in the concrete

Before adding the concrete, soak the trench with water and allow it to drain away. This prevents the soil sucking too much moisture from the mix too rapidly, which could cause the concrete to crack. Shovel the concrete into the trench. Slice into the mix with your spade to dispel air bubbles.

Compact the concrete by tamping the surface with the edge of a length of stout timber in a chopping motion so that it is level with the top of the depth guide pegs. Place a spirit level on top of the plank to check that the concrete is horizontal. Leave the pegs in the concrete.

Allow the concrete to set. If it dries out too quickly, it is liable to crack. During hot weather cover the concrete with old sacking dampened with water. You should not lay concrete during very cold weather. Do not walk on the concrete surface for 48 hours. Leave the formwork in place for one week.

STEPPED FOUNDATIONS

On sloping or uneven ground a stepped foundation trench is needed. You will need to measure the vertical height of the slope in order to determine how many steps the foundations should comprise. Divide this by the depth of an ordinary brick. When casting the concrete, start with the lower step. Use timber pegs driven into the base as a guide to the depth of concrete needed.

Fix a length of board at the front of the second (and subsequent) steps to retain the concrete for the level above it.

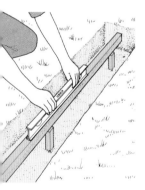

5 Drive in pegs so that they protrude by the depth of concrete needed. Check the pegs are level.

6 Soak the trench, then add hardcore where the ground is fairly soft and ram down well with a sledgehammer.

7 Pour in the concrete and work in by slicing into the mix with a spade. This dispels air bubbles.

8 Compact the concrete by tamping with a straight-edged length of timber and level it to the tops of the guide pegs.

Slab foundations

Slab or raft foundations are needed to support larger garden structures, and as a surface for paths and drives.

Preparation

Timber formwork is used to contain the wet concrete that will form the foundations until it has set hard. Set up stringlines stretched between wooden pegs at the perimeter of the proposed foundations, then dig out the topsoil until you reach firm subsoil. Compact the subsoil with a garden roller or by trampling over the surface with your boots. Construct the formwork as illustrated below.

Large slabs should be laid with a slight slope to one side in order to drain rainwater. An easy way to set the slope is by spanning across the formwork with a spirit level on a long plank. Place a small offcut of wood – called a shim – underneath the end of the plank at the proposed lower side of the slab. Adjust the depth of this formwork plank so that the spirit level registers horizontal: the slab will slope by the thickness of the shim which should be about 25mm (1in).

Adding the hardcore

You may need to add hardcore to the foundation base to give a suitably firm surface. The depth of hardcore depends on how soft the soil is and how thick the concrete slab will be.

Top the hardcore with a layer of sand to fill any holes which would otherwise be wasteful of concrete. Rake out the sand as flat as possible and finish off by drawing the back of the rake across the surface.

Laying slab foundations

1 Drive stakes into the perimeter of the proposed foundation and set horizontal.

2 Nail formwork to the stakes, butted end-to-face at the corners.

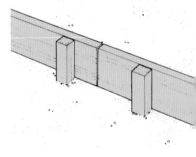

3 On the long slabs butt-join formwork boards end-to-end with extra stakes.

4 Add the hardcore to the foundations and compact thoroughly using a roller.

5 Tip the concrete from a mixing machine or barrow directly onto the foundations.

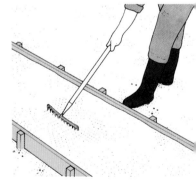

6 Rake out the concrete so it is level and just protruding above the formwork.

Slab foundations

Pouring the concrete

Use a garden rake to spread the concrete over the entire surface, so that it stands just proud of the formwork boards. Slice a spade into the mix at the sides several times to work the concrete well into place. Compact the concrete as shown below, right.

Finishing and curing

The rough texture left by the tamping beam is an ideal surface for building on, with a good key for mortar. But if you want a smoother finish – if the slab itself forms the finished surface – use a steel trowel or wooden float (a tool with a handle attached to a square wooden surface) with a circular motion to produce a finer texture. Alternatively, simply draw the

bristles of a stiff broom across the surface to give a ridged, non-slip finish. Cover the slab with heavy-gauge polythene held down at the edges by bricks. If a cold spell threatens, insulate by spreading a layer of sand over the polythene.

Adding reinforcement

Where your concrete slab will double as the surface for a drive, consider adding reinforcement, particularly if you have more than one vehicle, or own a caravan.

Reinforcement can be in the form of galvanized steel mesh, available from builder's merchants in rolls. A length with a 100 x 100mm (4 x 4in) mesh, made from 6mm ($\frac{1}{4}$in) diameter wire, is suitable for this purpose. Lay the mesh on the hardcore prior to casting the fresh mix.

MAKING A BUILDER'S SQUARE

Use a builder's square to check the corners of your formwork. You can make one from three lengths of straight-edged 50 x 25mm (2 x 1in) timber, screwed together to form a triangle in the ratio 3:4:5. A convenient size has sides measuring 600, 800 and 1,000mm (about 24, 32 and 40in) long. Use the builder's square to check the corners of the stringlines during setting out, and then the formwork, before you nail it to the stakes.

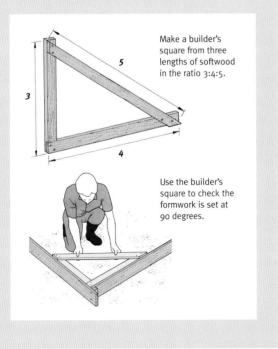

Make a builder's square from three lengths of softwood in the ratio 3:4:5.

Use the builder's square to check the formwork is set at 90 degrees.

Compacting the concrete

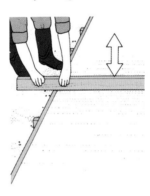

1 Compact the concrete using a stout timber beam with a chopping motion to help dispel air bubbles.

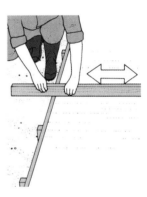

2 Level the concrete using the tamping beam with a sawing motion as you work along the slab.

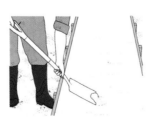

3 Fill in any hollows which appear using fresh concrete, then re-level. Tap the sides of the formwork to settle.

4 Cover the slab with heavy-gauge polythene and leave to cure for about four days before you walk over it.

Patios

A patio should be built where it will receive the most sunshine, although it is also desirable to site it close to some shade for very hot days. Alternatively, you can create your own shady area by constructing a pergola or awning over part of the patio.

Planning the patio

Consider the following points before you start constructing the patio.

Patio size As a rough guide to the scale of a patio, you should allow sufficient space to accommodate garden furniture for four people in addition to permitting passage through to the garden. The minimum practical size for this is about 3.7sq m (40sq ft).

Drainage The large area of the patio will prevent rainwater from soaking into the ground as normal, so you should take into account where the excess water will go. The entire patio must slope slightly – about 25mm in 1.8m (1in in 6ft) – towards the garden or flower bed, but not towards the house walls, or you could create a damp problem. If the ground naturally slopes towards the house you will have to incorporate a drainage channel at the end of the patio to divert the rainwater sideways to a suitable drainage point.

Existing drain runs It is likely that your patio will cover existing drain runs and possibly inspection chambers. You will either have to build up the walls of an inspection chamber to set the manhole cover at the new surface level, or else cover the existing manhole cover with a loose-laid paving slab for access in case of a blockage.

Surface materials A patio can be constructed from the same materials used for paths, including bricks, blocks, slabs, cast concrete – and even timber, with duckboards forming a platform on a concrete base.

Timber decking (see pages 110–115) can be quicker and easier to assemble than laying a patio but, unlike stone or brick paving, requires regular maintenance if it is to last.

Marking out the base

It is essential that you set out the base correctly to ensure the surface has a firm, flat foundation that will not collapse.

Use stringlines and pegs to mark the perimeter of the patio. Most patios adjoin the house and must be constructed so that the level is not higher than the damp-proof course (DPC) of the house walls.

Datum pegs A datum peg, made from 25mm (1in) sq softwood with a pointed end, is used to set the top level of the patio.

Marking out the base for a patio

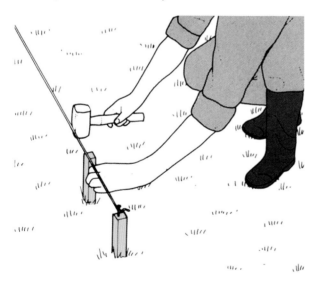

1 Stretch stringlines (preferably a coloured nylon twine) between pegs driven in at the perimeter of the patio, indicating the corners with more pegs set at the ultimate level of the patio.

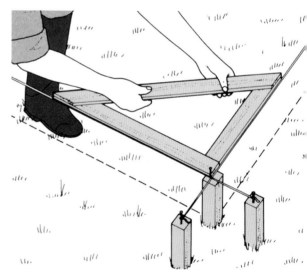

2 Check the corners with a builder's square (see page 93) to ensure that the stringlines are set at right angles. If not, adjust the pegs and string as necessary.

Setting the prime datum peg

Drive in the prime datum peg so that its top is at the height required for the patio. This must be at least 150mm (6in) below the level of the DPC to prevent rainwater splashing from the patio surface on to the house wall above the DPC.

In the top of the peg hammer a nail to which you can attach the stringline. Position a second datum peg at the other side of the proposed patio, and set it at the same level as the prime datum by spanning across the two pegs with a spirit level on top of a long straight-edged plank of wood. Or use a water level – a garden hose pipe, with transparent plastic tubing in either end, filled with water which is visible through the plastic. The water level will remain constant; align the water line at one end of the pipe with the top of the prime datum peg and use the other end to fix the next peg. For a wide patio you might need to drive in an intermediate datum peg. Fix a nail in the top of each of these pegs.

Attaching the stringlines

Attach stringlines – ideally, coloured nylon twine which is durable and easily visible – to the datum pegs.

Stretch the lines out from the house wall at each side and drive in pegs about 300mm (12in) beyond the area of the patio so you will have ample space to work. Fix another stringline between two more pegs to mark the outer edge of the patio. Indicate the corners of the patio by driving in more pegs. Check that the corners are set at 90 degrees using a builder's square, which is illustrated on page 93.

Fixing intermediate pegs

It is vital that the foundations of the patio are perfectly flat. Drive in more pegs around the perimeter of the patio at intervals of about 1.5m (5ft). Place a plank and spirit level on the prime datum peg and the adjacent perimeter peg and level the latter. Move on from the second peg to the subsequent perimeter pegs, levelling in the same way.

When the perimeter pegs have been set accurately, drive in more pegs at 1.5m (5ft) intervals over the entire surface of the base, levelling them to the outer pegs with the plank and spirit level. The top of each peg will be at the desired level of the patio.

Excavating the base

Dig out the topsoil (see page 92, for details) using a spade and a pick-axe for hard ground, then add 75–100mm (3–4in) of hardcore and ram this down well, using a garden roller or,

3 Level the pegs by spanning across the tops from a prime datum peg with a spirit level and plank. Tap down or raise the pegs as necessary until it is level.

4 Level the entire base by driving intermediate pegs at 1.5m (5ft) intervals across the surface and levelling them to match the height of the perimeter pegs.

Patios

preferably, a hired motorized plate compactor. This tool has a vibrating plate underneath, which will compact the hardcore thoroughly. Add a 50mm (2in) blinding layer of sand and vibrate this too, taking care not to dislodge the datum pegs fixed across the surface. The datum pegs should now protrude above the layer of sand by the thickness of the patio surface; if, for example, you are using bricks, this will be 760mm (2½in).

Edge restraints and formwork

If you are casting a concrete slab, fix formwork to the inside faces of the perimeter pegs, aligning the top edge of the planks with the tops of the pegs.

For other paving, some form of permanent edge restraint is desirable to stop the patio from creeping.

Where the patio abuts the wall of the house you can use the wall itself as a means of restraining the paving material, but you will still need to support the outer edges. There are various alternatives.

Precast concrete kerbstones are available from garden centres and builders' merchants. The kerbs usually have a bevelled top edge and may incorporate a moulded pattern for decorative effect. Dig a trench just outside the perimeter of the patio and bed the stones upright in 50mm (2in) concrete, with their top edge level with the datum pegs.

Brick edging looks particularly attractive with a brick or block paved surface. Again dig a trench and set the individual bricks (or concrete blocks) on end and side by side in 50mm (2in) of sand in a "soldier" course.

Timber edging can be used as an inconspicuous restraint for brick, block or slab paving. The timber must be thoroughly treated against rot with preservative. Attach the lengths to stakes driven into the ground so that their tops are level with the datum pegs, or fix to the outer datum pegs.

Dealing with sloping ground

Where the garden slopes away from the house you must build perimeter walls (see page 133) at the outer edges to create a type of stage on which to lay the patio.

The space within the walls can be filled with rubble and hardcore as a sub-base, then the paving laid on top as normal. Weep holes built into the perimeter walls will allow water to drain out: these can be simply unmortared vertical joints between brickwork or block-work at intervals.

You may wish to incorporate a flight of steps within the perimeter walls for easy access to the lower part of the garden (see pages 116–117).

Spreading the sand bed

Most patio materials can be laid on a 75mm (3in) thick bed of sand, either on dabs of fresh mortar or, in the case of flexible

5 Dig out the base to firm sub-soil using a spade or pick-axe. Remove all topsoil for re-use in another part of the garden. Take care not to dislodge the datum pegs.

6 Fill with hardcore and compact using a garden roller or motorized compacting machine, which can readily be hired. Add a blinding layer of sand and compact that too.

concrete block pavers, simply compressed into the sand itself without mortar (the edge restraints hold the blocks rigid).

It is not easy to spread a layer of sand over a large area and at the same time maintain the levels required, so it is usual to apply it in bays formed by 1.8m (6ft) lengths of 50 x 25mm (2 x 1in) wooden battens laid across the blinding layer of the sub-base.

Position a batten – resting on its narrower edge – along the perimeter of the patio and another about 1.2m (4ft) away along the patio site, parallel with the first. Support the battens with heaps of sand. Check across the tops of the battens with a spirit level on a plank to ensure that they are horizontal, then tip a barrowload of sand into the bay they form. Rake out the sand so that it stands just proud.

Level the sand to the tops of the battens by drawing a straight-edged length of wood along the battens. Fill in any hollows with more sand, then level off again. When you have spread out the sand in the first bay, carefully remove the outer batten and place it about 1.2m (4ft) away from, and parallel with, the second batten, forming another bay. Fill the gap left by replacing the batten with sand and level off with a trowel or short length of straight-edged timber.

Tip sand into the second bay and level it off, then repeat the process to complete the sand bed over the entire area of the patio.

SETTING A GRADIENT

The patio surface should slope slightly to drain off rainwater. On a flat site you should set one side about 25mm (1in) lower than the other. When setting out the base use a 1in 25mm (1in) thick piece of wood (a shim) under the spirit level on the lower side of the base to check that the level is correct.

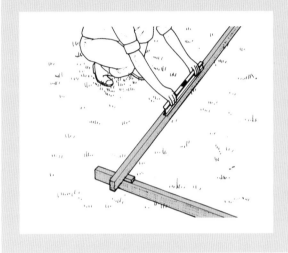

7 Set edge restraints such as precast concrete kerbstones at the perimeter of the patio to prevent the surface from spreading. Check that they are horizontal using a spirit level.

8 Add a sand bed over the sub-base onto which you can lay slabs, bricks or blocks directly. When covering a large area, divide the area into bays for easy spreading of the sand.

Laying paths

Planning a path

The first stage in making a path, whatever your choice of material as the surface, is planning the route it will take through the garden. The first rule in planning is that any path must lead somewhere, whether it is to a garden shed or ornament, or simply from one area of the plot to another.

Straight or angular paths will tend to segment the garden and give a formal appearance, whereas by incorporating curves you can produce a more natural effect. You should take into account the profile of the ground itself, both for the appearance of the path and for practical considerations: for example, a path sloping towards the house or other outbuilding will create a direct route for heavy rainwater to flow to the house walls rather than soaking into the ground as it would normally.

Draw a scale sketch plan and a side elevation of the garden to help you plan out the route of the path and any obstacles you might encounter. Consider also that looking at a curved path drawn from above on paper is quite misleading: in reality the curve will foreshorten. For an impression of what the path will actually look like, lower your eye to the level of the paper and look along the drawn curve.

Setting out the path

Whether you are intending to cast a solid concrete path or lay individual pavers, you must mark out the route on the ground, using strings stretched between pegs (or use a long hosepipe to help plot the course of a curved path).

Decide what use the path will be put to: if it is to be used for access with a wheelbarrow, be sure to allow enough width for passage. Two people walking side by side will require about 915mm (3ft) width for comfort.

Choosing paving materials

Your choice of paving materials depends on appearance and durability. The options are basically cast concrete, preformed concrete paving slabs, bricks, moulded paving blocks, gravel or asphalt. Natural stone, for example reclaimed York paving, is attractive but comparatively expensive.

Concrete is plain, dull and utilitarian but ideal for a heavy-duty path, or for areas of the garden where appearance is not an important consideration. It can, however, be enhanced by having an exposed aggregate surface. Once the concrete has been poured and levelled, a decorative aggregate – such as coloured chippings – is spread over the surface and tamped down using a plank of wood. This pushes the stones into the wet concrete, which is forced up around the aggregate to hold it in place.

Paving slabs are tough and durable and available in a range of colours and tones and various shapes and surface finishes. Square and rectangular slabs are most commonly available. The most readily available size of slab is 450mm (18in) square, and bigger slabs are sized in increments of 150mm (6in). Slabs suitable for path-laying should usually be about 50mm (2in) thick. Finishes vary: the slabs may have a smooth, non-slip surface, be riven with the appearance of split stone or textured with an exposed aggregate surface, or be patterned to give the appearance of bricks, tiles or cobbles.

Crazy paving (random paving) is made from broken concrete or stone slabs, and sold in many different sizes, shapes and colours by the square yard. It may look decorative but is not really a practical consideration if the path is to receive heavy traffic from garden equipment.

Bricks of many types, new or secondhand, are suitable for use as a path surface, and can be laid in decorative patterns or simple brick bonding arrangements. Do not use the more porous bricks, which are susceptible to damage by frost. Engineering brick is the hardest and, consequently, the best performer against damp. There is a wide range of bricks available, from white to brown, and including yellows and reds. Bear in mind comfort (for walking) and drainage before selecting a textured finish.

Concrete paving blocks – which are about the same size as bricks, and sometimes decoratively shaped – are laid in interlocking pattern on a sand bed. Finished to resemble old bricks, they are often textured to simulate real brick.

Gravel can be used for paths provided there is some means of edge restraint – a kerb of bricks on end, for example – to prevent it from spreading to adjoining surfaces. It should also be laid on a concrete base to avoid sinking problems. Lay a 50mm (2in) thick sub-base of coarse gravel mixed with sand topped with a 25mm (1in) thick layer of fine pea gravel, then roll the surface to compact it thoroughly.

Cold cure asphalt is sold prepacked in sacks for direct application to a prepared base and, although really intended as a resurfacing material, can be successfully used for a new pathway. Apply the asphalt to a hardcore base, rake level, then roll flat and compact. As an alternative finish you can embed stone chippings in the surface.

Cobblestones can be set in a 50mm (2in) deep layer of dry concrete mix that has been poured into a prepared shallow trench. Pack the stones tightly; tamp them level. Sprinkle the path with water to activate the concrete and to clean the cobbles.

Wooden paths are well suited to rural areas and a good way to recycle a fallen tree. Dig down 200mm (8in); level and compress a gravel and sand mix to a depth of 50mm (2in). Use 150mm (6in) deep sections of logs, cut whole from the

SETTING OUT CURVES

A path winding down the garden is attractive element of any garden design. It entices the visitor to explore its length, its shape suggesting that their are hidden places or features to discover just around the next bend.

The path should be sinuous and gently curving to draw the visitor along. If it bends too sharply, it will be difficult to manoeuvre garden machinery along the path. The route a curving path takes can be difficult to set out unless you make a scale plan of its size and route on squared paper. This will enable you to estimate the materials you will need and help you transfer the shape accurately to the site.

Using stringlines

Stretch a stringline along the site for the longest edge of the path area, and another at right angles for the width of the path area. Measure along the stringlines at right angles to them in increments that are relative to your scale plan to give you the correct positions for fixing marker pegs. Stretch more stringlines from marker peg to marker peg to translate the shape drawn on your plan to the actual site.

If pegs and stringlines must be removed to excavate the path, put them back after digging to serve as a guide for the formwork, which will provide a support for the concrete while it sets.

Curving wooden formwork

For a cast concrete path which incorporates curves you will need to construct timber formwork that follows the shape of the path.

Softwood planks, about 25mm (1in) thick, are most suitable, but slightly thinner planks, used with more stakes, will do. They must be as wide as the desired depth of concrete. Make a number of partial saw cuts (up to half the thickness of the wood) across the breadth of the formwork planks at about 125mm (5in) intervals so that you are able to bend the timber as necessary to the shape of the path. Drive in more stakes than are needed for a straight foundation in order to support the planks adequately without their springing straight. Nail the stakes to the outer face of the formwork planks.

For gradual curves the saw cuts should be on the outside of the formwork, but for tighter bends the timber is less likely to snap if the saw cuts are made on the inside of the curve.

Hiring road forms

On a particularly long path, buying timber formwork can be costly. Consider hiring metal road forms, which comprise flat metal lengths with attached stakes: flexible and rigid types are available for curved or straight paths respectively. The forms are, of course, removed once the concrete has fully set.

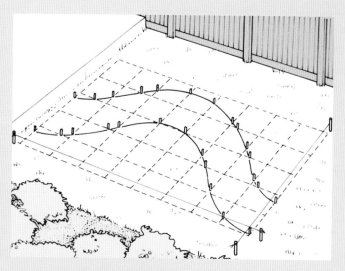

Marking out the curve using stringlines
Measure along the outer strings to points that correspond with the scale plan and drive stakes into the ground. Run stringlines from stake to stake to mark out the curved path.

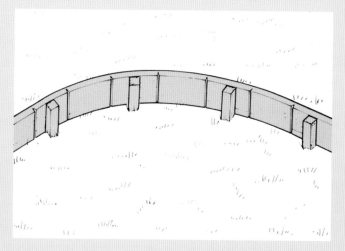

Creating curves in formwork
Form curves in formwork by making saw cuts across the planks at intervals, then bend the timber and secure to stakes. Cast the concrete within the formwork and remove when set.

Laying paths

trunk and thicker branches. Lightly sand down any sharp edges on the upper surface and arrange the logs on the base material, grain upwards. Pay attention to the size, shape and colour of logs in your design. Work them firmly into the gravel and sand, then pour more of the mixture between the logs. Using a broom, sweep the infill across the path, until it is flush with the top of the logs. Hammer down any logs that stick out of the gravel.

Low-lying plants can further enhance such a path; remove some of the sand and gravel mixture and replace it with the appropriate quantity and type of soil.

Laying the foundations

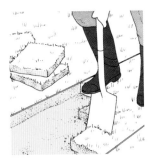

1 Dig out the topsoil within the stringlines, which are set 50mm (2in) wider than the finished path. Retain any turfs for re-use elsewhere.

2 Compact the base using a stout timber post, sledgehammer or garden roller. If using a post, wear thick gloves to protect your hands.

3 Add hardcore to the base and ram this down well with a sledgehammer or compact with a roller to a thickness of about 75mm (3in).

4 Blind the surface with a layer of sand spread about 50mm (2in) thick with a garden rake as a means of filling large hollows in the hardcore.

Preparing the sub-base

Most paths which are to receive normal loading from people and wheelbarrows can be simply laid on a firm, level base formed by the earth itself, without the need for a firmer sub-base. Set up stringlines to mark out the shape and route of the path, then remove topsoil or turf within the guidelines.

Where the path joins a lawn, plan to set the paving about 20mm (¾in) below the surrounding level so that you can mow the grass without damaging the mower blades.

Ram down the exposed subsoil with a stout timber post, or compact thoroughly with a garden roller. For a long path it is best to work in easily manageable bays rather than digging out the foundations for the entire run in one go. Check that the base is level using a spirit level on a long timber plank. Where the path follows the undulations of the ground, check that the base undulates consistently with ground level.

Allow a drainage crossfall to one side of the path using a shim of timber to set the slope (see page 92). Tip barrowloads of sand onto the sub-base and spread it 50–75mm (2–3in) thick using a straight-edged length of plank cut to the same width as the path.

Edge restraints

It is not necessary on fairly narrow paths to incorporate edge restraints to prevent the surface materials from creeping, although if you are casting a concrete slab you will have to construct timber formwork as described on pages 92–93. However, you might want to include some form of decorative edging purely for appearance. Garden centres and builders merchants stock a range of preformed edging, for example in a Victorian rope design. The edging is simply set, without mortar, in a slim trench at the sides of the paving.

If the path will abut a lawn, you can incorporate a mowing edge to make cutting the lawn where it meets the path easier and neater. See page 66 for details on creating a mowing edge.

Adding the hardcore

Where it is necessary to support heavy traffic or where the soil is soft, you should lay a sub-base of compacted hardcore. Tip a layer of about 75mm (3in) of hardcore into the sub-base and ram this down well using a sledgehammer or a garden roller, then top with a 25 or 50mm (1 or 2in) thick blinding layer of sand, raked level.

The base is now ready for laying your chosen paving material, whether concrete, slabs, bricks, or natural stone.

Expansion joints for concrete paths

Temperature variations cause concrete to expand and contract, and unless this is controlled a cast concrete path will crack at weak or vulnerable areas. Divide the path into bays about 1.8m (6ft) long by inserting a permanent expansion joint consisting of a length of preservative-treated softwood about 12mm (½in) thick between the outer formwork planks. To be fully effective the joints must be set at 90 degrees to the edges of the path, even when the path is curved. Support the expansion joint on dabs of fresh concrete, with its top edge flush with the top of the formwork. Pour in the concrete as previously described, then carefully tamp from each side of the expansion joint to avoid dislodging it.

Laying a concrete path

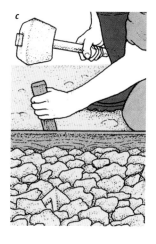

Dig a trench 10–15cm (4–6in) deep where the path is to be laid (a). Fill with hardcore and ram into place (b). Peg retaining boards 8cm (3in) deep along the sides (c).

Check for height and level with a straight edge and spirit level. Spread the concrete between the retaining boards, rake and tamp it, and level with the edge of a board (d).

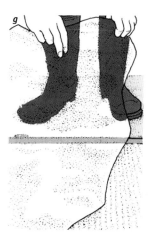

When the surface water has disappeared, smooth the concrete with a float (e). While the surface is still damp, brush with a stiff broom to roughen the surface (f).

Cover with polythene sheeting to protect the surface of the concrete and allow to dry for 5–10 days (g). A fortnight after laying, remove the formwork (h). The path is now ready to use.

Loose-laying paths

Paving slabs can be laid on a sand bed without mortar where there is likely to be minimal pedestrian use. The bed should be about 50mm (2in) thick: you will need to buy 0.5 cubic metre of sand for every 20sq metres of path (or 1.7 cubic feet for every 215sq feet). Where the path will receive heavier use, lay the slabs on mortar dabs (see page 104).

Prepare the base as previously described for foundations (see page 100) and spread the sand over the surface. It is important that the path is consistently level over its surface, so set each slab according to a common reference point such as a datum peg driven into the ground at the start of the path. The top of this datum peg should be set at the level required for the finished path.

Placing the slabs

Lift the first slab into position on the sand bed, placing one edge against the adjoining surface and lowering the other end onto the sand. Wiggle the slab slightly to bed it on the sand. Check the level: if the slab is not lying flat, tap with the handle of a club hammer to bed it down properly. If the slab is too low, lift it and trowel more sand underneath, then replace it and tap level.

Place the second slab alongside the first one, align their edges, then tap the second slab gently with the club hammer to bed it firmly in the sand. Adjust if necessary in order to maintain the correct level in both directions.

Butt the edges of the slabs up against each other or, for wider joints, insert pieces of hardboard between them. Avoid making the joints wider than about 12mm (1–2 in), or you will have trouble creating a level surface.

Finishing the joints

Once all the slabs have been laid on the sand bed you can fill the joints. Mix some sand and dry cement in the proportions 1:3 and brush into the gaps between slabs.

Either leave the joints as they are, or sprinkle water over the surface with a watering can fitted with a fine rose: this hardens the cement mixture enough to prevent the slabs from moving too much.

CUTTING PAVING SLABS

When you are laying paving slabs you will probably need to cut some slabs to fit around corners or at the end of the path. Where you have used a staggered design you will have to cut slabs to fit at the edges. Hydraulic stone splitters are available for hire to make short work of cutting slabs accurately, but there is no reason why you cannot simply cut the slabs with a club hammer and bolster chisel.

Measure the width of the gap you have to fill and transfer the measurement to the slab. Score the slab with a bolster chisel, then place over a length of timber on a firm flat surface and break along the score line by tapping firmly with a club hammer. Fit the cut slab with the slightly rough cut edge to the outside of the path.

Loose-laying paving slabs

1 Lay the first slab on the sand bed and set level with the top of the datum peg, checking with a spirit level.

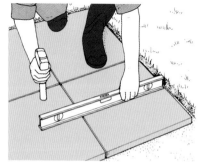

2 Level the slabs by tapping with the handle of a club hammer: adjust the sand level under slabs as necessary.

3 Fill the joints with a mixture of sand and cement, brushed in to fill the gaps; water in using a watering can and rose.

Crazy paving paths

Crazy paving comprises pieces of broken paving slabs laid to produce a complex, decoratively patterned surface. However, despite the apparently random effect of the paving, the pieces must be laid in a strict formula both for a symmetrical appearance and for strength.

The sides of the path are formed by a row of fairly large slab pieces which have at least one straight edge, placed outermost. Similar-sized pieces with irregular edges are positioned along the centre of the path while smaller irregular pieces are used to fill in the space.

Preparing the site
Crazy paving is obtainable from larger garden centres or building contractors in a choice of colours and thicknesses. Make sure you are given a good mixture of shapes, sizes and colours (unless you specify all one colour), and have them dumped as close as possible to the site. Alternatively, use natural stone, with its seams and marbling.

Stack the slabs, grouped by colour, shape and size, alongside the run of the path so that it is easy to select the types you require as you are laying them.

Prepare the base by digging out the topsoil. If the subsoil is not firm, dig this out too and replace with 75–100mm (3–4in) hardcore. Top with about 50mm (2in) of sand, raked and levelled.

Laying the perimeter pieces
Begin by placing a stringline at the required level. Place the perimeter pieces of crazy paving along the edges of the path, level with the stringlines, to check that they fit correctly. Mix some mortar, then lay the first stone on dabs of mortar, trowelled onto the sand bed. Press the slab down on the mortar dabs with a wiggling motion to bed it firmly, then lay the neighbouring pieces. Place a spirit level across the slabs to check that they are level.

Laying the central slabs
Dry-lay the larger slabs along the centre of the path, then return to the starting point, lift them one at a time, remove or add sand as necessary to give a level finish, and re-lay on four or five dabs of mortar trowelled onto the base.

Check that the central slabs are set level with the perimeter slabs using the spirit level. Place a stout length of timber across the entire path and tap this with a club hammer in order to level the slabs consistently: it is otherwise quite difficult to set each slab level with its neighbour.

Placing the small infill slabs
Fill in between with the small irregular pieces, bedded on single dabs of mortar. It is often easier to "butter" the back of the smallest pieces of crazy paving with mortar, scraping it off the trowel and furrowing the surface with the blade to aid adhesion. Use the timber and club hammer to tap the slabs level with the surrounding ones.

Pointing the joints
The gaps between the crazy paving slabs must be filled with a fairly wet mortar mix to hold each slab in place. The pointing should also be bevelled to drain surface water from the path. Once hardened, this filling will help keep the slabs in place.

Laying crazy paving

1 Bed the straight-edged slabs selected for the perimeter on dabs of mortar at the sides of the path.

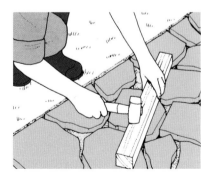

2 Lay the larger central slabs and smaller infill pieces in the gaps and level using a club hammer and a length of stout timber.

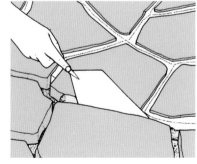

3 Point the joints between the crazy paving slabs with mortar, bevelled to drain water.

Mixed materials

For added interest in what would otherwise be a plain-looking patio, cut in areas of different paving materials such as cobblestones, bricks, gravel or timber for variation – or else construct planting areas.

Creating patterns

Mixing colours By mixing different-coloured paving you can create random or formal patterns. For example, you can highlight diagonal lines across the patio with red slabs contrasted with the overall green or buff ones; or you can pick out alternate rows of slabs in another colour, working from the perimeter of the patio forming squares within squares, and finishing with a solid block of, for example, four slabs at the centre.

Mixing shapes With hexagonal slabs, too, you can form interesting cut-outs by omitting units from the overall area. You may be able to mix hexagonal slabs with ordinary square or rectangular slabs of different colour.

Adding curves Some makes of slab are intended to be laid as part of a set, to make up an overall design impressed upon their faces. Other slabs are available with a segmental cut-out at one corner; these form a circular hole when four slabs are laid in conjunction.

Using bricks and timber

Brick paving Introduce areas of brick paving into a slab-laid patio to add texture and colour. For a geometric pattern lay an edging of brick pavers around each square slab. Experiment by laying the bricks flat, on edge – or even on end.

Timber Use lengths of rough-sawn preservative-treated timber in conjunction with slabs and bricks. Railway sleeper-sized blocks of wood embedded in the surface can be used to break up a plain run of slabs and can form shallow planting beds.

Log inserts Log rounds, preferably of hardwood which will last better against rot, can be set within an area of missing paving slabs, and the gaps around them filled with gravel.

Aggregates for the patio

To create an attractive feature within the patio, omit a number of slabs from an area of paving and fill the gap with decorative aggregates. Many types and colours, including recycled and reclaimed materials, are available, often pre-bagged.

Cobblestones are commonly about 50–75mm (2–3in) in size, and can be loose-laid within your feature areas, contained by decorative edging or simply by the edges of the paving slabs. Alternatively, for a decorative area on which you can walk, bed the cobblestones in a screed of mortar, pressing them as level as possible with a stout board and club hammer. Pebbles measure about 40–50mm (1½–2in) and can be used in the same way as the large cobblestones.

Gravel chippings, about 6mm (¼in) in size and made of rough-edged flint, come in various colours – they are often bagged up in mixed colours – and can be scattered over planting areas to reduce evaporation from the soil, or else used to fill isolated areas where slabs have been removed. They will precisely fill any shape of hole in the patio and can be laid right up against plants without doing any harm. Marine shell, crushed, provides a fascinating infill for feature areas on the patio, especially when whole seashells are included in the area for a distinctly seaside look.

Laying paving slabs

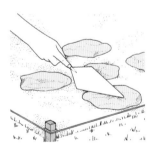

1 Apply the mortar dabs to the sub-base in the position of the first slab; trowel on five dabs, one at each corner and one centrally.

2 Lay the first slab on the mortar dabs, placing one edge first, then lowering flat. Tap level with the shaft of a club hammer.

3 Lay the remaining slabs, butting the edges together or slipping spacers between each. Check the levels with a spirit level.

4 Fill the joints with a dry mix of 1:3 cement and sand, then water it in with clean water using a watering can with a fine rose fitted.

Above left: Antique red brick-style paving made from high strength concrete, and therefore resistant to frost and wear and tear, makes an attractive paving surface for a weathered old-fashioned look.

Above: The material used for garden steps should blend in with their context. The durability of hand-dressed, natural sandstone make it an ideal material for use as steps.

Left: Wooden stepping stones are a practical if traditional form of garden path. If softwoods are used, they will require regular treatment with preservatives.

Left: In order for a wall or raised bed not to look out of place in a garden it is vital that the right material is chosen. Reproduction Cotswold stone blocks not only look authentic, but are easy to construct.

Below left: Fences make less solid barriers than walls, defining a space without necessarily enclosing it. Informal panel fences are made from naturally supple woods such as willow or split hazel.

Below: Although economical and quick to put up the strength of prefarbricated fences lies in the way they are attached between the posts.

Mixed materials

Small-scale paving

The alternative to a patio made predominantly of large-scale paving slabs is one comprising a surface of small-scale units such as bricks or concrete blocks (see pages 80–85). The benefit of these materials is that you have more freedom to create surface patterns by selecting a decorative bonding arrangement: basketweave, herringbone, caneweave, parquet, or even a simple stretcher pattern are possible – and you can even lay the bricks or blocks diagonally (see page 109). For visual relief in a large area covered with small pavers, you might still consider adding feature areas of different materials, including gravel, cobblestones, or bricks.

Laying cobblestones as infill into a paved patio

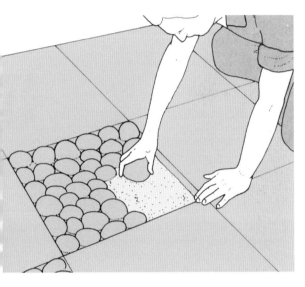

1 Cobblestones can be set in a mortar screed in feature areas within slabs or bricks. Spread out the mortar, then push in the individual cobbles about halfway, varying the colour mix.

2 Bed the cobblestones evenly by placing a straight-edged length of timber across the top (resting it on the surrounding paving slabs) to press down any high stones.

Define and soften a patio of square riven-faced slabs with borders of bricks.

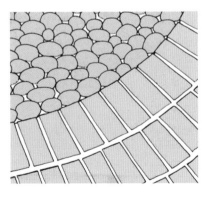

Create circular patterns with cobblestones and bricks – for example, surrounding a tree.

Decorative areas of planted gravel within areas of paving will avoid a plain appearance.

Paving: flexible pavers

Concrete paving blocks, known as flexible pavers because they are laid dry, without mortar, on a sand bed, can be used to create an attractively patterned and textured hard surface for a patio, or for paths and drives.

Paver formats

Flexible pavers roughly correspond to brick sizes, although they are normally about 60mm (2in) thicker. Numerous colours and textures are available. Select a colour that will complement the house; this may restrict your choice but the end result will be more acceptable than a contrasting scheme. Before opting for a textured finish, consider the function of the surface. An irregular finish is not ideal if you want to stand tables and chairs on the paving. Whether the chosen surface is smooth or textured, wet an area of one paver before you buy to check the colour change you can expect in rainy weather and to test slip-resistance.

In addition to uniform slabs, different shapes are also made, intended to interlock with neighbouring blocks to form a decorative bonding arrangement (see opposite page).

Bevelled-edge In its simplest form the paver may have a bevelled top edge, which accentuates the rectangular shape of the individual block when laid.

Fishtail Another popular type is the wavy-edged 'fishtail' block, often laid in a parquet design to give a characteristic rippling effect as if viewed underwater.

Angular There is also a geometric cranked rectangle block, which strictly speaking should be laid only in a diagonal stretcher bond. A "bow-tie" version of this creates a zigzag pattern across the paving when laid in stretcher bond.

Patterned face Some rectangular paving blocks have a pattern impressed in their top face, such as two, four or eight smaller squares which are intended to resemble a mosaic finish, or a series of diamond shapes for a studded effect.

Laying flexible pavers

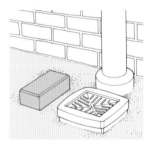

1 Check the position of gullies, down pipes and other obstructions in relation to the finished level of the paving blocks.

2 Place the blocks on the sand bed in your chosen pattern (here a parquet design), working from a walking board resting on the edge restraints.

Preparing the base

Concrete paving blocks can be laid on a prepared foundation of hardcore (see page 100), 75 to 100mm (3 to 4in) in depth, topped with about 50mm (2in) of sand. The edges of the paving must be lined with kerbstones, timber restraints or a row of blocks set on edge in concrete. Spread out the sand in bays, as described on page 97. To allow for the compaction of the blocks lay them about 10mm (⅜in) above the top of the edge restraints. Make sure that the sand bed is a block-depth less this dimension below the top of the edge restraints.

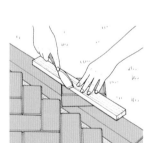

3 Set up stringlines across the paving as a guide to laying the blocks symmetrically, especially when creating a diagonal effect.

4 Mark blocks for cutting by holding them over the space they will fill and scribing with a bolster chisel against a straight edge.

5 Vibrate the blocks into the sand bed using a hired motorized plate compacting machine fitted with a sole plate (or use a carpet to cushion).

6 Brush sand into the joints between blocks and vibrate the surface again using the plate compactor to form a firm, flat patio.

Dealing with obstructions

Where the patio is built adjacent to the house walls there will be some obstructions to contend with, such as gullies and rainwater downpipes, which you must not cover. Use an individual block as a gauge to check how the paving will fit against these features: it may be necessary to sink the foundation lower to avoid complicated junctions, or else create a well around the obstruction using a row of blocks on end.

There may well be manhole covers within your patio area, which you must not block permanently. It might be necessary on your site to extend the height of the manhole walls to suit the new surface, or you may simply be able to loose-lay blocks over the manhole cover; these can be lifted in case of blockage or overflow.

Placing the blocks

Position the first block pavers against the edge restraints at one corner of the patio, following your chosen pattern. Lay only whole blocks, leaving any cut ones until last.

To ensure the blocks are bedded down sufficiently in the sand, place a stout length of timber across the surface and hit this sharply with a club hammer. Place the timber systematically in all directions to bed all the blocks level. Check with a spirit level held on top of the timber that the surface is flat. Use a shim of wood under the spirit level to set a drainage fall to one side of the patio.

Work on an easily manageable area, then move your walking board further onto the surface and continue laying the blocks. It is best to work from the corner diagonally across the patio, so the finish is flat in appearance.

Setting up guide strings

Laying the hundreds of small blocks needed for a patio is not difficult but it is tricky to keep the overall bonding arrangement consistent without some guides to work to.

Stretch a string between pegs across the patio, aligned parallel with the leading edge of the section of paving you are laying. Lay the blocks up to this line, then move the line across about another 1.5 or 1.8m (5 or 6ft) and lay more blocks up to it. This method of checking the alignment of the paving blocks is most important when you are laying blocks diagonally across the surface, as you have no outer guidelines to show you are laying them out of true.

Cutting block pavers

Most laying patterns used for block pavers will require you to cut some individual pieces for the edges. Using a club hammer and bolster chisel, mark off the amount to be cut by scoring with a chisel against a straight edge, place the block on a firm,

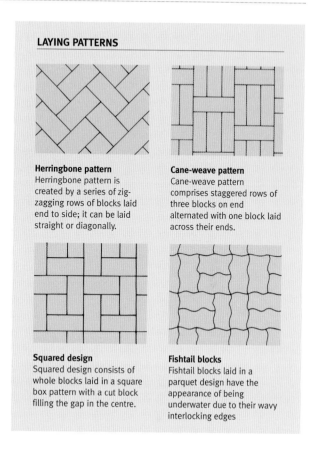

LAYING PATTERNS

Herringbone pattern
Herringbone pattern is created by a series of zig-zagging rows of blocks laid end to side; it can be laid straight or diagonally.

Cane-weave pattern
Cane-weave pattern comprises staggered rows of three blocks on end alternated with one block laid across their ends.

Squared design
Squared design consists of whole blocks laid in a square box pattern with a cut block filling the gap in the centre.

Fishtail blocks
Fishtail blocks laid in a parquet design have the appearance of being underwater due to their wavy interlocking edges

flat surface and strike the line sharply with the chisel and a club hammer. If you are laying a large patio, however, it is worth while hiring a hydraulic stone splitter. Always wear plastic goggles to protect your eyes from flying chips.

Compacting the paved surface

It is best to hire a motorized plate compactor for this task. Choose a machine which is fitted with a rubber bottom or sole plate to avoid damaging the faces of the blocks.

Spread a layer of sand over the blockwork to fill the joints, then operate the plate compactor. Run the machine across the surface: the vibrating sole plate will force the blocks well into the sand bed, and has the action of forcing sand up between the joints, making the entire area rigid and firm.

Add more sand to the surface and brush it into the joints with a stiff-bristled broom to work it well in. Follow with two or three more passes with the compactor to vibrate the sand into the joints.

Timber decking

A raised timber deck provides you with space outdoors for dozing, dining or soaking up the sun, and can be constructed using just a few specialist carpentry techniques. At its most basic the deck is simply a slatted (duck-board) platform resting on the ground as an alternative to slabs or concrete. When raised on stilts, equipped with steps, rails and even an awning or pergola, it can become a traditional-style verandah. You can adapt the design shown here to your own requirements, or buy a kit of components from a specialist supplier and assemble the deck according to the instructions provided.

A raised timber deck, incorporating a pergola for shade, makes an attractive addition to the side of the house, providing space for sitting out and dining, either on built-in or freestanding furniture. The deck surface – a series of slats with small gaps between – drains quickly after rain, and is a more comfortable option than concrete slabs. The deck is built on sturdy uprights mounted on metal plates bolted to concrete foundation pads. This method of construction makes it easy to deal with sloping ground levels: the posts are cut to the required length, while the deck itself is fixed horizontally to them.

Timber decking

The basic duckboard

A basic timber slatted duckboard platform can be constructed entirely from lengths of preservative-treated sawn or planed softwood measuring about 75 x 25mm (3 x 1in) on a concrete or slab surface. Assemble the duckboard on site.

Extremely straightforward to assemble, the platform consists of lengths of timber forming the bearers, which are spaced about 760mm (30in) apart and parallel with each other. The bearers should run in the direction of the slope of the surface on which it is being laid.

Lengths of the same timber are cut to span the width of the platform and placed across the bearers at right angles to them. Set the slats about 6 to 12mm ($\frac{1}{4}$–$\frac{1}{2}$in) apart, using an offcut of wood as a spacer so that the gap is constant across its length. If the platform is up to 3m (10ft) in width, you can lay full lengths of timber across; however, for wider platforms the lengths will have to be butt-joined. Stagger the joins at each side of the platform in alternate rows so that there are no continuous break lines across the surface.

Secure the slats to the bearers by hammering in 35mm (1$\frac{1}{2}$in) long floorboard nails, two per bearer position.

The raised timber deck

A more substantial structure can be constructed along the lines of a traditional verandah, normally attached to the side of a house with access via a door or french window. The deck comprises a number of upright posts set on concrete pads, with an arrangement of joists fixed on top, and attached to a stout wallplate bolted to the house wall. The decking itself is fixed over the joists. By extending the length of the uprights, a side rail can be incorporated into the design; extending the uprights even further allows you to assemble a pergola or awning over the deck. Seating can be incorporated into the main structure of the deck if required.

For access onto the deck, a simple set of timber steps can be constructed. If the deck is built over an existing door, direct access to and from the house is possible – you may be able to convert an existing window into a doorway for this purpose.

Planning the structure

Decide what you are likely to use the deck for, as this helps you determine its overall size: if you intend to dine outdoors, it must be sufficiently large to accommodate a table and chairs with space for people to pass behind when serving a meal. Where the deck will be used as a sunbathing area, space must be allowed for loungers.

Consider how the deck will appear when attached to the house wall: if it is fairly narrow – say about 3m (10ft) – and

projects out from the wall about 6m (20ft), it could resemble a pier at the seaside. However, a deck of this width running along the wall of the house would probably appear to be in better proportion. A squarer deck, on the other hand, is more in keeping with a corner location, set in the angle between two walls that meet at right-angles.

When planning your deck, particularly if it is raised, consider if it will overlook neighbouring gardens. It may affect your neighbours' rights to privacy and sunlight. In fact in some cases, timber decking structures require planning permission, so it is worth contacting your local authority prior to construction, especially if you are considering building a substantial or elevated deck.

Draw a scale plan of the garden on graph paper and mark in the intended position and size of the deck, plus access arrangements and other features which might influence the design. Draw a side elevation of the site to illustrate the way the ground slopes: the deck can be constructed on sloping ground by adjusting the length of the timber posts so that the deck surface is horizontal.

Set up stringlines and pegs to mark the perimeter of the proposed deck so that you can imagine the visual impact it will have on the garden and the house.

Timber requirements

Use the plans you have drawn to work out the amount of timber needed. The main structural components are made from two stock sizes of timber. For the below-deck supports, use 138 x 38mm (5$\frac{1}{2}$ x 1$\frac{1}{2}$ in) timber, with 75mm (3in) square timber for the above-deck supports. The dock joists should lie made from 138 x 38mm (5$\frac{1}{2}$ x 1$\frac{1}{2}$in) softwood, supporting slats of the same size timber laid flat rather than on edge.

Setting the concrete pads

The timber posts are supported on concrete pads cast on compacted hardcore. Each pad is about 400mm (16in) square and about 150mm (6in) thick. The tops of the pads should be level, but it is not essential to make them level with each other, as the length of the posts can be adjusted accordingly.

Use stringlines and pegs to mark the position of each pad on the ground. Allow for the pads to be spaced about 1.4m (55in) apart (measurements should be taken from the pad centres, not their edges). Measure out from the house wall the front-to-back dimension of the deck and mark the positions of the outer pads, then measure back toward the wall to determine the location of the remaining pads.

Dig out the earth and add the hardcore as necessary at each pad position, ram this down, then add and rake smooth the blinding layer of sand. Cast the concrete in this cut-out.

Timber decking

There is no need to set up timber formwork for the pad castings, as the sides of the cut-out will suffice.

The posts themselves are housed in metal plate sockets, which are set on each pad and secured with bolts to the wet concrete. Ensure that the sockets are aligned with each other, and square to the wall, by setting up temporary stringlines as a guide.

Remove any vegetation on the ground area which will be

below the deck, cover with a weed-suppressing membrane and then spread pea gravel over the surface.

Setting the supporting posts

The main supporting posts are made up from a combination of three 3m (10ft) lengths of 138 x 38mm (5½ x 1½in) timber bonded together with waterproof woodworking adhesive and secured with 100mm (4in) nails for strength, although they could be of solid timber. Each combination post has a 75mm (3in) square tenon cut at the base so that it will fit into the socket of the plate fixing attached to the concrete pad. Once cut, treat the tenons with preservative, then insert them in the sockets with their broad faces to the side of the deck.

On uneven ground the posts will not all be the same length so mark the finished height on each post. If a pergola is being incorporated into the deck, rest a length of timber on top of the lowest post so that it stretches across to the adjacent post edge. Set a spirit level on top of the timber, adjust until level, then mark the second post to the same height as the first. Repeat for the other pergola posts, then remove them one by one and saw to length.

Constructing a deck

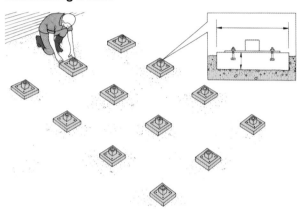

1 Concrete pads are set across the base of the proposed timber deck, and metal plate and socket fixings bolted down. The pads form the support for the deck's upright posts. Correct spacing is important. It does not matter if the ground is uneven, as the posts are cut to the correct level later, and the deck fixed horizontally.

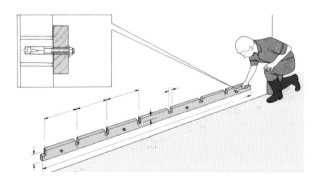

2 Attach a stout timber wallplate to the house wall, notched to take the ends of the deck joists. The plate is bolted to the masonry.

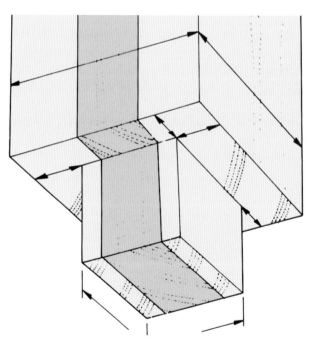

3 The main support posts are made up of three lengths of timber bonded together with glue and nails. The bottom end is then tenoned to fit into the plate sockets.

Timber decking

Fitting the deck joists

The deck joists are nailed around the supporting posts at the required height for the platform. You may also want to incorporate a split-level surface in the deck, in which case upper and lower joists will be needed.

Mark on the outer support posts the height for the underside of the joists, then measure the lengths required and cut from in 138 x 38mm (5½ x 1½in) timber. Hold the outer joists against the marked posts, set horizontal with a spirit level placed on top, then secure to the sides of the posts with 100mm (4in) nails or use galvanized screws.

Use four nails per post, arranged as the corners of a square. Butt-join the return lengths of joist timber end-to-face at external corners.

Installing a wallplate

Where the deck adjoins the house wall it is necessary to attach a stout timber wallplate for the outer joists and intermediate timbers to rest on. Measure the length required and cut from 138 x 38mm (5½ x 1½in) timber. Mark out notches 69mm (2¾in) deep and 38mm (1½in) wide on the top edge of the wallplate, spaced 423mm (16½in) apart, with a notch at each end to take the outer joists. Cut the notches using a saw and chisel.

Drill holes in the wallplate at 450mm (18in) intervals to take masonry bolts, hold against the wall and mark through the fixing holes. Secure the wallplate to the wall, ensuring that it is set perfectly horizontal, and at the correct height to coincide with the ends of the joists.

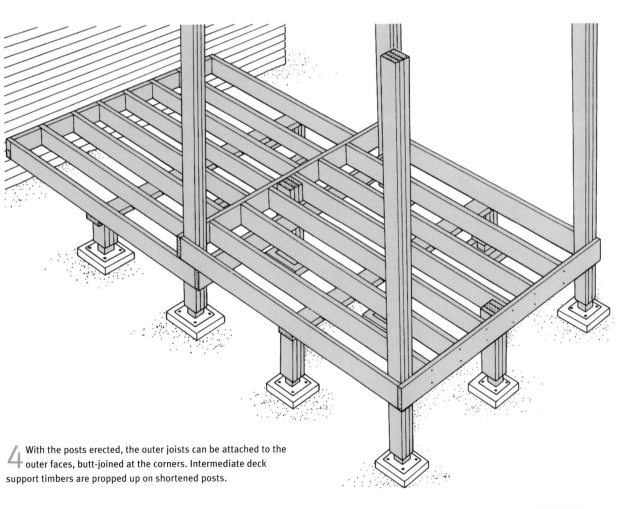

4 With the posts erected, the outer joists can be attached to the outer faces, butt-joined at the corners. Intermediate deck support timbers are propped up on shortened posts.

Timber decking

Fitting the intermediate deck supports
Intermediate deck supports are provided by lengths of 127 x 12 x 38mm (5 x ½ x 1½in) timber laid flat under the joists and supported on the combination support posts which have been cut down. Measure the distance from the base of each intermediate post to the underside of the outer joists and deduct 38mm (1½in). Cut the posts to this length and slot them in their sockets, supporting the deck support timber. Nail the deck support timber to the ends of the posts.

Fitting the joists
Cut the intermediate joists to length to span from the front outer joists to the wall, then cut notches to match those cut in the wallplate. The tops of the intermediate joists must be level with the top edge of the wallplate and the top edge of the outer joists. Fit the joists by setting their notched ends on the wallplate and butting the other ends against the inside face of the outer joist. Secure by driving nails through the outer joists into the end of the intermediate joists. Nail through the notched joints into the wallplate at the other end.

Laying the decking timber
When the outer framework of the deck has been erected, lay the decking surface. Cut all the lengths of timber to fit between the outer joists, then position them across the framework and

secure at each joist position with 75mm (3in) round wire nails. Space each of the slats about 3 to 4mm (⅛ to 3⁄₁₆in) apart for ventilation and drainage of rainwater from the surface.

Incorporating rails and seating
Side rails can be built around the decking by using the main supporting posts as corner supports. Nail lengths of 75 x 50mm (3 x 2in) timber horizontally across the posts, about 450mm (18in) from the deck surface. Fix intermediate supporting posts of 75mm (3in) sq timber between the deck surface and the rail: these supports should be notched to accommodate the rail near the top and at the bottom to fit over the edge of the outer joists, to which they are then nailed. Thinner balusters (the uprights) of 38mm (1½ in) sq timber can be nailed underneath the rail, spaced about 50mm (2in) apart, at each side of a small flight of stops leading up the front of the deck.

Intermediate posts can be used to form the framework of a built-in seating unit, clad with planks of thinner timber.

Incorporating a tree seat
If you have an attractive tree in your garden, within the proposed area of the raised decking, you will be able to incorporate this feature in the overall design of the unit. Construct a wall around the tree from bricks, concrete walling

5 Cut the decking slats to length and nail to the tops of the joists, using two fixings per joist. Leave a gap of 4mm (³⁄₁₆in) between each slat, using a wooden spacer as a guide.

6 Thinner balusters fixed under the rail form an attractive frontage to the decking. Set them at each side of a pair of intermediate posts fixed at each side of the entrance steps.

Timber decking

blocks, dry-stone walling blocks, or even timber, so that it protrudes through the floor of the decking by about 450mm (18in). Simple bench seating fixed to the top of the wall will provide a shady place to sit.

Preparing the foundations

Before you start to construct the decking to incorporate the tree, build the wall around the tree. For a masonry wall you will, of course, have to create suitable foundations on which to build. A basic strip foundation around the perimeter of the proposed wall will be sufficient (see page 88), although you must be careful not to damage the roots of the tree when digging the foundation trench.

Where the roots are large, you will have to bridge the foundation trench to avoid them; make sure that this does not unduly affect the stability of the wall. If the roots are small you may be able to trim them back a little (although this will have the effect of limiting the tree's growth above ground).

Making the seat

Cast the concrete foundations and allow to cure properly before building the wall. The total height of the wall depends on how high the decking is above ground level, but usually you will need to lay about ten courses of bricks to give sufficient height above deck level for comfortable sitting.

Lay the bricks in stretcher bond, turning bricks in alternate courses to continue the return walls. When the wall is built to the correct height, neaten the mortar joints and allow to set hard for at least two days. If you are using blocks, the principle of construction is the same.

The seat itself is composed of eight lengths of 75 x 25mm (5 x 1in) softwood screwed in pairs to three cross-pieces of 50 x 25mm (2 x 1in) softwood. Arrange the pairs around the walls, abutting them end-to-face. Attach the cross-pieces to each face of the walls using metal angle brackets screwed into wallplugs.

A timber seat unit

Create an informal timber tree seat protruding from the raised decking using railway sleeper-style wooden blocks stacked as for a retaining wall (see page 164). Allow about three courses of blocks above the level of the timber decking for a comfortable seat height. Connect the layers of wooden blocks with a metal band bent over the top and screwed through pre-drilled holes to a sleeper in each row.

Adapting the decking

Naturally, because the decking is pierced by the tree seat walling, you will have to adapt the structure accordingly. To do

this, you will have to construct a timber frame around the wall, and ideally fixed to it, in order to support the ends of the decking slats.

Run the slat support joists alongside the side walls of the tree seat and attach them with expanding bolts, as used to attach the wallplate. To support the ends of the joists running up to the front and back faces of the side walls you will need to fit secondary wallplates, in exactly the same way as the main wallplate, notched to accept the ends of the joists. With a timber sleeper wall, simply screw on the joists and secondary wallplates. Fix the decking slats to the joists, as previously described, nailing them additionally to the supporting timbers surrounding the tree seat walling.

DECKING SAFETY AND MAINTENANCE

Check, when you purchase timber for use in a garden deck, that it is suitable for its purpose – your supplier will be able to tell you if it meets the specifications for your proposed use. If using hardwood for the deck, satisfy yourself that it has come from sustainable sources. Softwood is a cheaper option, but it is more prone to rot and will splinter.

Raised decking structures should be surrounded by railings. Any elevated deck should, ideally, be checked by a building contractor who can ascertain its safety. Choose grooved timber planks for the deck floor as these offer more grip, especially if the decking has become wet or damp. All the metal fixings used in the construction of the deck should be galvanized to prevent them from rusting.

When working with wood, ensure that you wear suitable protective clothing – gloves will protect you from splinters, and remember that skin should not come into contact with treated or preserved wood for any length of time. When sawing or sanding wood, cover your eyes with goggles and wear a dust mask.

If you have a large quantity of treated wood waste to dispose of at the end of the project, contact a waste disposal contractor. Small quantities of off-cuts and sawdust can be disposed of safely, but do not be tempted to use preservative-treated wood or its sawdust as a mulch, nor add it to a compost heap. Do not burn preserved wood.

Regularly move any containers and furniture that sit on the timber and brush down the decking to keep it clean – using a stiff-bristled brush should remove any mildew or slippery algae. For a more thorough clean, garden centres and do-it-yourself retailers sell proprietary deck cleaners.

Perform an annual maintenance check to assess any cracking (wood expands and contracts) or if any parts of the deck have suffered rotting or attack from insects. Fix or replace any rotting, wobbling or warped planks or supports. Treat annually with a preservative or wood stain if necessary – choose an appropriate preservative and follow the instructions on application given on the container. If the deck is painted, repaint regularly, sanding down the old paintwork first.

Steps: introduction

When level changes occur in the garden it is essential that the transition can be made from one level to another as easily and comfortably as possible. Steps offer the most efficient way of changing levels. Besides being functional, they can make a significant contribution to the appearance of a garden, and are frequently used as major focal points. Steps give pedestrian access to the various parts of a sloping or split-level garden, while also providing a visual link between the separate elements – vegetable patch, lawn, beds, and so on.

Steps and their surroundings

Steps should be in proportion with, and the same width as, any associated paths. They should be planned to be in proportion with the particular wall or slope with which they are associated and also with the garden itself. When too small they will appear mean or insignificant; when too large they can easily look pretentious. There are basically two types of steps – freestanding or cut-in – although there are many variations in the construction materials.

Cut-in steps

Cut-in steps are used where you need to negotiate a slope or a bank. The shape of the steps is cut out in the earth itself and various materials used for the treads (the parts of the steps on which you walk) and risers (the vertical parts). Cut-in steps may be formal, regular flights or meandering and informal.

Freestanding steps

Where you need access from ground level to a higher, terraced level, freestanding steps are more suitable. Built either at right angles to the retaining wall of the terrace, or parallel with it, so standing proud of their surroundings, they are usually formal in appearance.

Step formats

Sketch out the position and shape of the steps on squared paper to help you to determine how they will look and how they will fit in with the existing garden plan. Perhaps most important is to draw a side elevation of the steps, which will show you just how steep they will need to be.

You will have to take into account certain safety criteria with regard to the format. If the flight is too steep, it will be tiring to climb. Where it is too shallow there is a danger of tripping. The following dimensions are typical for comfortable, safe walking:

Basic step types

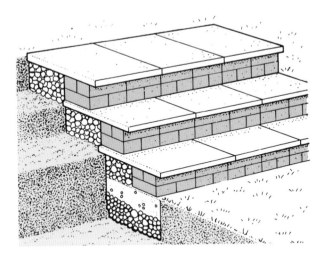

Freestanding steps

Freestanding steps are built between one flat area and another, and the bricks are "toothed into" the retaining wall to prevent the structures from parting. The perimeter walls that form the sides of the flight are built either on a raft foundation or on strip foundations under each wall.

Cut-in steps

Cut-in steps are built into a bank or slope, the shape of the flight sculpted in the ground itself, which forms the foundation. The bottom of the flight rests on a concrete strip footing. The bottom riser is built on the foundation and backfilled with hardcore, then treads are laid on top of this; subsequent risers and treads are built on the back of (or behind) the lower treads.

Risers should usually be 100–125mm (4–5in) deep, but may be up to 150 or 175mm (6 or 7in).

Treads should not be less than 300mm (12in) from front to back (sufficient to take the ball of your foot when descending without the back of your leg scraping on the step above). Consider who will use the steps: treads 600mm (24in) wide will accommodate only one person; for two people walking side by side make them 1.5m (60in) wide.

The nosing is the front edge of the tread, which should project beyond the riser by about 25mm (1in) to define the shape of the step with an edge of shadow.

Proportions for steps

A golden rule when designing steps is that every riser (the vertical plane) and every tread (the horizontal plane) should be consistently proportioned in the same flight. Where steps are created from natural materials such as rock or logs it can take some effort to achieve this, but an uncomfortable, even dangerous, ascent or descent will result if the steps are not as regular as possible.

About every 10 or 12 steps, there should be a landing to allow a short respite and the size of the landing should be a multiple of the size of the tread, front to back, again to allow smooth and safe progress.

There is a recognized relationship between the size of the riser and that of the tread: the deeper the tread, the shallower the riser should be. Garden steps tend to have deeper treads and shallower risers than their domestic counterparts, so they are less steep.

For reasons of safety, the risers of garden steps should not be less than 100mm (4in) or more than 200mm (8in). Their precise size, however, ultimately depends upon the height to be achieved and the space available and their style upon the design of the areas they will link.

STEPS OF DIFFERING STYLES AND MATERIALS

Steps contribute to the appearance of a garden, to the extent that they are often used as major focal points. They range from functional looking bricks and slab combinations to grander constructions that entice the visitor to explore another level

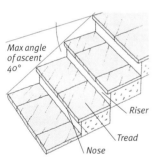

The angle of ascent should not exceed 40° in a garden. The nose is the upper and outermost front edge corner of tread.

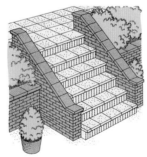

These brick and reconstituted stone steps are half-in and half-out of the slope, making use of the space at both top and bottom.

Curving steps are always intriguing. These are made of treated logs and consolidated gravel and are suitable for a woodland setting.

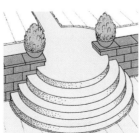

Semi-circular steps are one of the most popular styles. They are excellent for announcing a view from the top.

Making log and curved steps

Masonry steps can appear incongruous in an informal garden and their regular appearance may be a little hard in, say, a woodland setting or wildlife garden. In such instances, timber steps will often be more appropriate. Cut-in steps are more suitable for this type of garden, and using sawn logs as the risers is a quick and easy way to form an attractive flight.

In more formal garden settings, steps need not always conform to a straight format. Where you have enough space, consider creating a flight composed of circular or segmental treads to scale a graceful shallow rise in the ground, perhaps leading to a formal terrace beyond.

Log steps

At each step position, drive in stout, rough-hewn stakes to align with the nosing position at each side. Place a log behind the stakes so that they support it, then backfill with hardcore. Ram down the hardcore with a sledgehammer, then top with fine gravel as the tread surface.

You can also make up a single riser from two or more slimmer logs stacked on top of each other. As an alternative to using round logs you can obtain railway sleeper-type wood blocks sold specifically for use in garden construction. Fix the sleepers with stakes, as for logs, to create a more formal yet still rustic flight.

Turning the flight within the bank or slope is easily done by simply fanning out the logs or sleepers.

When using timber steps, be wary of the treads becoming slippery after rainfall. There is no truly effective way to prevent this from happening, but a chickenwire covering and keeping the steps clear of moss and lichen will lessen the risk of a slip.

Making curved steps

Mark out the shape of the steps with an improvised pair of compasses made from a length of wood attached to a stake with string. Cut out the rough shape of the circular treads and cast concrete slab foundations beneath (see pages 92–93). There is no need to make the foundation slab round, however; just cover the corners with soil after you have built the steps.

Use bricks or blocks laid on mortar to form the curving front edges of the treads, and fill the circles with gravel or cobblestones to create an attractive effect. You could even lay turf within the brick circles for a grassy flight of steps, but bear in mind that these would be very difficult to maintain and mow satisfactorily.

Circular landings

A variation on curved steps is to create circular landings, staggered and part-overlapping on a shallow slope. Use the same construction methods as for curved steps, adding compacted hardcore before the gravel.

A flight of log steps and brick-and-gravel circular steps

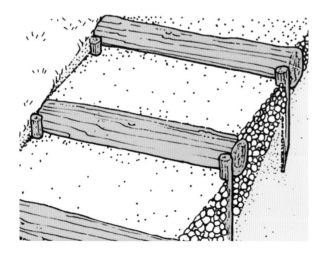

Log steps are created by supporting log risers with wooden stakes and backfilling with gravel.

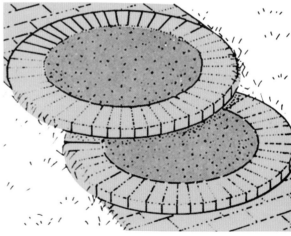

Circular landings are made from brick risers backfilled with gravel, stones or other paving material.

Profile boards

Profile boards used to mark out strip foundations (see pages 90–91) can also be used to set the building lines for constructing a set of garden steps. Use a pair of profile boards and strings to mark the front edge of the U-shaped foundation trench needed for the steps. For the side walls of the steps, set up profile boards at the front end, the strings intersecting the previously fixed ones at right angles.

Stringlines At the terrace wall, you cannot fix profile boards. Instead, connect the ends of the strings to the masonry of the terrace with masonry nails driven in at the correct height and width – check for accuracy with a spirit level.

Position the stringlines to correspond with the width of the brickwork or block-work you intend to use to construct the side walls.

Transferring guidelines Transfer the positions of the stringlines to a screed of bricklaying mortar trowelled onto the concrete strip foundation by running a spirit level, held vertically with a trowel blade held at its base, along the mortar.

SETTING UP PROFILE BOARDS

Profile boards, used in pairs, are utilized to indicate the position of the trench for when constructing strip foundations. Each profile board consists of a piece of wood nailed across two batons. These batons have pointed ends and can be driven into the soil.

Although the stringlines could simply be tied firmly into place, there is a danger that the string could move or slip. Instead, for greater accuracy, knock nails into the profile boards to correspond with the width of the building material and attach strings to the nails (shown right). Two sets of profile boards are required to mark out corners. Transfer the positions of the parallel stringlines to a screed of mortar using a spirit level for accuracy and a trowel to mark the mortar (illustrated below). This gives a line to follow when laying the first course of bricks.

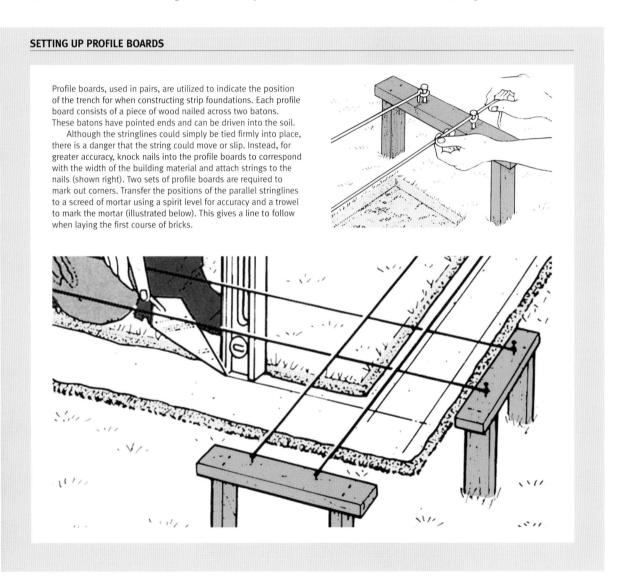

Casting concrete steps

Calculating the number of steps

To work out how many steps you will need, measure the vertical height you need to scale and divide this figure by the height of a single riser plus tread.

With a terraced site just measure the height of the retaining wall. On a sloping site the job is more complicated (see page 125). Drive a peg into the ground at the top of the slope and a length of cane into the ground at the base of the slope. Tie a length of string between the peg and the cane and set it horizontal using a spirit level. Measure the distance from the base of the cane to the string to give the vertical height of the slope: divide this by the depth of a riser plus tread to give the number of steps that will fit into the slope.

Safety features

Steep flights should include a handrail – about 840mm (2ft 9in) above tread height – on each side, which extends about 300mm (12in) beyond the flight, linked with existing fencing or railings for a unified scheme. Alternatively you could build a wall (at handrail height) at each side of the flight.

Flights comprising more than 10 steps should be broken halfway with a landing which provides a good resting place and can also break a fall. Take this into account when calculating the number of treads required.

The treads should slope slightly towards the front – a fall of about 1/2in (12mm) is adequate – so that rainwater will drain off rapidly. This is particularly important in winter, when ice would make the steps slippery and dangerous. For the same reason, choose only slab treads with non-slip textured faces.

Drainage from the steps

Although you should slope the front of the treads forward, this could cause damp problems where the flight faces a house wall. The considerable amount of water streaming down the treads must be diverted from the wall by creating a shallow cross channel at the base of the stops loading to an existing drainage inlet or gully.

On steps that run adjacent to walls it is also advisable to include drainage channels on the wall side of the flight, so that water can be taken from the surface of the treads.

Material options

The materials you choose should blend in with their context. For example, when building freestanding steps up to a terrace, use the same materials for the risers as were used for the retaining wall of the terrace; where the steps continue an existing path, use the same paving materials for the treads.

Many types of bricks, blocks, pavers, walling blocks and paving slabs are suitable for use in constructing garden steps. You can use bricks and blocks both for the risers and for the treads; face textures may be smooth, pitted or, in the case of decorative concrete blocks, resemble split stone. Slabs,

---

CAST CONCRETE STEPS

Cast concrete steps are made by constructing timber shuttering in situ, adding a hardcore backfilling, then topping with about 100mm (4in) thickness of concrete. The formwork tray must be be staked and braced to prevent the concrete from forcing it apart. As an alternative to using timber formwork you can construct the side shuttering from 20mm (3/4in) thick plywood.

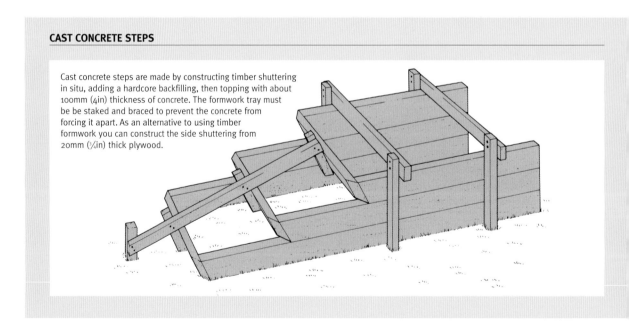

although suitable only for the treads, may be smooth-faced, riven, or even patterned for an ornate appearance.

Softening the appearance of steps

A flight of steps can appear harsh and angular unless you visually soften them in some way. Colourful edging plants introduced at the sides of cut-in steps will minimize the angularity of the flight. You can even plant low-growing species against the risers: this will reduce the harsh lines of the steps and clearly mark the change of level. On broad steps, place pots of colourful plants on the treads to create an avenue of foliage and flowers.

Casting concrete steps

A durable, if utilitarian, set of steps can be cast in concrete *in situ*. You can leave the concrete bare, or else cover it with other paving materials such as bricks, slabs or even quarry tiles. The steps are cast in timber formwork – known as "shuttering":

Tray shuttering One method of constructing concrete shuttering for garden steps is to make up a number of three-piece timber trays – one for each step – consisting of a pair of side boards with a front riser support fixed across. Use 200 x 25mm (8 x 1in) soft-wood for the trays, with the front edge of the side pieces sloping inward towards the bottom to make the top front edge of each tread protrude. Alternatively, form the sides of the steps from 20mm (³⁄₄in) thick plywood, cut to the stepped shape and fixed in place with stakes and braces.

For a tray construction, set the trays in position on the prepared foundations, remembering to slope them downwards by not more than 12mm (½in) for rainwater run-off. Support the side boards with 100 x 50mm (4 x 2in) timber stakes braced with horizontal timbers spanning the width of the flight: this is to prevent the considerable weight of the wet concrete from forcing the side boards apart. Brace the front riser supports with a diagonal length of timber staked to the ground at the base of the flight of steps, and fix wedge supports at each riser position.

Apply oil – old engine oil is suitable – to the inside faces of the shuttering to prevent the concrete from adhering to the wood. Fill most of the cavity inside the tray shuttering with hardcore, rammed down well and topped with a layer of sand to fill any large voids, leaving about 75mm (3in) depth for the layer of concrete.

Mix up the concrete, preferably using a motorized mixing machine, in the proportions 1 part cement : 2½ parts damp sand : 4 parts coarse aggregate.

Pour in the mixed concrete and work right into the corners of the trays. Tamp the mix well down, levelling it with the top of the formwork trays. Use a steel trowel to smooth the concrete. Reinforce the front edge of each tread on cast concrete steps by embedding a length of steel rod in the tread, spanning the width of the step.

Nail a length of wooden triangular moulding to the back top edge of each riser support shuttering, in order to form a bevelled nosing on each tread. This will prevent the concrete from crumbling, and at the same time avoid a sharp edge which could be a danger to young children using the steps.

Leave the concrete to harden fully for about four days, then remove the shuttering. Lay your choice of facing material directly on the concrete, bedding it in mortar. The finish on the steps should be even and slip-resistant.

Step sizes

The deeper the tread of any step, the shallower the riser should be. Garden steps are less steep than their domestic counterpart and they tend to have deeper treads and shallower risers – they are likely to have to bear regular and greater loads and be accessible in all weathers so do not rise very sharply.

As a general rule, the risers of garden steps should not be less than 100 mm (4in) or more than 200 mm (8in). The table below gives a range of dimensions for well proportioned steps, but this will depend on the style of the steps and the space available.

CALCULATING STEP SIZES

Low risers and deep treads generally appear more elegant, especially when the steps are broad from side to side. On the other hand, high risers and shallow treads look more purposeful.

Calculate step dimensions by comparing the horizontal space requirement and availability with a simple cross-section showing the height to be overcome. This will help to determine the correct riser-to-tread ratio. The amount of space available at the top or bottom of a proposed flight of steps helps to determine their position and form.

Riser (top-bottom)	Tread (back-front)
180mm (7in)	280mm (11in)
165mm (6½in)	330mm (13in)
150mm (6in)	380mm (15in)
140mm (5in)	410mm (16in)
130mm (5¼in)	430mm (17in)
115mm (4½in)	450mm (18in)
100mm (4in)	475mm (19in)

Making cut-in steps

These steps are cut out of the earth itself, to allow you to negotiate a slope or bank. Measure the vertical height of the slope (see box, opposite) to determine how many steps you will need to construct.

Building the steps

Mark out the shape and size of the flight of steps on the surface of the bank using stringlines stretched between pegs driven into the ground at the sides. Set up more strings horizontally to define the tread nosings. Working from the top of the flight, start to dig out the rough shape of the steps, and follow the instructions given below to create the steps. Note that the less you stand on the steps during construction, the better, so try to compact the earth from the sides.

On a large flight – more than, say, about 10 steps – it is advisable to cast a concrete footing in a trench at the base to

Making cut-in steps

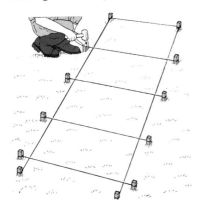

1 Set up stringlines and pegs to define the sides of the flight and the positions of the tread nosings.

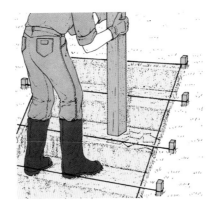

2 Cut out the rough shape of the steps using a spade, then compact the earth using a stout timber post.

3 Define the steps more accurately, according to the guide strings and the chosen size of risers and treads.

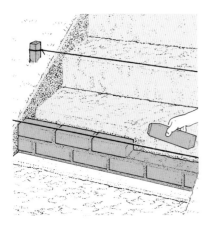

4 Lay the first riser on a concrete footing if necessary, building up two courses of bricks or blocks in a basic stretcher bond.

5 Tip hardcore behind the riser in the tread position, ram this down well, then top with sand to fill the hollows.

6 Lay the slab treads on a perimeter screed of mortar, aligning the nosings with the stringlines.

Above: It is important to choose a garden gate that is in keeping with its setting. Picket fences with a diagonal brace are among the easiest styles to make at home.

Left: A traditional painted wooden door will enhance a garden entrance. Doors and gates need to be made from the best materials and well maintained to ensure a long life.

Left: Steps are an obvious solution for uneven levels or for leading the visitor from one area of the garden to another. These semi-circular steps lead from a patio to a outdoor dining area enclosed within a wooden pergola.

support the bottom riser and prevent the entire flight from sliding down the bank. Dig the trench under the position of the bottom riser, about twice the front-to-back measurement of the riser, about 100mm (4in) wider than the step, and about 100mm (4in) deep. Ram hardcore into the base of the trench and top up to ground level with fresh concrete. Compact the concrete, level it and allow to set overnight.

Construct the first riser on the concrete footing using your choice of blocks, bricks or stone. Whichever riser material you choose, follow basic bricklaying techniques (see pages 130–131) and adapt the technique for the steps.

Cutting bricks or blocks

Stagger the joints between bricks or blocks by half the brick or block length in the first and second courses to form a basic stretcher bond. To maintain this bonding arrangement you will have to cut the end units in half. To cut a brick or block, score a line on the brick with a bolster chisel, place the brick or block on a firm, flat surface and strike with a club hammer and the bolster chisel.

Laying the first tread

Tip hardcore behind the riser and ram it down well – but take care not to dislodge the riser in doing so. Add more hardcore up to the base of the tread position and ram this down too. You are now ready to lay the tread.

Slab tread Lift a slab into position on the prepared base and align its top outer edge with the first stringline. If the fit seems accurate, remove the slab and trowel a screed of mortar

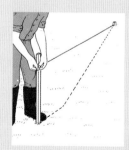

MEASURING THE SLOPE

Work out how many steps you will need to negotiate the slope by measuring the vertical height of the slope. To do this, drive a peg into the top of the slope and a cane at the bottom. Connect the peg and cane with string. The string must be horizontal to give an accurate reading – check this using a spirit level – then measure the cane from ground level to the height reached by the string.

If a whole number of steps is not possible (the measurement is likely to fall short or run over a whole number) you will need to dig out the ground at the base or add earth at the top.

around the perimeter of the riser. Alternatively, you can stick down the tread using five dabs or a complete bed of mortar; the latter is best for a flight that will be put to heavy use.

Press the slab onto the mortar and wiggle it to compress the mortar. If the step is two slabs wide, lay the second slab, leaving a small gap between the first and the second slab, to be filled later with a dry sand and cement (3:1) mix.

Use a spirit level to check that the slabs are level with each other; check also that they slope not more than 12mm (½in) towards the nosing for rainwater run-off. Tap the front edge gently but firmly with the shaft of your club hammer to give the correct slope.

Small-scale treads You can use bricks or blocks as the treads, laying them on mortar in the same way as slabs. Nosings should overhang the risers in the usual way. As with slab treads, ensure a slight slope towards the front for drainage.

Laying the remaining steps

The second riser can be laid on the back edge of the first tread, or immediately behind it on a base of hardcore topped with sand. Trowel a screed of mortar beneath the riser position and lay the bricks or blocks as previously described. Backfill with hardcore as before and lay the second tread. Continue laying risers and treads in this way to complete the flight.

To neaten mortar joints between bricks, scrape off excess and form a half-round profile by running a length of hosepipe along the joints. Brush a dry mortar mix between the slab treads, or else fill the joints with wet mortar and neaten the profiles. Point the back edge of the tread where it meets the riser above. Allow the mortar to harden for about one week.

7 Incorporate drainage fall by angling the treads slightly downwards towards the front. Use a shim to keep this angle consistent (see page 92).

Making freestanding steps

Freestanding steps should be constructed in the same or similar materials as the vertical terrace they are intended to climb, and ideally should be tied into the terrace as an integral feature.

Construct strip foundations to support the perimeter walls of the steps, and set up stringlines and profile boards as a guide to laying the masonry (see box, page 119). The strings should be aligned centrally on the strip foundation, spaced apart by the width of the bricks or blocks you have chosen.

Constructing the first riser

The flight of steps is made up of a number of plinths which are two courses of bricks or blocks deep. Each plinth is smaller than the lower one by the front-to-back dimension of the treads. The plinths, stacked one on top of the other, with their back edges flush, form the skeleton of the steps.

Start to build the first plinth on the strip foundations you have cast. Mix up some mortar in the proportions 1 part cement : 5 parts sand. Trowel a 10mm (⅜in) thick screed of mortar onto the strip foundation, then transfer the position of the stringlines onto this layer as illustrated on page 119.

Furrow the surface of the mortar screed with the trowel to aid suction and adhesion of the masonry.

Starting at the terrace side, lay the first course of bricks or blocks for the riser, lining up the edges with the scribed line on the screed. Wiggle the brick or block as you press it down to bed it firmly and evenly, then tap with the handle of your trowel. Butter the ends of the bricks or blocks with wedges of wet mortar to form the vertical joints and press into place against the previously laid piece.

At the corner of the riser, turn a brick or block at right angles to continue the wall onto the front face. Trowel mortar on top of the first course of masonry and lay the second course in the same way, this time staggering the joints by half, stretcher fashion.

Place a spirit level along the stretcher-bonded walls to ensure they are horizontal, and adjust if necessary. If the mortar joints are not applied at a consistent thickness, the perimeter walls will not rise evenly. Span across both side walls with the spirit level on a long straight-edged plank to check that they, too, are aligned.

Toothing in the steps

In order that the flight of steps is permanently and rigidly attached to the terrace wall, it is necessary to bond the riser side walls into it. This is done by "toothing in" – by chopping out alternate bricks or blocks from the terrace and inserting alternate bricks from the new walls into the hole by half their length.

Chop out the masonry carefully using a club hammer and cold chisel. Brush dust and debris from the hole and dampen the surface to avoid the masonry sucking too much moisture from the fresh mortar, which could cause it to crack. Trowel mortar into the base of the hole, and around the end of the new brick or block. Insert the brick or block into the hole and tap to bed it down.

Backfilling the plinth

Leave the mortar to set for a few hours before backfilling the plinth with hardcore. Tip in the broken bricks and rubble and ram well down. No hardcore must protrude above the level of the masonry walls.

Spread a layer of sand over the hardcore to blind the surface, filling hollows. Draw a length of wood across the walls to level and smooth the sand.

Laying the subsequent plinths

Reposition the stringlines as a guide to laying the second riser walls, stretching them between canes stuck in the ground just outside the concrete footings – at this stage the profile board will be of no further use and can be removed.

Construct the second riser plinth on top of the first, its front edge set back by the front-to-back dimension of the tread. Tooth the masonry into the terrace wall. Backfill this plinth with hardcore, top with sand, then build the remaining plinths by the same procedure until the flight has reached the top of the terrace.

As the plinth walls rise, check frequently that they are horizontal. You can check whether the walls are bowing outwards by holding a long spirit level or length of straight-edged timber diagonally against the sides: any curvature should be corrected before the mortar starts to harden.

Check also that the mortar joints are the same thickness throughout, using a gauge rod: this is made of a length of timber marked off in brick-plus-mortar joint increments. Held vertically against the plinth walls it will show where the joints become inconsistent.

Fitting the treads

When the masonry shell of the steps is finished you can add the treads. For slab treads, trowel five dabs of mortar onto the hardcore and sand base and lower the tread into place. Tap down with the shaft of a trowel, incorporating the drainage fall towards the front.

Lay the treads for the remaining plinths in the same way, then point all the mortar joints in the walls and between the slab treads. Allow the mortar to set fully for about one week before using the steps.

Making freestanding steps

Completing the flight

At the top of the flight of steps you should try to continue the run of treads into the existing surface at the same level. This is straightforward where the steps lead up to an existing paved area, but where the steps finish at a raised lawn or planting bed it is a good idea to run a path of slabs or bricks through it to give a sense that the steps lead somewhere. Steep steps should be fitted with handrails at each side, as for cut-in steps (see page 120), while large freestanding flights can be built with integral side walls, stepped as the flight rises, and capped with slab copings to match the treads. These should be at handrail height, about 840mm (2ft 9in).

Making freestanding steps

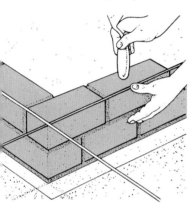

1 Lay the bricks for the first riser in two courses of stretcher bond, aligning the outer top edge with stringlines set up at the perimeter of the foundations.

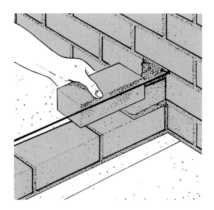

2 Tooth the risers into the terrace wall on alternate courses. Chop out a brick and insert the last riser brick into the hole by half its length, bedded on mortar.

3 Tip hardcore into the plinth and compact it thoroughly with a stout timber post or sledgehammer, taking care not to dislodge the newly laid brickwork walls.

4 Spread sand over the hardcore. Using a straight-edged length of wood, scrape the sand level with the top edge of the plinth risers ready to accept the treads.

5 Lay the subsequent risers over the first plinth, using the same bonding arrangement. Check frequently that the walls are not bowing at the sides.

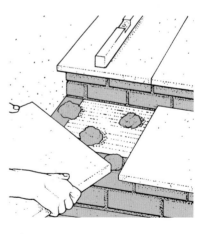

6 Bed down the treads on five dabs of mortar trowelled on the hardcore and sand base. Set the slabs level across the surface but sloping forwards slightly.

Walls: materials

Walls perform numerous functions in the garden, such as defining boundaries, screening unattractive views, dulling traffic noise and providing protection against the elements.

Choice of materials

The materials you choose to construct your garden wall must be suitable for the purpose you want it to perform. Bear in mind colour, texture, shape, and size when choosing materials so that the wall will not look incongruous. The clean lines of some types of bricks suit a formal design, whereas decorative walling blocks are more rugged in appearance and evocative of an informal, natural style. Secondhand bricks or stones are usually available from builder's merchants and demolition sites, and often have a more mellow, weathered look.

Natural stone blocks are laid without mortar to create a traditional dry-stone wall with its distinctive angled face, common as English field boundaries but just as successful when used in the garden. See pages 134–135 for more details.

Bricks

Moulded from fire-burnt clay or calcium silicate, bricks are made in standard metric units measuring 225 x 112.5 x 75mm, which corresponds roughly to the old imperial size of $8^{7}/_{8}$ x $4^{3}/_{8}$ x 3in. Compatibility of size is important where you intend to match a new wall with an old wall. The dimensions given for bricks are, in fact, nominal, as the actual size is $^{3}/_{8}$in (10mm) less all round to allow for the thickness of a mortar joint. Of the many types available, only three are suitable for garden walling.

Facing bricks, also known as stocks, have an attractive finish on the sides and ends and come in various colours with rough or smooth textures. Faced versions have only one or two attractive sides.

Common bricks are used where appearance is not vital, and are less costly than facing types. Commons have no special facing and are best painted or rendered. Do not use where they are likely to be subjected to heavy stress.

Engineering bricks are dense, smooth and impervious to water, and best for walls that will be exposed to dampness, or where part of the wall will be buried underground. Two classifications of engineering bricks are made – A and B – depending on their combined strength and water-resistance.

Colour and origin

Bricks are also known by a variety of names, which generally refer to their colour and texture, but often to their place of origin and the colour of the clay used in their manufacture – Flettons (from the Cambridgeshire village where they originated), Staffordshire Blues, Leicester Reds, Kentish stocks (in shades of yellow), Dorking stocks (in shades of pink) are examples.

Special-shaped bricks There is a variety of special-shaped bricks which are used to give a decorative effect to a plain wall, or to protect the structure from the effects of rain. Bullnoses and bullheads are rectangular, but with one rounded end for use as a stopped end on a garden wall.

Curved bricks are curved in length for use on rounded walls or arches.

Copings come in rounded, bevelled or chamfered format, and are set at the top of a wall to finish it neatly while throwing

---

BRICK BONDS

Bricks and blocks are generally laid in an overlapping "bond" to create a rigid structure and to spread the load to the foundations. There are a number of different bonds used for walls, the most basic of which are half-brick and single-brick walls.

Half-brick walls. Single thickness, half-brick walls are laid in a "running" or stretcher bond in which the bricks are laid end to end with their long stretcher faces showing. Alternate rows are staggered by half the length of the brick.

Single-brick walls. Double thickness, single-brick walls consist of parallel pairs of half-brick walls with courses of headers – or bricks laid across the width of the wall so that their end faces are visible.

Flemish Garden Wall bond has three or five stretchers to one header per course, the headers often of contrasting colour for decorative effect.

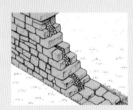

Dry-stone walls are constructed without mortar, using large edging blocks with smaller infill pieces, tied by large flat stones.

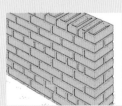

English Garden Wall bond has stretcher and header courses; three or five courses of stretchers to one of headers.

Reconstituted stone block walls are laid in the same way as bricks. Modular units span two or more courses at a time.

rainwater clear. They may overhang the wall thickness to give a lip that prevents water trickling down the face of the wall. *Corner pieces* are specially shaped copings that span a right-angle corner in a run of walling.

Bricks with frogs and holes

Some bricks have an indent in one face, known as the frog, which is intended to provide a good strong bond with the mortar. Normally laid uppermost, the frog is filled with mortar during bricklaying. Performing the same role, some bricks have holes pierced through their middles, into which mortar is forced as the joints are formed between courses.

Building piers

Straight walls of brickwork or blockwork more than about 915mm (3ft) high should be supported and strengthened by

the addition of a column, or pier, at 1.8m (6ft) intervals, and at each end of the wall. The piers should be linked with the bonding pattern used for the wall.

Forming corners

When turning a corner in brickwork you must maintain the bonding arrangement for strength and continuity. At its most basic, on a stretcher bond wall where bricks overlap each other by half, the corner is formed by turning one brick at right angles to form the return wing of the wall, then alternating bricks at subsequent courses to maintain the pattern.

It is good building practice to build up the corners and ends of a wall first, shortening each new corner by one brick and ending in a whole brick. This process, called racking back, gives the corners and ends a chance to become stable before the section between them is filled in.

Piers and corners in stretcher bond

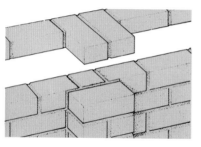

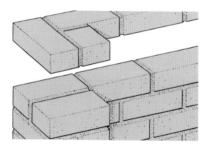

An intermediate pier is formed by alternating two bricks header-on with half brick and two three-quarter bricks in the next course.

An end pier in stretcher bond is formed by turning alternate bricks header-on and filling in at the courses between with half bricks.

A corner in a half-brick stretcher bond wall is formed by turning a brick at right angles, then alternating the bond on each course.

Special finishing bricks

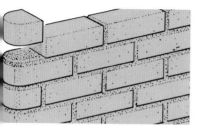

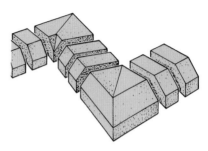

Bullnose bricks are rounded at one end to give a neat curved finish to the stop-end of a garden wall of single brick thickness.

Rounded coping bricks are mortared along the top of a wall, and overhang the sides slightly. Drip grooves allow rain to drain away.

Bevelled coping and corner bricks are used on the top of a masonry wall. The corner bricks match the chamfered copings.

Walls: laying

Bricks and concrete blocks enable you to construct straight, curved or angular walls anything from a couple of courses to several feet in height.

However, bricklaying is not a task to be undertaken lightly, and it is essential to learn the basic skills before embarking on a full-scale project. Master the techniques described below and adapt the methods to your particular requirements.

Setting out the foundations

Accurately setting out the foundations of a wall or other masonry structure is of prime importance if the wall is to be laid level, square and adequately supported.

For accuracy in laying the bricks, set up wooden profile boards at each end of the foundation trench, with stringlines stretched between them, spaced apart by the width of the wall – either 110 or 230mm (4½ or 9in) depending on whether you are building a half- or single-brick wall.

Bricklaying equipment

Start by familiarizing yourself with the tools you will need for bricklaying:

A bricklayer's trowel is used to pick up, shape and apply mortar to the foundation and the bricks. The shaft of the trowel is used to tap individual bricks or blocks into place.

A spotboard is a panel of chipboard, plywood or blockboard about 600mm (2ft) square, used to hold the mortar close to the wall you are building; mount it on a portable workbench or stack of bricks so that you can easily scoop off mortar.

A hawk is a smaller board fitted with a handle, with which you can hold small quantities of mortar while laying the bricks.

A spirit level is used frequently to check that individual bricks or blocks and complete courses are horizontal; the level is also used to check that the wall does not bow outwards.

A gauge rod is used to check that the mortar joints are consistently 10mm (⅜in) thick.

A bolster chisel has a sharp, straight edge for cutting bricks.

A club hammer is mallet-shaped and is used with a bolster chisel for cutting bricks. First, mark the break point by holding the bolster chisel at right angles to the brick and tapping the upper end gently with the club hammer. Repeat this on all four faces. Then place the chisel on the stretcher face that will be visible and give a firm stroke with the hammer.

Laying bricks

1 Set up profile boards, then spread a 10mm (⅜in) thick screed of mortar over the concrete strip foundation. Furrow the surface with the trowel as the improves the adhesion.

2 Butter the end of the brick with mortar, by drawing the loaded trowel across the end, forming a wedge shape. Furrow the wedge of mortar by drawing the trowel along it in ridges.

Walls: laying

Pins and strings are used to set each brick course horizontal (see illustration, page 132).
Buckets are needed for proportioning the ingredients of the bricklaying mortar,

A spade is needed for mixing the constituents that will make up the mortar on a hard, flat surface (such as a large square board laid flat on a path or drive).
A wheelbarrow is needed to transport quantities of bricks.

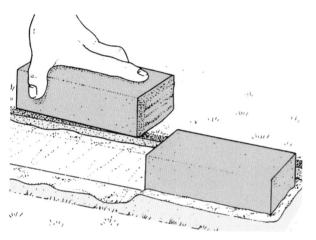

3 Lay the first brick on the mortar screed, flush with the end of the wall. Butt the mortared end of the second brick up to the clean end of the first laid brick.

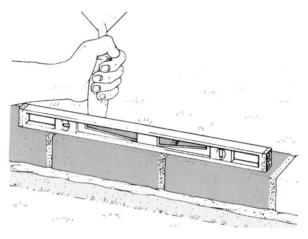

4 Place a spirit level along the course and tap the bricks horizontal using the shaft of your trowel. Pack under low bricks with more mortar to level them.

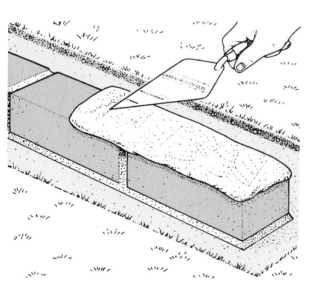

5 Trowel a screed of mortar onto the bricks of the first course, furrow the surface for better adhesion and position the second course of bricks on top.

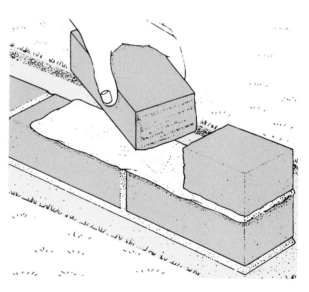

6 Lay the second course as for the first, but start off the course with a brick cut in half across its width to maintain the bond. Continue to lay further courses, checking the level as before.

Walls: building levels

Basic bricklaying techniques

Mix up the mortar and tip it onto the spotboard. Scoop up two or three trowel-loads and transfer the mortar to your hawk. Practise slicing off some mortar and scooping it onto your trowel by sliding the blade underneath. Learn how to place the mortar properly: hold the trowel over the site and draw it backwards sharply, turning it over at the same time so that a sausage shape of mortar rolls off the blade.

Using this action, spread a 10mm ($^3/_8$in) thick screed of mortar along the concrete strip foundation on which you are going to build the wall. Furrow the surface of the screed by drawing your trowel blade back along it in ridges.

Transfer the positions of the stringlines fixed to the profile board to the screed by running a spirit level vertically along each and scribing the mortar with a trowel blade.

Laying the bricks

Position the first brick on the screed of mortar, aligned with the scribed marks at each side, and flush with the proposed end of the wall. Press the brick firmly down, wiggling it to increase the suction. Some mortar will be squeezed from the sides of the brick. Scoop up the mortar from the base of the first-laid brick and use to form the vertical joint between it and the second brick.

Scrape the mortar off the trowel onto one end of the second brick, forming a wedge shape. Furrow the wedge with the trowel, then place the brick on the screed, mortared end butted up to the end of the first brick. Scoop up the excess squeezing and use to lay the third brick, and so on.

Check whether or not the course is horizontal. Adjust the bricks in height either by lifting low ones and packing out with mortar underneath, or by tapping with the shaft of the trowel to sink them further, as necessary.

To form the brickwork bond you must overlap the second row of bricks with the first, so that the vertical joints do not align. For a simple stretcher bond, spread a screed of mortar along the top of the first course of bricks and start the second with a brick cut in half across its width. Continue with whole bricks, finishing the row with a half-brick.

Continue to lay subsequent brick courses to complete the wall, using good building practice: checking levels, building to a guideline and racking back the ends and corners.

Pointing the joints

To neaten the mortar joints, press the blade of a pointing trowel against the vertical joints, bevelling the mortar to one side. Run the blade along the horizontal joints, pressing at the top to form a bevel; this will deflect rainwater from the wall.

BUILDING LEVELS

Check frequently that the brick joints are the same thickness throughout, that the bricks are laid horizontally, and that the wall does not waver from a straight line.
Racking back Build up the corners and ends of a wall first, stepping back the brickwork by half a brick each course: this allows you to check the structure for squareness. Stretch stringlines between the ends or corners of the wall as a guide.

Pins and strings Push a pin into the new mortar joint at one end or corner of the wall and stretch the string along the outside edge of the new course, securing it at the opposite end of the wall with a second pin. Raise the string and pins for each subsequent course.
Gauge rod Make up a 915mm (3ft) long gauge rod, marked in brick-plus-mortar joint increments. If the wall is rising properly the marks will be level with the top edge of each brick.

Make a builder's square (see box on page 93) use to check right-angled corners.

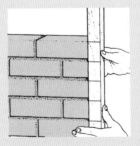

Use a gauge rod to check that the mortar joints are 10mm ($^3/_8$in) thick throughout the courses.

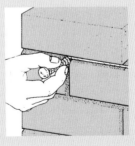

Use pins and strings to set up guidelines to which you can lay the brick courses accurately.

Build up the end and corners first, racked back, then lay the intermediate brickwork.

Walls: retaining walls

Retaining wall format

An earth-retaining wall can be constructed using the same basic building techniques described in this book. Remember that the wall must have sufficient mass and solid enough foundations to resist the lateral pressure of earth and water.

A typical single-brick-thick earth-retaining wall up to 1.2m (4ft) high will need strip foundations the length of the wall, 510mm (20in) wide (from front to back), and 150mm (6in) thick. Set the concrete strip in a trench 510mm (20in) below soil level.

The brickwork itself should be a minimum of 230mm (9in) thick (single-brick), bonded using Flemish or English Garden Wall bond (see page 128). Below ground level, use engineering bricks. If the wall rises above 1.2m (4ft) in height you must incorporate piers at each end, plus intermediate piers every 1.5 to 1.8m (5 or 6ft) if the wall is over 3m (10ft) long.

Metal rods tied to a concrete casting buried in the earth bank will give further stability. At the wall end, the rod is mortared into a brick joint; at the casting end the hooked rod is encased in the concrete as an anchor.

Resisting damp

Because the retaining wall is under considerable pressure from the earth it is holding back – and because part of it is actually underground – it is necessary to protect it against dampness.

Drainage The retained earth must drain freely from the back of the wall to prevent it from becoming waterlogged, so install plastic drainpipes extending through the thickness of the wall and sloping from back to front. The drainpipes should be positioned just above the lower ground level. Alternatively, you can leave "weep holes" in the ground-level course of bricks: unmortared vertical gaps between every four bricks.

Where the earth is particularly wet, however, it is best to lay land drainage pipes laterally in order to filter the excess water away.

Damp-proof membrane It is usual to coat the back face by applying several coats of bitumen emulsion using a brush.

Backfilling the wall

When the wall has been constructed and left for several days for the mortar to harden fully, backfill with earth to create the terraced effect. Tip loads of granular, porous material such as pebbles or gravel behind the retaining wall for good drainage, then add subsoil to within about 150mm (6in) of the top of the wall. Compact the gravel and the subsoil using a garden roller, then top up with good fertile topsoil. Leave the soil for a few weeks to settle, topping up if necessary.

CREATING TERRACES

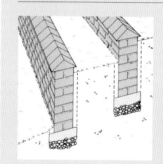

To create a series of terraces in steeply sloping ground earth-retaining walls are needed, to hold back the earth you remove. Build the walls on footings, then backfill with gravel, subsoil and topsoil to create the flat areas behind each wall. Incorporate drainage holes, and fit a polythene membrane behind each wall.

Resisting damp

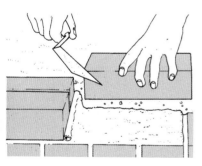

1 Insert lengths of plastic drainpipe in the retaining wall at ground level so that excess water can be channelled away.

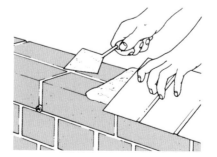

2 Fit bevelled coping to the top of the wall – which should be just above terraced ground level – to clear rainwater.

3 Attach heavy-duty polythene to the back of the retaining wall as a damp-proof membrane, then backfill.

Dry-stone walls

A natural stone wall has a distinctly rugged appearance which suits a country-style garden. The wall can be constructed as a freestanding structure, or as an earth-retaining support. Soil packed into the joints allows them to be used for planting.

Choose the hardest, most impervious stone that available, such as granite or basalt. You will need to allow about 1 tonne per cubic metre (just under 1 ton per 1¹⁄₃ cubic feet) of wall.

Aim to have the load of stone dumped close to the site. If you need to move the stone some distance, hire a sturdy builder's wheelbarrow.

How dry-stone walls are made

A dry-stone wall, although random in construction, must be made to a strict formula for rigidity and strength. It comprises:

BATTER FRAMES

The angled shape of a dry-stone wall is formed by wooden frames assembled to give the correct "batter". On freestanding structures the wall is narrower at the top, with the outer blocks laid to follow the shape of the batters, one either end of the structure.

Building a dry-stone wall

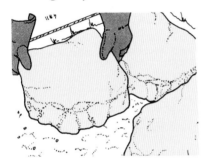

1 Lay one layer of large, flat foundation stones on the compacted earth sub-base, interlocking the irregular edges.

2 Build up the ends by several courses of regularly shaped edging blocks alternated with large, flat through stones.

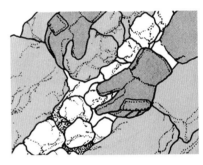

3 Place small infill stones into the cavity formed between the front and back facing blocks. Ram the stones down firmly.

4 Link the outer leaves of the wall by laying large, flat through stones at random intervals. Continue building the wall with the squarer edging blocks.

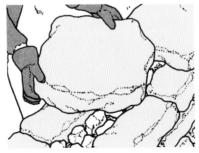

5 Fit a row of coverband stones across the top of the wall to close off the structure from rain. Ideally the row of stones should slope slightly for drain-off.

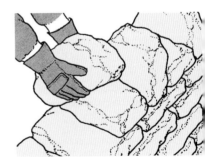

6 Place a row of coping stones along the top of the coverband, setting them on edge with a slight lean to one side, or in decorative buck-and-doe format.

Foundations Well-compacted and stable subsoil with large flat foundation stones on top.

Edging blocks Fairly regularly shaped edge blocks laid on the foundation stones form the front, rear and end faces of the wall, with a cavity in the centre.

Infill stones Small irregularly shaped "hearting" stones used as infill for the cavity between the edging blocks.

Through stones Long, flat stones called "random throughs" placed at random intervals across the wall, from front to back, in order to tie the outer faces together.

Coverband A row of large, flat stones laid at the top of the wall, on which the copings are laid.

Coping stones Flattish stones laid on edge along the top of the wall; they may be laid in a "buck-and-doe" format – laid alternately flat and on edge to create a turreted profile.

Setting the batter

A dry-stone wall must be built with a broader base than top for rigidity and to transmit the loading to the foundation stones. A typical batter, as the angled shape is called, is about 915mm (3ft) wide at the base and 300m (1ft) at the top.

Batter frames are used to set the angle during construction of the wall (see box, left). Make up a batter frame from lengths of 50 x 25mm (2 x 1in) softwood, nailed together in the wall's proportions. A batter frame is required for each end of the wall.

For an earth-retaining dry-stone wall, the back edge of the wall should be kept vertical to counteract the lateral pressure of the damp earth: fix the back upright straight and the front one angled back towards the bank.

Making the foundation

Mark out the shape of the base using string-lines stretched between pegs driven into the ground at the perimeter. Dig the trench to depth, removing the topsoil as far as firm subsoil. Compact the subsoil with a sledgehammer or garden roller.

Choose some large, flat foundation stones with at least one straight edge and lay in the base of the trench, interlocking the irregular edges for strength. Tap the stones down firmly with the shaft of a club hammer.

Constructing the wall

Stand the batter frames in position at each end of the foundation trench and link them with stringlines as a guide to building. Stack edging blocks on the foundation stones to form staggered vertical joins between courses. Lay through stones alternately to bond the smaller stones.

Build out from the ends of the wall using edging blocks, linking them with the end blocks with staggered joints. Follow the shape of the batter when placing the stones, so the sides start to slope inwards.

When you have laid three or four courses add smaller infill stones to the cavity between the edging stones. Tie in the two leaves, or "skins", of the wall with through stones.

Fitting the coverband and coping

When you reach the top of the wall, lay the large, flat coverband stones across the top, forming a lid to the shell. Finish off the dry-stone wall by setting a row of coping stones on edge, tilting them slightly one way to throw off rainwater.

MAINTAINING AND PAINTING WALLS

Repointing walls

 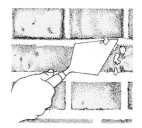

Repoint with a 1 cement, 1 lime, 5 sand mix. Scrape away old mortar to a depth of 2.5cm (1in).

Moisten the joints and pack mortar in firmly. Finish with a trowel to give a chamfered edge.

Painting walls

Remove loose paint with a wire brush. Use a chemical sealant if the bricks are in poor condition.

Apply a fresh coat of paint designed for use on exterior masonry.

Fences

There is a vast range of fencing styles, either custom-made or prefabricated, which serve numerous functions in the garden. You may want something practical yet attractive to stake out the boundaries of your property or simply make a utilitarian barrier. Certain types of solid fencing will provide a windbreak for the patio, while some semi-solid types will allow a gentle breeze to filter through at the same time as giving privacy.

Prefabricated panel fences

Prefabricated fence panels provide the quickest and most economical means of creating a solid barrier. However, panel fences are not the most rigid of structures, being generally constructed of inexpensive, fairly thin timber. Their strength lies in the way they are attached between the posts. Protection against the elements is provided by the bevelled coping strips nailed along the top to shed rainwater.

Basketweave The most popular type of prefabricated panel fence, basketweave panels are made from thin slats of larch or pine: these are woven horizontally around vertical slats in a basketweave pattern. Panels are fixed between timber or concrete posts by driving galvanized nails or bolts through the framing battens.

"Waney"-edged A version of the basketweave prefabricated panel fence. The horizontal planks have irregularly shaped lower edges, often with the bark attached, and overlap to form a solid barrier. The planks are fixed within a thin softwood frame, which is again nailed between the posts.

Trellis Trellis panels are often used to give additional height to a basketweave or wavy-edged panel. Trellis can be used as a lightweight fence in its own right. Semi-solid trellis makes an excellent screen for rubbish bins or a compost heap, where only a lightweight structure is needed.

Split hazel (wattle) or willow (osier) fences These are panels of basket work, available in a range of sizes and unsurpassed for an instant rustic look or for supporting plants. Wattle hurdle in particular weathers very quickly, becoming unobtrusive in a matter of weeks.

Post-and-rail fences

There are various versions of the post-and-rail fence, which is generally used at property boundaries. It basically comprises a number of horizontal rails nailed to or notched into the posts. The posts themselves may be round and the rails half-round in section, and they frequently still have their bark attached for a more rustic appearance. Within this category, these are the most commonly found fences:

Ranch-style Ranch-type fences have thin, planed planks of softwood nailed horizontally to short posts of softwood, or housed in slots cut in the posts.

Double ranch-style A semi-solid variation of the basic ranch-style fence, the double version has additional planks fixed to the opposite side of the posts in such a way that they coincide with the gaps between the planks on the other side.

Picket Often known as paling or palisade fencing, picket fencing forms an elegant boundary popularly used in front gardens, particularly in rural areas, and is traditionally painted in white gloss or treated with preservative.

Palisade True palisade fences are similar to picket types, but differ in that the vertical pales are butted close together side by side, forming a solid fence.

Hit-and-miss palisade fence This is made up of poles split in half lengthways and nailed to horizontal rails in a staggered pattern, providing complete privacy yet allowing the wind to filter through.

Closeboarded fences

Where good security at a property boundary is called for, perhaps the best type of fence is the closeboarded variety. It comprises stout posts with two or three horizontal triangular-section arris rails fixed between, usually housed in mortices (specially cut sockets or holes) cut in the sides of the posts. Vertical boards are attached to the rails in overlapping fashion. The boards are set on a horizontal gravel board in order to protect them from damp rising from the ground.

Metal fencing

Vertical bar fencing: unclimbable fence This is made of vertical round iron bars, looped at the top and held together with rails in rectangular sections. Usually associated with country gardens, this is a long-lasting alternative and it is usually painted.

Railings These are normally associated with town front gardens and were traditionally made of vertical iron bars with cast-iron finials or arrowheads. Railings are now manufactured in aluminium alloys and are available in a range of patterns.

Continuous bar fencing (estate fencing) This is a traditional means of enclosing fields or estates. The fence is made of horizontal wrought-iron straps and round vertical bars. It is still available, but it is expensive.

Wire mesh For practical fencing a wire mesh fence may be suitable. Although this fencing is often of utilitarian appearance, more elegant decorative types are also available. The mesh can be fixed between timber, concrete or angled metal posts.

Open-mesh The size of the mesh may be 10 to 100mm ($\frac{3}{8}$in to 4in) square. As protection against rusting, the wire may be coated in green plastic; alternatively the bare metal will be galvanized against corrosion.

Fences

Decorative wire Often found hooped at the top, decorative wire mesh is sold in rolls in heights from 4in to 3ft (100 to 915mm). The larger sizes must be attached to posts as for open-mesh fencing, but the pointed ends of the smaller types can be simply pushed into the ground.

Welded mesh Chain-link, or welded mesh, fencing is the toughest of the wire structures, the steel wire being welded at each junction.

Split-chestnut paling Stockade, or split-chestnut paling, fences are assembled from cleft chestnut stakes connected at the top and bottom with galvanized wire. The line wires are attached between stouter posts of softwood, usually diagonally braced, with intermediate posts to prevent sagging.

Spiked chain Used purely for decorative effect or to mark out a boundary without forming a solid barrier, spiked chain fencing consists of steel chains.

TYPES OF FENCING

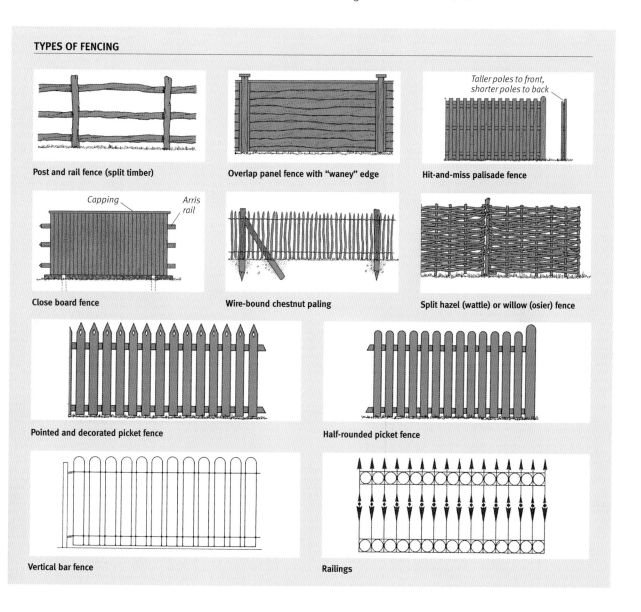

Post and rail fence (split timber)

Overlap panel fence with "waney" edge

Hit-and-miss palisade fence

Taller poles to front, shorter poles to back

Close board fence

Capping

Arris rail

Wire-bound chestnut paling

Split hazel (wattle) or willow (osier) fence

Pointed and decorated picket fence

Half-rounded picket fence

Vertical bar fence

Railings

Fixing fence posts

Preservative-treated fence posts are sold in standard lengths, although you will probably have to cut them to size. You must allow for sufficient depth of post to be sunk in the ground, plus an allowance for the posts to extend a few inches above the top of the fence panels. Cut the posts to length and mark the required above-ground height clearly around their girth.

Even if the posts have already been treated with preservative, soak the cut ends of the posts in a bucket of preservative overnight so that the vulnerable end grain absorbs the fluid. If the posts are untreated, make a preservative bath and soak the posts thoroughly (see below).

Marking out the run of fencing
The first job in erecting a fence is to mark out its position on the ground so that you can determine the number of panels, timber or wire mesh and supporting posts needed. Stretch

stringlines between pegs driven into the ground to mark the run of fencing, then use a batten the length of one fencing panel plus the width of one post to determine how many panels and posts you will have to buy.

Post fixings
While concrete posts are best set in a hole dug in the ground and encased in concrete, timber posts can he concreted in the same way, attached above ground level to concrete spurs, or fixed using a proprietary metal fence spike. Where a post is to be fixed to a solid surface, such as a concrete base slab, either embed it in the slab itself or attach it with bolt-on metal plates – these have a socket which takes the end of the post.

For posts which stand up to about 1.2m (4ft) high, dig a hole 460mm (18in) deep, but for taller posts dig down 610mm (24in) to provide more support below ground. Excavate the hole by a further 150mm (6in) to allow for a base of hardcore, which will let surplus water drain away.

Although a spade can be used to dig the hole, a post-hole borer can readily be hired and involves much less effort. It removes a core of soil less laboriously using a corkscrew action. To use the tool, place the blades at the required post position and turn the handle to gouge out the earth. The core of earth is removed by lifting the tool.

Setting the post upright
Ensure the post stands perfectly vertical by holding a spirit level against each face and adjusting it as necessary. Pack more rubble around the post to within 150mm (6in) of ground level.

Concreting in a post

1 Dig a hole using a spade or, for ease, a hired post hole borer, which lifts out a core of earth. Make sure you position the hole correctly.

2 Prop the post in the hole on a brick, with temporarily pinned-on braces, and set it vertical by checking each side in turn with a spirit level.

3 Ram hardcore into the hole around the propped-up post to support it firmly. Stop the hardcore short of ground level by about 150mm (6in).

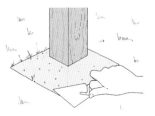

4 Trowel in the fresh concrete around the post and compact it to dispel air bubbles. Shape the mound so that rainwater will run off quickly.

WEATHER PROOFING

Capping the post tops
Trim the tops of the fence posts to a single slope or point to ensure that rainwater runs off rapidly. Treat the cut ends by soaking the posts overnight in a bucket of preservative. Alternatively, you can fit a preformed wooden cap to the square top of the posts, by nailing it on.

Making a preservative bath
Soaking the fence posts for a few days in a bath of preservative will ward off possible attack by rot as a result of contact with damp ground. Construct a preservative bath by building low dry-laid walls of brick that are stacked in stretcher bond but without mortar. Line the inside of the bath with a sheet of heavy-duty polythene, lapping over the sides of the brick walls. Fill the bath with preservative and lay the fence posts inside so they are completely submerged. Leave the timber to absorb the preservative for a few days (according to the manufacturer's instructions) turning each piece at regular intervals.

Fixing fence posts

Mix up a fairly dry concrete mix in the proportions 1 part Portland cement : 4 parts all-in aggregate, or use a dry ready-mixed fence-post concrete which is sold pre-packed in conveniently sized bags by builder's merchants and DIY stores. Shovel the concrete into the hole around the post so that it is just proud of the surrounding ground level. Compact the concrete with the offcut of post to dispel air bubbles, then shape into a neat mound so that rainwater will not be able to collect at the base of the post and encourage rot.

Installing a fence spike

1 Drive the spike into the ground using a sledge hammer and offcut of post (and fixing accessory).

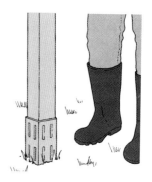

2 Check that the spike is vertical by holding a spirit level against each side in turn at frequent intervals.

3 Push the post into the collar of the fence spike. You may have to tighten integral bolts to secure.

It is best to leave the concrete to harden for about two days before attaching the fencing panels. If you use fence spikes, however, the panels may be attached as soon as the posts are correctly positioned.

Using fencing spikes

A fencing spike consists of a galvanized steel spike with a square, wedge-shaped collar at the top, into which the post fits, to be gripped by internal flanges. Some makes of spike have sockets which must be closed around the post with integral bolts. These bolts can cope with irregularly-sized posts (post dimensions are given only nominally, and sometimes you may have to pack offcuts of wood between post and collar to obtain a tight fit). Instructions for installing a spike are shown above.

To fit the post, wedge it into the collar and secure by tightening any integral nuts or driving nails into the pre-drilled holes. Plot the positions of the other post holes with your gauge batten and fix the remaining posts in the same way.

Concrete spurs

As with fencing spikes, concrete spurs avoid direct contact between ground and post, minimizing the risk of rot. Spurs are bought ready-made, with a single bevelled end and holes for attaching the post. Set the spurs in concrete, with the angled end uppermost. The lowest fixing hole should be just above the plug of concrete, so that the post is held close to, but not on, the ground. Ensure that the spurs are vertical using a spirit level. The post will be attached to the taller

spur-front, so calculate the distance between the spurs accordingly. Allow the concrete to set completely before bolting the wooden posts onto the spurs.

Aligning the posts

If the fence is to be straight and rigid, without warps, the posts must be erected so that they are precisely the correct distance apart to accept the panels (or other components such as arris rails), and properly straight and upright.

As you fix the posts check that they are aligned with the stringline. Test-fit a panel or rail between posts. Check also that the posts are fixed to the same depth by placing a long straight-edged plank on top and resting a spirit level on it. Adjust the depth of the posts accordingly.

CONCRETE POSTS AND FENCES

Most fences are supported by square-section timber posts. Concrete posts, however, are available for a rot-free, durable fixing for all types of fences. They are generally 100mm (4in) square, reinforced with lengths of iron rod embedded in them. Various moulded formats are made to cope with different fencing styles: drilled concrete posts are intended for supporting wire mesh fences, while mortised posts accept the arris rails of closeboarded or post-and-rail fences. Notched posts are made to accept the end of a diagonal brace needed for some types of fencing. Channelled posts are made especially for concrete fences, in which solid panels replace the usual timber type.

Fixing a panel fence

Panel fences are a quick and economical way of creating a solid barrier at a property boundary, within a plot as an efficient windbreak for the patio, or for demarcation of different areas within the garden. However, their appearance tends towards the functional (unless you choose split hazel or willow panels for a more natural look) and may not be appropriate for all garden settings. Even so, the appearance of a panel fence can be softened and made less obtrusive by using a coloured timber preservative to treat them, and by using the fence as a support to grow climbing plants and shrubs – perhaps employing the methods of creating plant supports illustrated on page 153.

If you are erecting a boundary fence, first mark out the run of fencing on the ground using stringlines and pegs. Remember that all your posts and fencing must be on the property side of the stringline.

Fixing the posts

Fix the first fence post (see page 138). Although you can erect all the fence posts first, spaced the correct distance apart, you may find it easier to fix them one at a time, using the next panel in line as an accurate spacing guide. This avoids the problem of misaligned posts.

With this progressive method of erecting a panel fence (illustrated below), it is better to use spike post fixings than to have to wait for each concrete support to harden before moving on.

Fixing gravel boards

You can install gravel boards beneath the panels to prevent the risk of damp earth touching the fence itself: the gravel boards are sacrificed in favour of the panels as they are easily replaceable.

At the base, nail 150mm (6in) lengths of 35mm (1½in) square timber vertically to the inner faces of the posts. Measure between these supports to establish the size of the gravel boards and cut lengths of 150 x 25mm (6 x 1 in) softwood to fit. Treat with a non-toxic preservative and allow to dry.

Position a gravel board between the posts and set it horizontal, checking with a spirit level placed on top. Nail the board to the vertical supports using galvanized nails.

Nail-fixing prefabricated panels

Prefabricated fencing panels can simply be slotted between the posts and secured by driving nails through the outer frame into the posts near the top and bottom and in the centre. First drill pilot holes through the frame pieces to prevent the thin wood from splitting when the nails are hammered in.

Place one of the panels between the first two posts on the run. Mount the panel on bricks so that it will be sufficiently high above ground level to prevent dampness, or else fit horizontal gravel boards and mount the panels on these.

Align the fence panel accurately so that it is vertical in all

Erecting a panel fence

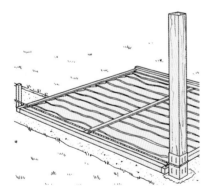

1 Mark out the fence run on the ground from the position of the first fixed fence post. Use a panel as a guide to fixing the remaining posts and a stringline and peg as a visual aid.

2 Use two-piece metal brackets to fix the fence panel to the posts. Make a T-shaped gauge to set the first half of the bracket the correct distance from the edge of the fence post.

3 Fix the second half of the bracket to the post about 25mm (1in) above the first half, using galvanised nails. Ensure that the brackets are fixed squarely or the panel will not fit.

irections, then place a spirit level on top of the panel to check that it is horizontal. Hammer 75mm (3in) galvanized nails through the pre-drilled holes.

Bracket-fixing prefabricated panels

Because the outer frame of prefabricated fence panels is quite thin, it is quite likely that splitting could occur in severe winds, and the fence may even blow down.

For a stronger fixing it is best to use proprietary galvanized metal support brackets, of which there are two commonly available types: a one-piece U-shaped channel (illustrated on page 142); and a pair of L-shaped fittings, shown being affixed in illustrations 2 and 3, below.

One-piece brackets Mark a centre line down the length of the inner face of each post and attach a pair of one-piece metal brackets centrally and squarely to the post, one near the top and the other near the bottom, using 50mm (2in) long galvanized nails.

You might find a further type of one piece bracket (see box, page 142), which has an L-shaped section, that is nailed to the inner face of the post and the outer frame piece of the fence panel. A further L-shaped bend in the bracket, which has a triangular leg, slots behind the timber frame piece to hold the panel tightly against the post.

Two-piece brackets Fix the brackets in paris, one about 25mm (1in) above the other, with the raised flanges at opposite sides, forming what is essentially a staggered channelling.

This type of bracket provides greater resistance to winds, as the staggered formation supports the fence panel at a greater width than the one-piece brackets.

To ensure that your position both halves of the bracket accurately, make up a simple gauge from offcuts of timber and use thins as a spacing guide. the gauge comprises a short length of wood with a cross-piece nailed on at right angles, so that it protrudes by the distance the brackets must be set away from the edge of the fence post. Hold the gauge against the side of the post with the cross-piece resting on the inner face, to which the brackets will be attached. Butt each bracket up to the end of the cross-piece and nail on.

Fitting the panels

With either type of bracket fixing you will have to lift up the prefabricated panel and slot it into the channels. With two-piece brackets it is best to push the panel between the top brackets from below, then pivot it down carefully and lower the bottom edge between the lower bracket fixings.

If using the one-piece brackets, you must lift up the panel and lower it into the top brackets, then gently feed it downwards and into the lower brackets.

With either type of bracket, secure the panel by hammering 50mm (2in) long galvanized nails through the pre-drilled flanges and into the slim panel edge framework.

Once the panels are held securely, you can remove the bricks from beneath them.

4 Feed the fence panel into the gap between the two parts of the bracket from below, then pivot it downwards and slot it into the channel formed by the lower pair of brackets.

5 Stand the fence panel on a brick (or fit a gravel board first) so that it does not come in contact with the damp earth. Secure the panel by nailing through the bracket flange.

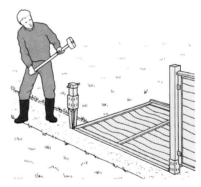

6 Fix the subsequent posts on the fence run by lying a panel on the ground, one end butted up to the previously fixed post; then drive a metal post spike into the ground at the other end of the panel.

Fixing a panel fence

Cutting down a panel

As your fence run is unlikely to be an exact number of whole prefabricated panels long, you will probably have to cut a panel to fit the gap at one end. Hold a full-size panel in the gap, against the posts, one end overlapping the previously fixed panel in the run. With a pencil, mark down the panel against the post to indicate the overlap. Continue the line around to the other side of the panel.

Use a claw hammer to prise away the upright batten on each side of the panel, at the overlap end. Reposition the battens on the inside edge of the pencil guidelines. One of the battens will be longer than the other, and this should project at the bottom of the panel.

With the panel lying flat on a hard surface, hammer galvanized nails through the upper batten, through the panel's slats and into the lower batten. Nail at each slat for a secure fixing. To prevent the nails from pulling out again, place a brick or concrete slab underneath, and use long nails which will protrude and be turned at the ends.

ONE-PIECE FENCE PANEL BRACKETS

One-piece fence panel fixing brackets are nailed to the inner faces of the posts and the prefabricated panels slotted into the channels they form, to be secured with galvanized nails. There are basically two types of bracket.

One-piece brackets
U-shaped brackets have holes pre-drilled in their backs for fixing direct to the fence post. Holes in the protruding flanges are for nailing the brackets to the panels.

Fence clips
Fence clips are nailed to the post and the side upright frame pieces of the panel, and the bracket clips around the frame to hold the panel securely against the post.

Support the panel firmly and saw off the protruding end of the longer framing batten. Next, saw off the surplus ends of the panel slats and the coping and bottom rails, using a panel saw. Cut as closely as possible to the outer edge of the newly repositioned side frame pieces. Fit the cut-down panel between the posts using nails or brackets as normal.

Dealing with sloping ground

A panel fence, because of its rigid format, cannot follow the slope of the land and instead must be erected in a stepped format between vertical posts (see page 151).

The triangular gaps left beneath each panel can be filled with shaped gravel boards if the gap is not more than about 150mm (6in) at its deepest. For greater gaps than this you will have to build plinth walls of bricks, reconstructed concrete walling blocks or natural stone. Build the walls once the fence posts have been erected, setting horizontal foundations into the slope so that the masonry can be laid straight.

Should the ground slope across the proposed line of fencing, the best solution is to build masonry retaining walls that will hold back the earth to form a terraced effect. Incorporate the fence posts into the wall, then erect the fence panels on top of this in the normal manner.

Fitting a trellis top

If you want to increase the height of a fence for, say, greater screening or to provide a frame for climbing plants, it is quite simple to add a trellis top. Allow for the depth of the trellis when calculating the length of the posts you will need, and fix the panels so that the appropriate space remains above the top of the fence panel.

With heavy-duty square-pattern trellis you can simply nail the outer uprights to the posts. With the lighter-weight type – especially the flimsy expanding diamond pattern – you should nail short vertical battens of 75mm (3in) square timber to the inner faces of the posts and attach the trellis to these. Alternatively, simply nail the trellis directly to the front faces of the posts.

Using concrete fence posts

Panel fences are easy to install using precast concrete posts. Other such posts have channels moulded in their sides, into which you can slot the panels without the need to make additional fixings. It is vitally important – as with any fencing job – to set the posts perfectly upright so that the panels will fit snugly in the channels.

Another type of concrete post has a recess in each side in which the fence panel is retained by metal brackets screwed to the outer frame pieces.

Fixing a closeboarded fence

Although close-boarded fences are available in prefabricated versions, this type of durable boundary is normally erected on site from separate components. The posts may be ready-mortised to take the horizontal arris rails, or you can cut the mortises yourself. A far easier option, however, is to fit the arris rails with special galvanized metal arris rail brackets.

Preparing mortises and arris rails

Mark the positions of the mortises for the arris rails on the posts. The arris rails should be set about 300mm (12in) from the top and bottom of the fence. Use a 25mm (1in) flat bit fitted in a power drill to drill out the bulk of the waste wood within the 75 x 25mm (3 x 1in) mortises, then neatly square off the corners with a wood chisel.

Arris rails are usually triangular in section, are made of preservative-treated softwood, and have ends that must must be hewn to fit into the post mortises – although for bracket fixings the ends of the arris rails can be square. Use a small axe to trim to the necessary wedge shapes. You could use a planer file or even a saw to shape the arris rails if you do not feel sufficiently confident using an axe. Treat the cut ends of the arris rails and mortices with preservative.

Erecting mortised posts and rails

For the traditional method of erecting a closeboarded fence, set the first post in concrete with its mortises facing the direction of the run, as shown below. Prop up the second post in its hole and insert the first pair of arris rails in the mortises.

AFFIXING ARRIS RAILS AND MORTISED POSTS

Arris rail
Galvanized metal arris rail brackets are nailed over the triangular-section arris rail and the pre-drilled flanges are nailed to the inner faces of the fence posts.

Mortised posts
Mortised fence posts take the wedge-shaped ends of arris rail; nails are hammered into the rail through the posts, using a club hammer to prevent jarring as they are driven in.

Make sure the flat backs of the rails face the back of the fence. Drive 75mm (3in) galvanized nails through the post into the ends of the rails to secure them. Check that the arris rails are horizontal. Assemble the next post-and-rail section in the same way; repeat to complete the run.

Erecting a close-boarded fence

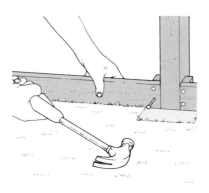
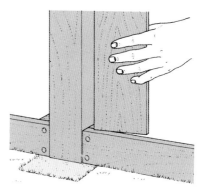

1 Set the first post in concrete and prop the second post in its hole. Fit the arris rails in their mortises, then level the entire assembly using a spirit level for accuracy.

2 Nail gravel boards of 150 x 25mm (6 x 1in) timber to short support battens nailed to the inner face of the posts. Recess the battens so that the boards fit flush.

3 Place the first feather-edged board on the gravel board, with its thicker edge against the post and its top edge aligned with a stringline stretched between posts.

Fixing a close-boarded fence

Using arris rail brackets

To erect a closeboarded fence using arris rail brackets, first install all the posts the correct distance apart and upright. Cut lengths of arris rail to fit snugly between the pairs of posts, then nail on the metal brackets: these are shaped to fit over the triangular section of the rails, and have right-angled pre-drilled flanges which fit against the face of the post. Drive nails through the flanges to secure the rails to the posts.

Attaching gravel and feather-edged boards

Nail 150mm (6in) lengths of 35mm (1½in) square timber vertically to the inner faces of the posts as supports for gravel boards on which the cladding will stand. Each gravel board should be flush with the outer face of the fence post.

Mark out and cut the feather-edged boards to the height required for the fence, between the top of the gravel board at the base and the underside of the coping strip at the top. The feather-edged boards are positioned so that the thick edge of one overlaps the thin edge of the other by about 12mm (½in).

The boards are attached to the arris rails with 50mm (2in) galvanized nails. Stretch a stringline between posts to indicate the top edge of the feather-edged boards, then stand the first board on the gravel board with its thick edge against the first post. Drive two nails through the board into the arris rail at the top and bottom.

Position the second feather-edged board on the gravel board, overlapping the thin edge of the first by 12mm (½in). Drive a single nail through the boards at each arris rail. Continue to work across the fence. Hold a spirit level vertically against the outer edge of the boards at intervals to check that they are upright, and adjust if necessary.

WEATHERPROOFING THE FENCE

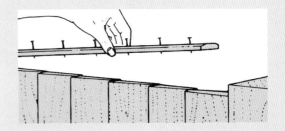

Fitting coping strips
Coping strips throw rainwater from the face of the fence and prevent moisture from seeping into the vulnerable end grain of the feather-edged boards. Cut lengths of bevelled coping strip to fit between the posts and place them on the top of the feather-edged boards. Drive nails carefully through the top of the copings and into the ends of the boards at regular intervals.

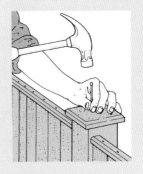

Fitting post caps
Weatherproof the top end of each fence post by nailing on a preformed chamfered post cap. The cap is slightly broader than the girth of the post so that rainwater will be thrown clear without trickling underneath and potentially causing the top of the post to suffer from rot.

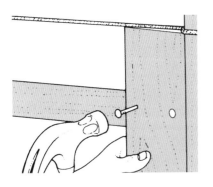

4 Drive two nails through the board into the top arris rail. Check the level of the board, then hammer in another two nails at the lower arris rail.

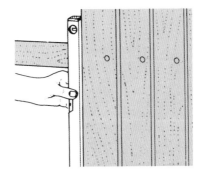

5 Add subsequent feather-edged boards using one nail per rail. Check with a spirit level that the boards are vertical – tap gently with a hammer to adjust.

6 Make a spacing gauge from an offcut of timber. Use to set each board so that it consistently overlaps its neighbour. Fix the board at the top, then slide the gauge down.

Picket fencing

Although ready-assembled picket panels are available, you may prefer to make up this attractive boundary fencing from scratch so that you can vary the design to suit your garden. It is sensible to assemble sections of picket fence flat on the ground and to secure the resultant panels to the posts in the same way as ready-made panels.

Cutting the rails to size
Set the 75 x 50mm (3 x 2in) posts in the ground between about 1.9m (6ft 6in) and 2.7m (9ft) apart, using concrete or using metal spikes. Cut arris rails of 50 x 25mm (2 x 1in) softwood to span between posts. Mark on the posts the proposed positions for the arris rails. Measure the distance between the rails. Lay the rails on a hard flat surface, spaced the correct distance apart, with their ends aligned.

Fitting the pales to the rails
Cut the pales to length as required and lay out on the pair of arris rails. Secure each pale to the rails with two 30mm (1¼in) long galvanized nails per fixing. Place the nails diagonally apart for a firmer fixing, and angle them inwards slightly.

Use a piece of timber the width required for the gaps between pales, as a gauge to spacing. Place the gauge in each gap and push the pales up to it as you work across the section. Fix all the pales to the rails, leaving about 100mm (4in) of rail protruding at each end for attaching the assembly to the posts.

Picket fencing

1 Assemble the picket fence on a flat surface by laying out the arris rails and securing the pales over them. Use a spacer to determine the positions of the pales.

2 Nail the picket panels to the fence posts, driving in two nails per arris rail. Ensure that the rails are horizontal and the pales are vertical by checking with a spirit level.

COMMON TYPES OF PALE

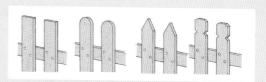

Four common styles of pale are the plain square-ended type, a softer rounded top, an angular pointed top, and a more ornately shaped Queen Anne format. One of these pale patterns can be used throughout a run of fence, or two or more alternated to create a more individual design.

Fixing the pale-and-rail assemblies
The procedure for fitting the pale-and-rail assemblies to the posts is identical to that for fixing prefabricated picket panels. Hold a panel against the posts, propped up underneath on bricks so that the pales clear ground level by about 60mm (2½in). Place a spirit level on the top arris rail and set the panel horizontal. Nail through the end of the top arris rail into the posts at each side, then recheck for the correct level before securing the bottom rail to the posts.

Make up and fix subsequent panels in the same way to complete the fence.

TURNING CORNERS

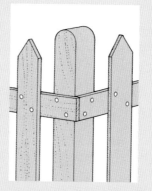

There are no particular problems involved in turning a right-angled corner with either ranch-style or picket fences, because the same post can be used for attaching both sections.

Fix the planks of a ranch-style fence or the arris rails of a picket type so that those on one side of the corner overlap the ends of those on the other side of the corner. The overlapping plank or rail should be on the front elevation of the fence for the neatest appearance.

Drive a nail through the overlapping plank or rail into the end of the overlapped plank or rail so that the join will not part.

Fixing a ranch-style fence

Post-and-rail fences, comprising vertical posts with horizontal rails nailed across them, take a variety of forms; all are quite straightforward to erect.

Ranch-style fences can be erected on site using separate components, while picket (or palisade) types come in optional kit form for easy assembly. With this type of fence, in which there are many vertical pales to attach to the rails, kit assembly saves time; however, check before you buy that the quality of the panels is acceptable, and the fixings strong, particularly where the pales are already attached to the rails.

Dimensions
Ranch-style fencing is an open-plan format for boundaries, usually painted white (or sometimes a colour) but often available simply treated with preservative stain for a more natural appearance. It consists of posts fixed at regular intervals, with horizontal cross-pieces of 120 x 20mm (4¾ x ¾in) planed softwood meeting at the centre of alternate posts.

Extremely adaptable, ranch-style fencing can be any height from a few feet up to about 1.8m (6ft). The planks should be spaced so that they present an aesthetically pleasing effect. There may be a gap of about 100mm (4in) between each pair of planks, for example, and between the top of the post and the top of the first plank, with a larger gap at the bottom between the ground and the base of the lowest plank.

Erecting single ranch-style fencing
Set main posts of 125 x 100mm (5 x 4in) timber in concrete in the ground at 2m (6ft 6in) intervals, with smaller intermediate posts – say, 90mm (3½in) square – midway between. The combination of larger and smaller posts will create an attractive rhythm.

As the planks are fitted to the outer faces of the posts, it is essential that the posts are precisely in line: check this during erection by placing a long straight-edged plank of wood across the outer faces of the posts.

Lengths of plank should meet in the centre of a post. However, to avoid a clean break down the fence where the planks meet, it is best to stagger the joints on alternate rails. Fix the first plank so that one end is flush with the outer edge

---

PLASTIC RANCH-STYLE FENCING

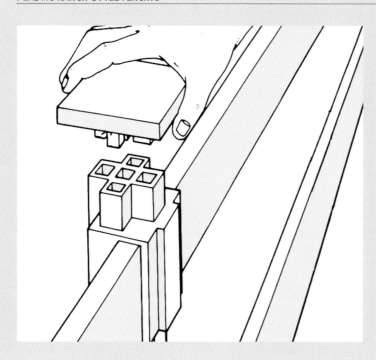

There are numerous makes of plastic ranch-style fencing available, but as this is a product that can be made from from recycled and waste material, do first consider purchasing a fencing kit manufactured from recycled plastic products.

Assembly details vary depending on the fencing kit purchased. Most, however, consist of hollow PVC posts which are concreted into the ground, with cellular plastic planks which push-fit into slots in the post, or which are connected by plastic sleeves themselves attached to the posts with plastic screw fittings.

Plastic caps have flanges which simply slot into the post tops, and they are normally glued into place. Likewise the hollow ends of the planks at the end of a run are fitted with end caps, which simply slot into place.

Fixing a ranch-style fence

of the first post on the run. Secure it in the middle to the intermediate post, then fix the other end halfway on the next main post. Run another length of plank from this post, across the next intermediate post and on to finish halfway at the new main post.

The next plank down should start at the end post and finish halfway at the intermediate post; a further plank should run from the intermediate post, fixed at the middle to the next main post, and finish halfway at the next intermediate post. This method will produce a more solid fence.

Attaching the planks

Nail fixings Ranch-style planks can be simply nailed to the posts using 35mm (1½in) long galvanized wire nails. At a butt-join use two nails, one above the other about 25mm (1in) in from the end of the plank. At an intermediate join, again use two nails but stagger them diagonally for a firmer fixing. Drive nails in at a slight inward angle to each other.

Screw fixings Using screws to attach the planks to the posts gives a much more secure fixing than using nails, although it takes longer to insert them. You will need a helper to hold the planks in place against the posts while you mark them in pencil to show the positions of the posts. Remove the planks and drill clearance holes through them using a 4.5mm (³⁄₁₆in) twist bit to take 37mm (1½in) No. 8 galvanized countersunk woodscrews. Recess the screw holes with a countersinking bit so that the screw heads will be sunken.

Hold the planks in place again and mark through their screw holes. Remove the planks and make starter holes for the screws in the posts using a 12mm (½in) diameter twist bit. Replace the planks, insert the screws and tighten with a screwdriver.

Double ranch-style fencing is erected in the same way as the single variety, except that identical planks are fixed to the opposite side of the posts to coincide with the gaps between the planks on the first side (see illustrations, right). Stagger the butt-joins the opposite way.

Notching the posts

A more durable and rigid form of ranch-style fencing can be constructed by notching the posts to take the horizontal planks. Before fixing the posts, lay them on the ground and mark the positions of the planks on one face of the post, using a plank as a template. Remove the plank and mark the sides of the post with the thickness of the plank minus about 6mm (¼in) so that the planks will protrude this distance from the posts. Chisel out the waste wood within the pencil lines in order to form the notches, then test the fit of the planks against the post.

Double ranch-style fencing

1 Screw or nail planks to the main and intermediate posts, with butt-joins between lengths occurring at the centre post. Ensure the planks are fixed horizontally.

2 Stagger the joins between planks on alternate rows to avoid a continuous break line down the fence at one post, which would tend to weaken the assembly.

WALLS, FENCES, AND GATES **147**

Fixing a post-and-wire fence

Wire mesh fencing, used as a boundary marker or a means to keep animals in or out, is stretched between posts of timber, concrete or steel. It is available in long rolls, in a choice of chain mesh, chicken wire, or a more decorative mesh with a hooped top. Most suppliers will sell a kit containing all the hardware needed for the type of mesh fence and post.

Wire fencing is less expensive than timber. It also provides a boundary that makes minimal disruption of the view. Although its appearance is not in itself attractive, wire mesh makes a good support for climbing plants; however, you need to choose suitable, lightweight varieties as most wire meshes are weak in comparison with alternative fencing materials.

Choosing posts
Concrete posts are available with holes to take the straining wires on which the mesh is stretched, while timber posts will probably require holes to be drilled for this purpose. Steel posts, which come in square, triangular or L-shaped section, are usually pre-drilled to take the wire. One advantage steel posts have is that the intermediate posts can simply be hammered into the ground rather than being set in concrete.

Preparing the posts
Concrete and metal posts need little preparation other than fixing in the ground with their pre-drilled holes facing along the run of the fence. However, timber posts (which should preferably be pre-treated with preservative) must be prepared prior to sinking them in the ground. Mark the height of the fence on each post, including an allowance for the post to protrude about 100mm (4in) at the top of the mesh. Mark the positions of the straining wire fixing holes and drill through the posts at this point using a 10mm (3/8in) wood bit. Treat the holes with preservative.

Set the main strainer posts in concrete, having made the post holes broader at the bottom than at the top to counteract the tensioning of the line wires. Fit the diagonal

---

BRACING THE OUTER POSTS

Install the upright strainer posts first and let the concrete harden fully. Dig a hole for each of the diagonal braces needed. Cut the braces to length from timber the same size as the posts.

To mark a brace for cutting, hold it in place against the side of the upright post, its bottom end resting on a brick in the hole. Mark the brace against the side of the post in pencil to give the correct angle for cutting. Saw along the line, then return the brace to the post, holding it against the side. Mark a notch about 20mm (3/4in) deep on one side of the post, then continue the cutting lines around to the opposite side.

Saw down the notch depth lines, then pare away the waste wood using a wood chisel. Slot the angled end of the brace into the notch and secure it by driving two nails, dovetail fashion, through it into the post.

Add concrete to the post hole to secure the diagonal brace and leave to cure in the normal way (see page 138 for instructions on the use of concrete with posts).

Set the main upright post first, then notch a diagonal brace of the same size timber into the inner face, about 150mm (6in) from the top of the post. Secure the brace to the post with two nails driven in at opposing angles to prevent it from pulling out.

Set the base of the brace on hardcore, then pack around with coarse concrete. Allow to harden before fitting the straining wire to the post.

Fixing a post-and-wire fence

braces to the outer posts (see box, page 148), and then erect the intermediate posts. The diagonal braces counteract the pressure imposed by the tightening of the straining wires.

Turning corners

If your mesh fence is to turn a corner you will need to install a special corner straining post. This type of post features a pair of diagonal braces set at right angles, and pre-drilled holes for the tensioning bolts and for other fittings.

Erecting on sloping ground

Although mesh fencing is flexible enough to cope with minor irregularities in the level of the ground – you simply set the base of the mesh a little way above the ground – it cannot accommodate a steeply sloping site. In this case you will need to create a series of steps in line with the gradient. At each change in level you must erect a two-way straining post and fit shorter lengths of mesh between.

On a slope, braces will be needed at each side of the straining posts to provide support in both directions. With steel and concrete posts you will probably have to order special posts made by your supplier following a plan of the sloping or terraced area. Note that the posts must also be longer than usual to cope with the difference between levels.

Attaching the straining wire

Eyebolts are used to attach the straining wire to the posts, and to the bolts you must fit stretcher bar brackets, which keep the mesh taut along its height. Slot the eyebolt into the hole in the post and attach the stretcher bar brackets, plus

their washers, to the other end. Do not tighten the fittings at this stage. Thread the end of the straining wire through the eyebolt, turn it back on itself and twist the end around the taut wire several times using a pair of pliers.

Fitting a turnbuckle

A "turnbuckle" can be fitted between the eyebolt and the straining wire to make it easier to adjust the tension of the wire. To fit this, attach the wire to the eye at the end of the turnbuckle and hook the other end onto the eyebolt attached to the post. Do not tighten the turnbuckle until the fence is ready for tensioning.

Tensioning the wire

Run the wire to the other end of the fence and cut it off the roll leaving about 150mm (6in) extra for attaching to the post. Fit a second eyebolt and connect the wire by threading it through the eyebolt and twisting it around itself.

Start to tension the wire from the turnbuckle or one of the eyebolts, tightening with an adjustable spanner. Tighten the fittings equally at each end of the wire. Over-tightening the wire could result in it snapping, so stop adjusting the eyebolts or turnbuckle when the kinks have straightened out.

With metal or concrete posts, fit additional straining wires in holes provided along the posts' length. With timber posts a straining wire at the top and bottom is sufficient.

Intermediate fixings

The straining wires must be held against the intermediate posts to prevent the mesh from sagging, although the fixings

Erecting a wire mesh fence

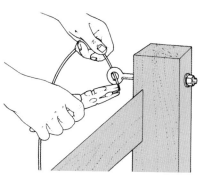

1 Fit the first eyebolt to the post without tightening fully, then attach the line wire and twist it around itself using pliers.

2 Thread a stretcher bar onto the end of the mesh roll, then attach the bar to the brackets attached to the eyebolts.

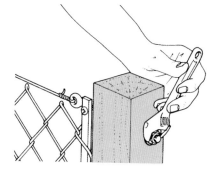

3 Tension the line wires using an adjustable spanner to tighten the nuts on the eyebolts, or tighten the turnbuckle.

Fixing a post-and-wire fence

must not hinder the tensioning of the wires via the eyebolts. With timber fences you can simply hammer staples over the wires to hold them in place, but with concrete and steel types you will need to fit wire "stirrups".

Cut lengths of 3mm (⅛in) galvanized binding wire and slot two through the pre-drilled hole in the post, then take them around the sides of the post and twist the ends around the line wire, which is stretched across the face of the post.

Fitting the mesh

A stretcher bar is fed through the end of the mesh to keep it taut along its height. Slot the bar through the free end of the roll of mesh, then bolt the bar onto the brackets attached to the eyebolts. Tighten the bolts with an adjustable spanner.

Unroll the mesh along the length of the fence and loosely tie it to the straining wires with twists of wire wound on using pliers. Shake the mesh as you go to even it out. At the opposite end of the fence, feed on a second stretcher bar at the line of links which just reach the straining posts.

Unravel a strand of the mesh beyond this stretcher bar by untwisting the top link with a pair of pliers. Bolt the second stretcher bar to the brackets attached to the eyebolts.

Tensioning the mesh

Pull the mesh taut on the straining wires by lightening the nuts on the eyebolts; these pull the stretcher bar brackets against the post. Once the mesh is evenly taut, secure it to the straining wires at 150mm (6in) intervals using twists of wire.

Should the mesh appear to sag, remove the stretcher bar and move it along the mesh one or more links to tighten it; then repeat the straining procedure.

Line wire plant supports

Wire frameworks enable you to support a growing climber while it is becoming established and to train it into the most suitable shape. Wires can be stretched horizontally between freestanding posts, forming a type of fence within the garden.

Post fixing It is not necessary to concrete the posts into the ground. Use 75mm (3in) square timber which has been treated with a preservative which is harmless to plants.

Trim the bottom ends of the post to points with an axe and, using a sledgehammer, drive them into the ground vertically about 900mm (3ft) deep at each end of the run.

Braces To counteract the tension of the line wires and the weight of the growing climber, brace the uprights with diagonal lengths of 75mm (3in) square timber nailed to the inside face about 150mm (6in) from the top. The brace should be sunk into the ground at the base. Dig a hole for the brace and place a brick or large stone in the base to wedge the brace against, then fill in with the earth.

Intermediate posts Drive in intermediate posts of 75mm (3in) square timber, without diagonal braces, at 1.2m (4ft) intervals.

Line wires Drill 10mm (⅜in) diameter holes through one of the outer posts, 130mm (5in) apart. Slot in galvanized straining bolts and retain with washers and nuts. Attach 2.5mm (¹⁄₁₆in) gauge galvanized or plastic-coated wire, twisting it back around itself.

Attach screw-in cup hooks to the opposite end post and attach the free end of the wires. Fasten the wires to the intermediate posts with wire staples hammered in: the wires should be held against the posts by the staples but not so tightly that they cannot be tensioned by the straining bolts.

Tighten the nuts on the straining bolts to stretch the wires taut, using an adjustable spanner.

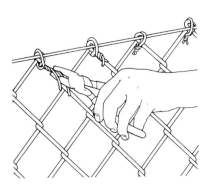

4 Secure the mesh to the line wires by winding on twists of galvanized wire at intervals along the run to prevent sagging.

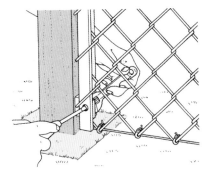

5 At the other end of the fence, slot on another stretcher bar and attach to the eyebolt brackets.

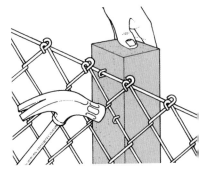

6 When the mesh is taut, secure it to the intermediate posts with in wire staples (or fit stirrups on metal or concrete posts).

Fences on sloping gardens

Where the ground level is very uneven it is usually necessary to build a fence or wall in a stepped format. Calculating the gradient is explained on page 125.

Stepping the structure

With rigid types of panel fencing such as closeboarded, woven or overlapping versions it is best, on sloping ground, to create a stepped foundation. Position the fence posts vertically, with their top edges set to a consistent slope. Check that the slope is consistent using a spirit level. Fix the panels as normal, leaving triangular gaps between their bottom edge and the slope. Fill in these gaps by cutting panels to fit the shape, or else remodel the earth underneath the square-based panels.

Stepping the foundation

In order to make solid plinth walls beneath a panel fence built on a slope, or to support a masonry wall built on a slope, you will have to construct a stepped concrete foundation (see page 91). Lay the concrete strip foundation between each post position using as formwork lengths of board spanning the trench and supported by timber stakes at each side. Work from the top of the slope, casting each horizontal section of strip foundation on the roughly shaped earth base.

When the first step is formed, move the board formwork down to the vertical edge of the next step and cast another section. Repeat this process. Cast the fence posts in the concrete slab at the given points, then leave the concrete to set before building the plinth walls.

ADJUSTING A SLOPE OVER A LARGE AREA

ADJUSTING A SLOPE OVER A LARGE AREA

Where the site is very uneven, and perhaps sloping too, work out the overall level and carry out any remodelling of the earth that may be necessary, for this exercise, use boning rods, which, together with a straight-edged plank and a spirit level, enable the level to be established by sight.

Boning rods are stakes with short pieces of wood nailed across near the top and bottom at right angles. Fix a short boning rod in the ground at the top of the slope and a longer one further down. Lay the plank between the two rods at the top and adjust the depth of one of the rods until the spirit level shows you that the plank is level. Then place a third rod lower down the slope, lining its top cross-piece by eye with the bottom cross-piece of the second rod. Proceed in this way down the slope. Then measure the various vertical dimensions and add them all up. Don't forget to subtract the height of the cross-piece from the ground at the top of the slope.

Setting fences on a slope

Post-and-rail fences can be built on ground that slopes quite considerably. Set the posts vertically as before, then fix arris rails at an angle that follows the lie of the land. Cut mortises in the posts to take the arris rails so that they slope at the correct angle: drill out the mortises first, then finish off with a chisel for accuracy. Fix the vertical pales of picket or palisade fencing vertically, with the bottom ends cut to a slope. Set the top edges to the same angle as the arris rails. The pales will be uneven in length, but each must be vertical.

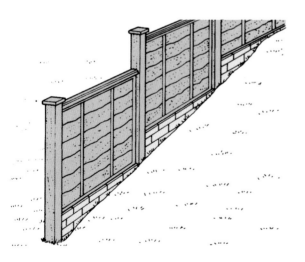

Rigid fence panels must be stepped down and the triangular gaps beneath filled with gravel boards, cut-down panels or brickwork plinths.

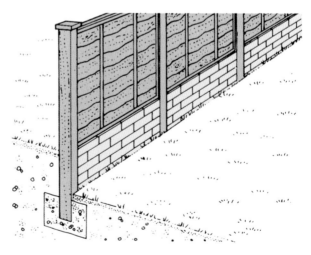

Building a retaining wall where a slope runs across the garden and erect the fence on top of this.

Fixing a trellis

Trellis is a versatile extension to a solid fence; it can serve, for example, as a means of increasing the height of a standard panel size. However, it is also useful as a lightweight fence in its own right. Trellis can also be fixed to a wall or against a fence as a means of supporting climbers and shrubs.

Trellis supports
Prefabricated wooden trellis panels in square or diamond pattern make an attractive support for climbers. Numerous types and sizes are widely stocked by garden centres and do-it-yourself stores.
Standard panels Pre-treated with horticultural preservative, standard trellis panels are commonly 1.9m (6ft 6in) high in a choice of widths.
Expanding trellis Sold in folded form, expanding trellis opens out concertina-fashion to make diamond-pattern panels.
Fan-shaped trellis Consisting of three or four uprights arranged side by side at the base, but fanning out to a broad top with cross-pieces pinned on to maintain the fan shape, this type of trellis arrangement is intended to be fixed against a wall to provide support for single climbing plants or shrubs.

Fixing the trellis
You will find that some trellis panels are pre-drilled for wall-fixing. To fix a panel to a wall, first hold the trellis in position and mark through the screw holes. Set the trellis down and drill holes in the wall to take wallplugs. Push in the wallplugs, then mount the trellis.

Trellis fixed to a wall or fence can be a problem when you need to repaint the wall behind or treat the fence with preservative. One way around this is to hinge the trellis panel to the wall at the bottom, and attach it to the wall at the top using a simple hook. When required, you simply release the hook and pivot the trellis down from the wall (shown right).

Home-made lightweight trellis
To make a lightweight trellis in diamond pattern for fixing to the top of a solid fence or wall, first draw out the area you want to fill as a square or rectangle on the ground. Cut pieces of 25 x 6mm (1 x ¼in) softwood to length and lay them diagonally across the marked-out area, parallel to each other and spaced about 50 to 75mm (2 to 3in) apart.

Cut more strips of timber to length and lay these diagonally opposite to and across the first rows of strips, forming the diamond pattern. Hammer 12mm (½in) tacks through the slats at the intersections, then turn over the lattice arrangement and tap the ends of the tacks to bend them over slightly, so preventing the strips from pulling apart.

Nail the trellis to a thin frame of softwood to give it additional support, then attach the frame itself to the fence posts.

Fixing trellis above a wall
Should you want to erect a trellis along the top of a masonry wall, you will have to attach it first to long upright battens, which you can screw to the wall.

Lay the trellis on the ground and position lengths of 50 x 20mm (2 x ¾in) sawn softwood, preservative-treated against rot, along its outer uprights. The battens should be just over twice the depth of the trellis members for a firm fixing to the wall. Nail the trellis to the battens, then lift the assembly and ask a helper to hold it in place against the wall.

Drill holes through the battens protruding from the base of the trellis at top, bottom and centre, and into the masonry. Push hammer-in frame fixings (a plastic wallplug with screw attached) into the holes and tap with a hammer to seat fully. Use a screwdriver to tighten the fixings; this causes the plugs to expand within the wall and secure the battens.

Fixing a trellis to a wall

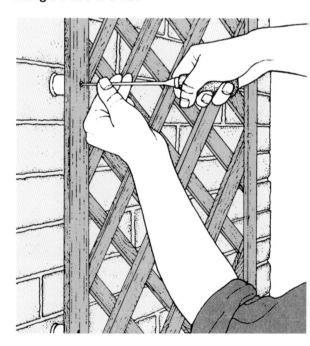

Fix trelliswork to walls with screws, using cotton reels as spacers to hold the trellis away from the wall, allowing plants to wind around it.

Making plant supports

As a means of giving height to a flat plot, or providing a colourful screen, climbing plants are invaluable. To grow well, all climbers, ramblers and scramblers need some means of support. Plants can be grown up walls and fences, but there are other structures of a more decorative appearance that can be erected purely for the plants' convenience.

Arches The rustic arch looks especially at home in cottage gardens covered in honeysuckle, roses or clematis. Larch poles (treated with a wood preservative to prolong their life) can easily be joined together in a suitable shape.

Pergolas A pergola is a series of arches linked together. Use rustic poles or treated timber and secure the bases of the posts as with those of an arch. Knock galvanized staples into the wood and tie plant stems to the frame with twine.

Tripods In small, flat gardens, tripods of larch poles can be used to support climbers in flower beds, so giving height to the planting. Simply knock treated poles into the ground 60–120cm (2–4ft) apart and fasten them together at the top with strong twine or wire.

Colonnades Useful more as a visual screen than an impenetrable barrier, the colonnade consists of a series of vertical posts linked by one or two stout ropes. The posts should be positioned 1.8–2.4m (6–8ft) apart. Plants growing on colonnades will need to be tied in regularly if the feature is to be seen to best effect.

Trees Garden trees that are past their best can be brightened up considerably if climbers are allowed to grow up them.

Plant supports on walls and fences

Plain-faced fences and most walls will need to be provided with some kind of plant support if climbers and wall shrubs are to be grown against them.

The traditional way of supporting climbing plants on walls and fences is to fix horizontal wires to the surface at 30–45cm (1–1½ft) intervals. These can be held in place with masonry nails if they are required for one season only, but metal vine eyes inserted into drilled and plugged holes provide a more permanent fixing. The wires will be held 5–8cm (2–3in) away from the wall, allowing the stems to twine around them. Wire netting is an alternative to trellising and wires.

Hinging a trellis for easy access

Hinge the base of the trellis, fixing it to a 5cm x 2.5cm (2 x 1in) wooden batten with brass hinges. Fix to a batten at the top with wing nuts.

Using wire and cleats

To support plants on walls, attach wires horizontally at 30–45cm (1–1½ft) intervals with masonry nails or vine eyes.

Gates

Whether you want a gate to confine children and pets to the garden, to improve your frontage, or to provide a measure of security, ready-assembled gates are available in a choice of materials and a host of styles. Choose a design with care.

Timber gates

Wooden gates suit most sites, although styles vary greatly.
Front entrance gates To mark a boundary in front of a garden path, and at the same time restrict the movements of children and animals, look for a gate that is about 900mm or 1.2m (3 or 4ft) high, which corresponds with the popular height of fencing and garden walling. A gate of this type normally comprises a pair of side uprights, with horizontal rails and, usually, exterior-grade plywood lower infill panels.
Side entrance gates Usually more utilitarian in appearance than front entrance gates, and normally about two or three times the height to discourage intruders, side entrance gates are traditionally the ledged-and-braced type. Three horizontal rails are braced with diagonal rails, and the cladding may comprise feather-edged vertical boards to blend with a close-boarded fence, tongued-and-grooved vertical boards, or else pointed-top vertical pales.

Drive entrance gates To fill a drive width of up to about 3m (10ft), you can install a pair of standard front entrance gates, but for wider than normal drive entrances you can choose from various models of farm-style gates.

A traditional five-bar gate consists of a pair of upright posts with five equally spaced horizontal bars between, and a diagonal brace fixed to the back to prevent the gate from sagging. The brace normally spans from the low part of the hinge side to the top part of the opening side.

Smaller versions of these gates doubled up with their large counterparts are often sold as a means of providing pedestrian access at a drive entrance. A band of metal usually links the two inner posts of the gates as a catch.

Hardware for gates

Most gates come without latches, hinges, or other hardware, and you will have to buy these separately. Select fittings that have a "japanned" finish (black glossy lacquer) or a matt black coating to prevent rust attacking the metal. Alternatively, choose galvanized metal fittings which have greater resistance to rusting and can be overpainted to blend with the gate if necessary.

Types of gates

Overlapping board gate Intended to match a run of wavy-edged, lap fencing.

Woven panel gate A side entrance gate made to fit in a run of basketweave fencing.

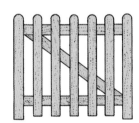

Paling gate The diagonal brace an ideal complement for a picket fence.

Diamond slatted gate A front entrance gate, a more rustic design.

Ornately scrolled metal gate Most suitable for an elegant front entrance.

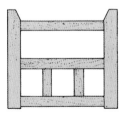

Standard timber gate A front entrance gate with plywood infill panels below.

Choosing gate accessories

Strap hinges Double strap hinges consist of a single strip of metal bent to fit along both sides of the horizontal rails of a timber gate. A preformed loop at the end slots onto a matching "hook", which is either bolted through the side post, hammered in, or set in the mortar joints of a brick pier.

T-hinges The simplest type of gate hinge, the T-hinge consists of a screw-on hinge flap for attachment to a wooden gate post with an elongated flap screwed to the rails of the gate.

Hook-and-band hinges With this heavyweight hinge, a separate screw-on hinge pin connects with a bolted-and-screwed-on metal strap fixed to the gate.

Reversible hinges A hinge which can be used either way up (and therefore at either side of the gate), the reversible hinge has a pin which is housed in a pair of screw-on cups.

Suffolk latch Used mainly for tall, side-entrance, closeboarded or tongue-and-groove clad gates, the Suffolk latch has a thumb-operated pivoting "sneck" (catch).

Automatic latch This consists of a hook screwed to the inside face of the gate's top rail, which links with a thumb-operated latch attached to the post: the latch fastens when the gate is pulled closed.

Spring closer A metal spring attached to the back of the gate at a diagonal angle between the hinge post and the hinged stile of the gate, properly tensioned, will push the gate into the closed position when released, engaging the latch.

Drop bolt Fixed near the bottom of the gate's opening stile on the inside face, a drop bolt can be released and engaged in a plate fixed to the ground to prevent a drive gate from swinging too far when it is closed.

Gate stop Fulfilling the same role as a drop bolt, the gate stop consists of a cast-iron seating fixed in a hole in the ground, with a lift-up flap to prevent the gate from swinging too far.

Gate holder To hold a gate open, a holding device consisting of a pivoting latch is fixed at ground level at the point at which the gate swings open, engaging with a loop.

Cabin hook To secure a single gate in the open position, a cabin hook consists of a slim length of hooked metal fastened to a screw-on plate, attached to the gate. A second plate with a loop is screwed to a post or wall to take the hook.

Metal gates

Metal garden gates are made either of mild steel, for lightweight gates, or wrought iron, a heavier and more durable material. Styles of gate for path and drive entrances are similar, and consist of traditional ornamental designs or plainer infills within an outer framework. Side entrance gates are usually taller than front gates, but based on similar designs.

Latches are usually attached to the gate during assembly, and are normally of the lever variety used on timber gates. Hinges, likewise, are normally fitted to the gate during assembly, and there is usually no way of altering the inbuilt hand (gates hang from one side or the other; either left-handed or right-handed).

Gate posts

Gates may be hung between timber, metal, or concrete posts, or else fixed between brick, stone or concrete block piers attached to a masonry wall. Select a material that will complement or blend with the gate and adjacent boundary.

FITTING GATE POSTS

Fixing Gate posts
Although gate posts may be set in concrete in the same way as fence posts, you should link the post holes with a bridge of concrete to form a single unit. This will make the sagging of individual posts less likely, and so reduce the possibility of the gates sticking or jamming.

Spacing out the posts
To set the correct width between posts, lie the gate on the ground and place the posts at each side, leaving a gap of 6mm (¼in) from the gate stiles. Place hardboard packing between the gate and posts, then temporarily pin battens of wood connecting the posts at top and bottom with an intermediate batten fixed diagonally.

Lift up the connected post assembly and position in the previously dug post holes. Prop the posts vertically with struts of timber while pouring in the concrete.

Dig a trench about 300mm (1ft) deep between the post holes, add hardcore to the base and top with fresh concrete. Compact the concrete level with the surrounding path surface. Leave for a few days until the concrete has hardened before hanging the gate.

Fitting timber packing at the piers
Where new piers are being built for a gate, the hinge pins and latch keep should be built in during construction. But when you are fitting a gate between existing masonry piers, it is easier to attach vertical lengths of timber packing to each pier and secure the gate hinges and catches to these. This procedure saves your having to cut into the masonry in order to fit the mortar-in type of fitting.

Stand the gate between the piers and measure the gap for the thickness of packing timber needed. Cut the packing posts, drill holes for the fixing bolts, then mark the positions of the holes on the piers. Drill holes for the bolts, then attach the posts using expansion bolts.

Drive gate posts
A heavy drive gate requires stout fixings at the posts to prevent the gate from sagging. At the opening side a standard fence post fixing can be used, but at the hinge side it is best to dig an extra-wide hole and secure a length of timber horizontally near the base of the post to act as an anchor.

Constructing a gate

Constructing a gate to your own specifications is quite straightforward, and uses only basic carpentry techniques and tools. With the rigid outer framework assembled, fit the type of infill cladding which best suits your garden design.

The frame components
The frame consists of a pair of stiles of 100 x 50mm (4 x 2in) hardwood (or planed softwood as a less expensive option) with top and bottom horizontal rails of 75 x 40mm (3 x 1½in) timber tenoned into mortises cut in the stiles. A diagonal brace of 100 x 19mm (4 x ¾in) timber is fixed between the stiles.

The infill cladding may be a row of vertical tongued-and-grooved boards, a latticework arrangement of thin slats, or plain plywood. The cladding is fixed to battens of ½in (12mm) square timber screwed to the inner perimeter of the outer frame members.

Marking out the joints
Mark out and cut the stiles to length and bevel the top ends inward for rainwater run-off. Mark out and cut the top and bottom rails to length, including an allowance at each end for forming the stub tenons: these should penetrate mortises cut

in the stiles by about 75mm (3in).

To prepare the tenons for cutting, first mark their length on each end of the top and bottom rails and square the lines around the timber using a try square and marking knife.

For accuracy, use a tool called a mortise gauge to scribe the tenons on the rails. Set the gauge's twin pins to the width of the tenon: 12mm (½in). Then with a rail set upright in a vice, score parallel lines down the sides as far as the scribed length marks and across the top of the timber. Mark out the other end of the rail, and the second rail, in this way.

Cutting the tenons
With a rail clamped in a vice at an angle of 45 degrees away from you, use a tenon saw held horizontally to cut down the waste side of the gauged lines as far as the length marks. Now reverse the rail in the vice and cut down from the other corner. Set the rail upright and saw down the triangle of waste that is left. Repeat for the other side of the tenon, then hold the rail flat and saw along the length mark to remove the waste. Complete all four tenons in this way.

Make shouldered tenons by marking 19mm (¾in) in from each side of the tenon and cutting down these lines. Turn the rail on its side and cut down the side of the tenon at the length mark to remove the piece of waste wood.

Cutting the mortises
Place the stiles side by side, inner faces pointing uppermost, and mark lines across both 10mm (6in) from the top and 25mm (1in) in from the bottom, using a try square. Place a tenon on the stiles, aligned with the pencil lines and mark the width of the tenon. Square the line across, then use the mortise gauge set to 12mm (½in), as before, to scribe twin lines between the joint width lines. This gives the width of the mortise. Repeat for the other three mortises.

Traditionally, mortises are cut solely with a mortise chisel, which takes some time and practice. Instead, it is acceptable to drill out the mortises using a 12mm (½in) diameter auger bit fitted in a power drill: first measure the length of the tenon (in this case, 75mm/3in) and wrap adhesive tape around the bit as a guide to drilling to the correct depth.

Clamp a stile horizontally in a vice or workbench, mortises uppermost, and drill out the bulk of the waste in a series of closely spaced holes within the mortise lines. Remove the bit when the tape guide reaches the top of the timber.

The mortise must, of course, be square-sided, so use a mortise chisel to pare away the remaining waste carefully. Repeat this procedure for all the mortises, then test-fit the tenons in the slots.

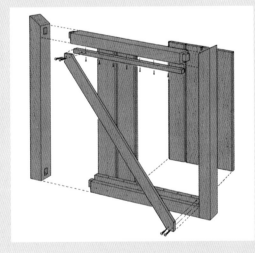

CONSTRUCTING A FRONT ENTRANCE GATE

A front entrance gate constructed from a simple mortise-and-tenoned outer frame with diagonal brace can be completed with your choice of infill panels or slats. Construct from hardwood for best weathering, or softwood if the gate is to be painted.

Below: A freestanding pergola
can act as an exciting
centrepiece to a garden – this
one acts as a leafy walkway
to seating.

Right: A sloping site, natural or otherwise, is necessary for the construction of a waterfall. If the garden has no natural slope it is quite easy to build an artificial mound out of soil.

Below left: There is endless scope for constructing pools, from the variety of shapes and sizes available to the kinds of surrounds, whether hard landscaping, planting, or a combination.

Below right: The desired jet of water in a fountain can only be achieved if the pump is large enough to emit the necessary flow and height.

Constructing a gate

Assembling the frame

Sand all the joints thoroughly and wipe off dust, then apply PVA woodworking adhesive to the tenons. Slot the tenons into the mortises and clamp the entire frame with a pair of sash cramps which fit across the gate pulling the stiles inwards. Check with a try square that the internal angle between rails and stiles is 90 degrees: if there is some misalignment you may be able to correct this by repositioning the sash cramps to pull the frame square.

Using a damp rag, wipe off any smears of adhesive that have squeezed out from around the joints, then set aside the assembly for the adhesive to dry.

The diagonal brace fits into the top opening-side corner and the bottom hinge-side corner. Cut the brace slightly overlong and hold in place. Mark the brace for cutting against the stiles and rails, then saw off the corners as marked. Fit the brace to the inner frame to which the cladding is attached.

Fitting the inner frame

Cut two lengths of 12mm (½in) square timber to fit horizontally between the stiles, and two more to fit between the first two, once they have been secured to the top and bottom rails.

Attach this inner frame, butt-jointed at the corners, with 25mm (1in) long rustproofed countersunk woodscrews. Recess the heads beneath the surface by countersinking the mouths of pre-drilled clearance holes with a countersinking bit.

If the cladding material is to fit within the top and bottom rails, position the inner frame back from the front face of the gate the thickness of the material you are using. Where you want the cladding – say, decoratively shaped pales – to protrude above the top rail of the gate, set the inner frame flush with the front face of the gate.

Screw the diagonal brace to the back edge of the inner frame, then invert the gate and nail on the cladding.

Attaching the cladding

The cladding can be attached with 35mm (1¼in) long galvanized lost-head nails. For pales, use 50, 75, or 100mm (2, 3, or 4in) wide softwood, 19mm (¾in) thick, with two nails per fixing to the inner frame. With panelling, drive in nails around the perimeter at 75mm (3in) intervals.

Hanging the gate

Before fixing the gate between the posts, check that there is sufficient clearance underneath for the gate to swing open

Positioning tapes for offset measurements

1 Prop the gate between the posts or piers on wooden blocks, with a gap of 6mm (¼in) at each side and 50mm (2in) below.

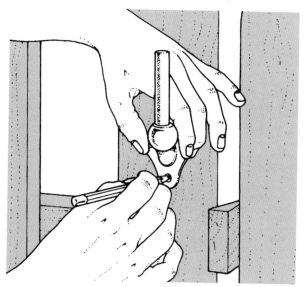

2 Fit the strap hinges to the gate first, prop in position and screw the lower cups onto the end of the hinge pins.

Constructing a gate

fully by positioning it against the hinge-side post and chocking it up in the fully open position, prior to fixing it between the posts or piers.

If there is sufficient clearance, chock up the gate between the posts or piers, with a clearance gap of 6mm (¼in) at each side, using wedges of wood. Raise the gate by 50mm (2in). How the hinges are fitted depends on the type you are using:
T-hinges With the gate in position, hold the hinges in place along the top and bottom rails and mark through the screw-fixing holes. Remove the gate and drill starter holes for the screws. Fit the long hinge flaps to the gate, then offer the gate up to the post and screw on the narrow hinge flaps.
Strap hinges Attach the strap part of the hinge to the gate, after drilling any bolt holes necessary, then prop up against the post, but in the open position. Mark the screw holes for the hook on the post, then screw the hook on.
Reversible hinges With the gate propped between the posts, straps attached, screw the bottom cups onto the post, then fit the top cups, retaining the hinge pin.

Attach a spring-closer across the gate and post by screwing the top bracket to the post and the lower one to the hinge stile of the gate. Fit the latch to complete the installation: with the gate closed, screw the latch mechanism or keep against the post, then fit the locking bar and screw on.

FITTING A SPRING-CLOSING DEVICE

A spring-closer is useful, especially where child safety is a consideration. This device, screwed across the post and gate on the hinge side, will pull the gate shut even when it is left open. An automatic latch will hold it shut.

Dealing with sloping ground

No part of the gate should come into contact with the ground when the gate is opened or closed. If your garden path slopes down towards the gate, work out the height the gate must be hinged at by getting a helper to hold it between the posts while you work. There must be a minimum clearance from the highest point on the ground of at least 30mm (1¼in).

With the gate held in position, mark the top and bottom positions of the gate on the posts, then cut wedges the correct size to prop the gate in place while you secure the hinges.

Where the ground slopes across the line of the gate, you will, of course, still have to fix the gate vertically, and tolerate a gap at one side: hinge the gate at the higher side of the slope, so that it will swing freely without scraping the ground.

3 Fit the top hinge cups to retain the hinge pins. Note that the bottom corner of the diagonal brace is on the side of the hinge.

4 An automatic latch is screwed to the gate post and its locking bar to the gate; a thumb-operated lever releases the bar.

Trompe l'oeil

The practice of deceiving the eye using *trompe l'oeil* techniques has been elevated to an art form. In garden design it is almost always used to make a garden appear larger.

There are four devices commonly used for this: optical illusion (often involving trellis), mirrors, murals, and false perspective.

Trellis

In this trellis *trompe l'oeil*, the view beyond is partly obscured – in reality, there is very little space. A dark-coloured wall with green ivy climbing up it, for example, gives the impression of distance. Should more space be available behind the trellis, plant grass or lay a light-coloured path with blue-flowering plants to suggest greater distance. Trellis *trompe l'oeil* can be free-standing, as this one is, or it can be fastened to a wall, but a free-standing trellis is best set with in a neutral foil, such as a yew hedge.

Mirrors

Mirrors are used to create a sense of space in confined spaces. Provided that they are made of weatherproof toughened glass and are strongly supported, mirror *trompe l'oeil* features can be used in a variety of situations.

In the example shown here, the mirror has been recessed into a moon gate, but it could just as well have been positioned a metre or so beyond the moon gate on a far wall thereby allowing hidden access to a path running behind the wall. This ploy makes the garden appear twice its real length, once the reflected image is added to the true distance between the front of the garden and the wall.

False doors or gates

False doors or gates are useful for *trompe l'oeil* and give the impression that there is more to the garden than there really is. In the example shown here, four small diamond-shaped mirrors are set into the door, making it appear that there is another garden beyond.

Half-thickness metal gates, which appear to be of normal thickness when reflected, can be used in conjunction with mirrors. The gates, which can be made to look authentic with hinges and latches, should be removable to allow them and the mirror to be cleaned.

Murals

Murals can be effective both indoors and out. A previously dismal basement has been transformed in this example by a simple, brightly coloured mural, using exterior quality paint. In conjunction with real potted plants, the illusion, while never entirely convincing, is fun and cheering.

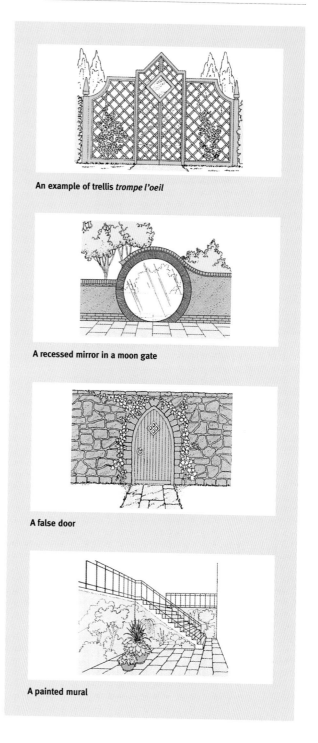

An example of trellis *trompe l'oeil*

A recessed mirror in a moon gate

A false door

A painted mural

Contours/planters

Shaping the contours of the land to suit your requirements is one of the basic principles of planning a garden, but one that is often neglected. Many people put up with gardens that are nothing more than flat, featureless expanses of earth, with no visual relief or outstanding features to attract the attention. This is particularly so with newly constructed houses, where the garden is likely to be a muddy wasteland of debris left behind by the builder. In fact, you can flatten a sloping site, if that is what your garden design requires; but often it is better to turn the slope to advantage. If you start with a flat site, you ran create terraced planters or undulating shapes without too much difficulty.

A log roll planter

A planter need not be a high structure between two ground levels. Even adding a contrasting edging to a flower border or a slightly raised lawn can provide a subtle but significant change of level that adds to the interest of the design.

Several manufacturers stock preformed half-round log sections, with flat backs, connected in a log roll. These are intended as an edging for borders, but equally well serve to make a raised planter or a division between terraces.

The heights of the individual logs in the rolls are typically 150, 300, and 450mm (6, 12, and 18in), and they come in 1 m (3 ft 3in) lengths.

The benefit of log roll edging is that it is very flexible and can cope with quite complex curves. To install the edging, dig a shallow trench around the path, lawn, or border, then unroll and insert the edging, and backfill with earth to hold it in place (illustrated below). Although the timber is durable, it is sensible to fix heavy-duty polythene behind the rolls in order to prevent the damp earth from touching them.

Reasons for changing the contours

Faced with a plain plot the most radical option of all is altering the shape of the ground. This is not just a means of creating more visual interest – it also provides the opportunity to erect original structures which will serve as additional planting areas.

Introducing earth-retaining walls into a basically flat site will immediately create a series of terraces, which you can plant out. Terracing a steeply sloping site has the benefit of making the plot more usable, workable, and attractive to the eye.

Changes of level in a garden can provide shelter from

Constructing a log-roll planter

1 Mark out the area of the planting bed and dig a shallow trench at the perimeter to take the rolls of log edging.

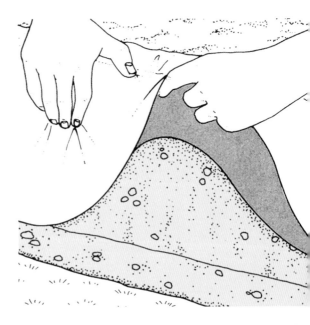

2 Drape heavy-gauge polythene over the back wall of the trench as a damp-proofing precaution to protect the timber edging.

prevailing winds or frost, and hence may be useful in the provision of, say, a kitchen garden. Slopes can also have the function of concealing an unsatisfactory boundary.

Introducing slopes

Remodelling the earth can produce interesting undulating profiles, often with the benefit of improving drainage to promote healthy plant growth. Beware of too drastic alterations, however, as the point of the exercise should be to make adjustments, not to introduce dramatic change.

Slopes should lie at an angle of not more than 30 degrees, because a bank steeper than this is liable to erosion by surface and underground water movement. The gentler a slope is, the wider the area it will require; but remember that steep slopes will be difficult to traverse.

A gradient of 30 degrees is manageable comfortably with a cylinder lawn mower. A hover mower can cope with a steeper slope – up to 45 degrees. When planting a steep bank, it is advisable to plant through a sheet of coarse netting pegged into the soil; this will retain the earth until the roots establish.

When introducing slopes into the garden, it is important to relate them to the main views. A view at right angles to the

contour lines tends to be more appealing than a view that falls away to one side or the other.

Cutting-and-filling

Using the "cut-and-fill" technique you can alter the existing levels. For the sake of economy, the cut should be equivalent by volume to the fill. Carting away excess earth, or bringing new earth to the site, can be an expensive operation. The procedure involves removing the fertile topsoil from the whole area of ground to be reshaped, removing the subsoil from one area of the site and moving it to another, then returning the topsoil to both levels. Take care not to leave subsoil exposed as a surface covering.

Drainage of the site

Free drainage from the higher terraced area is necessary to prevent the roots of plants from becoming waterlogged. Building rubble can be used to form the core of a raised planting bed. A problem with these structures is that the soil is likely to drain too rapidly denying the plants much of the nourishment they need and making it necessary to water the plants more frequently. This can be prevented by laying turves, grass-side down, on top of the drainage material.

The retaining walls of planters should incorporate some form of drainage to avoid trapping water. A simple plastic or clay drain pipe inserted across the thickness of the wall, protruding from the face near the base, will act as a channel for excess moisture. On masonry walls it is sufficient to omit the mortar from a few vertical joints between bricks or blocks. This in no way affects the stability of the wall, but it does keep the back face of the structure well drained.

Materials for planters

Raised planting areas are a means of compartmentalizing your garden, and are especially convenient for the elderly or infirm to work in because they can be designed to be reached without stooping. They can be constructed from a wide range of materials, the choice of which is often determined by the style of garden. For a formal patio-style town garden, for example, neat, angular brickwork planters are an ideal choice, perhaps linked to brick walls and terraces, flanking sets of stops, or built within an area of paving slabs. Choosing second-hand bricks and incorporating curves in the planter walls will lessen the angular appearance while still creating an effect that is well organized and neat.

If you would prefer to create a more natural-looking effect – for example, in a rural garden – timber enclosures or dry-stone retaining walls are perhaps more appropriate. Timber types can be constructed from planed, preservative-treated

3 Unroll the log edging and set it in the trench, with its back edge against the polythene. Backfill the trench with soil.

Contours/planters

timber, jointed for strength as a sturdy framework to contain the earth; or they may be nothing more than a series of rough-hewn logs sunk end-on in the ground as a basic retaining wall.

Natural stone walls will always appear rugged and random (see pages 134–135). Reconstructed walling blocks with riven or exposed aggregate faces offer the outward appearance of a natural material combined with the manufactured' regularity of brickwork.

Whatever material you choose, you should strive to soften the structures with masses of plants, either spilling over the edge of the planter, or actually growing from between the stones or timbers.

Around the planters

The treatment of the planters' immediate surroundings is as important as the choice of materials. If you have planned the garden so that it will provide easy access for equipment, a paved or gravelled area surrounding the raised planting beds is ideal. This also reduces the amount of weeding that will need to be done.

Alternatively, turfing the area around the planters will help

---

MAKING A "RAILWAY SLEEPER" PLANTER

When stacking sleeper-type blocks to form a planter, stagger the vertical joins between them in alternate rows, just as you would when laying bricks. It is important to anchor two or more sleepers, using metal hoops driven into the ground, if you stack them with their short side uppermost. Backfill with subsoil, then topsoil.

Some manufacturers produce miniature versions of the original railway sleepers. These often have one or more rounded faces for a sorter, more natural appearance.

Construct a raised planter from sleepers laid horizontally. Butt-join the sleepers at the corners.

Build up courses of sleepers to the height required for the planter. Stagger the vertical joints to give a strong, rigid bond.

them to blend in with the garden. The planters may also be made to rise from conventional flower borders, so that they are surrounded by plants. Paths wending their way through the plot will, of course, be needed with such a design, for access with equipment and for tackling periodic maintenance tasks.

Building retaining walls

Constructing an earth-retaining wall to introduce terraces to the plot is not a straightforward matter (see page 133).

The sheer weight of earth that must be held back calls for a structure that is built to rigorous standards. If it is to be over about 1.2m (4ft) in height, you should obtain advice on the structure from your local authority's Building Control Department.

"Railway sleeper" walls

In the past, ex-railway sleepers have been a popular choice for some garden features. However, as they contain potentially harmful chemicals to preserve them, their use in the garden is controlled. For instance, they must not be used as part of play equipment or where skin is likely to come in contact with them. In addition, ex-railway sleepers can leach tar or other noxious substances, particularly in warm weather. As an alternative, suppliers are offering sleeper-style wooden blocks for use in the garden. When laid as a single layer they require no support or fixings other than their own considerable weight. The sleepers, which generally measure 1.3m x 225 x 125mm (52 x 10 x 5in), can be laid directly on the ground as the edging to a border, path or other feature. A single height of sleeper will create a substantial low bed, but you can also stack the sleepers to make a high retaining wall (see box, opposite).

Log walls

Logs can be used to make sturdy planters with a natural, rustic quality. Stakes of the same wood can be used to secure the walls; they need to be sturdy and rammed well into the ground to brace the weight of soil in the planter.

Lay the bottom logs on the ground to plot out the position of the planter. Decide on the height of the planter in advance and cut the stakes accordingly. Drive the stakes in close to the end of each log.

At a corner where two logs meet, two stakes will be required; the ends of the logs should be bevelled. Build up the layers of logs behind the stakes, staggering the ends of each course of logs in relation to the course below. Attach the logs to the stakes using galvanized nails.

Interlocking logs

Another way to make a raised planter (or a fishpond or tree seat) is to buy flat-backed, round-faced logs with notches cut in their edges. Adjoining logs interlock to create a rigid yet lightweight structure, and it is possible to construct rectangular, hexagonal, or other shaped units. Preformed panels made of a row of connected logs can be attached with dowel fixings so that a planter can also double as a practical bench unit in the garden. Because of the interlocking construction, no further fixings are necessary.

Damp-proofing provisions

Any timber structure will succumb to rot unless it is specially treated, so it is essential that some kind of damp-proofing provision is made in the planter construction.

While a thorough treatment with preservative is vital, additional protection can be provided by a waterproof barrier between the retaining walls and the earth in the planter. Heavy-gauge polythene placed behind a log roll border or sleeper wall will act as a moisture bar.

Sandwich the polythene sheet between the timber and the earth, allowing it to protrude slightly at the top and bottom: future planting will conceal the polythene from view.

A further provision against dampness rising into the timber is to bed the retaining walls on a fine layer of gravel, which has the advantage of being free-draining.

A PLANK AND POST PLANTER

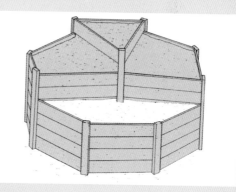

A plank-and-post timber planter can be built on flat ground, or into a slope. It consists of a number of posts supporting stout planks stacked one on top of the other to create a basic box to contain the soil. The box can be any angular shape, and divided into a number of bays.

Making a timber planter

This timber planter provides a neat growing area you can work on without having to stoop. No complicated carpentry joints are required to construct the planter, as the assembly makes use of the weight of the earth the box contains to force the side planks against the supporting timber posts.

Planning the structure
Construct the planter from 75 x 50mm (3 x 2in) sawn softwood for the supporting posts and 150 x 50mm (6 x 2in) sawn softwood for the plank sides. Try to purchase treated timber or treat the timber with a non-toxic preservative.

Sketch your garden and draw in the position and size of the planter to see how it relates to other features. Work the sketch into a scale plan drawn on graph paper so that you

Constructing a timber planter

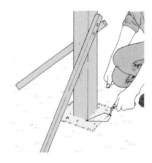

1 Set the perimeter posts in concrete, or use spikes to support them around the marked out area of the planter.

2 Mark cutting lines on the planks. The mitres will be forced against the posts by the pressure of the contained soil.

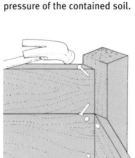

3 Place the bottom planks behind the posts. They should be long enough to finish at the middle of the posts.

4 Stack the planks behind the posts, level them, then secure them to the back of each post using galvanized nails.

can calculate the quantity of timber you will need to buy. Draw a side elevation so that you can work out the height of the various bays that divide the planter.

Setting the posts and plank sides
Mark out the overall shape of the planter on the ground using stringlines stretched between wooden pegs driven into the ground at the post locations. Dig the post holes and add hardcore to the holes. Set the uprights in the holes, propped vertically, and pour in concrete. Leave until the concrete is fully set. Alternatively you can use metal fencing spikes to set the posts: these are hammered into the ground and have a collar at the top into which the bottom end of the post slots.

Hold each plank, which should be longer than required, behind pairs of posts and mark off the cutting lines in pencil. Cut the planks to size using a power saw with an adjustable sole plate. Setting the angle of the sole plate will ensure an accurate fit for each plank.

Cut the planks as marked, then position them behind the posts on a layer of fine gravel to ensure rapid drainage of rainwater. You should aim to sink the bottom row of planks about 100mm (4in) below the surrounding ground level so that soil will not leak out onto the paving or other surface. Place a spirit level on the top edge of each plank and tap the plank horizontal with the shaft of a club hammer.

Stack the planks until you reach the finished height and secure by driving in two 75mm (3in) long galvanized nails at each end at an angle to each other.

Completing the planter
When you have constructed the outer framework of the timber planter you can start to divide it off into a number of separate bays, set at different levels. Intermediate posts can be fixed within the main box to support single planks, creating a gentle change of level, or else stacked planks can be used for a more dramatic terraced effect. Remember that the bottom planks should be bedded on hardcore and gravel both to prevent them from sinking and to improve drainage.

In spite of any preservative used on the timber, the planter will eventually succumb to the effects of the damp earth unless you provide a second line of defence. Pin sheets of heavy-gauge polythene to the inside walls of the planter and its bays before you fill it with earth: this will form a physical barrier through which the dampness cannot penetrate.

Once the skeleton of the planter has been constructed, you can fill the box with upturned turves to within about 250mm (10in) of the top row of planks. Add subsoil and compact lightly. Add topsoil to within a few inches of the top row of planks and leave to settle for about two weeks.

Making a brick planter

A masonry planter is not difficult to construct, following the basic techniques of bricklaying (see page 130). The structure need be no more than about six or eight courses high, so the provision of foundations is not a problem, unless the ground is especially soft. A planter can be on any sound, level surface.

Bricks and mortar

To make a planter about eight bricks long, two bricks wide and six courses high, you will need about 100 bricks. This will produce a planter that measures 1565mm (61¾in) long by 440mm (17¾in) deep (front to back).

Choose facing bricks, which have an attractive colour and facing texture, if the planter is to be freestanding, or obtain bricks similar to those used in other features in the garden.

An ordinary stretcher bonding pattern (which has bricks overlapping by half their length in alternate courses) is used in assembly; at the corners, a brick is turned at right-angles to the others and the bond continued.

About 80kg (176lb) of mortar is needed to lay the bricks, and this can be purchased as a dry ready-mix. Add water. Mortar of the correct consistency should hold the ridged shape when a shovel is dragged across the surface.

Building the planter

Dry-lay the first two courses of bricks on the foundations, without mortar but with finger-thick gaps between each brick, to check that the stretcher bond and the mortar joint thicknesses are correct and consistent.

Set up stringlines and pegs. Check that the corner of the planter is at right-angles using a try square. Remove the bricks about three at a time, and re-lay them on a mortar screed trowelled on the base. Tap the first brick into place with the handle of the trowel, aligning it with the stringline, so that the mortar joint is only 10mm (⅜in) thick. With the trowel scoop up the surplus mortar that is squeezed out and use to spread onto one end of the second brick, forming a vertical joint. Lay the third brick in the same way, then remove the next three loose-laid bricks and lay them properly on mortar.

Check that the bricks laid are set horizontally. Complete the first course of bricks, then lay the second on top, staggering the vertical joins by half the length of a brick. As the courses rise, use a gauge rod (see page 132) to check that the mortar joints are consistent and check the face of the wall for bowing.

Completing the planter walls

If you are using bricks with frogs (indents) on one side, these should be laid frog upward, so that the vertical mortar joint is made as strong as possible. The fresh mortar, trowelled onto each course, fills the frog and forms a key that prevents sideways movement of the courses. At the final, sixth course, however, lay the bricks frog downwards, so that the flat top faces of the bricks will give a smooth top to the planter walls. Alternatively, lay a row of specially shaped coping bricks along the top of the planter. These are available with a bevelled, chamfered or rounded finish, and are laid in exactly the same way as ordinary bricks.

Pointing the mortar joints

Neaten the appearance of the planter by pointing the mortar joints. To do this, use a length of hosepipe to rub the mortar, to form a neat, rounded profile. Leave the planter for four days so that the mortar can harden fully before adding the soil.

Damp-proofing the planter

As the planter will contain a considerable amount of earth, which will be damp for much of the time, it is a good idea to paint the inside of the unit with bituminous emulsion to prevent the moisture from soaking into the bricks. Leave the emulsion to dry thoroughly before adding the soil filling.

Allow surplus moisture to seep away by omitting the mortar from about three vertical joints between bricks in the first course on each long side.

Dig over the base of the planter to ensure drainage is not impaired and shovel a layer of pea gravel 25–50mm (1–2in) deep into the base to provide free drainage. Cover the ground with upturned turves (grass-side down) to prevent clogging, then top up with fertile topsoil. Allow this to settle for about one week before filling in any hollows and planting out.

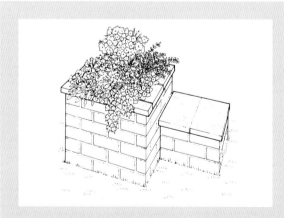

A brick planter can incorporate a low ledge, which can be used as a seat or as a plinth for a planted container.

Constructing a pergola

A timber pergola provides an ideal way to support grapevines, climbing plants, or bush or tree fruit. Once the plants are properly established, the foliage covering the pergola will also provide a cool and shady place to sit on hot summer days.

Alternatively, a pergola can be used as an arbour, or partially covered walkway. Entwined with roses, honeysuckle, or clematis, such a structure may simply terminate at a garden bench seat, or open into a gazebo. Built against a house wall, the pergola will even afford some measure of protection against rain, particularly if the foliage is lush.

The basic structure
A pergola is basically a stout timber framework consisting of tall upright posts with an arrangement of cross-pieces at the top, which form a semi-solid roof. The sides of the pergola may be left open, or else clad with trelliswork, planks, or fence panels, or garden furniture may be positioned between posts.

Unless the pergola is intended exclusively to support clinging climbers such as ivy or twining ones such as honeysuckle, additional supports to train plants over the pergola will be required. Numerous options are available:
Trellis Prefabricated trellis panels, or the expanding type of lightweight diamond-pattern trellis, can simply be pinned on to the supporting posts.
Line wires Galvanized wire, ideally coated with plastic, can be stretched between the posts and the existing top and additional bottom rails to form a vertical, horizontal or criss-crossing form of support for twining plants. Secure the line wires with hammer-in staples or nails, twisting the wire around itself using pliers. Alternatively, purchase some screw-in vine eyes to attach the wires.
Mesh Plastic-coated chain link garden fencing can be stretched to fit across the pergola framework and secured with staples. Alternatively, choose the lightweight green plastic mesh, which is fixed in the same way.

Once the climbers become established, support their stems by tying them to lead- or plastic-headed wall nails, driven into the main supporting timbers of the pergola.

The roof structure
The roof of the pergola is usually fitted with additional supports for climbers, in the form of cane poles, trellis, mesh or line wires stretched between eyebolts. It is important that the main roof beams are made of strong enough timber – 150 x 50mm (6 x 2in) sawn softwood is ideal – so that a person's weight could be supported. Snow can be very heavy, and the pergola must be able to withstand this loading.

The materials used to connect the roof timbers to the upright posts should be strong and rigid, and it is usual to use cross-halving joints for the longitudinal and cross-members. This joint, in which half the timber's thickness is cut

A freestanding pergola

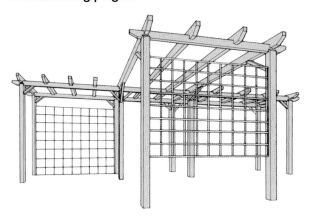

Construct a freestanding pergola over the patio to provide an area for sitting out under the shade of plants entwined around the structure's main beams and trellis panels. The pergola maybe a single unit, or two or three connected areas, furnished with patio seats, loungers, or a barbecue. Alternatively, construct the pergola as a leafy walkway.

An attached pergola

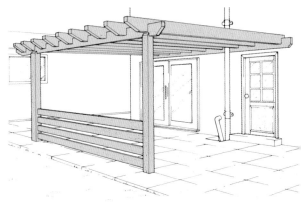

A pergola sited against the wall of the house becomes a partially covered extension to the living room, dining room, or kitchen with direct access, ideally through patio doors. This type of garden structure can also double as a carport during the winter months, when built over a suitable base such as slabs or pavers.

Constructing a pergola

Additional support for plants

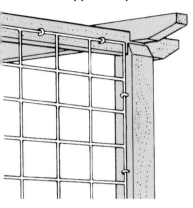

Galvanized chain link or plastic mesh can be stapled to the pergola posts and cross-rails as a plant support.

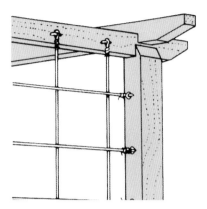

Line wires can be stretched vertically, horizontally, or in criss-cross fashion from eyes fixed to the pergola.

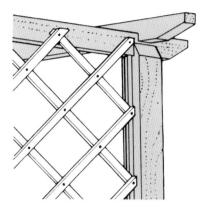

Prefabricated trellis in diamond or square pattern can be cut to fit across the posts and pinned on.

away to be restored when the pieces are connected, resists sideways movement and is unlikely to separate. Posts are normally notched to accept the roof timbers, or may have metal brackets attached.

Where the pergola is attached to the house wall, a stout wall plate is normally employed, bolted to tin- masonry and notched to take the ends of the roof timbers. A slope can be incorporated in the pergola roof, away from the house wall, in case subsequent glazing is required to convert the structure into, perhaps, a carport. There is no reason why sections of the pergola cannot be partially glazed using wired glass or plastic sheeting.

Types of pergola post

The supporting posts need not be timber. More substantial supports can be formed by constructing piers of brickwork, natural stone blocks, tubular or angled metal, or even cast concrete. For a classical appearance supporting columns cast in concrete could be used, possibly fluted and topped with capitals or incorporating decorative corbels or other scrollwork embellishments.

Design

The design of the structure and its size are important if the pergola is not to look incongruous. Many pergolas are made distinctive by their extending roof timbers, which are cut with bevels reminiscent of Oriental architecture: this design also protects the vulnerable end grain of the timber from the rain.

The shape of the structure may be rectangular or square, positioned over a patio or terrace. It can be made to follow the line of a path, or turn a right-angled corner in order to fit into a corner of the garden against a boundary wall or fence. More elaborate formats are possible, too, such as changes in the overall height of the pergola, in order to traverse a slope or to climb and cover a flight of garden steps.

There is plenty of scope for attractive designs. Variations in the height of the beams will give the pergola a sense of movement. This is very easily achieved by setting the poles or beams at different levels within brick or stone piers.

A rustic appearance is often more desirable than a formal effect. Complete tree trunks or straight branches will give an appropriately natural look, blending with climbers trained over the structure. Bamboo poles can also be effective.

When the uprights of a pergola are of masonry, it is important to provide a substantial roof structure. Too flimsy a superstructure will look disconcertingly out of scale.

The entrance to a pergola can be emphasized in various ways. One approach is to place a pair of matching ornamental features at either side of the entrance – for example, substantial containers, each planted with a tree or shrub, or a pair of urns or vases, or even statuary. Another way to provide emphasis is to add decorative braces between the supports and cross-pieces of the first arch.

It is also possible to construct a roughly circular pergola, using short roof timbers to connect the posts, arranged around a central feature, say a bird bath, statue or fountain.

Constructing a pergola

The position of a pergola will influence the effect it will have on the garden, and the kind of use you are able to put it to, so careful planning is required.

Planning the site

Because the structure is inherently angular, it is essential to align it with straight-sided features such as a garden wall or outbuilding, to avoid a disjointed appearance with spaces alongside that are awkwardly shaped and unlikely to be accessible.

Because of its height – probably in excess of 2.4m (8ft) – a freestanding pergola can appear to loom over surrounding features, or even to cast them in shadow. Conversely, if the pergola is placed in the centre of a lawn, for example, it might look marooned, or may block a pleasant view from the house.

It is best to opt for a site where the pergola can be made to blend in with its surroundings: for example, place it in a corner formed by boundary walls or the wall of a house and its extension, or run it along the side of a wall or fence, even attached to it. Where there is a narrow pathway running alongside the house, leading to a side entry or back door, consider erecting the pergola along the path as a leafy walkway.

A sunny aspect is important if vines or fruit trees are to be trained against the pergola, and one of its long sides should face a southerly or easterly direction (in the northern hemisphere) where it will receive sun for most of the day. Avoid placing the pergola in a location that is predominantly shaded by tall trees or buildings, or on a wall where it will receive little or no sunlight.

If the pergola is to be erected on a sloping or terraced site, remember that the top of the structure must be stepped to follow the gradient; otherwise it will appear too lofty.

Estimating materials

If one of the numerous kit pergolas available is to be used, everything needed to erect the structure to a given size will be provided. However, if the pergola is to be constructed to your own specifications, you will have to draw a detailed plan and side elevation, both to enable you to decide on the design of the structure and to calculate the lengths of timber and other materials you will require.

The greatest expense will be the timber, although if you choose a size that corresponds to standard floor joists – 150 x 50mm (6 x 2in) and 100 x 50mm (4 x 2in) – you might be able to obtain secondhand timber from a demolition site at much reduced rates. Do ensure, however, that it has not been treated with creosote or any other toxic substance. You will probably have to spend some time removing old nails from

the timber. Treat all the timber with a non-toxic preservative by soaking in a makeshift bath of fluid. If you buy new timber, make sure it has been pressure-impregnated with preservative.

Fitting a wallplate

For a single-sided pergola that is to be built against the house (or other) wall, a stout wallplate of 150 x 50mm (6 x 2in) timber will need to be fitted as a support for the roof timbers. Cut the wallplate to length and drill 25mm (1in) diameter holes through the face using a flat bit at the centre, 400mm (16in) in from each end, then at 50mm (2in) intervals.

Cutting notches for the rafters

The roof timbers can be located in notches cut in the lop edge of the wallplate. Mark out the position of each notch on the top edge with a pencil and a try square. Mark notches 50mm (2in) in from each end of the wallplate, then spaced at about 700mm (28in) intervals between. Continue the lines down the front and back of the wallplate for about 50mm (2in).

In order to incorporate a slight slope in the roof timbers, away from the house wall, make the depth lines of the notch about 50mm (2in) at the front and 30mm (1¼in) at the back. Draw a horizontal line at each side to indicate the depth of the notches.

Cut down the sides of the notches with a tenon saw, angling the cut toward the front if you are making sloping notches, then use a chisel and mallet to chop out the waste timber. Chisel out small pieces rather than attempting to remove large chunks, to avoid splitting the notch. Test-fit a length of roof timber in each of the notches.

Using metal brackets

Attaching the roof timbers to the wallplate with galvanized metal U-shaped brackets avoids having to cut separate notches, and the fixings are quite inconspicuous. Mark the positions of the roof timbers on the top edge of the wallplate only and fit the brackets after the wallplate has been secured to the wall.

Position the brackets and secure by hammering galvanized nails through the pre-drilled holes in the base of the channel. With the bracket-fixing method you cannot allow for sloping roof timbers unless you bevel the top edge of the wallplate.

Attaching the wallplate

Measure up the wall the height for the roof – up to about 3m (10ft) – and draw a horizontal line in chalk at this point using a spirit level and a plank as a rule. Lift the wallplate into place on the wall (with the help of an assistant) and align its bottom edge with the chalk line. Mark through the drilled holes in chalk, then remove the wallplate and drill holes in the wall using a 35mm (1⅜in) diameter masonry bit to a depth of 115mm (4½in).

Raise the wallplate again and align correctly, then insert 165 x 16mm (6½ x ⅔in) steel anchor bolts in the holes. Tighten the bolts in succession until you can feel the wallplate being pulled tightly against the masonry.

Preparing the posts

Cut the posts to length. The top of the main support posts should be notched to take the edge of the roof timbers, although intermediate posts can be fitted with brackets as for the wallplate.

In the top end of each main post, mark out and cut notches that are about 75mm (3in) deep and the width of the roof timbers. Bevel the square top of the posts on two sides so that rainwater will run off easily; neat bevels are also more aesthetically pleasing than square tops.

Erecting the posts

Erect the pergola posts after marking out their positions in relation to the wallplate and the drawn design. Use stringlines and pegs to mark out the shape of the structure on the

ground. Fit fence post spikes and slot in the posts, making sure the notches point toward the wallplate. Check that the posts are vertical by holding a spirit level against all four sides and adjust as necessary.

If the posts are to be set in concrete, leave them for about two days before continuing with the construction, so that the concrete will set properly.

Fitting the roof timbers

Measure the length of the roof timbers, allowing for an extension beyond the outer posts of about 150–300mm (6–12in). Bevel the ends of the timbers or mark out a more ornately shaped end and cut using a scrolling jigsaw whose blade is able to turn on its axis to the left and right.

Fit the roof timbers by lowering their back ends into the wallplate notches or brackets, then slot the front lower edges into the slots cut in the top of the main posts. Secure the timbers by driving nails through the pre-drilled upstands of the brackets, or hammer nails through the top edge of the wallplate into the sides of the notches.

Adding cross-piece rafters

The design of the pergola may include rafters fixed over the roof timbers at right-angles to them. These rafters, which can

Constructing an attached pergola

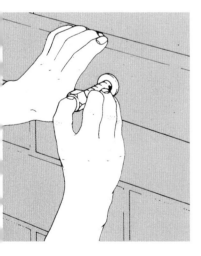

1 Secure the wall plate using steel anchor bolts. Remove the outer shell of the bolt and push into the wall before inserting the bolt through the hole.

2 Set the supporting posts in concrete or with fixing spikes or bolt-down plates, with the top notches aligned with the wallplate. Check all posts are vertical.

3 Metal U-shaped brackets offer the easiest fixing for connecting the roof timbers to the wallplate. Position the bracket and secure with galvanized nails.

Constructing a pergola

Erecting the support posts

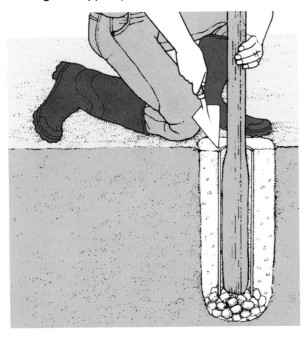

Sink wooden posts into concrete or into 60cm (2ft) pipes bedded into concrete. Replace the posts in the pipes when they rot. Always use treated timber.

be made of thinner section 100 x 25mm (4 x 1in) softwood, should be bevelled or decoratively shaped at each end, and should extend beyond the sides of the pergola by about 300–400mm (12–16in).

The rafters can be notched into the top edge of the main roof timbers, or fixed with U-shaped brackets in the same way as the main timbers are attached to the wallplate.

Bracing the structure
For rigidity, fit cross-braces between the roof timbers and the posts, and spanning across the roof timbers at a corner. This will help to prevent the pergola from flexing sideways or twisting during high winds. The best fixing is to set the bracing timber – use 50 x 50mm (2 x 2in) softwood – in notches cut in the roof timbers and posts. Cut the braces to length and hold in place so that the posts and roof timbers can be marked accordingly; then cut the notches.

Fit the braces and secure with nails driven through the top.

Shaping the rafters
Cutting bevels on the underside of the rafters and roof timbers has both decorative and practical functions. You can create a highly ornate effect by cutting complex curves in the protruding ends of the timbers – you could even create a fretwork effect by drilling holes in decorative patterns through the timbers.

Remember to treat all cut ends of the timber with preservative, even if you are using the pressure-treated type.

4 Lower the end of the roof timber into the channel formed by the fixing bracket and secure by hammering galvanized nails through the holes in the upstands.

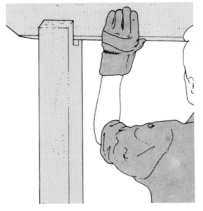

5 Locate the outer shaped end of each of the main roof timbers in slots cut in the top end of the supporting posts. The top of the post is bevelled for rainwater run-off.

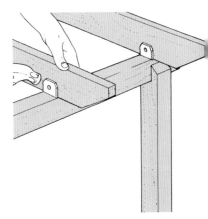

6 Rafters made of thinner timber can be fixed at right-angles across the main roof timbers. Notch the rafters into the roof timbers or fix with metal brackets.

Maintenance

When climbing plants are pruned in the autumn, the pergola that supports them should be inspected for signs of rot or if it has suffered attack by insects, which can damage and weaken the wood. If possible, climbing plants should be eased away from the pergola and the framework fully checked. Any infected wood must be replaced. New woodwork, and the cut ends of old woodwork, should be treated with non-toxic preservative or paint. Make sure that the preservative has fully dried before you restore any climber to its position.

Check any other materials used in the pergola. Replace any weakened wires and strengthen the fixtures if necessary.

BUILDING A GAZEBO

A gazebo is, strictly speaking, a summerhouse, belvedere, or pavilion sited in the garden in such a position that it will command an attractive view. In many gardens, the best position will be the corner of the plot, in the angle formed by the walls or boundaries with a view into the garden itself. The often elegant structure can also be a feature in its own right, containing built-in or freestanding seating, and possibly a table. Climbers can be trained up the sides of the gazebo and hanging baskets attached to the rafters.

Some gazebos have solid panelled walls, glazed windows and a door, while simpler versions may be just a lattice-roofed screen with trellis panels as walls.

Gazebos are available in kit form from major fencing manufacturers. It is easy, however, to construct a gazebo using standard fencing materials and trellis.

Mark out the plan of the gazebo on the ground using stringlines and pegs – it may be square, rectangular or a more complex hexagonal shape – and erect posts of 75 x 75mm (3 x 3in) sawn softwood about 2.1m (7ft) high at the corners.

Although the posts may be set in concrete, it is simpler to use fence post spikes. Where the gazebo is being assembled on a solid paved surface, use a post-fixing plate: the spike is replaced with a broad, flat plate which you bolt to the ground. Another version has an extension which is set in fresh concrete, for use where a spike is impractical.

Connect the tops of the posts with horizontal rails of 75 x 50mm (3 x 2in) timber, nailed into place, and fit diagonal braces at the upper corners. Construct a roof, pitched on four sides by linking rafters of 75 x 50mm (3 x 2in) timber to a central finial, shaped to a point and positioned at the apex of the structure. Notch the lower edge of the rafters to fit over the horizontal rails at the top of the posts and secure by skew-nailing (driving nails in through the sides of the rafters into the rails).

Clad the roof with preformed trellis cut to the triangular shape of each elevation and pinned on, or pin on a latticework arrangement of 25 x 6mm (1 x ¼in) slats cut to fit. Fix trellis to one, two, or three sides of the gazebo, leaving at least one side open as a viewpoint.

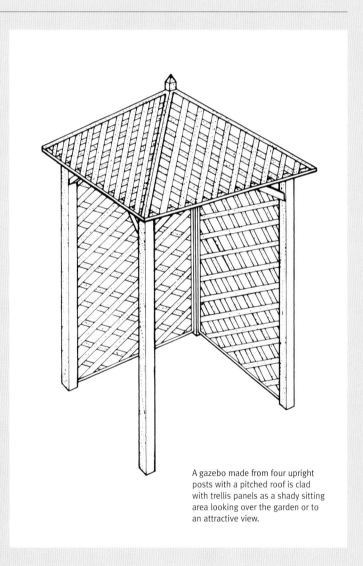

A gazebo made from four upright posts with a pitched roof is clad with trellis panels as a shady sitting area looking over the garden or to an attractive view.

Constructing a rustic arch

A rustic timber arch will add a touch of rural charm to your garden. Natural poles, available from garden centres with or without bark, are used to form the arch. Sizes are usually standardized; peeled, pressure-treated poles commonly come in 2.4m (8ft) lengths and 50–75mm (2–3in) diameters.

Designing a basic arch

A basic rustic arch should comprise two pairs of uprights concreted into the ground at each side of a path with a pair of horizontal rails fixed at the top and bottom, an intermediate pair of rails, and thinner 25 or 50mm (1 or 2in) diameter diagonal braces between. The top of the arch is made from two pairs of 75mm (3in) diameter poles fixed to a top piece, and to the side uprights. Further rails and braces can be added to create an attractive design. Although the supporting frame poles, rails and arch formers have basic joints cut for rigidity, the thinner bracing pieces can be fixed with nails.

Cutting the joints

All the joints and notches used to assemble the arch can be made with a panel saw and either a coping saw or a padsaw. You will also need a chisel to chop out the waste from some joints.

The top rails are located in 25mm (1in) deep V-shaped notches cut in the top end of each upright pole. Where the intermediate rails link the pairs of poles, cut V-shaped notches into the poles. Cut the rails to 600–900mm (24–36in) lengths and form V-shaped ends to fit into the notches in the poles.

Where a pair of poles cross, cut cross-halving joints: mark the diameter of each pole using masking tape and cut down the inside edges of the tape, on both sides, to half the depth of the poles. Remove the waste wood between the cuts using a chisel.

Treating the timber against rot

Lay out the poles and rails for each side of the arch and test-fit the joints. If they fit, disassemble and treat each joint thoroughly with preservative. The poles will need extra protection against rot where they will be inserted in the ground, so stand them to soak in a bucket of preservative overnight.

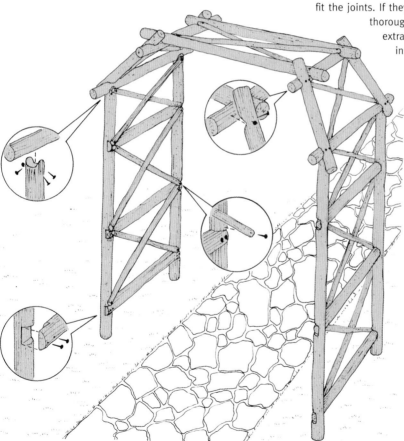

Assembling the frames

Assemble the sides of the arch with the upright poles laid out on the ground, then position the cross-pieces. Secure all the joints by driving 100mm (4in) long galvanized wire nails, which will not rust, through the joints themselves. Drive in the nails dovetail fashion so that they will resist being pulled apart. Nail the thinner cross-pieces to the side pieces to give the frames extra rigidity.

Erecting the side frames

Dig four holes to take the ends of the side frame poles and add a layer of hardcore to give a firm foundation and help drainage. Ram the hardcore down

The framework of the rustic arch consists of stripped or bark-covered irregular poles about 75mm (3in) in diameter, with smaller diameter poles used as intermediate bracing and decorative design. V-shaped or, as here, cross-halving joints are used in construction, strengthened by nails and screws.

Top: Unsightly rubbish bins or tools and furniture that have been tidied away can be hidden from view by a screen divide.

Above: Window boxes are an attractive option where space is at a premium; they can be constructed relatively easily.

Right: Glasshouses make an attractive as well as functional addition to a garden. This one is made from treated pine.

Left: Offering a summer extension to the kitchen, a barbecue can be bought purpose made although a brick surround barbecue is relatively simple to make.

Below: Garden lighting near a house not only highlights patios and terraces, but provides illumination to steps and acts as a deterrent to intruders once darkness falls.

Constructing a rustic arch

with a stout length of timber or a sledgehammer. Stand both assembled side frames in their holes and nail timber battens between the uprights to support the structure while the concrete hardens. Use dry-mixed fence post concrete, mix with water, and then tip into the holes. Pack the concrete around the poles to dispel air bubbles. Use a trowel to form a slightly domed top to the concrete infill to aid rainwater run-off. Leave the concrete to set overnight before fixing the arch top.

Fitting the arch top
Lift the arch top into position on the top of the side frames. There will be sufficient play in the upright poles to enable the joints to be pulled together, should they not align properly. Attachment of the top depends on the method of construction used. If the arch sides have a flat cross-rail at the top, laid in notches without protruding vertical members (as in diagram 5 below), the arch top should be notched on the inside edge of the angled poles, about 25mm (1in) in, to fit the cross-rail.

If cross-halved joints have been used, notch the angled poles on their sides and attach to the extended ends of the side uprights (see diagram 6 below).

Drill holes through the arch pieces into the top rails of the frame sides and insert 100mm (4in) long rustproofed screws to secure the structure.

Making a rustic arch

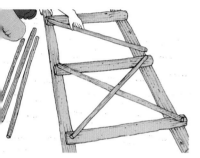

1 Assemble the arch sides on the ground before cutting the joints, with the braces of thinner section laid over the side uprights and cross-rails.

2 A Use a coping saw to cut a V-shaped notch about 25mm (1in) deep in the side of the uprights, then trim the ends of the cross-rails into V-shapes to connect.

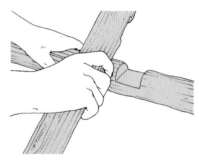

2 B Alternatively, cut cross-halving joints where rails intersect. Mark the diameter of each pole using tape and cut and chisel down the inside edges half the pole depth.

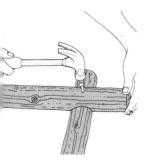

3 Secure all the joints with galvanized nails driven in at an angle to resist the natural flexing of the structure. Nail diagonal braces in place.

4 Bring together the rail and upright to test the joint. Trim with a chisel. Nail the joints together and nail on the diagonal braces.

5 Erect the side panels with uprights sunk in concrete-filled holes. Prop them up while the concrete sets. Lift the arch top onto the side panels.

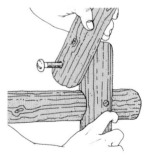

6 Secure the arch top to the side uprights as here, or to the top cross-rails using rust-proofed screws. The springiness of the structure prevents nailing.

Water in the garden

Some form of water feature is suitable for practically any garden style, as ponds and pools can conform to both formal and informal treatments. Lakes suggest informality while canals are formalized rivers, their slow movement suggesting tranquillity. Rills, for the most part, are narrow, fast-moving canals, waterfalls, and cascades. Either formal or informal, they are lively and dynamic, depending upon height, movement and sound for their success.

However, because of the focus drawn by any water feature in the garden, great care must be taken when choosing its form and placement.

Fountains

There is little to compare with the effervescing vivacity of fountains, although they are inherently formal features and can look a little out of place in informal pools. Wall fountains are extremely useful in confined spaces where an eye-catching feature is required in combination with the pleasant sound of running water.

Height, water pressure, jet arrangement, and droplet size determine the final form and effect. There are numerous fountain heads available from specialist outlets and catalogues which show exactly the type of jet produced. Apart from being beautiful, fountains also help to aerate the water.

When choosing a fountain be sure that the pool in which it is placed is large enough to catch all the water droplets, even on a breezy day. This will ensure that the surround stays dry and that water is conserved. Water loss through evaporation is greatest in fine droplet fountains.

Water features and wildlife

Any water feature in your garden will attract wildlife; a pond designed especially for wildlife that includes a variety of marginal plants, will attract a wider range of visitors. The pool will incorporate a stony beach area that gently slopes down into the water to allow the wildlife easy access.

Creating a wildlife pool is reasonably simple. They can be created with a butyl liner sandwiched between two layers of soil. Following the basic instructions for creating a pool given on page 182. At least one third of the pool edge incorporate a long gentle slope at an angle of 20 degrees, covered with stones and gravel to create a stony beach. The pool should be between 20–60cm (8–24in) deep, with shelves for marginal plants on the more sharply sloping edges. Do not worry about packing with the pond and its margins with plants – leave some space for natural colonization.

Maintaining water features

When designing and positioning a water feature, ensure it is neither in full sun all day nor in constant shade. Too much sun promotes excessive algae growth, while shade, combined with falling leaves and litter from nearby or overhanging trees, results in unhealthily low oxygen levels. Frequent cleaning will then be necessary. The condition of water is always improved with aeration by artificial means, with fountains and spouts, or by natural means using plants. Help this process by keeping approximately 30 percent of a pond surface covered with plants such as water lilies. This reduces water loss by evaporation and oxygen depletion in summer.

Formal and informal water features in the garden

Tranquil, still and mysterious, this lake reflects both sky and surround, thus increasing the sense of space.

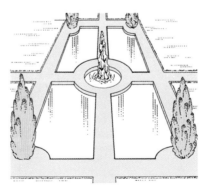

This formal pond's still, reflective surfaces are designed to contrast with the central pond, emphasizing its frothy central fountain.

A formal water feature on a small scale is appropriate in a small garden, especially as the pool surround doubles as a seat.

Water in the garden

Creating water features on slopes

Water always flows to the lowest level, apart from in very special natural circumstances sometimes found on mountains or moorlands where impervious soils create suspended water hollows.

Artificial pools on slopes rarely look convincing when the ground slope can be seen to continue beyond. To reduce the artificial impression, use the excavated soil from the pool area to create a bund (mound) on the low side of the pool. The bund should be a natural-looking shape if possible. Too uniform and the bund itself might suggest that the pool is not natural. When it is complete, plant up the bund with trees and shrubs, including evergreens. These will inhibit a through view and suggest that the slope has terminated. The pool or lake will then appear to be occupying the lowest area where water would naturally collect.

When creating a water feature on a steep slope, remember to include a flat area for access rather than allowing the slope to extend right down into the water, as this can be dangerous. On very steep slopes, when it may be impractical to create a single body of water, a series of minor stepped pools will look more natural and be easier to construct. Large areas of water on slopes will inevitably create logistical problems.

SAFETY FACTORS

WATER AND ELECTRICITY DO NOT MIX: ALWAYS USE WATERPROOF ARMOURED CABLE AND A WATERPROOF CONNECTOR

Always follow the manufacturer's instructions exactly when installing pumps, lighting, or any other electrically operated equipment. All electrical equipment must be operated in conjunction with a circuit breaker to protect against electric shocks; this device cuts off the electrical supply within 30 milliseconds should problems occur. Most pumps work directly from the mains 240 volt electricity supply. Armoured cable must be laid in a 50–60cm (20–24in) trench to protect it from being cut or damaged. Always have electrical connections inspected by a qualified electrician.

Make sure that there is sufficient space for the chosen water feature to work well aesthetically, practically and in terms of proportion. Allow plenty of room, too, for marginal planting. If uncontrolled, rampant plant growth can greatly reduce the open water surface.

Creating water features on slopes

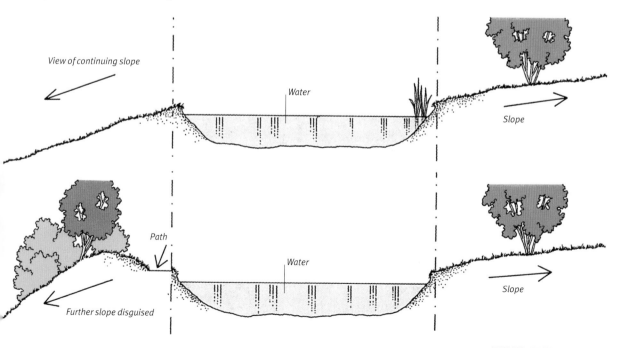

View of continuing slope

Water

Slope

Path

Water

Slope

Further slope disguised

Water in the garden

Water is used in the garden both for irrigation and as a feature, in the form of a pool or stream. Water allows a wide range of aquatic and marginal plants to be grown. Fish can be introduced, and amphibians such as newts and frogs may find their way to the pool.

Siting a pool

Position the pool where it can be seen to best effect and where the reflections on its surface can be enjoyed. Avoid siting a pool under trees. Not only will the shady conditions make for poor plant growth and minimal flower production,

but the pool will also become clogged with fallen leaves. An open site which is sheltered from strong winds is best. If pool lights or a pump are to be installed, make sure that the pool is within reach of the electricity supply.

Size and shape

Larger areas of water look more effective than small ones, so give the pool as large a surface as possible. Pools as small as 1.8m (6ft) long by 0.9m (3ft) wide may be constructed in small gardens but they will have to be planted carefully and maintained regularly if they are not to become overgrown bogs.

PUMPS

Pumps

All pumps work in the same way: an electric motor draws the water in through an input unit. This has a filter attached to it to filter out any leaves, twigs, and other debris. The output unit forces water out under pressure, the flow being adjusted by a flow-adjuster screw, and the whole unit is attached to a delivery hose or fountain assembly unit. With the addition of a T-piece, the pump will operate more than one feature.

Surface pumps

These are used to power fountains with high heads of water and streams and waterfalls with a large output. Surface pumps operate from a separate brick chamber built next to the pool. The pump chamber should be built at the same time as the pool itself, preferably in a position below the water level of the pool. If the chamber is above the water level, a foot valve and strainer must be used on the suction tube to retain the prime, which keeps the water pushing through. If the chamber is below the pool's water level, only a strainer is needed as the prime is maintained by gravity. The pump must not be housed where the vertical distance from the water level exceeds the suction lift of the pump. Make sure the pump chamber is dry and well ventilated. Build a single-layered running bond brick structure (see page 128) that will just accommodate the pump, incorporating an air brick in the top course for ventilation; use a paving slab for the roof which can be removed if access is required for maintenance.

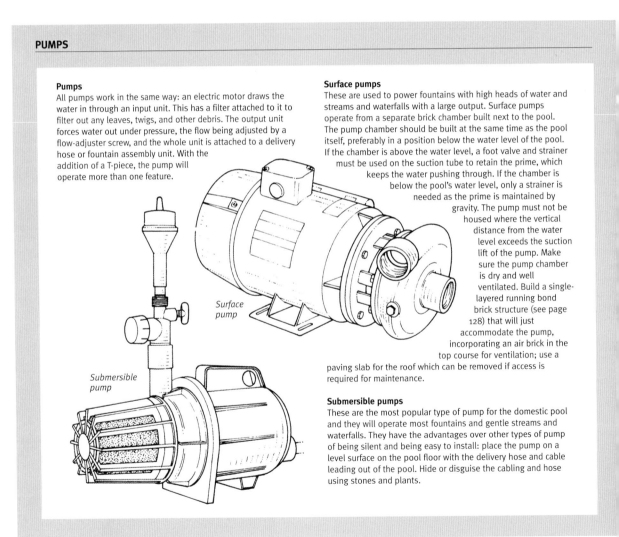

Surface pump

Submersible pump

Submersible pumps

These are the most popular type of pump for the domestic pool and they will operate most fountains and gentle streams and waterfalls. They have the advantages over other types of pump of being silent and being easy to install: place the pump on a level surface on the pool floor with the delivery hose and cable leading out of the pool. Hide or disguise the cabling and hose using stones and plants.

he water should be at least 38cm (15in) deep, though 45cm 8in) is more satisfactory. Pools with a surface area of more han 9.3sq m (100sq ft) may be 60cm (2ft) deep, and very arge pools up to a maximum of 90cm (3ft) deep. This depth vill allow the pool to heat up and cool down relatively slowly, nd it will ensure that fish can avoid being frozen in winter. ools less than 75cm (2½ft) deep may be more troubled by lgae than those of greater depth. The pool should contain teps or shelves where the water is about 23cm (9in) deep. his allows marginal aquatic plants to be positioned at the est depth.

The shape of the pool will depend entirely on the effect equired, but it is best to use bold and simple shapes rather han intricate ones. Formal pools (in the shape of rectangles, quares, circles, and ovals) can be constructed to fit into ormal gardens and terraces. Uneven shapes will create a more atural sheet of water in a natural garden. Experiment by aying a hose pipe or a trail of sand to mark the proposed hape of the pool and adjust the curves until the desired ffect is achieved. Mark the final shape with wooden pegs.

latural water courses

stream running through the garden will present the owner vith a superb garden feature, but also with some possible roblems. Moving water will not support water lilies and other quatics that need calm conditions; the speed and level of the vater may be very variable, fish will be difficult to retain, and he water may contain harmful mineral salts. Certainly, part of he stream may be dammed to make a pool, but the constant lisplacement of water and the infiltration of fresh supplies nay cause a build-up of algae and blanket weed. Trial and rror alone will reveal what can be done with individual arden streams, but the safest approach would be to establish

bog plants on the banks and to experiment with one or two marginal aquatic. Any changes to the bed or course of the stream may have to be approved by the local river authority.

The water supply

Where no natural water course is present, the pool maker will have to rely on the domestic supply both for initial filling and any subsequent topping up of the pool. Domestic supplies will have higher levels of mineral salts than the water in the pool, which has been modified chemically by plant and animal growth. Thus topping up with mains water can lead to faster build-ups of algae and weed. A garden pool must be managed with the aim of establishing a balanced ecology. A balanced pool will stay clear, and no single species of plant or animal life will become dominant.

Pumps

If a stream or waterfall is required on a flat site where water would not normally be expected to flow, then considerable site alterations need to take place. Changes in level are usually needed for this and, especially in an informal setting, the stream or waterfall must appear as an entirely natural phenomenon. In any event, an electric pump will be required to move the water around.

The advice of the supplier should be sought when determining the power of pump required. It is all too easy to choose a pump that is not powerful enough. Good catalogues will list a range of pumps and their performance ratings, expressed in gallons per hour, relative to the height and distance of the outfall or fountain head away from the pump. The higher and greater the distance over which the water is to be moved (known technically as the "head" of water) the more powerful a pump needs to be.

Waterfall: section through a butyl-lined waterfall

onstruct waterfalls starting at the bottom, overlapping the liner as illustrated. 'osition a submersible pump in the lowest pool, which must be sufficiently large so he water level does not drop too much when the pump is turned on.

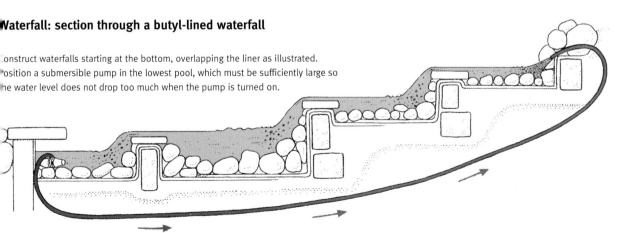

Creating pools

Various materials can be used as pool liners to create pools: the choice depends on their availability and the feasibility of construction or installation. Ease of access to the garden influences costs, not only to construction materials coming in but also to any excavated materials going out, so the volume of the pool is important.

Puddled clay

In areas with a clay soil, this technique has been used to create ponds for many hundreds of years. The clay must be flexible, impervious, and have a low silt content. A layer of lime used to be placed beneath the clay to discourage root penetration or animal activity which could cause the pond to leak. Today, low-grade plastic sheet provides a more economical and effective alternative.

The sides of a clay pond should not have more than a 20-degree slope: any steeper and the clay particles could slip downward, leading to water loss. Shrubs and trees should be planted well away from the edges of a clay pool and invasive aquatic plants such as willows, poplars, and some sedges

should also be avoided, as they could penetrate the clay, causing it to leak.

Liner pools

Flexible liners are less costly per unit area than concrete and are convenient. Butyl or PVC, for example, can have long lives though polythene is suitable only for short-term use. Flat sheet liners are not so easy to use in formal pools, which often call for awkward folding at any corners, but specialist firms can make liners to match specific pool shapes. If correctly fitted, flexible liners should not be visible above the water line and this is essential if the pool is to appear natural.

Rigid liners

Rigid liners, manufactured mostly from fibre-glass, are pre-formed in geometric or informal shapes to make instant patio or rock garden pools. Their artificial-looking edges can be disguised with rocks, plants, or grass. Old leaking pools can also be repaired using fibreglass sheets and resin.

Pool liners

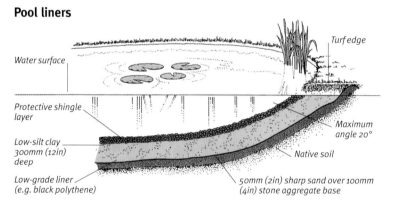

Water surface

Protective shingle layer

Low-silt clay 300mm (12in) deep

Low-grade liner (e.g. black polythene)

Turf edge

Maximum angle 20°

Native soil

50mm (2in) sharp sand over 100mm (4in) stone aggregate base

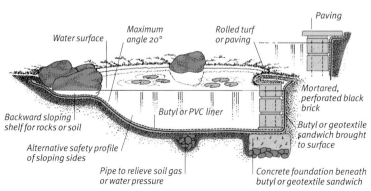

Water surface

Maximum angle 20°

Rolled turf or paving

Paving

Backward sloping shelf for rocks or soil

Alternative safety profile of sloping sides

Butyl or PVC liner

Pipe to relieve soil gas or water pressure

Mortared, perforated black brick

Butyl or geotextile sandwich brought to surface

Concrete foundation beneath butyl or geotextile sandwich

Rigid liners

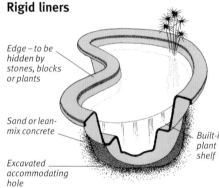

Edge – to be hidden by stones, blocks or plants

Sand or lean-mix concrete

Excavated accommodating hole

Built-i plant shelf

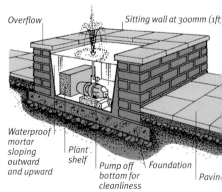

Overflow

Sitting wall at 300mm (1ft

Waterproof mortar sloping outward and upward

Plant shelf

Pump off bottom for cleanliness

Foundation

Pavin

Creating pools

Above-ground pools

If they are built with walls about 300mm (12in) thick and 450–600mm (18–24in) high, these features can also provide seating around their edges. Most materials can be used in their construction: real or reconstituted stone, brick or timber are all suitable, although the interior needs to be waterproofed either with waterproof mortar or a proprietary pond sealant.

In rigid pools the internal walls should slope upward and outward so that, in winter, expanding ice can move harmlessly upward, rather than outward as it will if trapped against vertical sides. An overflow at the proposed water level will also reduce the risk of ice lifting or otherwise damaging the pool coping.

Informal concrete pools

These should ideally be dish-shaped in section and deepest at the centre, whatever the plan form. This reduces the risk of cracking due to differential loadings, which is common where there are several separate deep areas. To be truly waterproof, concrete must be consistent in mix, well compacted, and be of uniform thickness not less than about 150mm (6in). If it is thinner than this, it will probably have to be waterproofed using a pond liner.

Rock or planting shelves should slope downwards and backwards to ensure stability. The edges of a concrete pool can be disguised with plants and rocks. A natural internal appearance develops more quickly if the concrete sides are textured rather than smooth.

Formal concrete pools

Formal concrete pools can be cast using shuttering, or they can be constructed as retaining walls over a base. In larger pools, steel reinforcement is needed to counter internal and external pressures. To prevent dissolved cement chemicals from harming aquatic life, fill the pool but wait at least six months before introducing any creatures into it. Then, change the water but do not scrub the pool sides. The spontaneous appearance of water beetles and daphnia is a sign that the water is uncontaminated.

Waterfalls

Although more ambitious in scope, the construction of a waterfall is not very different from that of a pond. Both concrete and flexible liners can be used to channel the water.

Concrete

Since concrete shrinks and expands in response to changing temperatures, often resulting in cracking, it cannot be used for the construction of long water courses. To overcome this, concrete streams and water courses are constructed as short overlapping units, as in the examples below and on page 181, with the rear wall of each section and the corresponding sides always higher than the anticipated water level. There is the added advantage, when a waterfall is constructed in this way, that a series of stepped, independent minor pools are formed. When the circulatory pump is switched off, water is retained in these minor pools and the stream does not run completely dry. The sides and bottom of a concrete stream or waterfall can be made attractive and natural-looking by placing stones or gravel against or on them.

Flexible liners

While flexible liners do not have the same thermal movement problems as concrete, it may be difficult to obtain very long and narrow strips suitable for forming stream beds.

To achieve the desired effect, shorter lengths can be used but overlapped. Smooth loose stones or rocks can be placed on the bottom and sides for a natural effect, but sharp stones may penetrate the liner and should therefore be avoided.

Informal *in-situ* concrete pool

Soil shelf with gravel shut off prevents capillary action and water loss in summer

Water surface

Pressure

Rock shelf slopes back

Brushed texture interior

Cleaning sump at centre

Minimum 150mm (6in) concrete (consistent thickness)

Rigid pool liners

Digging the base for a rigid liner

To fit a rigid or semi-rigid pond liner, prop the shell itself in place on bricks, boxes or wooden slakes and mark around its perimeter. Transfer the position of the outer rim of the liner to the ground by standing a spirit level next to it, and push a wooden peg into the earth at intervals of about 300mm (1ft) as you work around the liner.

Remove the liner and dig a line around the outside of the pegs, about 100mm (4in) away, removing them as you go. Dig away the topsoil to a depth of about 150mm (6in) and reuse this fertile soil elsewhere in the garden.

Excavate the earth further, copying the profile of the underside of the liner as closely as you can, but making it about 150mm (6in) broader all round. Check the depth of the hole by spanning across the lop of the excavation with a plank, then use a tape measure to measure to the base.

Remove all sharp stones and thick roots and flatten out any bumps. When you are satisfied that the hole is sufficiently deep, compact the surface by treading, then line the base and any shelves with a 25mm (1in) thick layer of sharp sand.

Fitting the rigid liner

Carefully lower the liner into the hole and shake it to settle it, then press it down firmly on the sand bed. Place a spirit level on a straight-edged length of timber spanning the rim of the liner to ensure that it is horizontal. Check the length and the width, then place the spirit level diagonally to ensure the liner is level that way, too. Chock up the liner temporarily until you can backfill it.

Filling the liner

Run a hosepipe to the pond liner and drape it over the edge, then start to fill the liner. While the water level rises, backfill with sand or sifted soil (with any stones removed). Use a

Informal pond shapes

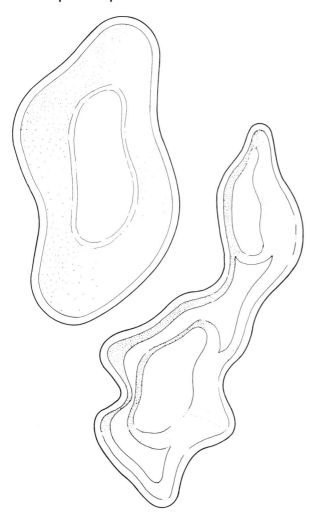

Informal pond shapes fit in best with most garden settings, and there is a range of rigid and semi-rigid preformed types in glass-reinforced plastic and PVC. Most types have moulded marginal shelves and deep centre pools, typically in kidney shapes, crescents and figure-of-eight formats. Alternatively, simply create the required shape with a flexible pond, as described on page 186.

STOCKING THE POND

As a guide to quantities, you should allow one bunch of plants per 0.3sq m (2sq ft) of surface water area. Marginal, shallow water plants such as water mint, marsh marigold, arrowhead, and yellow iris are ideal choices for planting out on the pond shelves, while deep water plants with large floating leaves, such as water lilies, water soldier, and greater bladderwort are ideally placed in the centre of the pond.

Lattice containers are used to pot the plants. Line them with hessian, using ordinary soil that is free from weedkiller and fertilizer, then top with a layer of pea gravel to prevent the soil from washing out.

Add the fish only when the oxygenating plants are well established: 1sq m of surface area will support 500mm (20in) of fish (1sq ft for 2in of fish). Therefore, a pond measuring 1 x 2m (3 x 6ft) will support 1m (3ft) of fish made up of 20 fish 50mm (2in) long.

small trowel (or your hands) to feed the backfilling under the marginal shelves, and pack it down firmly. As the liner becomes filled with water it will settle down on its bedding.

Setting the liner in sloping ground

In order to install a rigid pond liner in a naturally sloping site, excavate horizontally into the bank, shoring up the earth at the high side by constructing a small earth-retaining wall of brickwork or natural stone. The choice of material for this wall is determined by the style of garden and the shape of the pond itself: bricks will give a more formal effect, best suited to an angular pond, while stone or concrete blocks create a more natural setting in which an irregular pond is more suitable. The low side of the slope may need to be built up slightly, in order to even out the transition from the pond to ground level.

Fitting a rigid liner

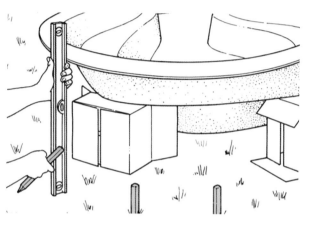

1 Set the rigid liner on supports and mark around its perimeter on the ground, using a spirit level and pegs as a guide.

2 Dig out the hole, following the profile of the liner. Use a plank spanning the pond to determine the depth at the centre.

3 Set the liner in the hole on a layer of sharp sand. Press it down to bed it firmly, then check the level across the rim.

4 Backfill behind the liner using sand or sifted soil, while a hosepipe fills the liner with water to settle it properly.

Flexible pool liners

Liners are well suited to the creation of curved pools. Use a garden hosepipe to plan the overall shape of the pond on the ground, experimenting with the shape.

Digging the hole

Dig out the hole for the pond within the guideline formed by the hosepipe. To create a split-level base, excavate the area to about 200 to 300mm (8 to 12in) deep, then, leaving a 225mm (9in) wide shelf around the perimeter of the excavation, dig over the remaining area a further 200 to 300mm (8 to 12in) or to a greater depth if required. Remove any large stones or roots that may puncture the liner.

Do not make the sides of the pond too steep. A gradient of about 100mm (4in) in a depth of 200mm (8in) should guard against collapse. Dig out any further planting shelves, or deeper areas required, and compact the soil by treading. Take care not to crumble the ledges as you compact the earth. Using a rake, spread about 12mm (½in) of damp building sand over the entire surface as a cushioning layer for the liner.

Underlining

Pond liners normally do not require any form of underlining apart from a cushioning layer of sand, but if the ground is very stony it is advisable to lay a polyester mat (available from a pond suppliers) over the excavated earth, prior to laying the liner. This will provide an extra cushion against rips.

Constructing a flexible liner pond

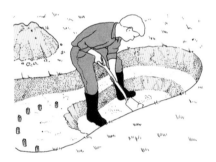

1 Outline the shape of the pond using a hosepipe, then dig out the base, using pegs for accuracy when gauging the depth at the centre and for the marginal shelves.

2 Set datum pegs at the edges of the pond and check the level. The pond must be set horizontal, even if the ground itself is slightly uneven.

3 Spread damp sand over the base and sides of the pond excavation to a depth of about 12mm (½in) as a cushioning bed for the flexible liner.

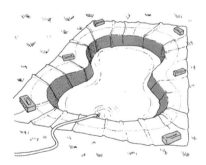

4 Drape the liner across the pond, weighted down with bricks at the edge. Fill the pond with water: the liner stretches into the shape of the hole as it fills.

5 Trim off the excess liner from around the perimeter of the pond, leaving an overlap of about 150mm (6in), which will be covered and secured by the edging.

6 Edge the rim of the pond with a row of concrete slabs or natural stones, bedded on mortar. The stones should overhang the pond by about 50mm (2in).

Flexible pool liners

Installing the liner

A flexible polythene or synthetic rubber liner will mould itself to the shape and size of the pond. To calculate the dimensions of the sheet, add twice the depth of the pond to its maximum length and width. For example, a pond with an area of 1.2 x 3m (4 x 10ft) and a depth of 600mm (24in) will require a sheet measuring 2.4 x 4.2m (8 x 14ft).

Drape the liner over the surface of the pond excavation and weight it down at the perimeter with a few bricks. Place a hosepipe into the pond and begin to fill it with water. The liner will be pulled into the contours of the excavation by the weight of the water. Brush out large creases with a soft broom, but do not worry about minor creasing as this is inevitable. Fill the pond to within about 50mm (2in) of the ground level.

Pleat the overlap neatly, then trim the edge of the liner with a sharp knife or a large pair of scissors, leaving a margin of about 300mm (12in). Fit the edging around the pond.

Laying the pond edging

The pool edge should normally provide a sharp transition between the water and the land. This forms a barrier to discourage roots of trees from penetrating the pool. If the garden is allowed to meet the pool edge, the soil – and the roots of nearby trees such as alder, willow, and poplar – would tend to suck out the water. But in some cases, particularly if you are hoping to attract varied wildlife to the pool, the liner can be merged into the edge and covered with soil so that some water overlaps at this point.

There are numerous ways to edge the pond. For example, where the pond slopes gently from the edges, set cobblestones directly on the liner, bedded in sand and cement mortar. Alternatively, set rocks on the marginal shelves, forming sunken walls, then plant the marginals in the recesses behind.

MAKING A RAISED POND

A raised or partially raised pond can be a focal point in a garden, especially when a fountain or other ornamental features are added.

To install a fully raised pond, set the liner on a compacted, level base and mark around its perimeter. Construct a wall around the liner using bricks, blocks, or stone-set on a strip foundation encircling the area of the liner. Build up the walls: no more than nine courses of bricks are necessary for a standard-sized liner.

Reposition the liner on a 25mm (1in) thick cushioning base of sharp sand, add about 150mm (6in) of water to hold the liner steady, then backfill between it and the wall with soil. Bridge the gap between the liner edge and the wall with an edging of paving slabs or other suitable material. For a less formal raised pond, a small rock garden or scree with rocky outcrops may be built as an alternative to the retaining wall. The rock garden should, of course, blend as naturally as possible with its surroundings.

If appropriate, the liner may be partially sunk into the soil and a low wall or rock garden constructed around it.

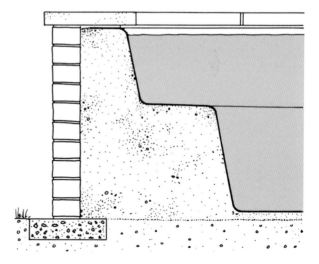

A typical planting arrangement for a garden pond, showing how the margins are used to hold plants in lattice containers while the deeper regions are home for water lilies and other deep marginal plants.

A raised pond can be made using a rigid liner resting on a sand bed at ground level, with a brick retaining wall built around it, then backfilled with earth.

Stepping stones

Stepping stones in water achieve the same effect as those in grass, allowing safe and easy access without creating unwanted divisions in the space. This is particularly advantageous where an uninterrupted flow is crucial to the design. Stepping stones look best if they appear to float just above the surface of the water, with a dark, narrow shadow.

Stepping stones can be of equal or of different sizes and their routes can be straight or curved, but for safety they must be spaced with care. The distances between the stones should take account of the differences in stride between adults and children. Normally, the gaps left between stones range from 150mm (6in) to 300mm (12in) but whatever is decided, it should be consistent.

The stepping stones should be large enough to allow plenty of room for the whole foot to be accommodated easily. Having to aim at a small stepping stone is not only inconvenient but potentially dangerous, so a minimum size of 500mm (20in) square is recommended.

Cross-section of stepping stones

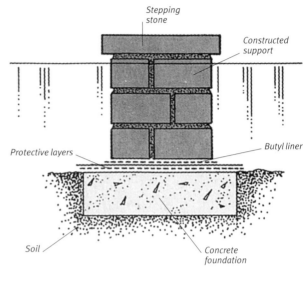

Stepping stone

Constructed support

Protective layers

Butyl liner

Soil

Concrete foundation

Artificial stepping stones

Jetties and beaches

Jetties are usually associated with larger areas of water where a boat might be useful or necessary, although they also provide a useful vantage point from which fish can be fed or admired, allowing a clear rather than an oblique overview. Some designs include jetties and boats in the smallest gardens, simply presented as a tableau.

Beaches provide access to and from the water for humans, animals, amphibians, and birds, while protecting the pool liner beneath, especially when flexible types such as butyl or PVC are used. A beach should comprise round pebbles or pea shingle rather than stones, which have sharp edges. To be convincing, the surface beach material should be of an adequate depth – at least 150mm (6in) is a good rule of thumb.

Many designers include beaches simply because they like the look of them, rather than for any practical reason. To help a constructed beach look as natural as possible, try to match any locally occurring stone or pebbles, even if only in colour. Beaches placed at the windward end of a pool need to be regularly cleaned because it is here that wind-blown scum and litter collects.

Jetty and beach combination

Siting water features

A pool, cascade, or fountain can be sited almost anywhere within your garden design depending on its size and scale – a fountain can be located on a wall, for example, taking up little space. However, in order for the water feature to continue to enhance the garden, certain factors should be considered when choosing its site.

Trees

When planning the site for a water feature, assess the amount of sunlight it will receive (shade inhibits the growth of aquatic plants). This is best done in summer when any trees will have their full covering of leaf. Consider also the shade cast by buildings, and bear in mind that in winter the sun will be lower in the sky and more shade cast.

A pool should not be sited within 5.5m (15ft) of any trees, as both spreading roots and falling leaves will cause problems.

Research the habits of the trees you plan to plant near the pool or are already growing there – some fruit trees such as cherry and plum can harbour aphids that will harm waterlilies and aquatic plants, while yew trees produce seeds that are poisonous to pondlife. Willow and poplar trees have vigorous root systems that can damage the structure of the pool.

Wind and frost

Select a sheltered position for a pool or other water feature if possible, where it is less likely to freeze. Check that the area is not in a frost pocket, however, as some sheltered spots can trap cold air. Strong winds can damage, or even overturn, marginal acquatic plants and sweep debris onto the surface of the pool. They can also blow the spray of a fountain off course so that water falls away from the pool. In addition, water evaporation will be greater in a windy site.

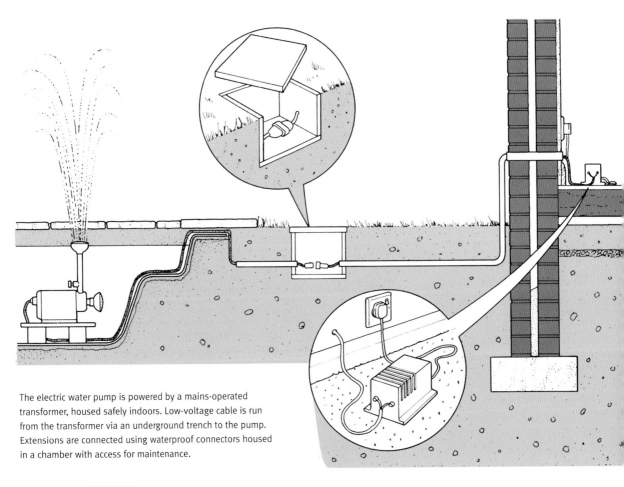

The electric water pump is powered by a mains-operated transformer, housed safely indoors. Low-voltage cable is run from the transformer via an underground trench to the pump. Extensions are connected using waterproof connectors housed in a chamber with access for maintenance.

Siting water features

Water Features

A wide selection of formal and informal features are readily available, many in kit form, from garden centres. Choose one that is appropriate in size and style to the site and garden setting.

Wall fountains These are are suitable for small gardens and many formal garden settings. Where water at ground level is inappropriate for reasons of safety, this could be considered a safe water feature. Wall fountains are available in many styles made from stone, metal, terracotta, and fibreglass. Tiny submersible pumps are housed in a water-filled bowl and pumped via a small bore-pipe to an outlet: in the example illustrated below, it is a lion's mouth.

Wall fountains can be used equally well as planters drained of water as a precaution against frost damage. A small-leaved decorative ivy would make a charming winter substitute for the trickling water of summer.

Solar-powered fountains These negate the need to fit a pump or provide electricity in the garden, and are energy-efficient. The base incorporates the solar panels which power the fountain. Solar fountains are simply placed into the pool, where they will float on the surface, and often have a selection of fountain heads to provide different spray patterns. One disadvantage is that they will not provide a cascade of water when it is not sunny or in the evening as they require light to work.

However, some models are fitted with batteries to provide a additional power so that they will work on cloudy days and at night. Some are even fitted with lights to illuminate the spray. More elaborate versions come with larger solar panels that are sited outside the pool, facing south, attached to the pump unit by a cord that is submerged in the pool.

"Bell" fountain These provide a more gentle movement of water than more upright flows of water. Low fountains are best for small catchment areas, as tall fountain heads and fine droplets can result in a pool being depleted through evaporation on breezy days.

Bowl fountain For a small patio this feature, which can be made safe for even young children if it is filled almost to the brim with black pebbles, is an ideal focal point. A small jet appropriate in height to the bowl's diameter brings the fountain to life, powered by a concealed pump. Line the inside of the bowl with a black pond sealant to make it waterproof and to make the water surface more reflective.

Sculptured fountain Sculpture has long been associated with water because of the attractive symmetry of the reflection. Sculpture, of a style appropriate to the garden, can be incorporated as a fountain head.

Rock pool Rock pools should look entirely natural: there should be no liner visible anywhere. If a series of pools is to be constructed, the bottom pool must be significantly larger than those above to ensure that it is not noticeably depleted when the pump activates the waterfalls.

Rill Originally a narrow stream running through a meadow, similar features can be formalized for garden use. The great landscape gardeners of the past included rills for their movement, sound, and as a gentle surprise.

Stream Make an artificial stream look as natural as possible and conceal evidence of liners at the bottom and sides by disguising them with turf, plants, gravel, or rocks.

If rocks do not naturally occur in the garden or are not used elsewhere, avoid lining the stream sides with them, as they will give a look of artificiality. If rocks do occur or are planned as part of a water or rock theme, place them as naturally as possible and place more in other areas adjacent to the stream. For continuity, use broken stones of a similar type to rest at the bottom of the stream.

WATER FEATURES

The examples shown here are a selection of formal and informal features.
1. Wall fountain spouting from lion's head.
2. Solar-powered fountain.
3. Small patio pool with a "bell" fountain.

Creating play areas

Although you can purchase pre-formed play equipment to build at home, it is reasonably easy to construct the apparatus to your own design, such as this raised play house incorporating a slide and climbing bars.

Ideally, if space permits, children should be allocated a separate area in the garden. This should be somewhere you can ensure their safety while at the same time protecting lawns and flower beds from the inevitable rough-and-tumble.

Boundaries

First of all, think about how you can provide some form of demarcation for the children's garden. Use a low barrier, say a simple post-and-rail type such as ranch fencing, to hem them in without their being out of sight from the house or another part of the garden. The fence should be substantial enough to stand up to rough play, but should not have pointed poles or protruding wires which could be dangerous.

As an alternative, a low wall may be built, but this is less

satisfactory as it is a more permanent structure and cannot so easily be removed once there is no further use for the play area. Provide a gate, fitted with a good latch on the opposite side, if you do not want young children to wander.

Surface materials

Choosing the most suitable surface for the children's garden depends on the age of the children and the use to which the play area will be put. There are various options.

Mulches Bark and woodchip mulches are more natural looking than many surface materials and will absorb much of the energy of falls. However, unless some form of barrier is provided it can drift into other parts of the garden and so requires regular raking. Special play area mulches are available pre-bagged from suppliers, and the mulch should be applied to a depth of at least 300mm (12in). Recycled rubbed mulches are also available.

Impact-absorbing play surfaces There are a variety of modular or tiled surfaces, designed for play areas, made from recycled rubber. Some mats can simply be underlaid with a geotextile membrane and placed over the ground or grass, whereas certained types of tile have to sit on a concrete base edged with shuttering. Wet-pour rubber, which looks like tarmac but is springy, sits on a prepared base and is suitable for large play areas.

Concrete slabs Although an area paved with slabs or cast concrete will offer the toughest, most hardwearing surface for a play area, it is not a sensible choice where small children will be playing; neither should it be used as a base for a climbing frame, slide or other structure from which they might fall.

Gravel Gravel, like concrete, is not the most friendly surface for boisterous games and also tends to create a mess throughout the rest of the garden as the stones are dragged along by feet.

Sand Suitable only for small areas such as underneath a climbing frame or at the end of a slide, sand will break a fall and prevent a potentially serious accident. However, it will attract neighbourhood cats and after heavy rainfall it remains wet for some time. Special playpit sand can be obtained pre-bagged from garden centres and DIY stores.

Grass A turfed area soon deteriorates if used for ball games. It is, however, the most suitable surface to use as a play area, and re-turfing the area in early autumn will allow it to recover and be ready for use again in spring.

Timber A timber decking, although not really practicable for large areas, can be useful as a surface for a play area that contains a climbing frame, where the deck can become part of the frame itself.

Pair of swings and swing bar

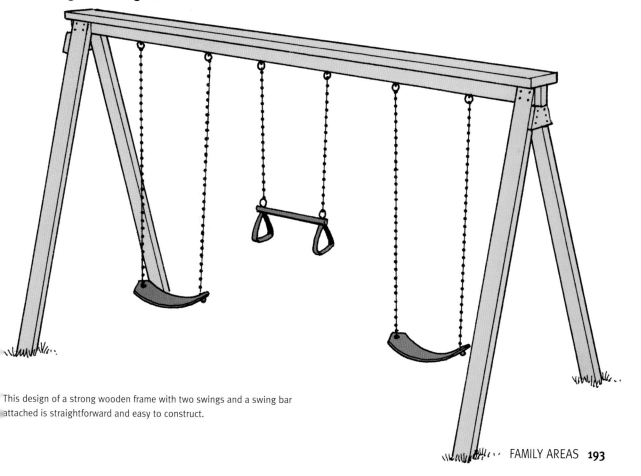

This design of a strong wooden frame with two swings and a swing bar attached is straightforward and easy to construct.

Climbing frames

The basic framework

A sturdy rectangular or square framework can be erected using 100mm sq (4in sq) planed softwood as the main supporting uprights, with intermediates of smaller-section 75 x 50mm (3 x 2in) timber. The top rail of the climbing frame should be constructed from the smaller-section timber, bolted to the main uprights and screwed to the intermediate posts.

For greater rigidity, cut halving joints at the corners of the surrounding top rail, and notch the intermediate bracing horizontals between the perimeter rails. The arrangement of the intermediate rails depends on the configuration of the climbing frame, and what facilities are to be included. The swing, knotted climbing rope, rope ladder, and climbing tyre are strung on eyebolts from the rails.

Lengths of 35mm (1½in) diameter hardwood dowel or steel rods are fixed into holes drilled in the supporting uprights to form climbing rungs and somersault bars, or fitted between the intermediate horizontal rails at the top of the frame to act as the monkey bars.

Building a metal climbing frame

A climbing frame constructed from tough steel tubing and proprietary galvanized metal couplings is easy to erect. The fittings are commonly available, and consist of a range of tee-sockets, single sockets, elbows, straight couplers, and end cups, which can be used to design the climbing frame. The structure is also easy to dismantle and move.

The steel tubes are sold either by the manufacturer of the fittings, or at DIY stores, builder's merchants or scaffolding suppliers. They come in a choice of six diameters from 21mm (⅞in) to 60mm (2⅜in). To join the tubes, simply slot on the fittings and tighten them using a hexagonal (Allen) key. Dig holes in the ground for the main supporting tubes, setting them in concrete if the frame is to be permanently sited. If the frame is to be moved, embed tubes of larger diameter into the ground in concrete supports and then slot the frame supports into these: the fit does not need to be precise, as the weight of the completed frame, and its span, will prevent it from wobbling.

Dig holes about 300mm (12in) deep and about the same square, fill with hardcore, and ram down with a stout length of timber. Set the lengths of tubing upright in the holes and pour in the concrete to retain them. Compact the concrete mix around the tubes so that it sets level with the ground.

Once the ground supports have been set, insert the uprights for the climbing frame and

Tree houses

CHILD SAFETY: GENERAL POINTS

A garden made for children must incorporate various safety features, both to protect them from harm and to prevent damage to nearby property and garden features. In addition to sensible precautions such as fencing off a garden pond or swimming pool, and overseeing games with paddling pools, slides, and climbing frames, make certain that the play equipment used has been safety-tested and approved.

Timber used to construct toys or play equipment should be sanded smooth to avoid splinters and snagged clothes, the edges bevelled and the corners rounded. Check that there are no nails or screw-heads protruding from components, and always use rustproof screws and nails so that in the event of a scratch the risk of a wound becoming septic is lessened.

With large-scale equipment frequent checks are necessary to ensure its safety. The surface of a slide must be free from snags or protruding fixings and should incorporate a guard rail at the top.

The stairs up to the slide must be secure and slip-resistant. A seesaw should be fitted with a buffer underneath the seat to cushion the user against jarring.

Check that all joints used to connect play equipment are sound before a child is allowed to use it, and check regularly for splits and other defects that may develop. Timber should not be painted as the paint film can conceal dangerous cracks or other faults. Instead, apply a clear, non-toxic varnish to timberwork. Similarly, with smaller toys, any paint used must be lead-free to avoid the risk of poisoning.

Keep the play area a suitable distance away from glasshouses, conservatories, cold frames, and house windows, to minimize the possibility of damage from balls or other missiles.

The kind of toys and play equipment you construct for the garden will depend on the ages, interests, tastes, and physical capabilities of your children.

connect them to each other by inserting lengths of tubing into the sockets in the upright; these tubes should be horizontal so the pairs of sockets must be level.

Build the climbing frame up to the preferred geometric shape, remembering to connect all exposed ends of the tubing to form a series of interlinking square frames.

Tree houses

If you have a suitable, and suitably sited, tree with a strong trunk in your garden, a tree house can become a favoured play area. Similar techniques and guidelines

apply for the construction of a simple tree house as for the climbing frame. Take care in the siting of the tree house – neighbours might not appreciate it if impinges on their privacy.

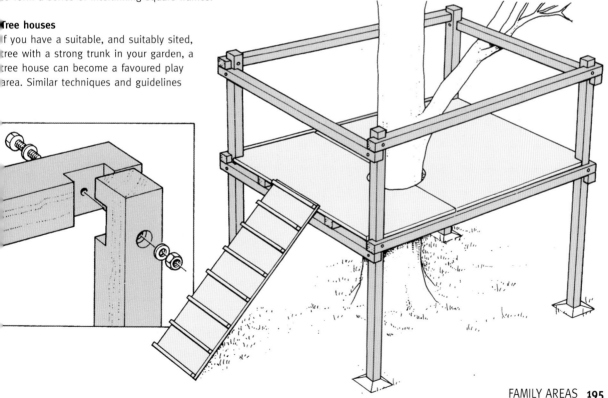

A sandpit-paddling pool

A dual sandpit and paddling pool, specially designed so that the water and sand will not mingle, is an attractive addition to a play area.

The basic frame

The design of the sandpit/paddling pool is simple: it consists of a rectangular box made from planks of wood and divided into two halves by a pair of planks, fitted with a slatted wooden seat-cum-lid, with storage space underneath it. The sandpit and paddling pool areas are fitted with slatted lift-off covers to keep out animals and debris that would foul the sand and water. The unit is straightforward to construct using old floorboards or skirting boards, or new planed timber planks measuring about 150 x 25mm (6 x 1in).

Preparing the joints

The corners of the frame are connected using simple halving joints. First cut the boards to length, bearing in mind that they should be about 300mm (12in) longer than the finished size of the box, to allow for the overlapping joints.

Stack the long and short boards together so that they are aligned at one end. Tape them together while you mark out the joints. With the stacked boards lying flat, measure in from the end a distance of 150mm (6in) and scribe a pencil line across at this point against a try square. Continue the squared line around one edge of the stacked boards and onto the opposite side.

Now measure a distance of 25mm (1in) in from the scribed line and scribe a parallel line around the boards in the same way as before: this gives the thickness of the joint, which is equal to the thickness of the timber. It is best to measure the actual thickness of the board, as given dimensions are only nominal, and slight differences may occur. Measure across the boards from a long edge a distance equal to half the width of a board and scribe a line at this point, connecting the parallel lines at right-angles to them. This gives you the depth of the joint. Release the boards from the tape and continue marking lines around onto the opposite face of each individual board. The boards which were central in the stack must be marked according to the parallel lines marked on one edge. Mark the joints on the opposite end of each board in the same way.

Cutting the halving joints

Cut the halving joints by placing the boards, stacked and taped together again, in a vice or workbench jaws. Saw down the parallel lines from the scribed edge as far as the joint depth lines. Repeat for the joints on the other end of the boards.

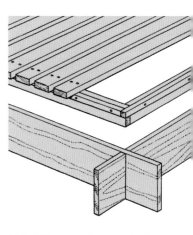

Slatted lids are made from a simple framework which slots into the compartments.

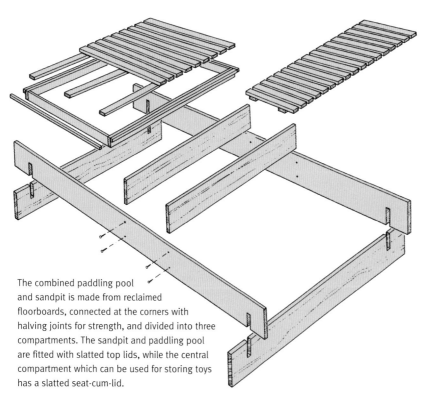

The combined paddling pool and sandpit is made from reclaimed floorboards, connected at the corners with halving joints for strength, and divided into three compartments. The sandpit and paddling pool are fitted with slatted top lids, while the central compartment which can be used for storing toys has a slatted seat-cum-lid.

A sandpit-paddling pool

Free the boards and chop out the finger of waste from each using a wood chisel.

Assembling the basic box
Slot the halving joints together to form the rectangular box. If necessary, dismantle and make any adjustments to the component parts. Continue to reassemble the box without adhesive until you are confident the pieces will fit, then dismantle the box again and apply PVA woodworking adhesive to the joint faces, then reassemble. Clamp up the joints and set aside until the adhesive has dried.

Fitting the dividers
Measure the distance between the two long sides of the box frame and cut two lengths of board to fit. Mark guidelines on the inside of each side board for positioning the dividers: as a guide, these should be about 600mm (24in) apart. Slot the dividers between the sides of the box and drill clearance holes for screws through the side boards and into their ends. Insert screws and tighten to secure the dividers.

Making the slatted lids
The slatted lids for the pool, sandpit, and storage area are simply loose-fitting, although the storage box/seat lid with hinges could be attached to one of the dividers.

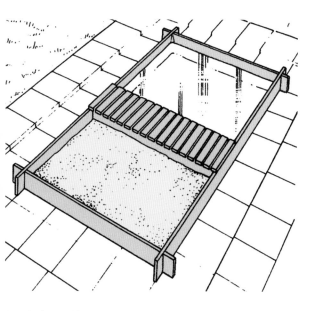

Contain the sand by setting the entire unit in a sunken area lined with slabs, surrounded by a higher skirt of slabs.

To make a basic slatted lid, construct a simple butt-jointed frame of 50 x 12mm (2 x ½in) softwood to fit inside the perimeter of the sandpit or paddling pool compartment using nails to connect the pieces. Now pin a ledge of 25mm sq (1in sq) softwood around the frame, aligned with the top edge.

Make up a slatted square of softwood to fit within the butt-jointed frame as the lid by pinning 50 x 12mm (2 x ½in) slats of soft-wood at right-angles to formers (battens) of the same timber, spaced near each end of the slats, and one centrally. This assembly slots into the butt-jointed frame, and is nailed to it. The ends of the slats, which should be fit spaced about 12mm (½in) apart, should overlap the framework so that it finishes flush with the outside edge of the thin ledge fixed around the butt-jointed section.

Drop the completed slatted top into the compartment of the main box to check the fit. Assemble a matching top for the other compartment. The slatted top for the divider compartment is of simpler construction: simply pin slats to a pair of formers cut to fit along the inside edges of the dividers. Finish the unit by applying clear preservative or preservative stain.

Alternatively, substitute the slatted compartment tops with solid tops of exterior-grade plywood, fitted with a central handle for lifting. Plywood tops need to be thoroughly treated with preservative, then coated with exterior-quality varnish to protect the wood from the weather.

Fitting a pool liner
The paddling pool section of the unit must be fitted with a flexible pool liner to make it waterproof. Cut a square of vinyl liner to fit within the compartment, lapping up the sides, and just over the edges. Pin the liner to the top edge of the compartment and trim off the excess with a sharp knife. At the corners, fold over the flap of liner and pin this in place, too.

Emptying the pool is simply a matter of lifting the box frame to pour out the water. As an alternative, drill a hole through the side of the end plank and the liner and fit a plastic tap used for water butts. The vinyl liner must then be sealed to the board at the hole, using waterproof adhesive, to stop the water seeping behind the liner.

Constructing the base
Concrete paving slabs make the most practical surface for this construction, and should be laid in an area about one slab wider than the box itself all around, with a further slab-wide paved area beyond at a slightly higher level. This is done by sinking the main surface about 100mm (4in) below ground level, with the higher skirt of slabs at ground level. This confines most of the sand to the play area.

Dustbin screens

It is not very appealing to have to look at rubbish bins in the garden. However, they can be concealed from view by constructing a simple screen.

Designing the screen

A basic screen can be an open-ended, three-sided structure consisting of two end piers and two corner piers. If the screen is to be used to conceal dustbins, it should be built on concrete raft foundations (see page 88), with the solid base doubling as a dry base for the bins themselves. The height of the screen will depend on how tall the dustbins or wheelie bins are that you wish to conceal, and the width of it on what it will contain.

Building a pier

Start the construction by dry-laying (laying without mortar) the first row of bricks on the base, turning or using half-bricks to form the bases of the piers. Mark out on the concrete base the shape of the screen wall by drawing around the bricks in chalk. Remove the blocks. Mix some mortar on a large board on a nearby hard surface or in a wheelbarrow. It is easiest for a project of this size to use a pre-bagged, dry-mixed mortar to which just water is added.

Trowel a bed of mortar onto the base in the position of the first pier, furrow the surface to aid adhesion and suction. Tap down the first brick with the shaft of your trowel and check that it is level by placing a spirit level across the top. Following the instructions for bricklaying given on page 130–133, creating a stretcher bond wall, turned at 90 degrees to form the corners.

The mortar joints between bricks must be consistently 10mm (⅜in) thick, and this should be checked frequently as the wall is built. It is also important to ensure that the wall does not bow outward. Check this by holding a spirit level or straight-edged length of timber across the face of the wall: any unevenness will be obvious. Correct any misalignment before the mortar hardens.

Fitting capping and coping

Neaten the appearance of the wall and help deflect rain from its joints by bedding bevel-topped coping stones along the three side walls. These stones overhang slightly at each side. To protect the tops of the piers, fit square cappings on the pilasters, bedding them on mortar.

Smooth all the mortar joints by running an offcut of garden hose along the setting mortar to give a half-rounded profile.

If appropriate, paint the screen with exterior emulsion paint to camouflage it or to blend with other paintwork.

Making a screen to conceal bins

1 Hold your spirit level against each side of the pier in turn to check that it is vertical.

2 Lay the bricks, following the instructions given on pages 130–133, using a single thickness stretcher bond.

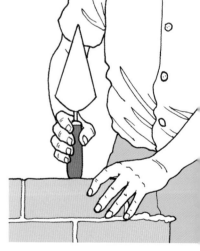

3 Tap down each brick as you go, then check the course is horizontal using a spirit level, further adjusting as necessary.

Compost containers

Types of compost heap

The ideal size for a compost heap, which will produce the most rapid results, is about 2m (6ft) square, and 1.5m (5ft) high. A selection of proprietary ready-made compost bins are available, or you can make the enclosure yourself.

Ready-made containers Metal-framed compost containers are commonly wire-mesh boxes fitted with a hinged access panel, or else little more than a strong, black polythene sack held in a metal cradle: holes in the side of the sack provide the necessary aeration. Plastic containers include an open-topped round format with preformed holes in the sides for aeration. There are even tough plastic compost containers available which are mounted on a cradle. If these are turned every day, they can produce compost in as little as 21 days.

Timber compost containers are available constructed from a number of interlocking planks, which enable you to disassemble the surround for access to the compost inside.

Home-made containers Do-it-yourself assembly compost containers take many forms. Erect side walls from breezeblocks stacked up without mortar, alternate courses staggered by half their length. For airflow to the base of the heap, raise the container walls on bricks laid on edge. Another method is to create a wooden container from planks nailed to vertical posts set in concrete or to fencing spikes. For access to the heap, the front planks should be removable, preferably slotted into a channel formed by slim battens fixed to the supporting posts: simply slide the planks up and over. Again, provide aeration by spacing the planks apart by about 50mm (2in), using timber spacers. Fit a lid of corrugated plastic.

Corrugated iron or plastic panels, held between timber posts driven into the ground, can be used as the basis for the walls of a compost container. Rest the panels on bricks on edge, or on drainpipes laid on the ground, to introduce an air supply to the centre of the heap.

CORRUGATED COMPOST CONTAINER

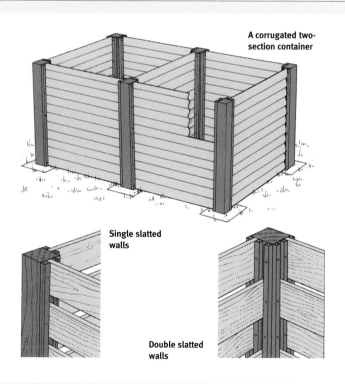

A corrugated two-section container

Single slatted walls

Double slatted walls

Make a compost container from 4in (100mm) square, preservative-treated, sawn softwood posts, fixed vertically at each corner of the proposed unit, bedded in concrete or fixed with fence spikes.

It is sensible to divide the heap into two to separate the compost still under production from that which is already useable. A panel of corrugated plastic, or of timber slats held between intermediate posts, which can be slid out if necessary, can be incorporated into the design of your compost container

Where you are making a two-section container, include intermediate posts (top). Fit pairs of 25mm (1in) square vertical battens to the sides of the posts to form a central channel to take the wall panels (shown left). The walls themselves may be nothing more than sheets of corrugated PVC roofing material (as in the top diagram: the side of the container is cut away to indicate the corrugations of the material).

Alternatively, use prefabricated sections comprising horizontal planks nailed to uprights: the planks should be spaced about 2in (50mm) apart for aeration of the heap (far left), or else staggered at each side of the uprights as double-slatted walls (shown left).

Building a barbecue

Barbecues, now very popular adjuncts to the garden, can offer a versatile summer extension to the kitchen. They may be purchased in a wide range of designs, or constructed for use in a permanent position in the garden.

Siting the barbecue

Although correct design of a barbecue is crucial to its working efficiently and safely, picking the site is of equal importance.

Avoid siting the grill close to open windows, where curtains could billow out and catch light or where smoke is likely to waft through neighbours' windows. The barbecue unit is usually box-shaped and built of non-combustible materials such as bricks, concrete blocks, or stone. It has an open back (where the cook stands) and an open top.

MAKING A LOOSE-BRICK BARBECUE

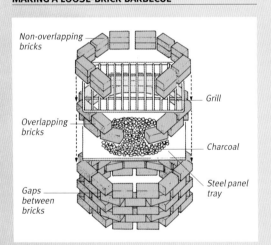

Non-overlapping bricks

Grill

Overlapping bricks

Charcoal

Gaps between bricks

Steel panel tray

A temporary barbecue, which can be dismantled for storage during winter, can be made by stacking bricks dry, without mortar. It can be built in a circular, triangular, square, or hexagonal shape. A basic circular unit will use about 100 bricks; other shapes will need more. As well as being easy and quick to construct, it is a very efficient structure – the honeycomb bonding arrangement used to raise the walls ensures a plentiful supply of air to the charcoal for good combustion.

Lay the bricks on a prepared base with 50mm (2in) wide gaps between each brick. Continue to stack bricks, alternating the staggered bond with each course, until you reach the seventh. Place a sheet-steel panel across the top of the brick walls as a fuel tray to hold the charcoal, then add two more courses of dry-laid bricks on top of which a slatted grill is placed.

Add another two or three courses of bricks around the back of the unit to act as a windshield for the cooking area.

Cooking height The barbecue should be constructed so that it is perfectly stable, with its grill set at the most convenient height for cooking – normally about nine or ten courses of bricks from ground level.

Cooking control The barbecue needs a supply of fresh air to burn correctly, and this can be provided by building in an updraught flue to the grill area. Construct a permanent barbecue on concrete strip foundations, from half-brick thick walls arranged in a U-shape. The grill and charcoal tray are placed either on adjustable-height brackets set in the mortar joints, or on fixed supports formed by turning bricks at right-angles in relevant courses to protrude from the walls.

Laying the bricks

Prepare strip foundations using profile boards and stringlines as a guide to setting out. Realign the stringlines to indicate the position of the walls of the unit, then trowel in a 10mm (⅜in) thick screed of bricklaying mortar onto the prepared foundations. at one side of the barbecue. Furrow the surface and lay the first course of bricks end to end. At the corners, turn a brick at right-angles so that its end abuts the side of the last brick on the side wall, forming a mortar joint between the two.

Lay the second course of bricks, starting with a brick cut in half across its width to maintain the stretcher bond. continue to lay courses of bricks, staggering the vertical joints alternately, until you reach the fifth course, on which the support ledge is built. At the fifth course, lay a row of bricks at right angles to the walls, abutting them side by side and placing them on edge rather than flat down. The bricks should overlap the walls at each side evenly. Continue this row of bricks along the back wall of the unit.

Add a further three courses of bricks in stretcher bond on top of the overlapping bricks: this forms a narrow ledge on which to rest the cooking grill and the charcoal tray. Build another ledge at the tenth course of bricks, then add another three courses in stretcher bond to complete the main part of the barbecue unit.

Building a work surface

The easiest way to add a worksurface is to construct a low plinth wall in bricks about six courses high, set on a separate strip foundation parallel with one of the side walls of the barbecue. Lay the sixth course of the plinth wall on edge.

Cut a panel of 9mm (⅜in) thick exterior grade plywood or chipwood to fit between the plinth wall and the ledge protruding from the side of the barbecue, the other side of which supports the charcoal tray. Complete the barbecue unit by neatening the mortar joints.

Building a barbecue

Making a brick barbecue

1 Lay five courses of bricks, then add a sixth on edge, overlapping the side walls on the three sides to form a ledge for the charcoal tray and work surface.

2 Build up the side and back walls in stretcher bond by another three courses; add the tenth on edge, then add the windshield.

PROPRIETARY BARBECUES

Purpose-made barbecues include the so-called hibachi type; made of cast iron or cheaper, thinner steel, this is the simplest model. The tabletop type is basically a simple tray which contains the charcoal, with handled grill trays; these slot in at one of several height settings for adjusting the ferocity of the cooking. Hibachis are ideal for use on a homemade brick-built barbecue surround, because all that is required is a flat surface at the cooking height on which the feet of the tray can rest.

Freestanding barbecues made of lightweight steel (often wheeled) offer portability and a more controlled cooking environment than a simple hibachi. They usually feature adjustable cooking heights via ratchet lever or multi-position grill housings, a built-in windshield, and battery-powered rotary spit attachment.

Other, even more complex, barbecues such as the kettle type are intended for freestanding use, and may incorporate wheels for mobility, but they should not be moved when alight. The kettle cover serves as a windshield when raised, and pivots or hinges over the cooking to convert the barbecue into an oven, infusing the food with the cooking aromas and smoke. Versions are available with rotating spit attachments.

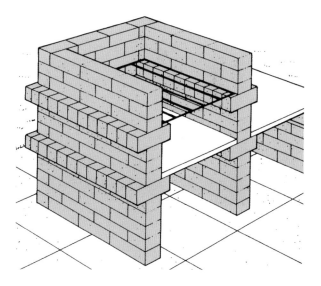

3 Place the shelf and worksurface on the ledges and slot in the charcoal tray and grill above. Point the mortar joints; leave to set. Leave for a few days before lighting the barbecue.

Putting up an awning

An awning can enhance any garden and can also add to the appearance of a house, shading a terrace or seating area, allowing it to be fully used when otherwise it may be uncomfortably hot and bright, as well as offering protection from light summer showers and some privacy.

Awnings for shade

As a way of quickly creating an area of shade within a garden they are ideal, and instantly bring shade where cover from vegetation would take time to grow. Awnings provide another useful function when placed over a window or glass doors; in shading the interior of south-facing rooms from direct sunlight they keep the room cooler and help prevent fading of and damage to furnishings from the sun's rays.

Awnings work well in a small garden – being retractable or removable, they will take up little space when not in use. Depending on type and the material they are constructed from, some awnings need to be stored indoors during winter. Retractable models normally just need to be closed up and secured over the winter months, and awnings need to be dismantled or retracted if strong winds threaten as these can damage the awning.

Awnings as shelter

Don't forget that if an awning is left open during heavy rain, this can soon collect in a pool and can damage the structure or material. Do consider how rain will drain away from the awning and from the area below it, and disperse any water by raising the material, ensuring that there is nothing below the edges to be drenched when the material is lifted. Some awnings are shaped to allow rainwater to flow away, which is worth considering in wetter climates and if the awning is to act as a shelter from rain.

Types of awning

There are several types of awning, many of which can be purchased direct from suppliers who may also fit it as an extra service. The internet is a good source to evaluate the models and types available.

Motorized models have retractable arms that swing out and back to open and close the awning. Powered by electricity, these are operated using a wall mounted switch and take any effort out of manually closing a large awning. Some models even have remote control units to open and close them, which can be useful on cloudier days and if sudden showers are likely. More expensive are climate-controlled awnings which have sun and wind sensors programmed to open and close the awning automatically as the weather changes.

Manually-operated awnings tend to be cheaper than motorized versions, and are opened and closed by turning a hand crank. Provided the awning is maintained properly, the manual operation should not take much effort.

Fixing an awning to a wall

1 Mark the position of the first hook on the wall using chalk. Measure the position of the second hook from this point.

2 Using a masonry bit of an appropriate width for the anchor bolt, drill a hole at the centre of each cross.

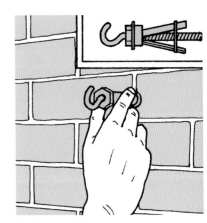

3 Insert the hook attached to the anchor bolt. The bolt will expand to provide a firmer grip as it is tightened.

Putting up an awning

The framework of the awning should be constructed from coated aluminium and stainless steel, to provide a strong, lightweight frame. The fixings should be made from stainless steel for strength and durability.

Simple awnings are much cheaper, easy to create, and fix to the wall (see illustrations, below); rather than retract them they are rolled up and unhooked from the wall.

Choice of material

Whichever type of awning you select for your garden, choose a material and pattern that is appropriate to your garden design and one that will enhance the appearance of the house. A wide range of colours are available, with many variations of the typical striped awning on sale as well as single coloured ones.

The material chosen my simply add a splash of sunny colour or the colour chosen can harmonize with other features in the garden – for instance, blues and blue-and-white stripes can work well in maritime gardens for a nautical touch, or green tones would complement a deck stained with a green-coloured wood preservative.

Do remember that dark colours absorb heat, so lighter colours are more appropriate for achieving optimum levels of shade. Ensure the material you choose for your awning will block out UV radiation, especially if it is intended to shade a play area for children. Fabrics can be specially coated to block

sunlight and repel moisture – these are generally easier to keep clean and are more fade-resistant.

Creating an awning

One of the benefits of creating your own awning is a wider choice of material. Instead of a cloth, it is possible to use a split-bamboo blind to add a more tropical ambience.

Hanging an awning from hooks in a wall creates a simple awning that can easily be removed when not in use.

Once a suitable sized piece of material has been chosen, eyes should to be affixed to holes punched into each corner. The next step is to mark on the wall the positions of the hooks. Once the location of the first hook has been marked, measure along the wall and indicate the position of the second hook. Remember that this distance needs to be slightly shorter than the width of the awning itself as the fabric is not to be taut, but will dip.

The hooks need to be attached to expanding anchor bolts to secure them firmly to the masonry. Drill a hole for each of the bolts using a masonry bit. Screw the hooks tight, ensuring that the hook remains vertical.

The wall-side of the awning is hooked into place. Two poles (cut to a length shorter than the height of the hooks to allow the awning to slope forward) support the outer edges of the awning. Attach a guy rope at both outer corners to stabilize the poles.

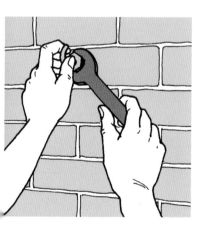

4 Hold the hook straight as you tighten the bolt with a spanner, in order to keep the hook to the vertical.

5 Once the hook and bolt are fully tightened and secure, the back corners of the awning can be attached to the wall.

6 The outer edges of the awning are supported by poles cut to a length to allow the awning to slope downwards.

Garden buildings: general information

Glasshouses, sheds and summerhouses can play an important part in the garden, but for best results they should be thoughtfully sited and carefully maintained.

Site and choice

All buildings should be easily accessible from the dwelling house. If electricity and water services are to be incorporated then the nearer the buildings are to the mains supply the cheaper and more convenient will be installation. Do not erect buildings on exposed sites and in the case of glasshouse avoid frost pockets and excessively shady spots. Bear in mind that shade angles alter considerably over the course of the year. All buildings should be sited clear of overhanging trees. Make sure that the ground is well drained, and that there is adequate provision for access when the ground is wet. Check with the local authority to see if planning permission is required for the structure to be erected.

There are so many different glasshouses, sheds, and summer housese available. Buy from a reputable manufacturer who has had plenty of experience in making garden buildings, and inspect the erected model before deciding to buy.

Materials

Sheds and summer houses may be constructed from ordinary deal (often Baltic pine) or from western red cedar. The latter is more durable and consequently more expensive. It is essential that both types of wood are treated with preservative to prolong their life. Western red cedar looks attractive unpainted and is the more durable wood. Many manufacturers supply buildings which have been pre-treated; others supply the preservative which must be applied by the purchaser.

Glasshouses are available in western red cedar, deal and aluminium alloy. The latter needs no maintenance, though on sites which are exposed to sea winds and spray a timber house might be a wiser choice, for salt is known to corrode some aluminium alloys. Some manufacturers supply alloy

Prefabricated foundations

Bed the corners of ready-made foundations in concrete placed directly on the soil. Fix the building to the foundations, following the maker's instructions.

Constructing foundations for a building

1 Mark out the area of the building and place canes at the corners. Measure the angles and ensure they are 90 degrees.

2 Excavate a trench for the foundation one spit deep and a spade's width wide between the canes.

3 Half-fill the trench with rubble or hard-core. Ram it firm. Use hardcore of even size and free of plaster rubble.

Garden buildings: general information

houses which are coated with white or green acrylic paint for protection and to improve their appearance.

Choose a glasshouse that pleases the eye, is strong and well made, large enough for the needs of the garden, and well equipped to allow good ventilation and light transmission.

Foundations

Solid foundations are essential for all permanent garden buildings, both to hold them level and to reduce the risk of rot and corrosion. Some manufacturers offer ready-made steel or precast concrete bases for their buildings. These are simply laid in place on firm ground, bolted together, and checked with a set square and a spirit level before the building is erected on top of them. It is wise to bed the corners of these foundations in concrete to ensure stability in high winds. The laying of foundations is shown below; further information on slab foundations is given on page 89.

Maintenance

All timber buildings should be coated with a suitable preservative once every two or three years. Apart from retaining the smart appearance of the building, painting or preserving will also lengthen its life.

Glasshouses should be thoroughly cleaned once a year in winter or early spring. The contents should be removed, fixed stagings and the main structure should be scrubbed down with a diluted solution of a proprietary horticultural disinfectant, and all debris removed. Thoroughly clean pots, containers, and

---

RE-GLAZING THE GLASSHOUSE

Immediately replace any panes of glass that are accidentally broken. Remove the old glazing sprigs with pliers and take out all the broken glass. Remove the old putty. Lay a bed of new putty and push the new pane of glass into place. Secure the pane with new glazing sprigs, which are knocked into place using a light hammer. Clean off excess putty with a damp knife and clean the glass with a damp cloth.

---

equipment before restocking the glasshouse.

Hinges and catches on windows and doors should be oiled regularly throughout the year to keep them operating smoothly. All glass, particularly in glasshouses, should be kept clean to allow maximum light penetration. Carefully clean overlaps between panes. Re-glaze any broken panes, as shown above. In aluminium alloy glasshouses (and in some wooden models) this may simply be a matter of removing the broken pieces and slotting in a new one which is held in place either by clips or grooves.

4 Position a brick at the ends of each trench and check that the eight bricks are at the same level.

5 Mix concrete from six parts ballast and one part cement. Pour into the trench up to the top of the bricks. Tamp it level.

6 When the concrete is dry, cement a row of bricks into place using 4:1 mortar. Lay a felt damp course over them.

Erecting a garden shed

A shed is an essential garden feature in which to store tools and equipment as well as bulky items for which no storage space is available elsewhere. Many shed kits are available and it is not difficult to erect them, with help, in a few hours once the foundations have been prepared.

Timber and roofs

All timber used in shed construction must be treated with preservative to combat rot. Softwoods need treatment at least every two years. There are two types of shed:
Pent roof Sheds with a pent roof, which slopes in one direction only (high on the door side; low towards the back), offer limited headroom overall. A window is normally included in the front or front side wall so that a workbench can be placed underneath for good light and sufficient headroom.
Apex roof For good headroom overall, an apex roof shed is the best choice: here, the roof slopes on two sides and has a central ridge and there is plenty of space in which to work as well as for storage.

Preparing the foundations

Erect the shed on a firm, flat surface such as a cast concrete base, or precast concrete paving slabs. Buy enough slabs to cover the base on which the shed is to stand with an overlap

of about 100mm (4in) all round. Mark out the base with stringlines and wooden pegs, then remove any vegetation and large stones from within the area. Dig out any turf and topsoil and use them in another part of the garden if possible.

Compact the earth and flatten the surface using a garden roller, then fill in any hollows with soil and roll again. Rake a 150mm (6in) layer of sharp sand over the base, then bed the paving slabs in this. Tap the slabs down firmly. Butt the slabs up against each other and check that they are level across the surface using a spirit level. Note that the entire slab base should slope gently – by about 25mm (1in) – in one direction to ensure rapid drainage of rainwater.

Assembling the shed floor

A kit shed usually has a prefabricated floor of chipboard (or floorboards), which is sometimes fitted with slim reinforcing battens resting on stout timber bearers. Place a layer of bituminous felt underneath the bearers so that damp cannot rise, and set the floor on this base. Check that the floor is firm and steady: if not pack underneath it with offcuts of timber.

Erecting the wall panels

Most panels must be bolted together, and you will need help to hold them in place while they are being fixed. First, place

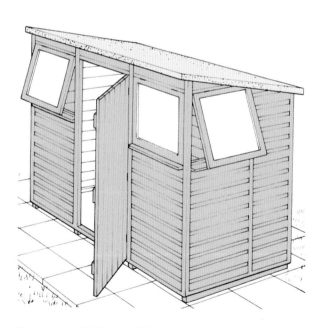

This pent type shed has a roof that slopes in one direction, usually towards the back.

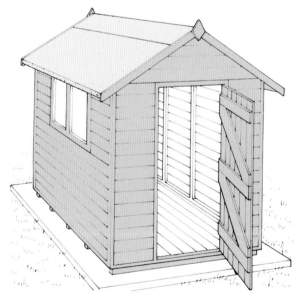

This apex-roof shed has a pitched roof sloping on two sides from a central ridge offering plenty of headroom.

Erecting a garden shed

Erecting a kit shed

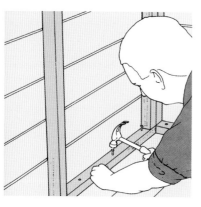

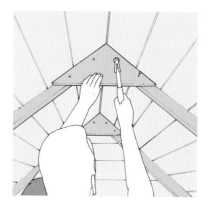

1 Fix the wall panels. The wall panels are lifted onto the floor and temporarily secured with bolts. Nail the wall panels to the floor, then tighten bolts to secure them.

2 Bolt the back and wall panels together loosely. Trimming battens may be required to seal the join between the panels at external corners.

3 An apex roof is nailed to the wall battens, then reinforced with plywood ridge plates. The final stage is to lay felt on the roof for waterproofing.

the back panel and one side panel on the floor and temporarily secure this with the bolts: screw on the nuts fairly loosely. Lift up the remaining two wall panels and fit the bolts – again, not too tightly.

Measure the diagonals inside the shed to check that the walls are square. Tighten the nuts with a spanner.

Position the four walls correctly on the floor – you will probably find that they are intended to overhang by about 25mm (1in) – then secure them by hammering nails through the lower reinforcing batten frame into the floor supports, at about 300mm (12in) intervals.

Fitting the roof panel

The roofs of small sheds are normally the pent type, which is far easier to fit than the pitched type. A pent roof is usually supported at the front on a header beam, which is secured to the top of the front wall panel, and supported at the sides on tapered battens fixed to the tops of the side panels.

Position the header beam and side battens and secure them by driving screws up through the wall panel frames The roof itself will simply be a panel of chipboard large enough to overhang the walls of the shed so that rainwater will run off clear of the walls. To secure the roof panel, lift it onto the roof bearers and align its edges with the walls to form a consistent overlap all round. Nail to the supports below.

To fit an apex roof, nail the roof braces to the wall frames, and reinforce underneath the ridge at each end with a nail-on

plywood plate. With larger apex sheds, however, purlins may need to be fitted and rafters to support the weight of the shed roof.

Fitting the roof covering

Some roof panels are supplied already felted as protection against the weather. However, if the panels are plain, fix sheets of bituminous roofing felt to the surface to make them waterproof. Cut a strip of felt from a 10m (33ft) roll to fit across the width of the shed. Lay the felt on the roof at the back, or lowest edge, so it overhangs by at least 100mm (4in). Fix the felt to the roof panel with 12mm (½in) long galvanized large-headed clout nails at 100mm (4in) intervals.

Fit the second strip of felt to the roof so it overlaps the previous strip by about 4in (100mm) and secure it with nails as before. With some smaller prefabricated sheds the roofing felt is simply secured by nailing slim preservative-treated battens across the overlapping layers.

Trim the excess felt so that it overhangs the roof by about 2in (50mm), then fold it over and secure with nails to the underside of the roof panel. Nail on a thin fascia board to cover the felted side and front edges, leaving the lower one, the back edge, free so that rainwater will run off.

Complete the shed by hanging the door and fitting any openable window frames that may be included with your model. Glaze the window frames without using putty by pinning the panes into the rebate.

Making a window box

City gardeners and flat dwellers are particularly reliant on containers to bring colour and plant interest to windowsills, steps, paths, balconies, and patios, but even large gardens benefit from the addition of containers. Containers on terraces and beside paths add variety of scale to the garden design, and allow small plants to be singled out for attention and enjoyed in detail. However, container-grown plants require more care than those grown in open ground.

Windowboxes

Wooden or strong plastic troughs are especially suitable for use as window boxes. They should be at least 15cm (6in) wide and 20cm (8in) deep, and as long as the window ledge. Choose plain colours which will be unobtrusive – the plants should provide the interest and brightness. Holes in the base are essential to allow free drainage, and the trough should be fitted with two or more feet to hold it 2.5–5cm (1–2in) above the window-sill so that excess water may escape.

Wooden boxes are easy to make. Ordinary planed deal may be cut to the required dimensions and fastened together with brass screws, which should be lightly greased to allow the box to be dismantled if necessary. To make the box last paint it with primer and exterior quality paint or coat it with polyurethane varnish or timber preservative. Allow all preservatives to dry off before planting up.

Proprietary plastic troughs may not have enough drainage holes. Use a drill to make more before planting. Window boxes and troughs on balconies can be a hazard because of dripping water, damp, or even falling boxes. Standing the box on a galvanized or plastic tray will prevent drips. The danger of falling boxes, however, is far more serious. The window box or trough on a balcony must be absolutely secure, especially if placed where it could fall on anyone.

Planting the windowbox

Choose colourful plants for the window box to make a bold statement. Alternatively edible plants are handy for a kitchen windowsill, such as herbs or small-leaved salad crops.

Plant up as shown on the next page, or alternatively place plants in pots in the box and surround the pots with gravel. The plants may be changed when they fade for new ones prepared beforehand.

Making and planting a window box

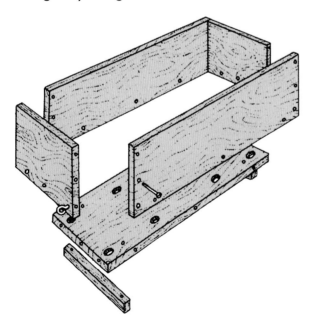

1 Construct the box from wood, using brass screws. Paint or treat with preservative. Fit low feet to hold it clear of the sill.

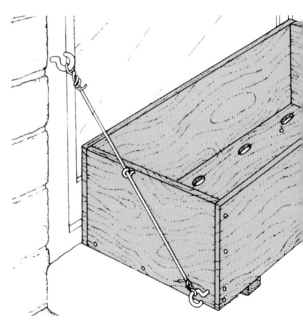

2 Anchor the box to the wall or window frame, using screw eyes and wire or chain, to prevent accidents.

Making a window box

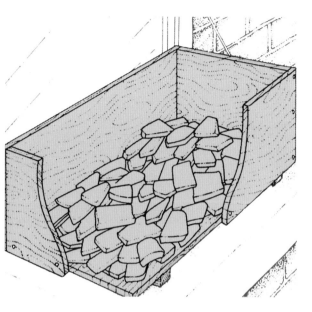

3 Place a layer of drainage material such as crocks or coarse gravel in the bottom of the box, for adequate drainage.

4 Fill to within 5cm (2in) of the rim with moist John Innes No.2 potting compost or a soiless equivalent.

5 Water the plants, knock them from their pots, and plant in the box, carefully firming the compost around the rootball.

6 Alternatively, place plants in pots in the box and surround with peat or gravel.

Installing electricity in the garden

However self-sufficient a gardener may be, the installation of outdoor electrical wiring and apparatus should always be left to a qualified professional. The dangers posed by faulty wiring and the use of poorly maintained electrical devices can never be overstressed, and the presence of moisture in the garden exacerbates the possibility of receiving electric shocks.

Electricity is potentially lethal, and stringent safety measures are essential if electrical equipment, especially outdoor equipment, is to work correctly and without endangering life.

Having established this principle, it is as well if the gardener understands some of the requirements which must be met when a power supply is being installed. It is sometimes possible for the gardener to do a certain amount of preparatory work to ease the electrician's task and lessen the expense. Consult the electrician before starting any such work.

Alternatives to electricity

If you are considering installing lighting in the garden or want to run a fountain in a pond, and are daunted or unhappy at the prospect of having a power supply run into your garden, or simply wish to conserve electricity, there are alternatives to electrical installations. For garden lighting there is an ever increasing range of reasonably priced solar light fittings that need no wiring (see page 213); and for ponds many solar-powered fountains and water features (see page 191) can be installed almost instantly. However, without electricity to power them, solar items need to be placed in a situation that allows them to receive plenty of sunlight.

For those who are uncomfortable trailing cables behind hedgecutters, garden trimmers, and blowers, cordless versions are available. These have limited running time, need to be recharged, and tend to be pricier (and heavier) than cabled tools, but offer a greater level of safety.

Electrical installations

One method of supplying power to garden buildings and to pumps in water features is to use a pre-assembled kit that is easy to install, allowing the cable to be plugged into the

A PERMANENT OUTDOOR ELECTRICAL SUPPLY

An outdoor electrical circuit linked to the household supply must be installed by a qualified electrician. Under new wiring regulations, your local authority Building Control Department must be advised of the proposed work. The home or landowner is responsible for ensuring that a competent person carries out this work, and there are penalties for not doing so. These regulations have been applied to protect householders from unsafe electrical installations. For further information, contact the local authority's Building Control Department.

Any installation should include a unit that incorporates a residual current device (RCD) which disconnects the supply automatically when faults are detected.

Underground cables

1 Dig a trench for the cable at least 60cm (24in) deep, 50cm (20in) under paths and other hard surfaces.

2 Protect the cable by placing a row of roofing tiles over it in the trench, or run through special protective conduits.

3 Lay warning tape, coloured with black and yellow stripes, along the top of tiles to indicate the presence of a live cable.

Installing electricity in the garden

mains supply in the house. These usually incorporate a residual current device (RCD), and have weatherproof switches and junction boxes.

If, however, the power supply is to be wired in to the house circuit, a competent electrician must do this work. New regulations govern fixed electrical installations in the UK, and any contractors employed to do this work must be registered as competent by a recognized scheme.

Cables and power points

When a power supply is to be run from a dwelling house to a garden shed or glasshouse, or to outdoor lighting points, the safest course is to have the supply cable laid underground. Overhead cables not only present safety problems – unless they are carefully positioned, for example, there is the risk of them being chafed by branches – they also look unsightly.

When electricians lay a supply underground they should use a fully armoured cable, for it can stand a certain amount of damage should it be struck inadvertently when the garden is being dug. To minimize the likelihood of such an accident, all armoured cable should be buried to a depth of 50cm (20in) under paths and hard surfaces, and to a depth of 60cm (24in) under lawns, beds, and other cultivated soil. Before the soil is filled in, tiles and warning tape (which is tape striped yellow and black to indicate a hazard) should be laid on top of the cable to remind yourself or anyone else that there is a live cable below.

The circuit must have its own fuse or RCD, and the cable itself must be of a sufficient size and capacity for the job it will be used for: a cable that can take 3kW of supply should be adequate for most garden needs.

Gardeners can save money and avoid possible damage to plants by excavating the trenches themselves to the specifications of the electrician who is to carry out the wiring. A permanent record should be kept of the position of underground cables and this information should be passed on to new occupants when a property changes hands.

Circuit breakers and plugs

Plug-in circuit breakers are inexpensive and should always be used where the circuit is not protected by an RCD. Employ the test button on the circuit breaker before use. If the circuit breaker trips, assess the fault or action that has caused the trip. If a circuit breaker trips regularly for no apparent reason, then replace it.

All switches, sockets, and plugs used outdoors or in a glasshouse must be weatherproof; those used for domestic supply indoors are not suitable. Control boards especially designed for glasshouse use are available (see page 219).

(see page 219)

SAFETY PRECAUTIONS

When electrically powered lawnmowers, hedgetrimmers, and other tools are used in the garden and the circuit itself is not protected by a residual current device (RCD), always use a plug-in circuit breaker (illustrated top left). Use only equipment that complies with the relevant British Standard and has been tested for safety.

Check that metal-cased power tools are properly earthed before use. Plastic-covered power tools will be double insulated but should still be used with a three-cored extension cable.

Before switching on the current, check all equipment for worn or loose parts and check flex and extension leads for damage to insulation and loose connections. Should a cable be damaged, cut out the damaged section and join the two ends with a purpose-made weatherproof connector (shown above). Cables should never be fixed with tape.

Wear appropriate clothing and footwear when using a mower or trimmer. Do not use electrical equipment in damp conditions.

Most electrical apparatus is now supplied with a plug already attached. If you need to fit a plug yourself, ensure that the plugs is weatherproof and has a suitable fuse. Again, regularly check plugs for damage or deterioration.

Other safety measures

Always unplug any equipment that needs to be adjusted: for example, if a blade or setting needs to be altered on an electric mower, or when a flex needs to be untangled. Be aware of the position of cables – keep the cable behind you when using trimmers and mowers and work away from the cable. If cables do become damaged, repair using a special connector. Never be tempted to tape up any breaks or damage.

Replace worn cables. If an electrical item has been stored away for any length of time, for instance an electric mower that has spent the winter in a shed, check that it is not damp before using; the cables may have become kinked through lack of use, so examine them carefully for any wear or damage. Get an electrician to check any electrical item if you have any doubts at all about its safety.

Garden lighting

Lighting can be used to great effect in the garden to illuminate beds and borders, pools, fountains, and trees, creating a magical ambience in the garden at twilight and at night. It can define the route of paths and drives once the natural light has faded. Lights – including coloured ones – embedded into a patio or into decking, allow the area to be enjoyed as the sun goes down, and make any seating area into a focal point in its own right.

It can be designed to highlight those parts of the garden that are viewed from the house, thus allowing the garden to be enjoyed after dark. If the observer is indoors the internal lighting and the barrier of the house windows will make it hard for the eye to appreciate the garden lighting. Very powerful bulbs will therefore be necessary to overcome this. It may also be worthwhile fitting dimmer switches inside the house to enhance the effect of the outside lights.

Securing lamps

Push lamps fitted with spikes into firm soil or turf. Direct the beam onto features you wish to highlight.

Positioning lamps

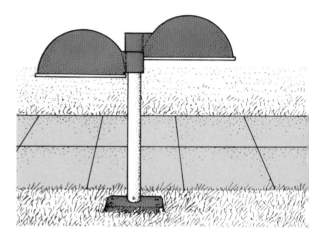

For functional lighting of paths and steps, use mushroom lamps directed downwards. This avoids dazzle.

Fix all exterior spotlights to walls or posts. Use them to create ambience or to light an area directly.

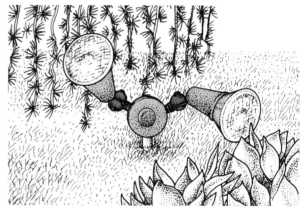

Illuminate trees and shrubs with floodlights placed low down and shining up into the foliage.

Garden lighting

Solar powered lights are becoming increasingly popular, and the range available ever growing. They save on electricity costs and negate the need to run electric cables into the garden, and the lack of cabling means that solar lights can be repositioned quickly and easily. However, they need to be placed in sunny positions to enable them to recharge, and the light that they emit is gently glowing rather than bright.

Installing a circuit

A garden lighting system must be installed by a qualified electrician: it can be extremely dangerous if the equipment is incorrectly installed or is unsuitable for outdoor use. The mains cable should be laid underground. The sockets must be fully weather-proofed and a circuit breaker should be fitted. Keep the cable which runs from the socket to the lamp as short and as obviously displayed as possible to minimize the risk of damage. The cable must be weatherproof, resistant to ultra-violet light and vermin-proof, and all equipment should be properly earthed.

Low-voltage sets are also available. A transformer, housed inside, usually converts mains voltage to a 12-volt supply. The lights are a weak source of illumination but the cumulative effect can be attractive and the lights can be moved around the garden to create a diversity of moods.

Choice of fittings and positioning

Choose only those lamps that are especially constructed for use in the open. They must be waterproof, resistant to corrosion, and able to withstand frost, snow, and damp. Most garden lamps are made of aluminium alloy or high impact plastic. There is a wide selection of different styles and colour of lamps, but choose something that is in keeping with the style of the garden.

Experiment to find the best positions for garden lights, but do bear in mind the following points. Make sure that all the lights point away from the onlooker. A tree or large shrub can be floodlit to act as a backdrop to a carpet of low-growing plants in the foreground. Alternatively, use floodlights to illuminate large areas in a pool of light; and position smaller spotlights to pick out specimen trees or shrubs. Spotlights turned on garden pools and streams can be especially effective, but they can also be positioned under the water to give waterfalls and fountains another dimension. Use only fully waterproofed lights especially designed for pools.

Securing the lamps

Dome lamps have spikes that are simply pushed into the ground to hold them firm. Others may possess drilled brackets which will have to be mounted on the house wall or a

convenient garden building, or on a wooden post which has been treated with preservative and knocked into the ground in front of the plants to be lit.

If lights are to be positioned in trees among the branches, they should either be firmly screwed to a strong branch, or secured with padded brackets that can be adjusted to prevent constriction and any harm to the tree.

TYPES OF GARDEN LIGHT

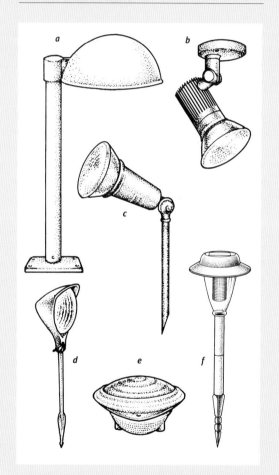

Mushroom lamps (a) light paths and steps. Spotlights (b) can be fixed to any solid surface, or to spikes (c) so that they can be moved. Pool lights (d) can be floating or submerged and floodlights (e) coloured. Covered solar lights (f) angle the light downward and so are ideal for illuminating paths and driveways.

Installing security lighting

Lighting can enhance the appearance of your home and garden, and obviously provides a means of visibility as dusk and darkness falls. The use of lighting within the garden for different purposes – to illuminate a pathway or create an ambience, for example – has already been mentioned on pages 212–213, with examples given of the different outdoor light systems available. However, lighting is also used close to the house, the garage, and in the garden, for reasons of security.

External lights are a deterrent for intruders (who prefer to act under cover of darkness) but also have more positive functions: they can lead visitors to your door and illuminate paths, gates, and doorways when it is dark to welcome your way into your home.

Security lighting

Decorative lighting – such as a wall-mounted lamp – installed close to a front door to allow the inhabitants to find their way in more easily after dark and, for example, to save them from fumbling about for keys and the door lock, has some value as security lighting, in that the light itself acts as a deterrent to intruders. However, the disadvantage of these is that the light needs to be switched on as darkness falls and switched off in the morning (or turned on before dark if returning to the house later that night).

More appropriate for security are lights that activate as someone approaches (which also serves to warn you of their presence) or switch on and off automatically as dusk falls or the sun rises.

Types of security lights

A range of security lights types and styles are widely available and can prove quite inexpensive. Select the type and choose a style appropriate to where it will be fitted – illuminate doorways and porches with softer, glowing lights. You do not

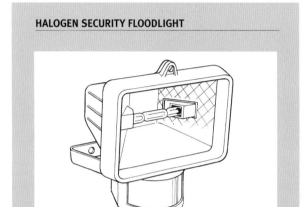

HALOGEN SECURITY FLOODLIGHT

Halogen floodlights are commonly used as a form of exterior security lighting. They incorporate a motion sensor that will detect any movement within a designated area, causing the light to come on. The light can be tilted in any direction to ensure that it illuminates the area intended – it is important that it does not become a nuisance to any neighbours.

Installing a halogen security light

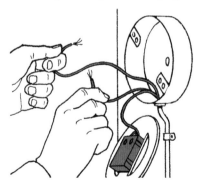

1 Turn the power off. If replacing an older light fitting with a new security light and motion detector, disconnect the existing unit.

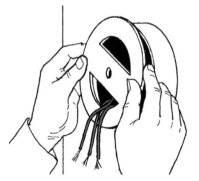

2 Fit the weather gasket and ensure it is secured evenly in place. Fit the front part of the new unit, tugging on each wire and connection to make sure it is secure.

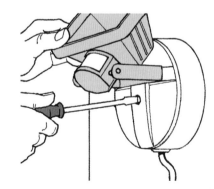

3 Secure the light fitting with screws and tighten. Finally, adjust the light and the sensor so that the appropriate area is targeted and illuminated.

Installing security lighting

want to dazzle yourself or any genuine visitors as you approach the front door. Wall-mounted spotlights (see pages 216–217) are ideal for downlighting paths that run alongside the house, while areas around the garage or where you wish to strongly illuminate parts of the garden are more suited to more utilitarian floodlights.

For many properties, the best security lighting solution is to use a low-voltage light fitted within a bulkhead (a bulb encased in a frosted glass cover) or porch light that comes on as dusk falls and switches off as it becomes light in the morning. Although this means that the light is constantly on during the hours of darkness, using a low-power bulb that provides a gentle glowing light is more energy efficient than other security lights. These cost little to run, and provide a softer light than halogen lights. A further benefit of this is that fewer shadows are cast.

Solar powered security lights are another option when a low level of lighting will suffice. These do not require any wiring and are therefore easy to install – but obviously need to be positioned where they will receive enough sunlight to power them throughout the day.

Perhaps the most widely available solution for security lighting are floodlights activated by movement. These either have an integral PIR (Passive Infra Red) sensor fitted to detect movement, or are connected to the light separately, and are usually high intensity tungsten halogen lights. The security benefits of these are that they are triggered by a person entering your garden, alerting you to the presence of a visitor (wanted or unwanted) to your property while surprising and making visible any intruders. They are fitted with photo-sensitive cells so that they do not switch on during the day.

As halogen floodlights can cause an uncomfortable glare and cast shadows (that could create hiding places), a light of no more than 2000 lumens (150Watts) should be installed. The timer governing the switching off of the light after it has been activated should be adjusted, if possible, to minimize the time the light is on.

Positioning security lights

Don't forget that any security light needs to be positioned in a location that prevents anyone tampering with, or disabling it. Ideally, the light should be fitted at a minimum height of 2.75m (9ft).

Security lights should always be angled so that they illuminate only your property, and must not shine into the windows of neighbouring houses. They should be positioned in such a way that they detect and illuminate people only within the boundaries of your property.

In addition, the movement detector needs to be set so that it is not triggered by people walking past your property nor set off by cats, small animals or wildlife, or even by the swaying of foliage in high winds. If it is caused to be flashed on by such events regularly through the night, it will soon become a nuisance both to yourself and to your neighbours, and the security function itself diminished as it will be thought of as an unreliable warning system to be ignored.

Ensure as well that any light that has an infra red sensor is not placed near a heating flue or other sources of heat, as these can trigger activation of the light. Obviously, the sensor should not point at the light or any other light source.

Careful positioning is also required to prevent the creation of dark shadowed areas close to the area you wish to illuminate.

If a neighbour is unhappy with your installation of security lighting, it is advisable to be understanding and take their complaint seriously. They can complain about light pollution to the local authority. Adjust your light to shine in a different direction and angle it downwards. If this does not resolve the problem, consider fitting a hood or shield to restrict the area that will be illuminated.

Replacing an external light

If a new external light is to be wired into the mains system, it is better employ a qualified electrician to perform this task. However, if you wish to replace an existing external light with a security light fitted with a PIR, this is more straightforward.

Start by switching off the power supply, and use a circuit breaker to ensure that the power is off. Remove the old light and the plate covering the wiring to expose it. If the new fitting will not fit the existing back plate, remove this and replace as well.

Disconnect the existing light fitting and check that the wiring is in good order. Connect the new unit using wire nuts, then pull on each connection to ensure that it is secure.

Push all the wiring back into the unit, and if there is a weather gasket in the fitting to protect from moisture, make sure that the gasket seal is even all around the unit. Place the front of the fitting against the back of the unit and affix with screws. Tighten to ensure the fitting is firmly in place, tilting the light out of the way to access and screws.

If the security light does not come with the bulb already fitted, take care when handling the bulb and use a cloth – touching the bulb can damage it and shorten its life.

Take time to position the sensor carefully so that the light will only detect the movement of people within the boundaries of your property. Aim the light itself so that it will illuminate the area required, not create shadows, nor become a nuisance to others.

Installing wall-mounted lights

Exterior lights fixed to the wall of a house, or on a wall within the garden, are a good way of providing illumination and help to create decorative effects in the way they are used. If lights are intended to create atmosphere rather than provide a means of lighting a doorway, say, or for security reasons, use them sparingly and position carefully so that they are not overwhelming.

As a form of illumination, spotlights are both functional and decorative, used to highlight specimen trees and shrubs, or a feature within the garden or to shed light on a flight of steps.

Levels of lighting

A well-lit house and garden looks welcoming. Never over-light the garden as this may simply make it look just as it does during the day, yet slightly harsher. On the other hand, just having the odd light illuminating a path or doorway may give a feeling of distance and remoteness. A soft, glowing porch light on its own can look attractive, but a stronger light source in the same position can look harsh and utilitarian. Careful placing of lights should create a feeling of security and also reveal a different look to the architecture and planting of the house and garden.

Power sources

If electricity is being run into the garden (see pages 210–211) then any external lights can be run off this circuit. Using mains electricity allows almost limitless possibilities for external lighting systems and permits quite elaborate lighting schemes to be planned and installed. However, with the requirement to carefully bury any cables (see Installing electricity in the garden, pages 210–211), it may not be a straightforward task if you decide to change this scheme at a later date.

More energy efficient than mains-powered lights are low-voltage lighting systems, connected via a transformer to the mains supply (see also page 213). These tend to be cheaper and safer to install. With low-voltage lights, there is no need to bury the cables connecting them into the soil, making them much simpler to lay. These systems are also easy to adjust and move if you decide to change the positions and emphasis of the lights, a benefit if you intend to illuminate different plants and different parts of the garden as the seasons change. A disadvantage of low-voltage lights is that power is lost the further from the transformer the light is, and there is a limit to the number of lights that can be run.

Solar-powered lights need to be positioned where they will receive the sun's rays, but they will not be as powerful as lights connected to the mains electricity supply. They will be at their least powerful on dark winter nights, which may be when the illumination is needed the most. This is offset by their ease of installation and they are more appropriate if a softer, glowing light is required.

Spotlights

As exterior lights, spotlights direct a beam of light in one direction, and are of particular use in drawing attention to specimen plants, a pool or a piece of statuary. Their directional nature means that they can be located some distance from the item they are highlighting, which is useful

Installing a wall-mounted light

1 Mark the wall to show where the drill holes are to be fitted, using the back plate of the fitting as a template. Make the marks clearer, if necessary, before drilling.

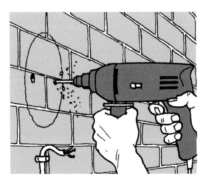

2 Drill a hole at each of the marked positions, making the holes slightly deeper than the length of the wall plugs that you are using to fit the light.

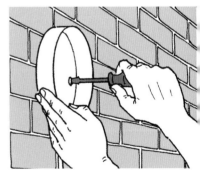

3 After inserting a wall plug into each hole, fix the back plate of the light fitting securely to the wall using a screwdriver and masonry screws.

Installing wall-mounted lights

as they can then be connected to the mains supply when attached to a wall or other hard landscaping.

When run off mains power, spotlights can be bright, with a strong beam that casts dark shadows, lessening any attempts to create a warm ambience. This can be rectified by using frosted or coloured lenses. Alternatively, position the spotlight so that its beam bounces off plants or another object, thus diffusing the light it supplies. Cross-lighting an object with a pair of spotlights reduces the shadows cast. Carefully used, spotlights create drama; overdone they can overpower their surroundings.

Long-bodied spotlights are an ideal choice; the length of the fitting means that the bulb is recessed and some way back from the lens, preventing glare. Selection of the fitting should also be based on its appearance: copper ones will weather over time to blend more with its surroundings, while chrome light fittings may be more appropriate to contemporary garden designs. Spotlights come with various filters: coloured filters or frosted lenses will created softer lighting effects. Similar to spotlights are spread lights that produce a wide arc of light and are useful for downlighting larger areas and backgrounds.

Fitting a wall-mounted light

If there is cabling in place to attach a wall light to, fitting one is a reasonably easy task. If, however, the fitting of the light requires rewiring or connection directly into the mains power supply, then this is a job best left to a qualified electrician.

Begin by turning off the mains electricity. Mark on the wall, using the back plate of the light fitting as a template, the position of the drill holes. If necessary, remove the back plate and make the marks clearer.

At each of these positions, drill a hole into the masonry. This hole should be slightly deeper than the length of the wall plugs that will be inserted to take the masonry screws. Next, insert a wall plug into each hole, then fix the back plate of the light fitting securely to the wall using a screwdriver and masonry screws. A power screwdriver will make this task easier.

Connect to the power supply by connecting the cable to the terminals in the front cover of the light fitting. Ensure the wiring is secure and in place before fixing on the front cover. Then bolt the front cover to the back plate, tightening the nuts with a spanner. Insert the lightbulb into the fitting, screwing it into place. Check that the light fitting and the cable are firmly secured to the wall, and get all electrical connections approved by a qualified electrician.

Angle and adjust the light so that is illuminates the area, or features, it has been installed to highlight. Spotlights mounted on knuckle joints allow them to be swivelled and tilted to direct the beam of light.

Colour and lighting

The bulbs chosen have an effect on the quality of light they supply. Tungsten lights give a warm, yellow light to create mood and atmosphere, whereas halogen bulbs produce a sharper light. Coloured filters bring drama to a lighting scheme, but should not be over used. Coloured downlighters or spotlights will bring a two-dimensional effect to the features they illuminate.

4 Once the cable has been connected to the terminal in the front cover of the light fitting, the front cover can be bolted to the back cover.

5 Insert a light bulb into the fitting. Before turning on the power supply and testing the light, check that the fitting and bulb are firmly in place.

6 Turn the light on and adjust it by tilting until it illuminates the area intended. Lights like these are ideal for spotlighting features in the garden.

Electricity in the glasshouse

A mains electricity supply in the glasshouse is a considerable aid in the propagation and growth of a wide variety of plants. Lighting also allows the glasshouse to be used on winter evenings. While heating by electricity can be expensive compared with other fuels, growing aids such as propagating cases, extractor fans and soil-warming cables can only be run on mains electricity.

Sophisticated computer systems can be installed in the glasshouse that integrate and control lighting, heating, ventilation, watering and humidity. These offer convenience and negate the need to regularly check the glasshouse environment, but are an expensive investment for the amateur gardener.

Lighting

Light in the glasshouse can be used to stimulate plants as well as to supply general illumination. Light is the factor that most frequently limits plant growth in glasshouses during the winter. Additional lighting, using high pressure mercury vapour lamps, is used commercially to stimulate the growth rate of various crops. However, it is seldom economic for amateurs because of the high equipment and running costs. Special lighting installations are useful however as an aid to propagation. Extra light will help to maintain the growth of rooted cuttings of deciduous plants during autumn and early winter when they would normally lose their foliage and cease growth for the season.

Lighting can also be used to increase the day-length, or period during which there is enough light for growth to go on. Some plants will not flower unless they have a certain number of hours light per day. This process is used commercially, but due to cost is seldom viable for the amateur.

When choosing lights, assess running costs, energy conservation, ease of maintenance, and bulb-changing of lights, and also the flexibility of the systems available.

Fluorescent strip lights are most commonly used for lighting glasshouses. Cheap to buy and to run, these do not emit heat and are energy-efficient but replacement bulbs can be costly and awkward to fit. Fluorescent lamps need a large reflector fitted above them to be really effective. They are suitable for propagation, hung directly above a propagating unit, or are available with red coatings or filters, which enables them to be used in the later stages of plant development, such as induction of flowering.

Fluorescent lights should be treated as a supplement to, and not a replacement for, natural light.

Growlamps have easy-to-screw-in, energy saving bulbs. The fittings are small, with an incorporated reflector, and can be positioned directly over a propagating unit or a group of plants. They do not produce excessive heat. Relatively inexpensive, they produce a full spectrum of light for year-round use, from propagation to flowering.

Envirolights – these fluorescent lamps are more energy efficient than other types yet still emit the same amount of light. Like fluorescent lights, they emit more blue than red spectrum light, unless specially coated or fitted with a filter.

High Pressure Sodium Lamps these are heavy and emit heat and noise, so need to be housed outside the glasshouse. The ballast allows the lamps to reach the high voltages required for their operation. These lamps are not very energy efficient, although the use of reflectors does help to reduce running costs. They produce the best quality of light for all-round plant growth, from propagation to flowering. The heat these lamps emit can make them unsuitable for propagation areas.

Ventilation

An electric extractor fan should be mounted high up above the glasshouse door. Provide ventilation at the other end.

Mist propagation

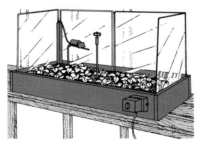

Mist units produce a humid atmosphere. Ideally suited to cuttings, they are often used with soil-warming cables.

Heating

Electricity may not provide the cheapest form of heating but it is clean, flexible and efficient. Fan heaters will expel their heat quickly, and care must be taken to position them where the heat can be evenly distributed and not blown directly on to plants. Some fan heaters can also be used to cool the glasshouse in summer, but they can be expensive to run. Fan heaters are useful adjuncts to other heating systems, or used on their own to provide background heat.

A thermostat is essential to control the heating: a good quality thermostat

Electricity in the glasshouse

GLASSHOUSE CONTROL PANEL

If the glasshouse is fitted with a mains supply, it is worth adding a special control panel. This is a switch and socket panel which is fitted to the end of the mains cable. It allows all electrical apparatus to be controlled from one safe, fused point, avoiding the installation of several sockets, each of which is a possible source of trouble. Only the mains supply has to be connected. The panel should include a residual current device (RCD – see page 211). Such panels can be bought with adjustable fixings to allow them to be mounted between two glazing bars in any size of glasshouse.

is required that has a narrow differential so that the temperature stays within a very narrow margin of the desired setting, rather than oscillating widely. Regardless of the method of providing heat chosen, a good thermostat will reduce heat wastage and running costs.

Soil and air-warming cables can be used to heat beds and propagating cases. Such a form of heating is cheap and is only applied where it is needed, not diffused as with general heating systems.

Heatwave panels are a method of heating bench tops within the glasshouse, allowing seed trays and plant containers to be placed on a heated area and moved more easily than those planted into trays or beds containing soil warming containers. The panels are made from coated heating elements sandwiched between layers of aluminium, and can be easily stored when not in use. Use only those electrical heaters

designed specifically for glasshouse use which meet the appropriate British Standard – domestic types are likely to be dangerous in the humid glasshouse environment.

Air circulation

Air circulation is vital if the glasshouse atmosphere is not to become excessively humid, hot, or stale. An electric extractor fan positioned high up at one end of the glasshouse will draw out the hot, humid air and, provided that some ventilators are open, fresh air will be drawn in.

A simple circulating fan can be similarly positioned to keep the air moving and avoid a stagnant atmosphere. This is particularly valuable in winter when air temperatures must be maintained at a reasonable level and frost avoided.

Automatic motorized vents, which are electrically operated, are a more sophisticated option. These rely on temperature sensors to open and close individually, or they can be linked with an overall computer regulating system so that they can respond to subtle changes in conditions in the glasshouse.

Electric propagating cases

Mains electricity in the glasshouse makes possible the use of heated propagating cases. These can be used for raising seedlings, cuttings or grafted plants. The combination of warm growing medium and relatively cool air provides the best possible growing conditions for many plants. The heat is supplied by cables in the base of the soil tray. Propagating cases should have a thermostat so that the correct temperatures can be maintained for the plants grown.

Mist propagation

Cuttings of many shrubs, herbaceous, and pot plants root more quickly if they are sprayed regularly with a fine mist of water. The mist propagation unit is a system for automating this operation. A moisture-sensitive "electronic leaf" governs the frequency of the spray which is emitted through fine jets mounted above the plants, and soil-warming cables provide the necessary bottom heat to prevent the growing medium from becoming too cold. Alternatively, more efficient control switches operate the mist spray according to light intensity.

Mist units are often used in conjunction with electric soil-warming cables, which are controlled by a separate thermostat.

A further sophistication is having the mist unit controlled via a glasshouse environmental control system. Information on temperature as well as on humidity are fed into a computer that controls the system. Misting rates are then altered in response to more subtle changes in conditions within the glasshouse.

Choosing garden furniture

The choice of outdoor furniture is largely determined by the garden's basic design and the way in which the furniture is to be used.

Choosing styles

The design of the furniture should complement the style of the garden. Rustic timber items are best suited to an informal or wild garden, whereas modern sets in steel or plastic may be more suitable for patios. Elegant, ornate cast-iron tables and chairs may be preferred in a formal courtyard scheme.

Benches Simple benches can be used in most parts of a garden. More formal style park benches are often effective when placed against a wall, hedge, or fence.

Chairs Basic metal chairs have a foldable tubular aluminium frame with fabric seat and back, while a more comfortable option is the canvas-seated, wooden-framed director's chair, which usually has an adjustable back. Cast-iron Victorian-style chairs are durable, if rather uncomfortable, with highly ornate pierced patterns. Lighter-weight, non-rusting cast-aluminium versions, and even plastic ones, are also available.

Dining sets Purpose-made garden dining sets are available in traditional hardwood to classic designs, or in lightweight metal or plastic with a modern, streamlined look; usually there is an optional central parasol. Modern garden dining chairs are typically foldable and fitted with removable upholstered cushions. For family picnics, a timber trestle table with integral bench seats is ideal (see page 222), and can be fitted with a central parasol shade.

Loungers Deckchairs are still hard to beat for lounging in the sun, and fold flat for storage – some types have leg and arm rests. For sunbathing, a basic metal-framed sun-lounger with fabric stretch cover is suitable, and some versions may have padded, upholstered covers, and adjustable headrests.

A luxurious touch in the garden can be provided by installing a swing seat with awning. These are commonly made with a steel tubular frame, often plastic-coated, and must be dismantled and put in storage during the winter.

Materials

Furniture falls into two main categories: that which can be left outside permanently and that which you must store indoors.

Plastic is undoubtedly the most durable material, and can be left outdoors without showing signs of deterioration. It never needs painting – a wash will suffice. However, it can appear utilitarian.

Metal is commonly used for garden furniture frames, although it is susceptible to rusting. However, galvanizing, painting, and plastic coatings will usually protect the vulnerable metal – provided the surface is not chipped or scratched. Aluminium will not rust, is much lighter than iron and steel, and can be cast to make traditional-style furniture.

Timber is the best-quality material for garden furniture, but it is also one of the most expensive and requires regular maintenance. Hardwoods can be left bare to weather to an attractive tone, while softwoods (with the exception of cedar, which weathers naturally) must be treated with preservative, or else painted to withstand the elements.

Regular maintenance

Whatever type of furniture you choose, ensure that all joints are firm and sturdy, and that metal fixings are galvanized to prevent rusting. On a regular basis, you should lubricate all pivots, hinges, and screw heads to prevent them from binding. Protect metal-framed chairs from corrosion during the winter by applying oil or a spray-on wax moisture-dispersing product which simply wipes off the next season.

Treat softwood furniture with colourless preservative, or repaint immediately prior to the summer season. Apply stain, varnish or oil to hardwood furniture before putting away in store, or before bad weather threatens if the furniture is to be left outside permanently.

Secondhand furniture

New garden furniture can be expensive, especially if you opt for items made from hardwood. As a money-saving option, items of furniture originally intended for indoor use may be obtained secondhand.

Junk shops, car boot sales, and stripped pine outlets can yield bargains in the form of old church pews, dining chairs, and tables. Stripped of any previous varnish, the pieces can be treated with preservative and resealed with varnish or paint if preferred. As such pieces are not intended for use out of doors, however, it is best to keep this type of furniture under the partial cover of a pergola or awning.

Built-in garden furniture

Built-in seating and tables may be readily incorporated into a patio garden. When building a timber deck, for example, it is not complicated to install integral bench seating or a built-in table (see pages 114–115).

Encircle a favourite tree in the garden with a bench seat fitted around its trunk: proprietary kits can be obtained, or a slatted top on a sturdy frame mounted on posts can be constructed.

During the construction of a brick- or stone-built terraced patio, it is possible to include plinth walls, running along the top of a raised planting bed, to form the base for a slab-topped seating unit.

Choosing garden furniture

Making a garden bench

For those with even modest carpentry skills, making your own garden furniture is not only a rewarding activity but also likely to be much less expensive than buying ready-made pieces.

Making a garden bench

A simple garden bench can be constructed by erecting two piers of bricks, natural stone or concrete blocks on a strip foundation base. The piers should be no more than about 450mm (18in) high for comfortable use.

Cut four lengths of 150 x 35mm (6 x ½in) planed softwood or hardwood to fit across the top of the piers with an overhang of about 150mm (6in) at each end, and screw these to three battens of 75 x 50mm (3 x 2in) timber, fixed at right-angles to them near each end and across the middle. Space the planks about 12mm (½in) apart. The bench top can rest loosely on the piers, or be attached with screws.

The basic design of the bench seat may be adapted by adding a slatted plank backrest supported on vertical timber posts screwed to the back edge of the masonry piers.

Making a picnic table

The popular type of picnic table with integral bench seating at each side is straightforward to construct: the components are simply bolted together or screwed into place.

A PICNIC TABLE: EXPLODED VIEW

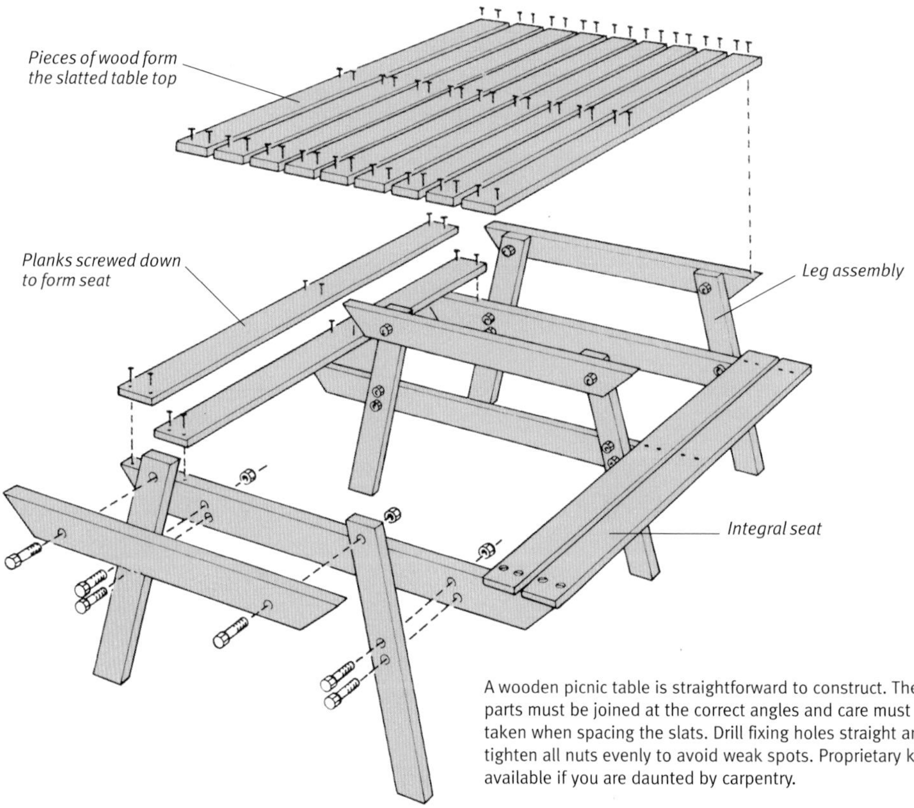

Pieces of wood form the slatted table top

Planks screwed down to form seat

Leg assembly

Integral seat

A wooden picnic table is straightforward to construct. The timber parts must be joined at the correct angles and care must be taken when spacing the slats. Drill fixing holes straight and tighten all nuts evenly to avoid weak spots. Proprietary kits are available if you are daunted by carpentry.

Making a garden bench

The table is supported on three leg frames of 62 x 35mm (2½ x 1⅜in) softwood, each comprising a horizontal top batten with pairs of legs bolted to it, splayed apart at the base. Planks of 150 x 35mm (6 x 1⅜in) planed softwood are screwed to the top of the leg assemblies to form the tabletop. The seats are formed by screwing pairs of planks to horizontal battens of 62 x 35mm (2½ x 1⅜in) bolted across the leg assemblies, about 450mm (18in) above ground level.

Assembling the legs

Mark off six 914mm (36in) long legs from a length of timber, then saw each to length. Cut the base and top of each leg to an angle of about 30 degrees, using a sliding bevel as a guide. Mark out and cut three top rails for the leg assemblies from the same timber. These should be about 914mm (36in) long, the ends cut to an angle so that people sitting at the table will not graze their knees on the sharp edges.

Lay the legs on the ground in pairs, with the top rails on top. Drill through both pieces to take 10mm (⅜in) bolts, insert the bolts, fit washers, and tighten the nuts securely but not too tightly at this stage, with an adjustable spanner. Repeat the procedure for the other two leg assemblies. All nuts are securely tightened when the assembly is completed.

Fitting the seat formers

Mark out and cut three 1.5m (60in) long pieces of 62 x 35mm (2½ x 1⅜in) planed timber, with angled ends, to use as the seat formers; these also help to brace the leg assemblies.

Lay a leg assembly on the ground and place a brace over it so that it protrudes equally at each side and its top edge is 450mm (18in) from the base of the legs.

Drill pairs of holes through the brace into each leg and insert bolts. Fit washers, then screw on the nuts. Tighten the nuts with an adjustable spanner so the leg and seat former assembly is rigid. Fit the other braces to the remaining leg assemblies.

Assembling the table framework

Cut nine 150 x 35mm (6 x ⅜in) planks to a length of 1.5m (60in) to form the tabletop and the seats. Assemble the table framework by drilling pairs of screw clearance holes in each end of each plank, then centrally, to coincide with the positions of the top rails and seat formers of the leg assemblies.

Screw the planks to the seat formers of the leg assemblies so that the framework will be freestanding. Next, screw the remaining five planks to the top rail of each leg assembly. Leave a gap of about 12mm (½in) between each of the planks on the seats and the tabletop: both the seats and the tabletop will overhang the ends of the supporting frame members slightly.

Drill a 35mm (1⅜in) diameter hole through the centre of the middle tabletop plank so that you can insert the stem of a parasol: the base of the parasol can be driven into the lawn, or filled into a proprietary parasol support under the table.

Apply preservative to all parts of the picnic table and allow to dry before using.

Positioning tapes for offset measurements

   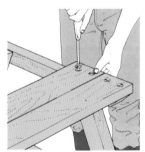

1 Bolt pairs of legs to a top rail to form the basic leg assembly of the picnic table. Make sure the ends of the legs and the rail are cut to the correct angles.

2 Cut the seat formers to length and bolt across each pair of legs, about 450mm (18in) from the base. The formers will act as a brace for the leg assemblies.

3 Assemble the table framework by screwing pairs of seat planks to the protruding seat formers. The table framework will then be freestanding.

4 Screw the planks to the top of the leg and seat assemblies, spacing them about 12mm (½in) apart. Treat the entire picnic table with preservative.

Glossary

Acid soil Soil with a pH value below 7.

Aggregate Particles of and or stone mixed with cement and water to make concrete.

Alkaline soil Soil with a pH value over 7.

Arris rail Horizontal rail, triangular in section, used in closeboard fencing.

Axes Notional or actual sight lines around which a garden is designed.

Ballast Sand and gravel mix used in making concrete.

Batter The slope of the face of a wall that leans backwards or tapers.

Bearer Another term for joist, used, for example, in a pergola to support lateral, overhead cross-beams.

Blocks Building units moulded from concrete, also called breezeblocks. Decorative versions are reconstituted blocks made from natural stone aggregates.

Bolster chisel A chisel with a wide blade, used in conjunction with a club hammer for breaking and cutting masonry.

Bond The pattern or arrangement that brick or stones have in paving or walling.

Brick trowel A trowel used for handling and placing mortar in bricklaying.

Builder's square A large try square, used for checking squareness in building walls or laying foundations.

Bund A mound of soil grassed or planted over, usually to appear naturalistic.

Butt-jointed Paving bricks or stones which touch, with no mortar or sand between them.

Calibration Inscribed or printed markings at regular intervals on instruments used to take measurements.

Cement Fine grey powder, a mix of calcined limestone and clay; used with water and sand to make mortar, or with water, sand, and aggregate to make concrete.

Claw hammer Heavyweight general-purpose hammer, with a claw at the back for levering out nails.

Closeboard A type of fence consisting of vertical overlapping feather-edged boards attached to arris rails between posts.

Club hammer A heavy hammer used in building work, usually with a chisel.

Cold chisel A long, slim chisel used for cutting or breaking masonry.

Concrete Sand, cement, and aggregate, mixed with water to form a hard building material for blocks, slabs, and foundations.

Coping The weatherproofing layer at the top of a wall, such as bevelled wooden strips or cast concrete pieces used to deflect rainwater from the face of a fence or wall.

Course The individual horizontal layers (for instance of brick, stone, or blocks) that go to make up a wall.

Cross-beams Part of an overhead structure, such as the timbers that form the top of a pergola.

Cross-fall Where the ground, lawn or paving slopes from side to side. Usually deliberately introduced to shed rainwater from an area.

Cross-section A drawing showing the changes in level, internal nature, or workings of a design, structure, or plot of land.

Datum A wooden peg set at a particular position, forming the point from which measurements are taken during the laying of slabs or concrete or used with range poles to assess the ground level when surveying a plot.

Datum pole Usually a coloured, banded pole stuck into the ground as a visible indicator of the position of the datum.

DPC (Damp-proof course) An impervious layer or sheet built into or applied to walls to prevent damaging water penetration.

Elevation A scaled drawing of any vertical element (eg a wall) or one side of the element itself, such as the north-facing wall of a house.

Fall A downward slope for rainwater drainage.

Feather-edge The edge of a wooden board in closeboard fencing, which is narrower at one side than the other.

Float A wooden tool used for applying and smoothing cement renderings and concrete with a fine texture.

Focal point The termination of a view that utilizes a distinctive artefact, sculpture, tree, etc. These usually lie at the end of an axis.

Footing Narrow concrete foundation for a wall, or the base of garden steps.

Frog The angled depression in one or two faces of some bricks.

Galvanized A protective coating of zinc to prevent nails, screws, and other materials from rusting.

Geotextile A membrane used to stabilize ground and protect flexible pool liners, for example, from external or internal damage.

Gravel boards Horizontal lengths of timber at the base of a fence to protect the cladding from rising damp.

Grid line Notional lines, usually forming squares when at 90 degrees, used in marking out and for recording changes in level – eg at the points where the grid lines intersect by 90 degrees.

Groundfall Where or how the ground changes in level by becoming lower.

Handsaw Saw with a flexible, unsupported blade used for cutting solid timber and man-made boards.

Hardcore Broken bricks, concrete or stones used as a sub-base beneath foundations and paving.

Hardwood Timber cut from deciduous trees. Not necessarily hard in a wooden sense, hardwoods should be certified as coming from sustainable sources.

Joist A horizontal wood beam used to support a floor, deck, or wall.

Marginal Plants that will grow on the edge or border of, for instance, a pool. Also the term for the sunken marginal shelf around the edge of a pool on which such plants can be grown.

Mastic A non-setting flexible compound used to seal joints.

Mitre A joint formed between two pieces of wood by cutting bevels of equal angles at the ends of each piece.

Mortise A rectangular recess cut in timber which receives a matching tongue or tenon.

Mulch A layer of material – organic materials, plastic sheeting, gravel, etc. – placed upon the ground to reduce water-loss through evaporation, to inhibit weed growth, and to moderate soil temperatures. Usually placed on the soil around plants.

Nosing The front edge of a step, often protruding from the riser.

Offset A measurement taken at 90 degrees off a main base line measurement.

Overlay A means of testing ideas or modifications to an existing plan or photograph by drawing on tracing paper and laying over the plan.

Pan A hard layer of soil beneath the surface.

Panel In fencing, any prefabricated section, usually made of woven larch strips in a thin frame.

Pavers Small-scale blocks or bricks used in path and patio laying.

pH The degree of acidity or alkalinity, eg of a soil.

Picket (or palisade) A post-and-rail fence with thin, usually pointed, vertical pales attached to the rails.

Pier The thickening of a wall at the ends or an intermediate point in order to give it added strength and stability.

Pilot hole A small-diameter hole drilled prior to the insertion of a woodscrew, as a guide for the thread.

Planter An enclosed container for soil used as a planting bed.

Range pole Calibrated colour-banded poles used to aid the measurement of garden sites.

RCD Residual current device. A safety device fitted to an electrical circuit or plug that breaks the circuit to prevent electric shocks.

Render A thin layer of cement mortar spread on exterior walls to give a smooth, protective finish.

Riser The vertical part of a step.

Roving pole A range pole which is moved around the garden during level finding and surveying.

Running bond Basic bricklaying bond that consists of stretcher courses with alternate rows staggered by the length of half a brick.

Rustic poles Poles, used for fences and arches, which are irregular in shape, and which sometimes have bark attached.

Scree The smaller broken rocks and gravel at the bottom of a rock face or cliff that results from natural weathering processes.

Screed A thin layer of mortar applied to give a smooth surface on which to build brick or block walls, or as a finish for concrete.

Seasoned Describes timber which has matured to reduce sap and moisture content, making it easier to work. Has greater resistance to rot.

Sett A cube or block of hard stone used for paving or edging.

Shuttering Vertical timber boarding, behind which concrete is poured to mould it to the desired shape and size.

Slabs Moulded concrete units in various sizes and finishes, used as paving.

Soakaway A pit filled with rubble, into which water drains and percolates into the earth.

Softwood Timber cut from coniferous (cone-bearing) trees.

Spike A metal preformed spike with a collar at the top used in fixing fence posts and other vertical timbers to the ground.

Spirit level A tool with a bubble vial used for checking horizontal levels; some types have a vertical vial and angle-finder.

Stretcher A brick that is laid horizontally with its length parallel to the wall.

Subsoil The layer of soil below the topsoil.

Tamp To pack down firmly with repeated blows, as when casting concrete.

Tenon A projecting tongue on the end of a piece of wood which fits into a corresponding mortise.

Topsoil The upper layer of dark fertile soil in which plants grow. Below this lies the subsoil, which is lighter in colour, lacks organic matter, and is often low in nutrients.

Tread The horizontal part of a step.

Triangulation A system for measuring a plot of land where it is divided into a series of notionally-linked triangles.

Try square A tool for checking right-angles.

Wallplate A horizontal timber beam placed along a wall to support joists or rafters, spreading their load.

Wall tie A strip of metal or bent wire used to connect sections of new masonry together, or to strengthen existing masonry.

Warps Twists in lengths of timber; such timber should be rejected.

Water table The level in the soil below which the soil is saturated by ground water.

Weep hole A small hole at the base of a wall that allows absorbed water to drain away.

Xerophytic plants Plants tolerant of very dry habitats and able to withstand periods of drought.

Index

Page numbers in italics indicate illustrations and information boxes

A

access issues 18, 24, 28, 40, 41,
    68
alpine gardens 64–5
arches 153, 174–5
asymmetrical gardens 41, 42, *43*
awnings 202–3

B

bar fencing 136, *137*
barbecues 81, *176*, 200–1
bird tables 55
blocks *80*, 81, 98, 107, 125
boulders 62, 65, 81
boundaries 11, 12, 24, 33, 48,
    49, 192
bricks *71*, *105*
    barbecues 81, 200–1
    bonds 46, 81, 84–5, *128*,
        132, 133
    cutting 125
    damp-proofing 133
    edging 66, 96
    foundations 88, *89*
    frogs and holes 129
    laying 130–3, 198, 200
    paths and drives 46, 98
    in patios 96, 104, *107*
    paving 83, 84–5
    planters 81, 88, 163, 167
    pointing 132, *135*, 167
    posts 169
    steps 81, *117*, 125
    stretcher bonds *128*, 129
    symbols *27*, *80*
    tools for laying 130–1, *132*
    types 81, 128–9

C

changing levels *see under*
    ground levels
chestnut paling fences 137
children and gardens 18, 50–1,
    57, 121, 154, *160*, 191, 192–7
climbing frames 51, 193, 194–5
closeboarded fences 136, *137*,
    143–4, 151

compartments in gardens 37,
    41, 163
compost containers 199
concrete *80*
    aggregate 84, 98
    blocks 81, 98, 107
    buying 81, 90
    cast 81, 88, *120*, 121
    expansion joints 100–1
    for fixing posts 138–9, *155*
    flexible pavers 96–7, 108–9
    foundations 81, 88, 89, 90,
        91, 92, 93, 108
    kerbstones 96, 108
    maintenance 66
    mixing 81, 90
    pads for decking 111–12
    paths 98, *99*, 100–1
    paving 81, 84
    posts 138, *139*, 142, 148, *169*
    reinforcing 93
    safety issues 57, 193
    in situ 84
    spurs 138, 139
    steps *120*, 121, 122, 125
    textured 62, 84
    in water features 183
conservation issues 9, 65, 80
cottage gardens *20*, 48

D

decking *20*, *72*, *83*, 85, 110–15
    built-in furniture 111, 114–15,
        220
    concrete pads 111–12
    decking gardens 62, *63*
    duckboard platform 110, 111
    foundations 111–12
    joists 111, 113, 114
    lighting 212
    maintenance 59, 66–7, 94, *115*
    with pergolas 111, 112
    planning 111
    in play areas 193
    rails 114, *115*
    raised 110, 111–14
    in roof gardens 70, 73

safety issues *115*
    supporting posts 111, 112, 114
    symbols *27*
    tree seats 114–15
    uneven ground 112
    wallplates 111, *112*, 113
design principles 22–31
    basic principles 22–3
        balance 22–3
        continuity 22
        harmony 22, 28, 41, 77
    composition 38–9
    cross sections 30–1, 41
    drawing up plans 26–9
        drawing boards *28*
        outline plans 28, *29*
        symbols 26, 27
    scale and proportion
        constructed elements 24
        feasibility 25
        focal points 25, 37, 38, 44
        horizontal surfaces 24
        interest 25
        simplicity 24–5
        small gardens *20*, 24
        vertical elements 24, 33,
            35
disabled gardeners 74–5
drainage 86–7
ditches 87
    "French drains" 87
    land drains *86*, 87
    patios 94, 96, *97*
    in paving 41
    in planters 163
    roof gardens 70
    rubble 87
    sloping gardens 41, 96, 163
    soakaways 87
    steps 120, *125*
    in walls 41, 87, 133, 163
dry gardens *54*, 58, *59*, 62, *63*,
    66, 70, 77
dustbins 39, *175*, 198
dwarf conifers 64, 65

E

electricity
    for awnings 202

cabling *179*, *190*, *210*, 211,
    213, 216, *219*
circuit breakers and plugs
    179, 211, 213, 215, *219*
for garden buildings 204,
    218–19
in glasshouses 218–19
for heating 218–19
installing 210–11
permanent supply *210*
for propagation *218*, 219
pumps *179*, *180*, 181, 183,
    190, 210
safety issues *179*, 210, 211
tools 66
for ventilation *218*, 219
see also lighting
exposed sites 60–1, 70

F

false doors or gates 161
family gardens 18, 50–1, 192–7
fences *13*, *106*, 136–51
    concrete posts 138, *139*,
        142, 148
    concrete spurs 138, 139
    in establishing ground
        levels 14
    fence posts 138–9, 140,
        142, 143, 146–7, 148–9
    fence spikes 138, 139, 140
    fixing 140–50
    foundations 142, 151
    gravel boards 140, 144
    marking out 138, 140
    metal 136–7, 148–50
    plant support 140, 150, 153
    proportion issues 24
    on sloping gardens 142,
        149, 151
    timber 136, *137*, 140–7
    tools 138, 139, 140–1
    trellis 136, 142, 152
    types 136–7
    weatherproofing *138*, 144
    see also types of fence
focal points 25, 37, 38, 40, 44, 45
formal gardens *20*, 42, *43*, 68,
    118

foundations 88–93
 brick 88, *89*
 decking 111–12
 fences 142, 151
 garden buildings 88, 89,
  204, 205, 206
 paths 90, 100–1
 patios 95–6, 108
 raft foundations *see* slab
  foundations below
 slab foundations 88, 89,
  92–3, 96, 100, 118
 stepped *91*, 151
 steps 88, 118, 119, 122, 125,
  126
 strip foundations 88, *90*,
  91, 119, 126, 133, 151
 tools *93*, 119
 tree seats 115
 walls 88, 90, 130, 133, *134*,
  135
front gardens 28, 46–7
function 9, 10, *19*, 18–21, 25, 42

G
garden buildings 204–7
 foundations 88, 89, 204,
  205, 206
 gazebos *173*
 glasshouses 20, *175*, 204,
  218–19
 greenhouses see
  greenhouses above
 maintenance 204, 205
 materials 204–5
 metal 204–5
 re-glazing *205*
 screening 38, 39, 68
 sheds *38*, 39, 74, 206–7
 siting 204
 timber 204, 206
garden furniture 220–3
 benches 220, *221*, 222–3
 built-in 111, 114–15, 220
 choosing 220
 maintenance 220
 making 220, 222–3
 materials 58, 220
 metal 58, 220

plastic 54, 220
 for seaside gardens 58
 tables 220, *221*, 222–3
 timber 58, 80, 220
 tree seats 114–15, 220
 types of 220, *221*
gardens for the disabled 74–5
gates *123*, 154–56, 159–60
 constructing 156, 159–60
 drive entrances 46, 154, *155*
 false 161
 front entrances 154, *156*
 gate posts 155
 hanging 46, 159–60
 hardware 154–5
 hinges 155, *159*, 160
 latches 155, *160*
 metal *154*, 155
 moon gates 161
 side entrances 154
 on sloping ground 46, 160
 spring closers 155, *160*
 timber 154–5
 types of *154*
grassed areas 13, 34, 66, 77,
  193 *see also* lawns
gravel
 gravel boards 140, 144
 mulch 62, 66
 paths 98
 for patios 104
 paving 73, 74, 82, *83*
 for steps 118
 symbols 27
 types 82, *83*
ground levels
 changing 13, *151*, 162–7
 contouring *see* changing
  above
 cutting-and-filling 163
 in decking 112
 establishing 13, 14–16
 in foundations *91*, 151
 in measurement plans 12, 13
 see also sloping gardens

H-L
hedges 24, 33, 51, 60, 61, 68
herb gardens 48, 68

holiday homes 58–9
horizontal surfaces 24, 33, 34,
  35, *56*, 62, 77
hosepipes 14, *15*, 16

informal gardens 20, 42, 45, 49,
  64–5, 68, 118
irrigation systems 59, 62, 66,
  70, 73

lawns
 edging 66, 98, 100, 162
 in family gardens 51, 192
 maintenance 66, 100, 163
 proportion issues 24
 in sloping gardens 41, 163
 tools 162, *211*
lighting *176*, 212–19
 colour 212, 217
 decking 212
 greenhouses 218
 installing *212*, 213, 214–17
 patios *176*, 212
 security lighting *176*, 214–15
 siting *212*, 213, 216
 solar-powered 210, 213, 216
 trees and shrubs *212*, 213
 types 212, 213, 216–17, 218
 on walls 40, *212*, 216–17
 water features 210, 213
logs *117*
 log rolls 162
 log rounds 85, 104
 paths 85, 98, 100
 in patios 104
 for planters 162, 164, 165
 safety issues 118
 steps *117*, 118
 in wildlife gardens *52*, 55
low maintenance gardens 58–9,
  66–7

M-N
materials
 for awnings 203
 choosing 34–5, 48, 62, 65,
  80–5
 conservation issues 9, 65
 covering material 34–5

garden buildings 204–5
garden furniture 58, 220
 ordering *13*
 paths 82–5, 98, 100, 103
 patios 94, 104–9
 for paved areas 34–5, 44,
  62, 82–5
 planters 163–4
 steps *117*, 120–1
 walls 128–9
mirrors 44, 161
movement 34–5, 56, 77
mulches 13, 62, 66, *115*, 192–3
murals 161

natural gardens
 see wildlife in gardens
nest boxes *52*, 55

P
palisade fences 136, *137*, 146
panel fences 136
 basketweave 136
 bracket-fixing 140, 141, *142*
 cutting down 142
 fixing 140–2
 gravel boards 140
 marking out 140
 nail-fixing 140–1
 posts 140, 142
 on sloping gardens 142, 151
 trellis 136, 142
 "waney"-edged 136, *137*
 wattle or osier 136, *137*, 140
parking spaces 18, 46–7
paths
 brick 98
 concrete 98, *99*, 100–1
 curved *99*
 edge restraints 98, 100
 expansion joints 100–1
 in family gardens 51
 foundations 90, 100–1
 gravel 98
 laying 13, 98–103
 from logs 85, 98, 100
 loose-laying 102
 materials 82–5, 98, 100, 103
 paved 98, 102

Index

proportion issues 24
  in screening 39
  setting out 98, *99*
  stepping stones *20*, 85, *105*
  timber 98, 100
  tools 99, 100, *101*, 102
patio gardens *44*, 60, 61
patios *19*
  adding interest 104, 107
  building *13*, 94–7
  drainage issues 94, 96, *97*
  edge restraints 96
  excavating 95–6
  foundations 95–6, 108
  lighting 212
  marking out 94–5
  materials 94, 96, 104–9
  obstructions *108*, 109
  patterned 96, 108, *109*
  planning 94
  proportion issues 24
  sand bed 96–7
  screening 39
  in sloping gardens 96
  timber 96, 104
  tools 94, 95–6, *97*, 109
paved areas
  in front gardens 46
  in hot, dry gardens 62
  maintenance 66
  materials 34–5, 44, 62, 82–5
  patterned 82–3, *84–5*, 96,
    107, 109
  proportion issues 24, 35
  in sloping gardens 41
  in small gardens 44
  see also paving
paving
  brick 83, 84–5, *105*
  composite 85
  concrete 54, 81, 84
  crazy paving *19*, *71*, 82, 98,
    103
  drainage 41
  drives 46
  flexible pavers 96–7, 108–9
  flexible systems 82
  foundations 88–9, 90, 108
  in gardens for disabled 74

gravel 54, 73, 74, 82, *83*
  maintenance 66
  materials 82–5
  paths 98, 102
  patios 96, 104, 107–9
  paving slabs 84, 89, 98, 102,
    104
  resin-bonded aggregates 85
  safety issues 66, 74
  size 24, 35
  small-scale 107
  stone *72*, 74, 82–3
  symbols 27
  timber 85
  see also paved areas
pergolas *13*, *124*, 157
  attached *168*, 169, 170–2
  constructing 168–72
  in decking 111, 112
  designs 169
  freestanding *168*, 170
  maintenance 172, 173
  planning 170
  plant support 153, 168, *169*
  posts 169, 171, 172
  roofs 168–9, 170, 171–2
  for screening 39, 45
  for shade 62, 70, *110*, 168
  siting 28, 32
  in sloping gardens 170
  symbols *27*
  wall plates 169, 170–1
perspective
  false perspective 36, 44, 45
  see also trompe l'oeil
  horizontal surfaces 56
  plans 36–7
  pools and ponds 56
  small gardens 36, 44, 45
  space issues 34, 36–7, 44,
    45, 56
  water gardens 56–7
photography 10, *13*, 37, 39
picket fences 136, *137*, 145, 146
planning permission 39, 79, 111,
  204
plans
  budgets 18
  composition 38–9

drawing up 26–9, 30
  function plans 18, *21*
  implementation 13
  information gathering 10–16,
    18–21
  measurement plans 10, 11–13
  outline plans 28, *29*
  perspective issues 36–7
  planting plans *13*, 23, 76
  for screening 39
  site assessments 14–16
  surveys 10
  triangulation 11–12
  see also types of garden
plant supports 140, 150, 153, *169*
  see also trellis
planters 162, 163–7
  brick 81, 88, 163, 167
  constructing *162–3*, *164*,
    165, 166–7
  damp-proofing 162, 165,
    166, 167
  drainage issues 163
  filling 166
  with logs 162, 164, 165
  maintenance 162, 165, 166,
    167
  materials 163–4
  plank-and-post *165*, 166
  "railway sleeper" *164*, 165
  in roof gardens 73
  stone 164
  surroundings 164–5
  timber 163–4, 165, 166
  see also window boxes
planting
  cottage gardens 48
  dry gardens 54, 62, 77
  exposed sites 60, 61
  family gardens 51
  on fences 140, 150, 153
  front gardens 46
  habits 76
  horizontal surfaces 77
  informal gardens 49
  low maintenance 66, 67
  planting plans *13*, 23, 76
  pools and ponds 56, *184*, *187*
  rock gardens 65

roof gardens 70, 73
  sloping gardens 40
  on steps 121
  on walls 40, 153, *153*
  window boxes 208, *209*
play areas 18, 50, 51, 85, 192–7
play structures 51, *192*, *193*,
  194–7
pools and ponds
  above-ground 183, *187*
  concrete 57, 183
  constructing *13*, *20*, 158,
    182–7, 196–7
  filling 184–5
  formal *178*, 183
  frost damage 183, 190
  informal 183, *184*
  lighting 210, 213
  liners 52, 178, 182, 183,
    184–7, 197
  maintenance 178–9
  paddling pools 196–7
  perspective issues 56
  plants 56, *184*, *187*
  proportion issues *24*
  puddled clay 182
  pumps *180*
  rock pools 191
  safety issues 57
  siting 62, 180, 190
  sizes and shapes 180–1
  in sloping gardens 179, 185
  symbols *27*
  water supply 181
  for wildlife 28, 52, 55, 178,
    180
post-and-rail fences 136, *137*,
  146, 151, 192
    see also palisade fences;
    picket fences; ranch-style
    fences
post-and-wire fences 148–50
productive gardens *20*, 48, 68,
  69
proportion 24–5, 34–7
  horizontal surfaces 24, 33,
    34, 35
  movement 34
  pools and ponds 24

small gardens *20*, 23

steps 116, *117*, 120

vertical elements 24, 33, 35

see also under design

    principles

R

railings 136, *137*

raised beds 39, 64, 74, *106*

ranch-style fences 136, 146–7,

    192

rock gardens 64–5

roof gardens 70–3

S

safety issues

    of concrete *57*, 193

    of construction 79

    decking *115*

    disabled gardeners 74

    electricity 179, 210, 211

    of front gardens 46

    play areas 51, 193, *195*

    protective clothing *17*, 79, *115*

    rock gardens 65

    roof gardens 70

    sloping gardens 40

    steps 118, 120

    timber *115*, 118, 165

    water features *57*, 179

sand 85, *89*, 193

sandpits 193, 196–7

screening 18, 38–9, 68, *175*, 198

seaside gardens 58–9

secret areas 39, 45, 51

shade 34, 37, 62, 70, 77, *168*,

    202

shelter belts 60, 61

shrubs

    in family gardens 51

    in garden design 76

    lighting *212*, 213, 216

    low maintenance 66, 74

    for screening 38

    for shade 62

    for shelter 61

    as vertical elements 33

    and water features 182

sloping gardens 40–1

access issues 40, 41

adjusting *151*, 162, 163

drainage issues 41, 96, 163

fences 142, 149, 151

flat areas, creating 41

gates 46, 160

lawns 41, 163

maintenance 66

patios 96

paved areas 41

pergolas 170

in plans 13, 22, 30–1, 40, *41*

planting 40

pools and ponds 179, 185

safety issues 40

space issues 41

steps 40, 41, 120, 122, 125

terracing 13, 33, 40

vertical elements 33

walls 40, 41

water features 179

small gardens *20*, 24, 36, 44–5,

    48

soil

    conditions *89*

    drainage systems 86–7

    and foundations *89*

    improving 87

    pH meters 16

    soil testing 16

    types 16, 87, *89*

space 32–41, 44, 45, 56

spiked chain fences 137

stepping stones *20*, 85, *105*, 188

steps *19*, *105*, 116–27

    brick 81, *117*, 125

    cast concrete *120*, 121

    circular landings 118

    concrete 122, 125

    construction *13*, 118, 119,

        120, 121–2, 125–7

    curved *117*, 118

    cut-in 116, 118, 122, 125

    drainage issues 120, *125*

    formats 116–17

    foundations 88, 118, 119,

        122, 125, 126

    freestanding 116, 120, 126–7

    log *117*, 118

materials *117*, 120–1

profile boards 119

proportion issues 116, 117,

    120

safety issues 118, 120

in sloping gardens 40, 41,

    120, 122, 125

softening 121

step sizes 116–17, 121

stringlines 119, 122

tools 119, 121, 125, 126, 127

toothing in 126, *127*

types of 116, *117*

stone 80

    artificial 81

    crushed 82, *83*

    natural 81, 82–3, 164

    patterns 82–3

    paving 74, 82–3

    planters 164

    reconstituted 83, *117*, *128*

    setts 82

    walls *128*, 164

structure 22, 32–41, 48, 65, 68

style 9, 10, 42–3 *see also* types

    of garden

surfaces

    asphalt 82, 98

    cobblestones 98, 104, *107*,

        118, 187

    coconut shell chips 85

    decking 110–15

    granulated bark 85

    impact absorbing 51, 85, 193

    paths 98–109

    paving 82–5

    pebbles *72*, 83, 104, 169

    for play areas 192–3

    setts 85

    shingle 82, *83*

    tarmac 82, *83*

    see also types of surface

T

terraces 18, *19*, 24, 33, 40, 120,

    126, *133 see also* patios

timber

    choosing 80

    conservation issues 80

defects 80–1

fences 136, *137*, 140–7

for garden buildings 204, 206

garden furniture 58, 80, 220

gates 154–5

hardwood 67, 80

maintenance 59, 66–7, 80,

    138, 165, 173

paths 98, 100

patios 96, 104

paving 85

planters 163–4, 165, 166

for play areas 193, 194, *195*,

    196

posts 138, 148

preserving 67, 80, *138*, 165,

    172

railway sleepers 118, *164*, 165

safety issues *115*, 118, 165

softwood 67, 80

tools *17*, 79

    boning rods *151*

    for bricklaying 130–1, *132*

    builder's squares *93*

    for changing levels *151*

    for disabled gardeners 74

    drawing boards *28*

    for fence fixing 138, 139, 140–1

    for fence posts 138, 139

    for foundations *93*, 119

    hand-held levels *15*, 16

    for lawns 162, *211*

    for paths 99, 100, *101*, 102

    for patios 94, 95–6, *97*, 109

    range poles 12, *15*, 16

    spirit levels 14, *15*, 16, *17*

    for steps 119, 121, 125, 126,

        127

town gardens *20*, 44–5

tree houses 195

trees

    in family gardens 51

    in garden design 76

    lighting *212*, 213, 216

    low maintenance 66

    plant support 153

    for screening 38

    for shade 62

    for shelter 61

symbols *26*
  as vertical elements 33
  and water features 182, 190
trellis
  on fences 136, 142, 152
  on pergolas 168, *169*
  for screening 39, 136
  in *trompe l'oeil* 161
  on walls 152, *153*
trompe l'oeil effects 44, 161

V-W

vertical elements 22, 24, 32–3,
  35, 38, 39, 62

walls 13, *106*, 128–35
  brick 81, 128–9
  capping and coping 135, 198

construction *13*, 130–5, 165,
  198
corners 129, *132*
damp-proofing 133, 162, 165,
  166, 167
drainage issues 41, 87, 133,
  163
dry-stone walls 28, 81, *128*,
  134–5, 163
in establishing ground levels
  14
foundations 88, 90, 130, 133,
  134, 135
lighting 40, *212*, 216–17
materials 128–9
painting *135*, 198
piers 129, 198
plant support 40, 153, *153*

pointing 132, *135*, 167
proportion issues 24
retaining walls 40, 87, 133,
  162, 163, 165
for sitting *40*, 74, 167, 220
in sloping gardens 40, 41
stone 128, 164
symbols *27*
tools 130–1, *132*
water features 53, *158*, 178–9,
  181, 188–91
concrete 183
fountains 62, *158*, 178, *180*,
  181, 190, 191
jetties and beaches 189
lighting 210, 213
liners 183
maintenance 178, 189

natural water courses 181
pumps *179*, *180*, 181, 183,
  190, 210
safety issues *57*, *179*
siting 62, 190–1
in sloping gardens 179
solar power 191, 210
stepping stones 188
streams and rills 180, 181, 191
waterfalls 53, *158*, 181, 183
see also pools and ponds
water gardens 56–7 *see also*
  water features
wildflower meadows 52
wildlife in gardens 28, 51, 52–5,
  178, 180, 189
wind 58, 60–1, 70, 190
window boxes *175*, 208–9

Acknowledgements

Mitchell Beazley would like to acknowledge and thank the following for supplying images for use in this book. For a list of stockists for Stonemarket, please see www.stonemarket.co.uk, for Jewson Lanscaping, see www.jewsonlandscaping.co.uk, and for Simply Greenhouses, see www.simplygreenhouses.co.uk

Front cover: *above left*, *right* Garden World Images/F Davis, *below left* Andrew Lawson/design: Nicola Lowe, *below right* Stonemarket; back cover: *above* Andrew Lawson/design: Oehme and van Sweden, *below* Andrew Lawson/Bosvigo, Cornwall.

1 Octopus Publishing Group/Sue Atkinson; 2 Garden World Images/D Warner/design: Nicholas J Bolt; 19 Octopus Publishing Group/Jerry Harpur; 20 *above left* Octopus Publishing Group/Michael Boys, *above right* Andrew Lawson/design: Andrew Card, *below* Octopus Publishing Group/Stephen Robson; 53 *left* Garden World Images/D Bevan, *right* Garden Picture Library/John Glover; 54 *above* Giulia Hetherington, *below* Octopus Publishing Group/Paul Barker; 71 *above* Garden World Images/D Warner, *below left* Octopus Publishing Group/Jerry Harpur, *below right* Octopus Publishing Group/Sue Atkinson; 72 *left* Garden World Images/Matt Keal, 72 *right* Octopus Publishing Group/Stephen Robson; 105 *above left*, *right* Stonemarket, *below* Octopus Publishing Group/Michael Boys; 106 *above* Stonemarket, *below left* Octopus Publishing Group/Mark Bolton, *below right* Jewson Landscaping; 123 *above* Garden World Images/F Davis/design: Roger Platts, *below* Stonemarket; 124 Octopus Publishing Group/Peter Myers; 158 *above* Octopus Publishing Group/Sue Atkinson, *below left* Octopus Publishing Group/Paul Barker; *below right* Garden Picture Library/Lorraine Pullen; 175 *below left* Octopus Publishing Group/Steve Wooster; *below right* Simply Greenhouses/Kybotech Ltd; 176 *above* Garden World Images/F Davis, 176 *below* Clive Nichols/design: Patrick McCann.

The publishers would also like to thank Barbara Haynes and Simon Maughan at the RHS for their editorial help; also Maya Albert of the RHS Gardening Advice Service for her advice on using electricity in the garden.